"Yiddishe Mamas"

✡ THE TRUTH ABOUT ✡ THE JEWISH MOTHER

Marnie Winston-Macauley

Andrews McMeel
Publishing, LLC

Kansas City

07 08 09 10 11 RR4 10 9 8 7 6 5 4 3 2 1

ISBN-13: 978-0-7407-6376-2
ISBN-10: 0-7407-6376-8

Library of Congress Control Number: 2006932271

www.andrewsmcmeel.com

ATTENTION: SCHOOLS AND BUSINESSES
Andrews McMeel books are available at quantity discounts with bulk purchase for educational, business, or sales promotional use. For information, please write to: Special Sales Department, Andrews McMeel Publishing, LLC, 4520 Main Street, Kansas City, Missouri 64111.

For the Jewish Mother . . .

With a majesty, often misunderstood and misrepresented. May our legacy be recognized. May our daughters continue this legacy in truth. May others recognize this truth: That today, in our chaotic world, may we all feel the comfort and wisdom of the Jewish mother.

A LITTLE OY
"Little Children Little Troubles,
Big Children, Big Troubles"

A LITTLE JOY
"Each Child Carries His Own Blessing into the World"

Contents

Preface xi

Acknowledgments xiii

Introduction xv

**CHAPTER 1: THE JEWISH MOTHER: IS SHE OR
ISN'T SHE AND WHO IS SHE?** 1

Is There Such a Thing as a "Jewish Mother?" 2

Stereotypes: A New Approach 5

So Who Then Are We? An Overview of the Ethno-type 9

**CHAPTER 2: FROM MY YIDDISHE MAMA TO THE
YIDDISHE YENTA: HOW COULD THIS BE—AND WHY?** 29

Media: Looking Back 29

Assimilation: Mama-Dramas and
the Sons Who Created Them 34

"Them" and Us 42

"The Poll:" Nineteen Non-Jewish Perceptions
of the Jewish Mother 46

A Mother Is a Mother Is a Mother?
What Makes Us Different? 59

**CHAPTER 3: JEWISH MOTHER JOKES: INSULT,
INSULATION, OR JUST PLAIN FUNNY** 65

Jewish Jokes: Why and What Are They? 67

Attitudes and Attitude 72

**CHAPTER 4: THE JEWISH MOTHER EXPERIENCE
AND EXPERIENCED: A BISSEL OF INFORMATION,
COMMENTARY, DEBATE, ANECDOTES, AND HUMOR** 77

On Coming to America 77

Mama-loshen: *Yiddish and Yinglish* 80
On Giving Birth . . . and a Little Sex 92
Kidfirst—the Oys and Joys 95
Jewish Mothers and Daughters 107
Jewish Mothers and Sons 114
Marriage and Mothers-in-Law 128
Bubbes *(Grandmas)* 137
Nakhes *(Pride)* 143
How Are You? Don't Ask—Cleanliness and Health 146
Essen *(Food)* 151

CHAPTER 5: YES, THEY, TOO, ARE JEWISH MOTHERS **171**
Pioneer and Colonial Jewish Mothers 171
This Land Is Our Land 186
Yentls! Scholars, Rabbis—and Jewish Mothers 198
Feminism and Activism 210
Jewish Mothers in Business:
    Forces to Be Reckoned With 242
Jewish Mothers and Sports 250
Jewish Mothers Everywhere 259

CHAPTER 6: JEWISH MOTHERS—DIDJEW KNOW? **263**
Albert Einstein 263
Queen Victoria, Moshe Montefiore,
    and Rabbi Nathan Adler 264
When Harry Met Sally 264
Jean Lafette 265
Wrongway Uncle 265
Sarah Bernhardt 266
Lorne Greene 266
Adah Isaacs Menken 266
Charles Dickens and Mrs. Eliza Davis 268
Hedy Lamarr 268
Véra Nabokov 269
River Phoenix 270
The Jewish Bride 271
Mrs. Yetta Bronstein 271

Anna Cohen Kopshovsky...271
Julia Query...272
Bruce Adler, the Bluegrass Rabbi
    and His Wife, Donna..272
Eduard Bloch...273
Rita Katz...273
John Stossel..275

**CHAPTER 7: JEWISH MOTHERS—
COURAGE BETWEEN THE TEARS**...**277**
The Inquisition...278
The Holocaust...279
Strange and Wonderful Bedfellows: Non-Jews.............293
Be Mad, Mother, Be Mad! The Horror Continues..........301
Our Homeland..303
Shalom..309

Epilogue...317
Appendix 1: The Aleph-baiz of
    Jewish Mother Humor.......................................321
Appendix 2: From These Roots:
    Jewish Mothers to Us All................................331
Selected Biographies..335
Selected Bibliographies..351
About the Author...362
Interviews..364

Preface

When my editor, Patty Rice, and I first discussed doing a book on the Jewish mother we never imagined that what would start as a relatively simple assignment (some facts, anecdotes, interviews, and humor) would grow—and grow—and continue to grow, into a far more complex and inclusive book.

Since writing *A Little Joy, A Little Oy* in 2002, plus calendars of the same name and the *Yiddishe Mamas 2007 Calendar*, I've gathered and stored thousands of facts—many from scholarly sources. There were, however, deep-felt meanings and sensibilities that wouldn't lend themselves to a calendar format.

When I began the interviews for this book, I realized immediately that there were issues of great significance that needed to be addressed.

I asked several basic questions: Is there such a thing as a "Jewish mother?" If so, what are our characteristics and how are these similar and different from all mothers? And what was it that spun our image from adored sentimentality—to neurotic interlopers?

I found vast differences of opinions among those I spoke with about roles, assimilation, and media representations. Suddenly, the "simple" forced me to look deeper and further.

In reading books about or for Jewish mothers, I realized that most, if not all, were bios, interviews, or subject-driven collections about food, humor, language, and, of course, religion.

However, I failed to find books that bridged themes, via using multiple approaches to understanding the Jewish mother—a book that includes interviews, facts, humor, and anecdotes among other things. So, I decided to write one. This approach has been a daunting and risky venture; a journey into areas that have already been deeply explored by mavens.

On the positive side, I hoped that by viewing the Jewish mother from many angles, the material will, when taken together, prove an insightful *portrait* of the Jewish mother.

It also intended to shed more light on scholarly material, in a readable, informative, and entertaining manner.

Although there are women who have contributed mightily to their communities and the world, they are not included since this book is about Jewish *mothers*, and that's where I stayed. All the women discussed are or were mothers, by giving birth or through raising children. As I defined the term, they were born into Jewish families, converted, or, if one parent was Jewish, have identified themselves as Jewish and raised Jewish children. I also included women and men who have no children, but had something important to contribute about Jewish mothers—their own and others.

There is also a special section on how *non-Jewish* women view Jewish mothers, since we may tend to be isolated within our own thinking. The results were surprising. The material chosen is not exhaustive, but *representative*. The focus is on the Jewish mother of Ashkenazi (or Eastern European) descent, as they comprise the vast majority of Jews in America and in the world.

Scores of interviews were conducted over a period of several years. The complete list is included in the Bibliography section, along with selected short biographies.

Here are a few who contributed:

Dr. Ruth Gruber, Dr. Carolyn Goodman, Dr. Myrna Hant, Dr. Eileen Warshaw, Rabbi Sally Priesand, Rabbi Bonnie Koppel, Rabbi Shira Stern, Blu Greenberg, Lainie Kazan, Judy Gold, Tim Boxer, Jackie Mason, Theodore Bikel, Mallory Lewis, Bill Dana, Mayor Oscar Goodman, Congresswoman Shelley Berkley, Tovah Feldshuh, Marilyn Michaels, Joanna Gleason, Michael Medved, Marta Sanders, Eileen Fulton, Amy Borkowsky, John Stossel, Binyamin Jolkovsky, Harry Leichter, Liz Abzug, Zora Essman (mother of Susie Essman), Melanie Strug (mother of Kelli Strug), Kaye Ballard, Marty Allen, Mrs. Danny Gans, Julie Cobb, Rabbi Yocheved Mintz, Rabbi Bob Alper.

Acknowledgments

The job of putting together such an ambitious project was not merely daunting (OK, moderately meshugge), but absolutely required the serious help of many people. (Unfortunately, none typed. Oy.) Without the generous time of those I interviewed, I'd be quoting myself, so to all who gave me that time, I'm deeply grateful.

There were many mavens I turned to for their vast fund of information and support. In particular, I'd like to thank author Tim Boxer, who knows "everything" about "everyone," and was incredibly generous with his "everything." Binyamin Jolkovsky and Harry Leichter were invaluable in providing source material, as well as their own views, anecdotes, and experiences. Dr. Ruth Gruber, a true legend, gave me so much of her valuable time and insight. Dr. Myrna Hant, an expert on Jewish mothers, along with media, was a fountain of information, as was Dr. Eileen Warshaw, who not only knows her Jewish pioneers, but can tell a story better than Louis L'Amour. Rabbis Sally Priesand, Colonel Bonnie Koppel, and Yocheved Mintz were enormously helpful and provided religious explanations with enthusiasm and joy.

On a personal level, I *don't* thank the lady I brought in to help clean up the *schmutz* (dirt) while I was working. When I asked her, at 9:00 a.m., if she was thirsty, she polished off the vodka and disappeared. Also, I'm *not* thanking the company that made the electronic hoodinky and turtle girdle I had to wear after spinal surgery, which gave me such an allergy I scratched my way through the writing. (I know. I'm kvetching.)

I do, however, wish to thank my husband, Ian, who took over the meals (and now has an uncommon relationship with take-out), my son, Simon, the critic, who thought the book "wasn't half bad." Also, my various publishers and editors of my *Ask Sadie* and other columns, Michael Chihak, editor and publisher; Lorrie Cohen, assistant news editor; editors Dina Doolen, Gabrielle Fimbres, and the staff of the *Tucson Citizen*; Caroline Orzes, publisher of *Jewish Life and Style*; and, once again, Binyamin Jolkovsky of Jewishworldreview.com and Harry Leichter of schmoozenews.com. Sherry and Dr. George Ritter, as always, are simply *there*, and I adore them, as I do my cousin Stephanie Winston, who is part advisor, part "sister." Then there's Dr. Howard Cohen, the greatest mensch (good person) I know, whose spirit, unbridled support, and love informs and enriches everyone he touches. My enduring love as well for Craig Kelso, my oldest and dearest friend.

Then there are my publishers. I owe a great debt to my friends at Andrews McMeel Publishing—the editors, art department, publicity department, and sales. Patty Rice, my editor, who, with graciousness and understanding (not to mention humanity), has been right there with me, along with her right hand, Katie Anderson. Copy chief Michelle Daniel was a terrific resource. Designer Diane Marsh did a beautiful job of Herculean proportions. Michael Nonbello, calendar editor, who took a chance on me, has been with me for over ten years. I also want to thank their staffs who pick up the phone when the others don't want to talk to me. Then there's Jennifer Collet, public relations, whose generosity and support can't be described—here's a lady who not only knows her stuff, but supplied one hundred copies of *A Little Joy, A Little Oy* calendars and books to our service people overseas. And of course, none of this would be possible without Hugh Andrews.

Introduction

Q: How many Jewish mothers does
it take to change a lightbulb?
A: *"Don't worry, I'll just sit here in the dark."*

Q: Why don't Jewish mothers drink?
A: *It interferes with their suffering.*

Q: What is the most common
disease transmitted by Jewish mothers?
A: *Guilt.*

We've all heard them. The Jewish mother stereotypes, borne of ridicule, heightened by Borscht Belt comics, portrayed in media—and casually accepted by Americans who go for the joke, the easy *zetz* (punch). And so, we have become the "cartoon." The prototype of the overzealous, overinvolved, overworried, overprotective, overnurturing, overbearing presence that has invaded popular culture.

There have also been scholars who have written volumes on the etymology of the "Jewish mother" as an ethnic subgroup that has no precise peer in other cultures. But some, in defense, have even denied the existence of the "Jewish mother," or, like the Biblical Deborah, waved swords, to swash away the images.

But those who have looked beyond the stereotype are not being heard loud enough. There are few popular spotlights on our reality. But then, the quick sound bite, the joke, is easier. It ends with a laugh, a "period."

As a journalist, I've been forced to look beyond that period. At the commas, the exclamation points, the 5,000-year-old clauses that have come before.

I've also been forced to examine my own experience as a Jewish daughter and mother and critically evaluate many viewpoints to arrive at my own truth. The journey has been an emotional one, and yes, tears have been shed. Self-examination is always emotional, if done honestly.

In every stereotype, there is an element of truth. I recall my late mother ripping the heads off photos of boys who dumped me. (The litter blanketed Queens, New York.) She also had a great sense of humor. My brother would have been born later, if my mother hadn't been having cake with Rose and Birdie—two of the funniest women alive. With Marty Allen's looks and Totie Fields's timing, the pair could fell you with a story. (Is it so unusual for two women to suddenly accuse each other of adultery—then chase each other on the El train in Brooklyn—simply to make the ride to work more interesting?) My mother's hysteria brought on labor pains. I can't think of a nicer way.

My grandmother was hilarious, though she didn't know it. Her entire reason for living after the death of my grandfather was "to move in" with us. From her mission came stories and anecdotes only a Carl Reiner could write. When my mother was in intensive care, my grandma somehow got through on the phone. She had to tell my ailing mother that "Harry Truman died." Only moderately sympathetic, my mother replied, "That's too bad," to which Gram responded, "I bet Bess will now move in 'mit' Margaret!" My mother, near death, laughed.

Yes, my grandmother sounded selfish. But then we look *beyond* at the woman who bribed border guards to get to America before the Nazis took over, leaving her birth family behind—forever.

This is why I had to look *before* the period. I needed to see how the backgrounds and religion of these women played a critical role in the "stereotype." The joke had a predecessor. And without examination, the meaning—and truth—is lost. And so are we, in trying to understand the underlying mind-set and principles that are far more important than the joke—a recent invention.

Many Jewish mother stereotypes are about intrusion, child-first suffocation, lack of boundaries, and wanting a good match for their offspring.

Yet these "traits" are also the very qualities—protection, education, nourishment and survival during pogroms, throughout the Holocaust, and other incalculable calamities—that have kept us alive and intact these 5,000 years.

In this work, I hope you will see the special soul of Jewish motherhood. You will read of the sacrifices, the extraordinary belief in the future through our children that Jewish women over the centuries have possessed. Our religion, from its earliest beginnings, knew that women have an internal fortitude that complements the male's outward leanings. You will see greatness, not only of woman heralded, but of unsung Jewish mother heroes, who are valiant every day of their lives.

You will also read fascinating facts, anecdotes, and yes, humor that was vital and kept us going while we were running—always running. Jewish women simply—are funny. We often cry when we're happy and laugh when we're suffering. So yes . . . there are "the jokes."

In the end, my truth is visual. I see an image of a very rare, precious tapestry, growing with each generation adding its own distinctive, complex pattern. Through thousands of years, the tapestry reflects our intricacy, complexity, and vibrance. And from it, we hear the echoes of women who have taken on as much as shoulders can bear and then some. We hear the strains of music, laughter, wisdom, tears, outrage, *tzedakah*, courage, *involvement* . . . and we see our children who have made extraordinary contributions to our culture and to humanity.

The jokes, then, are a part of this tapestry—before the "period." *But when viewed in this light, they become, to me, celebrations.*

And I worry. I worry the world will not know us. I worry that as the Jewish mothers assimilate and turn into pencil-thin blondes filled with Botox, who, in the words of Abraham Cahan, have become "alrightniks," will we worship "things" and lose the very gifts we have been given?

I worry, as we get more unaffiliated, or, as my friend Rabbi Yechoved Mintz calls it, "unfullfiliated," in this culture. The daunting task then, for the modern Jewish mother, is to reconcile the positive benefits of assimilation, without sacrificing our sense of Judaism and our parent-child purpose in a world that, more than ever, needs to believe in the power of the Jewish mother. Yes, it requires change and modification—but knowing what and how to modify is the great challenge.

At the start, I thought I was writing this for my ancestors. Today, I am sure I'm writing this for my descendants, who, I pray, will look *before* the periods—and add to our majestic tapestry in their own unique way. After all, what right does one stitch have to ignore the design?

"Yiddishe Mamas"

CHAPTER 1

The Jewish Mother:

IS SHE OR ISN'T SHE, AND WHO IS SHE?

"The Jewish mother." Never has one tiny adjective evoked such a firestorm. Make a speech in front of any Sisterhood meeting and play a little word association. Wear protective gear. A barrage of answers will tumble out among reverberating all-knowing laughter: "Loves her kids—to death!" "Always with the food!" "She won't *take* a 'no.'" "Oy, the *guilt*!"

And then, as the titters subside, slowly other associations emerge: "Kids come first." "Smart." "Funny." "Determined." "Cares." "You can count on her." And . . . "I miss her."

There you have it. The core. The essence of a peculiar conundrum that Jewish mothers and their children have been facing for the better part of the last one hundred or so years, as many of these mamas have left their small European towns (shtetls) to come to the Golden Land.

As one of "the chosen people," whose history is one of oppression, exile, and calamity, the modern Jewish mother is faced with the problem of imparting our heritage while ensuring that our children "make it" in the secular world. The balance is often, in the words of Tevye, "as shaky as a fiddler on the roof." It requires the balance of a ballet master teaching Jewish practices while helping the child comprehend the death of 6 million; teaching values, pride, courage, and activism or *tikkun olam* (our responsibility to try and heal the world) in a world where millions would like to see the extermination of our homeland. And the ultimate landing is to raise children who are unafraid and proud to be Jewish.

Can we *be* all those things?

But more, do we *want* to be all those things?

1

IS THERE SUCH A THING
AS A "JEWISH MOTHER"?

Zora Essman, the delightful, funny mother of comedian/
actress Susie Essman, who's currently barbing with great success
as the foul-mouthed wife of Larry David's wimpy agent on *Curb
Your Enthusiasm*, has just called me, out of breath. It seems she
just got off a bus with twenty-five Hadassah women.

"I don't know if there's a Jewish mother," she says, then quickly
talks about the ladies on the bus. "The Jewish mother I know is
a well-educated woman, a social worker, a psychologist. [Mrs.
Essman is a linguist and former college teacher.] Every mother
of my class and education level is the same. We share the same
values. We all get something from our backgrounds . . . a certain
style." Clearly, Mrs. Essman sees a commonality, a familiarity she
shares with her companions. And then . . .

"When my friends and I get together, we're all in our seventies
and eighties, we all say, 'My daughter she did this and this—she
married this one, she's dating this one, I told my daughter not to
do this or that' . . . and we all say *don't tell the daughter*! *Then* we
talk about Bush."

We have it! We see the highly educated, often hysterical, classy
lady who isn't about to buy into a stereotype "morph" as the
conversation continues into one of the classical traits we associate
with Jewish mothers.

THE JEWISH MOTHER: "IS THERE OR ISN'T THERE?"
AND WHY THE HESITATION TO ADMIT IT?

"There's *probably* a 'Jewish mother,'" says Melanie Strug,
mother of Kerri Strug, who made Olympic history in 1996,
when, with torn ligaments, she nailed her final vault, landing
the gold for the U.S. Women's Gymnastic Team. Mrs. Strug,
a determined, child-first mother, then goes on to describe the
"probably."

"She over cares, over worries, is very concerned about the
kids . . . making sure they get a good education, a happy social
life. Mom does everything for the kids."

Dr. Burt Strug, her husband, adds:

"Did you mention obsessive-compulsiveness?"

"In the minds of others a Jewish mother can be either a very nurturing, supportive, enriching woman or the opposite, a martyr, a nag, who demeans," offers Rabbi Yocheved Mintz.

"Some think of her as overbearing, a yenta," adds Dr. Ruth Gruber, who saved countless lives during the Holocaust and whose life was made into the film, *Haven*.

"But the women I see around me are not. I love the truth and beauty about Judaism. [The Jewish mother] is warm, takes pictures with her heart. There's something about being Jewish that comes from the heart, the soul, the *neshuma*."

These women are setting the record straight. They have to. In only decades we've gone from revered to needing a team of image consultants. There was a time Sophie Tucker singing "My Yiddishe Mama," or Yiddish theater star Boris Thomashefsky—who could slip a tribute to "mama" into *Hamlet*—reduced audiences to heaving, sentimental sobs.

No more. Over the years, we've watched media characters such as Fran Fine, Rhoda Morgenstern, Paul Buchman, Jerry Seinfeld, and Grace Adler, among many, virtually scouting places in Boca, not in tribute, but to get rid of their kvetching (whining), interfering, critical, loudmouth but "funny" moms—oh, who they love.

Today, nourishment is portrayed as forced feeding, while succor and family sacrifice has become "suffocation."

And Jewish mothers are supposed to accept this brutal image? *Feh*! These are the daughters of shtetl moms! Women trying to survive in poor Eastern European towns, who, shlepping Sabbath candles, were running, running, running—from pogroms, starvation, and death camps—some sacrificing their lives, holding their religion and their children close. They often bribed their way to a new land, using chutzpah, smarts, grit—to make it here and to keep their families whole and Jewish, so their children would do better, and therefore add to the world, and give them *nakhes* (pride).

"Is there a Jewish mother? Definitely," says Dr. Myrna Hant, visiting scholar at the Center for the Study of Women at UCLA "There is truth in stereotype, but do you want to say I'm a Jewish mother and have others formulate a whole litany of who you are? The modern Jewish woman isn't like this."

"We are stereotyped incorrectly as overbearing, unable to cut ties with children, unable to see beyond the limited family. This does Jewish women a great injustice," says Rabbi Shira Stern, who has a pastoral counseling practice. Rabbi Stern (the daughter of Isaac Stern) adds, "There are any number of ways of expressing Jewish motherhood. And yes, there are women who let their children actually cross the street without holding their hand—once they have the skill."

"I have one, a Jewish mother," says critic, and syndicated conservative radio talk-show host, Michael Medved. "I do try to avoid the term as it evokes unpleasant stereotypes which are mostly wrong," though, he admits, "any doable stereotype has some basis in reality."

> "'THE TIME TO MAKE UP YOUR MIND ABOUT PEOPLE IS NEVER,' AS PHILLIP BARRY WROTE IN *THE PHILADELPHIA STORY*. YOU THINK YOU KNOW SOMEONE, YOU DON'T. WHEN YOU STEREOTYPE THEY BECOME UNKNOWABLE. IT'S LAZY."
> —Joanna Gleason, actress/director, daughter of Monty Hall

"How many Jewish mothers spend their evenings in smoky clubs saying obscenities, and then the next day drop the kids off at Hebrew School?" says comic Judy Gold, a Jewish lesbian mother of two boys.

So much for "stereotypes."

STEREOTYPES: A NEW APPROACH

Stereotypes! The very word calls up an odious Stepford image. A plaster mold, fixed, from books, TV, and film that "defines" who we are. A Jack Klugman nose, a Sylvia Fine finger in frozen Sara Lee, a Helen Seinfeld having an attack over her son's libido during . . . shhh *Schindler's List*.

Jackie Mason, who became a hit with his show *The World According to Me*, has taken the "stereotyping" heat. But he's the first to defend it by saying, "If I were Margaret Mead, they'd call it anthropology."

It's a great sadness that this negative, unbalanced stereotype is a dangerous cheat turning many a Jewish mother away from claiming many of the magnificent characteristics we *do* share. Just as many Italians are offended by perceptions that all are members of organized crime, some Jewish mothers are faced with similar feelings of outrage. So much so that many of us gag at the very term, "Jewish mother." After all, who wants to be typed as Sylvia Fine?

So, naturally, while the Jewish people I interviewed were able to name characteristics, they were reluctant to "stereotype."

Is the answer to deny there is such a phenomenon as "The Jewish mother"?

No. Just as each individual group shares belief systems, attitudes, and values, I believe we do as well. PC aside, each religion and culture, whether Italian, Irish, or the Zoa tribe, all hold commonalities that not only bind them together, but are also evident in their thinking and behavior.

But the question remains, how do we bridge the gap between the loathsome cartoon cut-out image and the very real characteristics that we, as part of a great tradition, share?

I came up with a solution (at least for me). I call it *ethno-typing*. "Ethno-typing" allows us to treasure our uniqueness as a group and as individuals without falling into the trap of carbon copying all Jewish mothers.

Ethno-typing also carries with it no positive or negative judgment. Like an examination of any ethnic group, it allows us to look at our history, our biology, our values and characteristic traits, without prejudice or the quick sound bite.

Another "proof" that the ethno-type exists is *tribalism.* We Jewish mothers are marvelous at "recognizing" one another. In my own vast experience with the matter, we "get each other." And if in doubt, we may fish like Ahab, or at the very least, wonder "Is she Jewish . . . ?" *Not that it matters,* but . . . it does; it affects the way we communicate and shorthand our feelings.

Many of us simply feel a little more comfortable, safer, and freer with those with whom we share a common background—including a history of *tsouris* (trouble). A simple example is the use of what we call Yinglish—thanks to Leo Rosten. If our background is Eastern European, our mothers and grandmothers spoke Yiddish. Language is a critical component of culture and bonds us.

Even today, non-Yiddish-speaking Jewish mothers all understand some basic Yiddish and the Americanized version, Yinglish. Find me a Jewish mother who doesn't understand the universal cry, "Oy!" (There could be trouble here.) "Oy vey!" (It's getting worse.) And "Oy gevalt!" (Forget it altogether.) And most understand the myriad of words we have for luck and personalities—good and bad—and pepper "mazel," "chutzpah," and "shlemiel" (among more dastardly Yinglishisms) into our conversation with another member of "the tribe."

> "Jewish women are vital,
> you can pick them out in a crowd."
> —Dr. Myrna Hant

"There is something that feels comfortable when I'm with other Jewish mothers," says Zora Essman, mother of comedian Susie Essman. "I feel the difference, the sharing of experience."

Although actress Julie Cobb, daughter of actor Lee J. Cobb and Yiddish theater star Helen Beverley, was not raised in a traditional Jewish family, and has married "out," she relates that now that she's dating a Jew, she's experiencing new feelings. "It's a cellular knowing, a humor, a sensory feeling that goes deep," she says. "It's in the DNA. It's *sachel* (understanding, common sense, smarts), passion. I think it's possible that [in my past relationships] I may have been holding back a little."

It's in the DNA!

Four Jewish mothers who lived 1,000 years ago in Europe are the ancestors of 40 percent of all Ashkenazi (Central and Eastern European) Jews alive today! This remarkable finding was reported by an international team of researchers in 2006. Dr. Doron Behar of the Technion-Israel Institute of Technology and geneticist Karl Skorecki, with worldwide collaborators, sampled DNA from 11,452 people from sixty-seven populations. The researchers found that the mtDNA of some 3.5 million of the 8 million Ashkenazi Jews in the world (among 13 million) can be traced back to only four women carrying a distinct mtDNA, which was virtually absent in other populations. Behar and Skorecki's team refers to this phenomenon as a "founder effect"—when one or a small number of people have a huge number of descendants. "What the study also shows," Behar said, "is that Jewish mothers are highly valued for a good reason. This I could tell you even without the paper."

Tribal pride intact, we take on the whole of us, carrying that pride—and humiliation—to all Jews. When Son of Sam, David Berkowitz, was finally captured after his spree of serial murders, I recall my own mother saying, "Thank God, he was adopted!" It seems thousands of Jewish mothers were also sighing with relief, including comic Judy Gold's mother.

"My mother is one of those Jewish women who think that Jewish people are perfect," says Judy Gold. "Like when they picked up David Berkowitz, the Son of Sam, I thought she was going to have a heart attack. She called me two days later and left a message: 'He was adopted. Talk to you later.'"

We also share the *nakhes* and the inclusiveness when a Jew "makes it" or "breaks through." Decades ago it was John Garfield, then Tony Curtis. I heard it growing up. "Did you know Tony Curtis's real name is Bernie Schwartz?" And "Lauren Bacall was raised right near here!" Einstein, Bernard Baruch, Arthur Miller, Neil Simon, Sid Caesar, all were stars—Jewish stars. Their inclusiveness fascinated and delighted our mothers. Hey, they were family.

The late great playwright Wendy Wasserstein claimed that while her mother wasn't religious she harped on Jewish pride. In *Stars of David*, she reported her mother knocking on the television when someone came on, to tell her he was one of us. "She told me Barry Goldwater was one of us."

✡

GRANDMA MARKOWITZ, AN IMMIGRANT, WAS HAVING TROUBLE GETTING ACCUSTOMED TO THE STRANGE WAYS OF THIS NEW COUNTRY, BUT SHE WAS EXTREMELY PROUD OF THE AMERICANIZATION OF DAVID, HER GRANDSON. ONE AFTERNOON, DAVID BURST INTO THE HOUSE, YELLING: "*BUBBE*! THE YANKEES WON TODAY!"

"*AZOI* (REALLY?!)!" SAID GRANDMA. "SO TELL ME, IS THAT GOOD OR BAD FOR THE JEWS?"

✡

Tribalism does not only carry a community feeling, but an all-encompassing one that fuels our maternal mission.

SO WHO THEN ARE WE?
AN OVERVIEW OF THE ETHNO-TYPE

We're not wallflowers, according to Michael Medved. "She knows values and insists her children share them, live them. She treasures tradition. The keeper of the family welfare . . . that's her purpose in life," he says, adding, "She's romantic, educated, very up on the latest trends, cognizant of what's going on in her world around her, and how it affects the family. She's thrifty, but not opposed to spending, even extravagantly on her children, if it will further their position in life. Her waking hours are spent figuring out ways to make her child and husband more successful and she will sacrifice."

SACRIFICE: THE FAMILY: KIDFIRST *COMES* FIRST!

The Jewish mother will stand by her child, under all circumstances. Her love is constantly available and unswerving. No shlep is too much of a sacrifice. Both historically and religiously, the children have been the Jewish mother's *job*.

Melanie Strug, for example, describes her home when the children were growing up as a "cafeteria." As they were all involved in athletics, she was *forever* shlepping. "I picked one up at six, got another at seven, got another at eight," she says. "Our home life was centered around the kids. I'm a Jewish mother in the sense that the children came first."

"She resides in Brooklyn," joked Binyamin Jolkovsy, editor in chief of Jewishworldreview.com. "But she's selfless, puts her children above herself, sees her role as nurturer and molder of character and conscience. That's how the Jewish mothers in my environment are and I hope each and everyone lives up to that 'stereotype.'"

"Driven!" adds Dr. Eileen Warshaw. "Our careers come second, if it's good for the children."

Sacrifice and exceptional commitment to children is echoed by Orthodox author, lecturer, and feminist, Blu Greenberg, who proudly talks of her five children and nineteen grandchildren.

"She's me. She's very sensitive, compassionate, feely, huggy, kissy," says Jody Lopatin of Romanian ancestry, who, in addition to raising four children, was head mistress of an Orthodox Danish preschool. "But she's also sturdy, very strong, a mother hen who will protect her children—and anyone else's children."

And this devotion often knows few bounds. The Jewish mother ethno-type is not "minimalist." Children are not merely given opportunities, but are often pampered, to bring joy to both mother and child.

"Who puts a child in costume on a plane and privately buys out a candy store for the *passengers* to give to your five-year-old so she won't miss trick or treating?" laughs educator, political bigwig, and CEO of Rayburn Musical Instruments Company, Rona Ginott, describing a trip to Italy during Halloween. "I valued making life happy for my kids. I was gratified when that happened. I wanted to experience Halloween with my child."

And where is the Jewish father in all this? Despite media mocking, many are strong, involved, and share their wives' vision for the children. My own father was such a man. Yet . . . I understand the old joke "I decide the big things, like who should be president and how to achieve world peace. My wife decides the little things, like where we should live, and how we're raising the kids." This still exists in some Jewish families.

"The Jewish woman doesn't even pretend her husband is the boss. Italians and Greeks do. If mommy's not happy, nobody's happy," quips Mallory Lewis, daughter of Shari Lewis.

> "She is the glue that keeps the family together and makes it successful. The Jewish mother is very committed to her children and has her foot up her husband's butt."
>
> —Dr. Eileen Warshaw, executive director of the Jewish Heritage Center of the Southwest

"Your husband is secondary to our role as mothers," says Rona Ginott. "I did whatever I had to, to help my child first."

"Kids come first . . .
even before the husband."
—Dr. Burt Strug

"We did expect the kids to do well," says Melanie Strug. "My husband was working all the time. Moonlighting so our kids could have the best education, private schools, training—whatever they needed," she adds.

The majority of Jewish fathers no longer spend their days studying Talmud, which formerly gave them status within the Jewish community. Instead, *today's* status and a father's contribution is *gelt* (money) and *power*, making the money and the "connections" within and outside of the community to further his child and his family. NOTE: There are those within the Jewish community who don't necessarily see this change from spiritual to financial status as a good thing.

Annoyed and backburnered at times, these men usually take enormous pride in their wive's indefatigable spirit and commitment to their children.

What of the rest of family? Important, yes. Especially to support the survival and success of the children.

"Kerri visits her older sister once a month, and lives minutes from her brother. We're a very close family," says Melanie Strug. "If Kerri's air-conditioning unit doesn't work she calls her brother."

Commitment to family may be sacrosanct, but peace and harmony? That's another matter. Our ethno-type often includes what, to outsiders, may seem a peculiar scene. In my own family, there was the odd coexistence of absolute loyalty and constant kvetching about various family members. For example, there was the spendthrift who couldn't pay his mortgage, but wore silk underwear. And the "rumor-spreader." Then there was the family "matriarch" who redecorated our house, then invited guests to live in it—while my mother was out shopping. And who could forget the miser who ordered half the menu, stuck you with the check—and took home the leftovers.

All families have them, but the Jewish mother talks, debates, and argues—sometimes fiercely. These family fightin' words might put a scare into many non-Jews. To the Jewish mother "letting it out," then coming together in passionate forgiveness, is perfectly normal. And even with a litany of complaints, she'll still expect the group to rally for celebrations, holidays, and deaths. This dichotomy has been the fodder of Jewish humor for years.

✡

MR. MANDELBAUM: "WHY DON'T THE LEADERS OF THE WORLD REALIZE THAT NATIONS CAN SOLVE ALL THEIR PROBLEMS IF THEY JUST DECIDE TO LIVE TOGETHER LIKE ONE BIG FAMILY?"

MRS. MANDELBAUM: "BITE YOUR TONGUE!"

✡

Rich Mrs. Schwartz bought herself the most expensive co-op in New York for her and her daughter. Then she invited her exclusive friends to come see. When they got to the ballroom, her visitors gasped over the exquisite antique table that ran from one end of the room to the other. "And in this room," she said, "I can entertain our entire family from Brooklyn—God forbid!"

STUDY, *MAMALA*! HOW SWEET IT IS!

Education, particularly Jewish education, is not only a mantra that is deeply embedded in Jewish history and tradition, but also a celebration! It was a religious expectation for young boys in the shtetl, but it also represented the very future of Judaism—a way to keep the boys and girls who also learned the rudiments and were drilled by mama in her Jewish duties as *baleboste* (housewife) safely in the fold.

Picture it. A nineteenth-century mama, weeping with joy, dressed in little more than rags, carrying her six-year-old son in a prayer shawl, along with an apron filled with cake, honey, nuts, and raisins, for his first day of cheder (school). After his first "aleph" (the first letter of the Hebrew alphabet) the goodies are given out, with the child of the hour at the head of the line to celebrate his special day—the start of his formal learning.

Such an occasion! One that set the Jewish community apart. When 90 percent of the world was illiterate, the typical Jewish male over six was learning to read and write, often in at least three languages, including Hebrew, Yiddish, or Ladino.

Early on, while the men were studying, *someone* had to inspire, support, keep kosher, light candles, raise the children with values, milk the cows, earn a living, and make sure the house didn't collapse! Like Rachel, wife of the great Rabbi Akiva who sacrificed when he left for years to study Torah, the Jewish mother sees education as a sacred obligation—and revels in the *nakhes*, the pride of raising learned children.

"25,000 miles! My wife drove a total of 25,000 miles—back and forth—from Coolidge to Tucson so our son could study for his bar mitzvah," described Sig Lieberman, a former Arizona mayor with pioneer roots. "This is the sacrifice she made to keep the children involved in Judaism."

When Mrs. Levy was called for jury service, she asked the judge whether she could be excused.

"Listen, Mr. Your Honor. I should admit now, I don't believe in capital punishment."

"Madam," the judge explained, "this is not a murder trial, it's a civil lawsuit. Mrs. F. is suing her husband because he used the entire $15,000 she was saving to pay for her children's education to play the horses."

"Mr. Your Honor . . . about capital punishment. In this case, I could be wrong."

"I was a permissive mother," says Dr. Ruth Gruber, who sent both her children to Reform Sunday School. "But I was always very concerned about education. Education is what counted, never a car, a lethal instrument!"

"My brother had to travel two hours to get to an all boys Jewish school," says Harry Leichter, creator of the over 5,500 Jewish Web sites, www.Haruth.com and the *Schmooze News.*

Today, the dedication to education remains of prime importance, but there has been a shift to secular learning, representing a critical cultural change. Once the learned Jewish scholar was prized; now however many assimilated Jewish mothers look to the professions more than religious accomplishment—as status and success, or "making it," in the New World.

> "TO ME, SCHOOL WAS MOST IMPORTANT.
> I THOUGHT YOU CAN'T MAKE A CAREER
> OUT OF GYMNASTICS."
> —Melanie Strug, mother of Kerri Strug,
> who, in addition to Olympic Gold, holds a BA in
> communications and a master's degree from Stanford

"Homework! If one of my girls missed a day of school, there I was," chuckles Rona Ginott, "shlepping in the snow, the rain to get it for them. Heaven forbid they should miss something!" All that shlepping worked. Her oldest daughter is a Harvard graduate and attending Yale Law School and her younger sister is not far behind.

"I scanned into my computer my son's brilliant report cards and am happy to mail them to anyone who asks. Education is the most important thing in our family," says Mallory Lewis.

Does this dedication work in the secular world? You bet. There are more Jewish doctors than Jewish children on work release.

According to Dr. Bruno Halioua, author of *Meres Juives des Hommes Célèbres* (*Jewish Mothers of Famous Men*), about 12,000 of France's 150,000 physicians (8 percent) are Jews, whereas

Jews make up only 1 percent of the country's overall population of 60 million.

"We got to talking about our mothers," he said. "And I realized that most of my Jewish colleagues . . . got into medical studies because we were prompted to do so by our mothers. It's the same all over for the children of Jewish immigrants—medicine or law!" laughs Dr. Halioua. "I think that is the secret of Jewish mothers, in giving not only love like all mothers, but tremendous self-assurance to their children."

> **A**s the 2,000-year-old man, Mel Brooks claimed to be the first Jew to study medicine at the big medical cave. (It took a week.) His mother, he said, was the first one in history to coin the phrase "This is my son, the doctor."

EXCELLENCE!

" You're absolutely certain your progeny is perfect!"
—Mallory Lewis

Alright. OK. Sure, Jewish mothers have wildly different MOs. Whether she's the "'A' is good, now, let's talk A-plus" sort, or as Rona Ginott calls it, "a facilitator," who sets the tone by example and opportunity, the pursuit of excellence is part of our ethno-type.

"I was raised with the compulsion to do the best!" says Dr. Gruber. "'Why didn't you get 100?' I was asked, if I got a 99."

"I could do no wrong," says Theodore Bikel. "According to my mother, I was a genius!" He adds that this particular characteristic was not always helpful. Though his mother was supportive of his performing, the truth is, her expectation of perfection "was wrong . . . we all do wrong."

"The desires for high achievement are . . . characteristics that are disproportionately common in the Jewish community," says Michael Medved.

Although Jews represent one-fourth of 1 percent of the world's population, we have won over 20 percent of all Nobel Prizes awarded since its inception in 1901, and yes, some, like Rosalyn Sussman Yalow, have been Jewish mothers.

This hope, vital to the Jewish mama's spirits, is often met with an equal opposite reaction: Never (OK rarely) "satisfied," excessive worry, and protection.

I DON'T GET (MUCH) SATISFACTION, OR . . . THE KVETCH

There's a correlation between the *expectation* of excellence— and satisfaction. While the Jewish mother takes great pleasure from a child's success, with the bar set high, true satisfaction is not easy to come by—or to hold onto. A history colored by adversity, apprehension, exile, and fear of being sandbagged by "the evil eye," brings with it the constant expectation of disappointment. Many of us rain on parades—in advance. Better we should expect the worse—so when the rain comes, we've already put up the umbrella.

"[The Jewish mother] finds something wrong . . . with everything," remarks Judy Gold. "If we're leaving for a trip tomorrow, she'll say: 'Tomorrow! There'll be the worst traffic in the world!' If you suggest brunch . . . " 'Go *out* for brunch? It's too crowded. No one's going out.'" (Now, that's some logic.)

Neil Simon is a master at portraying this ethno-typical characteristic. In his *Brighton Beach Memoirs,* the mama sends her son out for a quarter pound of butter twice a day. Why not a half pound? "Suppose the house burned down this afternoon? Why do I need an extra quarter pound of butter?" she explains.

Even God is not immune.

A Jewish mama and her little girl walked along the beach when a gigantic wave rolled in and swept the child to sea.

"Oh, God," lamented the mama, her face toward heaven.

"This is my only baby! The love, the joy of my joy! Please God! Bring her back to me and I'll go to synagogue and pray every day!"

Suddenly, another gigantic wave rolled in and deposited the girl back on the sand safe and sound.

Mama looked up and said, " . . . she had on a hat. . . ."

✡ ---

THE RABBI WAS GIVING HIS USUAL SERMON, AND SENT THE CONGREGATION HOME WITH A REQUEST. "OUR SYNAGOGUE IS COLLECTING GOODS FOR THE NEEDY. PLEASE BRING ANYTHING YOU HAVE IN YOUR HOMES YOU CAN SPARE."

SUDDENLY A MOTHER OF FIVE CALLS OUT: "EXCUSE ME, RABBI, BUT DOES *TSOURIS* COUNT?"

--- ✡ ---

A classic story socks a double whammy . . . listen.

Yankele finally got married, although his mother wasn't thrilled with his choice, Elsa, a "smart-nik" therapist, who his mama thought had too much control over Yankele. On his birthday, she bought him two ties, one striped, one plaid.

"Oy, which to wear?!" worried Yankele when going to Mama's. He finally decided on one.

"I see, you're wearing the striped one," said Mama. "What . . . ? The plaid you don't like?"

So when he visited the following week, Yankele, to make peace, wore *both* ties.

When his mama saw this, she grabbed her head between her hands and sobbed, "Oy! See . . . ? I always knew, eventually, that wife of yours would turn you meshugge [nuts]!"

WHAT? ME WORRY: HIGH ANXIETY—MAMA'S LAW

And what fuels the pessimistic "kvetch"? In a word, worry. "Jewish mothers . . . we assume the worst," says Blu Greenberg.

> "Jewish mothers suffer from terminal anxiety."
> —Judy Gold

Forget Murphy's Law. Chances are his real name was Murphosky and his mama taught him: "If anything can go wrong, it will."

"'*What if* . . .' That's my wife, Ruth," chuckles Harry Leichter, creator of the *Schmooze News*, www.schmoozenews.com. "She'll figure out every single thing that could possibly happen. '*What if* . . . the children don't get a Jewish education? *What if* . . . we move to Minneapolis and have to drive six hours to take the kids to Hebrew school? *What if* . . . we move to Montana? Maybe there's a shul in Montana?' She's a worrier . . . money, bills, the kids, parents. The 'what if . . . ' is an analysis of every possible scenario."

I can still remember my late mother's face, peering out of a window at 1:00 a.m. if I wasn't home from a date. She gave me "the basic silent look" for two days, which I suppose she felt was equal to her two hours of suffering.

I'm a worrier. When my son was two, his pediatrician wrote on his chart: "MOTHER: LUNATIC," which could be due to the fact that I thought a hernia in a two-year-old might be malignant. It's in the DNA. The ethno-type no doubt contains a W-strand—for Worry. The *kinder* (children) are not only our cultural future, but a projection of ourselves—especially for the more extreme ethno-typical mother, who re-stapled the cord. And this constant "worry" has become our lead media stereotype "for the laughs."

Yet, "worry and pessimism is a product of our history," explains Rabbi Felipe Goodman. And God knows we've had a lot to worry about during our 5,000-year history.

"I worry," reports Julie Cobb, superb actress, much like her parents, Lee J. Cobb and Yiddish theater and film star Helen

Beverley. "I'm taking a Kabbalah class with my twenty-two-year-old daughter, yet I worry about everything. Is she happy? Is she safe? What's she eating? Is she exercising?"

AND SPEAKING OF FOOD . . . *ESS*, MY CHILD!

Food . . . the universal expression of love, is particularly important for a culture that has gone without. The Jewish mother is usually not happy unless she's feeding—*somebody*. Where food was scarce mama often sacrificed to make sure the *kinder* could eat. As newspaper editor and comic Laurie Cohen, who's in a constant battle over food and weight, says, "I always heard children are starving in Europe!" And of course, they were.

The preparation and serving of food in Judaism—obeying kosher dietary laws—is critical spiritually, and this responsibility falls to the Jewish mother, as we'll see later. Even today, when food is available and Kosher Lite, or picking and choosing from the Laws (if at all), is practiced by many Jewish mothers, still, the very *offering* remains a sign of hospitality and most of all, a capable *baleboste* (homemaker).

> ## "The Jewish mother is incapable of not offering food to everyone who walks in the door."
> —Mallory Lewis

The fabulous Jewish author, feminist, and scholar, Blu Greenberg, agrees. "In that sense, I'm a Jewish mother. Food. It always was important my children should not go hungry."

"My mother's from the school that the minute you walk in the house you have to eat," said Susie Essman in a 2003 interview, describing her mother, Zora. "She asks, 'What can I get you?' and if I say, 'Nothing,' the question just continues."

"One Thanksgiving, there were only six of us, and she had two twenty-pound turkeys—plus brisket. Not to mention the eight sides and fifteen pies and cakes. And halvah. I went onstage that night to do stand-up and I just read the menu from her dinner."

When I spoke to mama Zora, she had a slightly different take on the matter. "My kids don't know this part of me . . . a lot of it is, but it's really not me. The fact is, I do make two turkeys on Thanksgiving but . . . I'm trying to please everybody . . . one likes this dressing, another likes that dressing. My children say I have a brisket under my skirt . . . not me."

"*Ess ess ess!*" quips Harry Leichter. "My mother made me pregnant with all the food she gave me. She wanted to make sure I was healthy. She cooked steaks for me every day, even though she worked an eighteen-hour day. On weekends, there were seven courses."

The remarkable thing about my mother is that for thirty years she served us nothing but leftovers. The original meal has never been found. This oft-repeated hilarity was said by the late Calvin Trillin.

My own *bubbe* was the Empress of the Leftovers. She loved seltzer, which years ago was delivered in those marvelous blue or clear bottles that spritzed. When she came to visit, we noticed an odd pattern. There were eight or nine half-filled glasses of water in the fridge. Since she couldn't put the unused seltzer back—she *saved* it. She wondered where the bubbles went till her dying day.

---✡---

MOLLY AND JENNY RAN INTO EACH OTHER AT A DELI. "I HELD ONE FANTASTIC DINNER PARTY LAST NIGHT," SAID MOLLY. "I HAD OVER MY SONS, THEIR WIVES, AND MY SEVEN GRANDCHILDREN. I HAD SO MUCH FOOD THAT WHEN THEY WALKED TO THEIR CARS, THEY WERE DOUBLED OVER."

WITHOUT MISSING A BEAT, JENNY ANSWERED, "FROM YOUR HOUSE THEY COULD WALK?!"

---✡---

PROTECTION . . . OK, OVERPROTECTION

"They all have contact with their children every single day."
—Judy Gold, comedian

"When Kerri was in Texas, I went every couple of weeks to Houston. She's my best friend," says Melanie Strug. "I talk to her almost every day, as well as my older daughter."

Love and protection were partners in shtetl survival when life was brutal and enemies abounded. The two are still partners, and yes, there are moms who are comfortable with space, but the Jewish mother has a long memory, and often feels if a little involvement is good, a lot may be better. The tie between mother and child has been so historically intertwined that even now, letting go to some of us feels a little like letting go of ourselves. When it goes too far, the result can be overprotecting—or smothering. And of course, it can even be hysterical.

"My mother called just a couple of years ago to remind me not to sleep on my stomach because she said she heard on the news that sleeping on the stomach is the number-one cause of sudden infant death," says Amy Borkowsky, comedian and creator of two volumes of the hit comedy CD and book, *Amy's Answering Machine: Messages from Mom*. Using real messages from her mom, Amy Borkowsky became a comedy hit.

If you take kidsfirst, add worry, along with a dollop of heavy sacrifice and involvement, you get more connections than Sprint.

"When I was seven, I was once two hours late for dinner. My mother attached an egg timer to my belt. When it went off, that was when I went home," laughs Judy Gold, who is keeping the worry/protection tradition alive. "Once, when I had to be at an audition, I asked one of my son's teachers to walk with him and bring him home at six. Nothing at 6:15. By 6:20, I'm walking the streets hysterical! I called the head of the school, freaking out! They finally got home at seven. They were playing Game Boy. Here, I was going crazy assuming the worst."

"Phone Home" wasn't invented by E.T. (But no doubt Steven Spielberg heard it somewhere.)

"She has a map with pins so she can trail us," chuckles Harry Leichter, describing his mother-in-law, when he and his wife are traveling. On normal days, "She wants the kids (now early boomers) to check in twice a day. If we're not home by five, she asks 'where were you?' She wants to know exactly where we are at all times. And if we don't call her, she'll call us."

Like a Jewish Mrs. Claus, somehow, the Jewish mother "knows" if her kids have been naughty or nice. The intimate relationship gives the Jewish mama what she believes is special insight bordering on mystical powers—and if not? Logic.

THE REINS . . .

Control is a natural consequence of worry. Keeping tight reins was a role that was vital in shtetl life, where, as outsiders in a hostile world, religious tradition and survival was constantly threatened—and even the *kinder* understood the roots, often viewing mom as a majestic figure.

Esther suspected hanky-panky between her son Gerald and his roommate, Debby, though Gerald denied it. After one visit, Gerald noticed the gravy ladle was missing, so he sent "mama" a letter: "Dear Mama: I'm not saying you did take the ladle, I'm not saying you didn't. But the fact remains it's been missing since you were here."

Mama answered: "Sonny: I'm not saying you do sleep with Debbie, I'm not saying you don't. But the fact remains, if she were sleeping where she belongs, she'd have found the ladle already."

"Strong personalities and opinions!" says Mexican-born Rabbi Felipe Goodman, spiritual leader of Temple Beth Sholom, in Las Vegas, when describing Jewish mamas. "They want the best for the people they love and will stop at nothing. They'll also tell you to put on a sweater when *they're* cold."

"Rigid," offers actress/ singer, Lainie Kazan, who drew raves for her Mama role in *My Big Fat Greek Wedding*.

"She's domineering, but then you can also call the Jewish mother an aggressive survivor."

When these women came to America, however, the very traits that meant survival in the shtetl community were seen as "neurotic," especially when the youngsters who were "insiders" became desperate to move "out" into a world of freedom—including freedom from Mama's control. Disharmony between mother and child developed rather suddenly, and pain was the result, which provided fodder for both humor—and shrinks.

> "SHE WAS ALWAYS VERY CONTROLLING AND
> I WAS TRYING TO REBEL. SHE TOLD ME TO
> PRAY TO GOD . . . I WENT TO THE WINDOW
> AND PRAYED TO GIVE ME PEACE. [SHE DID]
> TELL ME TO WEAR CLEAN UNDERWEAR—IN
> CASE OF AN ACCIDENT."
> —Dr. Ruth Gruber

"[My mother] was a mixture of lovable, but she was more tyrannical than she'd like to believe," says the versatile actor/singer Theodore Bikel. "She devoted herself to being overly protective of me to the point where after she died, she 'kept' family away from me which was eminently disturbable."

IT COMES FROM LOVE, OR DON'T FEEL GUILTY

I'm hiding under my desk, but . . . hey, it came up—once or twice. Of course not all Jewish mothers operate using manipulation and guilt (other people do it too). But face it. A large dollop of sacrifice, even when seen by the children as love, can be a mega guilt-producer.

While the environment may have changed, the shtetl impetus to sacrifice for the *kinder*—if not for food, then for private schools, dancing lessons, college, or making a lavish bar mitzvah or wedding—persists as part of our kidsfirst ethno-type.

Yet, the flip side, especially when "sacrifice" is no longer equated with survival or Jewish values, is guilt. And in our brave new world, the benefactors are not always thrilled with the price.

"My parents come on the phone: 'What size is your dining room? I'm thinking of getting you a dining set. We ordered it for ourselves, but we'll see if the guy can drop it off to you from Florida to Arizona—and we'll live with the old one,'" describes Laurie Cohen, newspaper editor and comic. "Then, my mother tells me to 'run get measuring tape.' I don't have one. 'OK, so go get a ruler. Go the store, get a ruler, then come right home and call us.'" Oy!

The most famous example is the classic, oft-repeated Mike Nichols, Elaine May routine, "Mother and Son," where his mother claims to have waited by the phone for three days, near fainting from hunger, because she didn't want her mouth to be full when her son called. Even his explanation that he was busy sending up the Vanguard led her to kvetch, "it's always something."

"What is the other side of the mother's bountifulness?" poses Dr. Myrna Hant. "The major obligation of the child is to bring *nakhes* [joy] to his mother . . . it is the epitome of life's goodness. Defining success in the shtetl, as success in any culture, is complex and dependent upon many factors. Certainly, for the daughter success [was] defined as marrying well, being an efficient and skillful housekeeper . . . conducting a Yiddish *hoyz* [Jewish house] . . . keeping harmony in her family . . . being the mistress of a beautiful household, a real *baleboste*. For a boy, success [was] defined as scholarly prowess in Jewish studies."

HIGH INTENSITY AND HUMOR . . .
"*MAMALA*, CAN YOU HEAR ME?"

Jewish mothers make lousy mimes. Boom! Passionate, open, with both a natural and trained flair for the verbal, you know where she stands and how she feels. Always. About most everything. And there's an excellent chance you'll hear it over and over again.

Jewish mothers are also funny. Yes, I believe funnier than many other ethno-types. (Think Swedish.)

She's born into a religious tradition of Talmudic argumentation, honed by *mama-loshen* (Yiddish), the ultimate language of feeling, humor, wit, irony, misery, judgment, triumph, and intensity—she's "out there." She's vocal. She's passionate. And she's sharp.

Recall the scene in Woody Allen's *Annie Hall* in split screen. Alvy Singer, having dinner with his girlfriend's "proper" (if not insane) non-Jewish family, as he compares it with his own—a wild madding free-for-all. The volume alone is an ad for Miracle Ear, as his family argues, yells, and debates.

I chose this scene because, despite Allen's exaggerated portrayal, I've rarely seen a quiet Jewish home—especially over food. Some of the most enjoyable moments of my life were over the family dinner table listening as the adults talked, argued, and laughed. The Jewish mother has flair and drama, whether in agony or ecstasy.

Of course not all Jewish mothers are kvetchers or hollerers, but the ethno-type is high verbal—in praise, in criticism, in advice— in doing laundry, or yes, even in organizing a labor strike. As you will see in ensuing chapters, the other side of "out there" also spirits determination and a fearlessness to express opinions that go beyond "sweaters" and "clean underwear."

"WORLD, CAN YOU HEAR ME?"
ACTIVISM, COMMUNITY, PHILANTHROPY

Our religion and our cultural tradition instructs us to be change-makers. *Tikkun olam* is our responsibility to try and heal the world. And not just within the world of the Jews, but injustices to all peoples. Silence to the persecution of others is not an option for the Jewish mother.

"Responsibility and commitment are deeply indebted in the Jewish notion convenant," says religious feminist author Blu Greenberg. "We take this responsibility and partnership with our children."

In the pursuit of justice or fairness you'll rarely find the timid. If the Jewish mother is demanding and sometimes "loud" or outspoken, she's a fighter. She's out there shaking up "the system."

My paternal grandmother, a Russian immigrant to Canada, was legion. She fell in love with a much older widower with two children. Despite disapproval from her family, she leaped from a window and hopped on a horse, and the two lovers took off.

Within ten years or so, she had four more children, and she, too, was widowed and without funds while still in her twenties. Not only did she raise all the children, she ran a farm, took in sewing, was a magnificent cook, provided shelter and food for family from the old country, and still found time to work with a Jewish girls club. When a store raised the price of milk by a penny, she led a strike—and won.

"What a mouth she had on her!" says the family.

Her name was Manya and she died before I was born. As is the custom, I was named for her and take great pride in this amazing woman. Her unsung story is one of millions of typical Jewish mamas of her day—and today.

History is rife with examples of the Jewish mother, acting on her beliefs with almost unprecedented chutzpah! These attributes of strong verbal skills, courage, an acute sense of values, and determination have given rise to some of our most influential civic leaders, activists, and feminists—from Biblical Jewish mothers to pioneers, to modern-day Yentls such as Bella Abzug, Blu Greenberg, Betty Friedan, Barbra Streisand, Rabbi Bonnie Koppell, and Susan Weidman Schneider. These are but a few Jewish mothers, among many, who have changed the world, as well as our view of the Jewish woman.

WHOSE LIFE IS IT, ANYWAY?

Does the ethno-typical Jewish mother live through her children? Some do, not all. But as the *kinder* was the shtetl mother's job, the buck stopped with her. If you were a CEO and your company explodes, are you not shamed? Blamed? And so it was with the Jewish mother. Her children were her bailiwick, and her "success" judged naturally by the success of her effort.

> This is not exclusive to the Jewish mother. Even a Trump shleps his offspring on the air as his "true apprentices" and rarely fails to mention their education at Wharton.

"Many do live vicariously through their children. . . . It's for them," says Dr. Eileen Warshaw. "I feel it was the same way in the shtetl. They felt the child's success or failure would reflect on themselves."

Comic-singer-impressionist painter Marilyn Michaels had her maternal hands full. She was the daughter of Jewish entertainment royalty as the child of the late famed cantoress, Fraydele Oysher and Metropolitan opera basso, Harold Sternberg, and niece to the legendary cantor and Yiddish star, Moishe Oysher.

My son and I attended her son's birthday party when he was four or five. Grandma Fraydele was there. This tiny woman with the booming voice "encouraged" the boy to sing, which he finally did: "God Bless America." Grandma's response? "That you call singing?! Who's gonna applaud for that?" Marilyn gave me a withered look.

LETTING GO

Giving up the job of raising, advising, and being involved is not an easy task for any mother, but for one who is kidfirst it's a tough balancing act—knowing when and how to hold on—and when to tape our mouths shut.

> # "The Jewish mother feels her job isn't done even after death. You're never too dead to be a Jewish mother."
> —Mallory Lewis

"You're there for them when they're struggling, when they're adolescents," says Zora Essman. "Then you have to let go. It's hard to do. It's hard not to say when to brush your teeth."

Yet, despite the jokes and complaints, many adult children, while "protesting" overprotectiveness, nevertheless are grateful for the ongoing support and love they receive.

"Five years ago I was having some medical problems," says actress Joanna Gleason, who's married to Chris Sarandon. The couple has four children between them. "I was sleepless, agitated. I called my mom at 2:00 a.m. She's at my house in three minutes flat. She climbed into bed with me, and later cooked." Her mother, Marilyn, is still all about support for her grown children, a fact Joanna fiercely admires and emulates. "My mother is a Jewish mother, totally. Like all the women in my family, she's a maven in a crisis, a self-possessed talented woman, a nurturer. We all behave the same way . . . protective, focused, and we keep a benign distance. We know when to push, when to let go—and how to make our children feel safe."

Of course not all mamas, particularly several generations ago, were quite so educated on the art of letting go. My maternal grandmother, Bella, was Polish. She met my grandfather, Alec, a Russian, while he was on the run from the Russian Army with my infant mother. (So, who wasn't?) Leaving their families behind, they got to America in the 1920s through bribery and boozing the border guards. She was one tough, critical, controlling mama but then, she had to be.

When my mother married, grandma had to take backseat. During one decision-making discussion, she ventured her opinion. My father disagreed and explained patiently that now he and mom would make their own decisions. Shocked at being outsourced, Grandma screamed: "OY!!! I'm no longer the Cap'n, I'm only the Foist Mate!" Anchors oy vey!

THE ETHNO-TYPE: A MARVELOUS MYSTIQUE

The Jewish mother: loving, nurturing, sacrificing, child-centered, bossy, verbal, tribal, overfeeding, hilarious, protective, "out there," an activist—a woman whose background has been molded by religion, tradition, unbearable hardship and loss, and hope. All of these are the Jewish mother, but interpreted by each of us in our own unique way. Where we stand on the continuum varies, but almost all share most of these cultural traits and hope to pass them on to our children as part of our great legacy.

From My Yiddishe Mama to the Yiddishe Yenta:
HOW COULD THIS BE—AND WHY?

In seventy or so years, our complex, multidimensional, ethnotype Jewish mom has gone from love songs in praise to a sitcom insult. She's the butt of every joke, the cause of every neurosis, the one who poohs on her children's parades, hacks through emotional borders, manipulates to gain her own ends, and is as sensitive as roadkill.

Jewish women, just like all women, have grown through education, feminism, and power. We have had the opportunity to be ourselves with far greater freedom and recognition than ever before.

Yet oddly, today, the Jewish mother is still portrayed as the most negative *caricature* of the shtetl mother.

As Jewish males predominated in TV and film, a great deal of our image has been manufactured by them and whether directly or indirectly, we have become the negative by-products of assimilation.

MEDIA: LOOKING BACK . . .

In the 1940s and 1950s we got a glimpse of the Jewish mother through the incomparable Gertrude Berg, as Molly Goldberg, in what many consider the first true sitcom. The show, which started on radio, then moved to television, targeted the cultural differences between immigrant parents and their new-world children. During the show's thirty-year run, the Goldbergs, like many immigrant families, "moved on up" from a New York tenement, to the Bronx, and finally to Connecticut.

Molly, buxom and benevolent, was the family fixer, who, in her Mollyisms, or cracked Yinglish, used common sense, wisdom, and compassion as her tools to advise her family—and anyone else in her orbit. Through Berg's highly skilled writing and performance, every show revealed a love for mankind and acceptance of human behavior. She was likeable and personal with her audience and reflected the trials, hopes, and patriotism of many immigrant groups of her time—but in a nonthreatening way, which was acceptable to postwar viewers of many religions and races.

So much for positive ethnic images. After *The Goldbergs* ended in 1955, Jewish women mostly disappeared on air for two decades. The babies had boomed, many leaving generations between themselves and the shtetls. As families ran from their ethnic city streets to "melt" into suburbia— and the Land of Assimilation—the Vanilla families took over. The Nelsons, the Cleavers, the Andersons, and the Stones reigned in Main Street, USA, representing the generic American family archetype.

Then, in the 1970s came Rhoda Morgenstern (played by non-Jew Valerie Harper), Mary's best gal pal on *The Mary Tyler Moore Show*. When *Rhoda* spun off, enlarging the role of her Jewish mama, Ida Morgenstern (Nancy Walker), the change from warm-hearted shtetl mom started. The turbulent 1960s that pitted parent against child while bringing new world abundance to the Jewish mother became a part of prime-time TV, film, and books. The result was a reinvention of the Jewish mother, who, born or raised in America, was portrayed as a mélange of nurturing and devouring, manipulative, pushy, judgmental, demanding, insufferable—and "loving." The message was clear: Children were locked in mama-prison and their attempts to break out brought the laughs. Big ones.

As second bananas, the Jewish mother proved the perfect foil for their "long-suffering" children in shows such as *Mad About You*, *Seinfeld*, *Will and Grace*, and *The Nanny*.

Sylvia (Renee Taylor), Fran Fine's mother in *The Nanny*, is the quintessential pain in the *tuchus* (behind) with her all-consuming interest in: her daughter getting married, food, and greed. Guilt . . . constant one-line guilt, was the MO, as "Sylvia," when thwarted, asked "Fran" to, among other things, feel her for lumps.

More, even her *stereotype* was flawed. Not only was she tasteless and tactless, most attempts at the redeeming moment between mother and child just weren't, well, believable as the formula was objectifying and the quick joke.

In Sylvia's world, for example, greed came before kidfirst. In one episode, when it was thought there was a baby mix-up at the hospital, she was willing to give up her daughter to a classy Black woman—with money.

This would never happen.

> "THE TV STEREOTYPE IS UNFAIR, EXAGGERATED, UNBALANCED, EMBARRASSING, RIDICULING, AND EXTREME," SAYS BLU GREENBERG. "ON THE OTHER HAND, THEY CAN'T TAKE AWAY WHAT WE'VE ACHIEVED—THE VALUES OF THE JEWISH MOTHER."

In *Seinfeld*, there was no attempt at redemption with George Constanza's mother, played by the marvelous Estelle Harris. The same is true of the Jewish mothers (Susie Essman, among others) in *Curb Your Enthusiasm*. Larry David takes no prisoners in his group. They're all equal opportunity obnoxious, pretentious, paranoics, doomed to view life as universal *mishegoss*, and meet it mouth-on, with their own Mega-*mishegoss*.

The exception (on TV) was *Brooklyn Bridge* (1991), set in the 1950s, that showed Jewish mothering and grand-mothering as bountiful, beloved, and balanced. Sadly, few wanted to watch beyond a few seasons.

Today, the Jewish mother media stereotype has become the prototype for mothers of all stripes.

Mama-bashing is now universal. If these women aren't actually vipers, then many fall into the "Smart Wife Saves Tuchus of Stupid Male" category.

Most notable is Lord of the Wimps, Ray Barone: OK, he's a harmless guy but no hero. Why? Because, he's been "fixed," neutered, by "Everybody [Who] Loves" him. Mostly . . . the moms.

Ethnic moms, especially those of Italian descent, such as Marie Barone, are hard hit. Marie sets a new standard for the maternal stereotype as part harridan, part wolf, who acts with a vengeance—that "comes from love." Ray's put-upon wife, Debra, while far more aware, also grows a few unflattering fangs, coming out of most frays with "Wife Knows Best" tattooed on Ray's psyche.

Black moms, on the other hand, have faired better, thanks to Bill Cosby's influence. Claire Huxtable is the very soul of the modern mom, who can balance her law career while raising five children with a firm (if not sarcastic) hand in place. Child-first, this is a professional family with the affluence to provide for their brood. *The Jeffersons* and *Good Times* portray the wise matriarch, who, again, is both peacemaker and the conscience of the family.

Even the WASP mother (the perennial back-seated and obedient June Cleaver) is no longer immune. Jamie Buchman's mom in *Mad About You* evoked trembling in her daughters at the mere thought of a visit. Although she was portrayed as a constantly smiling, "life is good," woman whose MO was steeped in denial, her code-speak was like something out of *Through the Looking Glass*. Will's mother in *Will and Grace*, played by the glorious Blythe Danner, was the consummate stereotype of the WASP mom, who not only *talked* in code-speak, but was concerned with keeping up appearances and was steeped in emotional denial, which she handled through a very proper (and very extended) cocktail hour. (In crime shows, the WASPy mom is often *rich*—and in denial—with a son who has an eye tick and collects flesh-eating moths under mama's radar.)

In *Sex and the City,* though none of the *characters* were born Jewish, and their mothers are not seen on air, whenever they're mentioned, they usually bring about eye rolls, and trips home are about as welcome as a ring, courtesy of Cracker Jacks.

Yet one can't help but notice, that for all the kvetching about mothers, recent hits have reinvented almost precisely the same ethno-type in their "new" family groups—their friends.

The *Seinfeld* "four" are rife with "Jewish mother" stereotypes— without the Jewish mother. Argumentation for one. No debate is too petty. With almost Talmudic logic, the group might be found arguing about the possibility of "over-drying." It's laundry by Talmudic review. While George loathes the "insanity" of his babbling mother, within his new "family" of pals, could he be *more* of the stereotype in high decibel?

Group kvetching forms the core of the comedy. The "we four against the world— which is out to get us," plus the never-ending picayune debates are a close replica of the very traits they loathe in their parents. If you add a few years to the group, they would fit neatly with their mamas—arguing over temperature control, early bird specials, and pens that write upside down.

Will and Grace, along with friends Karen and Jack, form yet another faux "family." The Jewish Grace is not unlike her overbearing, narcissistic, yet charming mother. Will maintains his mother's rather formal rigid, appearances-first stance. Grace, like mama, is all about, well—Grace.

Will and Grace does have two important distinctions worth mentioning. It is the first prime-time sitcom since *The Goldbergs* to feature a marriage between a Jewish man and woman. When Grace and "Leo" Markus stood under a chuppah to wed, viewers saw a major Jewish character who didn't "trade out" or become the oddball mate, as foil for the more stable WASP, such as Paul and Jamie, Fran and Maxwell, Dharma and Greg, or Rhoda and Joe. Furthermore, the audaciously Jewish Grace is not the primo resident neurotic. Jack and Karen make Grace (even when she's singing) seem almost "regular"—an unusual and positive TV turn.

It could be that the need for "family," connection, involvement, and intimacy, burdensome as it may be, is still around. Because if we don't get it, we simply reinvent something like it—and call it "friends."

Comic films and books in popular culture haven't treated the Jewish mother—or any mother—much better. While some have been depicted as loving, the majority are harridans in films, for example: *My Favorite Year, Lovers and Other Strangers, Meet the Fockers, Annie Hall, Goodbye Columbus, Throw Mama off the Train*, and if you can imagine, Jane Fonda in *Monster-in-Law*.

And in books, there was the breakthrough seller, *Portnoy's Complaint* (1970), by Philip Roth who, in one passage, describes his mother as a woman who might actually be "too good"—as weeping and suffering, she ground her own horseradish, checked every "crease and seam" in his body, and whose house was so spotless, you could eat off the bathroom floor.

Comedy albums abounded. *How to Be a Jewish Mother* is based on the book by Dan Greenberg who "advises" the Jewish mother to sit with a daughter who is without prospects, and tell her you wish to go into the coffin with a smile on your face . . . so, maybe a professional man may not be so important (after all, her father was in ladies' buttons); besides, by then, mama will probably be dead anyway.

"On film, a real man has to be dueling, some supremely threatening force, something powerful, primal, and difficult," says author, film critic, and radio personality Michael Medved. "In domestic dramas, in so many films, novels, and stories involving Jewish men, they are involved in a constant duel with a mother—and you have to make that mother monstrous."

ASSIMILATION: MAMA-DRAMAS AND THE SONS WHO CREATED THEM

Earlier I wrote of the sons in media who helped shape the negative image of the Jewish mother. How did this transformation from adoration to comic strip occur when these shtetl families came to America? Like most change, it was a process, fueled by assimilation. In the shtetls, Hebraic traditions, sacrifice, protection, involvement, and making sure the kids were in the fold, were *essential* to keeping the family Jewish, together—and alive. I believe when these mothers came to America, they found themselves "outsourced" as their children wanted to fly and grab a piece of the American Dream and status, which was hard to reconcile with their Jewishness, and their mothers' expectations.

In the very early days of TV and film, this dual tug was expressed, but Mama was still an adored part of the equation. In the iconic *The Jazz Singer*, a classic story of assimilation, Jack Rabinowitz (Al Jolson) faces a life-changing choice. Does he sing as a cantor on Yom Kippur, or fulfill his duties as "Jack Robin," the jazz singer? In 1927, Hollywood's first feature-length "talkie" includes a memorable excerpt between mother and son after his father, the cantor, dies. In the dialogue, Jack promises his mama, that if he's a success, he'll move them to the Bronx (a step up), buy her a nice pink dress, and take her to Coney Island.

This critical speech sent Jack and his mother on their way to a new and untried future. One where, for the first time, the son had to take mama by the hand in this alien world. Her role was changing. She was no longer the sure moral center. Now, as a stranger in a brave new world, she was being led by her child— one whose religious values were being usurped by secular values in a fervent desire for acceptance.

> **"THERE HAS TO BE ALTRUISM TO REINFORCE EVERY STEREOTYPE. TODAY, IT'S ABUSED. WE'VE LOST OUR SENSE OF PERSPECTIVE WITH ASSIMILATION."**
> —Binyamin Jolkovsky

The next giant step in the change of image was the development of the Jewish comedian. Within a generation, Jewish sons were honing a new craft and a new view of "mama," as writers and comics in the Borscht Belt.

The Borscht Belt, in New York's Catskill Mountains, refers to the summer resorts Jews began to frequent in the 1940s. Initially bungalow colonies, known as *kuchaleyns,* they grew, due in part to "restricted" hotels. The Concord, Grossinger's, Granit, Kutshers, the Nevele, the Pines, Raleigh, Brickman's, and Brown's, became full-service luxury resorts and turned the area into what was called "the Jewish Alps." With virtually unlimited food, *shadchens* (matchmakers) and *tummlers* (underpaid social directors), young comics looking for a break, "apprenticed" by doing everything from acting as Master of Ceremonies to calling Simple Simon. These legendary hotels peaked in the 1950s and 1960s.

Male comedians who got their start or regularly performed in Borscht Belt resorts include: Jerry Lewis, Jackie Mason, Buddy Hackett, Woody Allen, Freddie Roman, Morey Amsterdam, Milton Berle, Carl Reiner, Shelley Berman, Mel Brooks, Lenny Bruce, George Burns, Red Buttons, Sid Caesar, Jack Carter, Myron Cohen, Norm Crosby, Bill Dana, Rodney Dangerfield, Shecky Greene, Mickey Katz, Danny Kaye, Alan King, Robert Klein, Jack E. Leonard, Don Rickles, and Henny Youngman, among others.

This group of mostly first-generation Americans became the founders of Borscht Belt humor, which was fast, frequently deprecating, and often used "Mama" material. The wonderful film *Mr. Saturday Night* is an excellent representation of the Borscht Belt.

Many of these comics, plus others, became writers, producers, as well as stars of TV and film—and some became the fathers of the Jewish mother stereotype, which continues today by mostly second- and third-generation sons.

After all, TV and film was (and remains) significantly Jewish in its origins, and in those who are in control as producers, network executives, and writers. As first-generation writers and comics, many not only found themselves in conflict with their family's shtetl ideas, but they also found those ideas fertile sources of "subversive" humor.

Jackie Mason, a rabbi, never did tell his father, also a rabbi, he was running up to the Borscht Belt to perform. In one interview I did with him, I asked how he thought his father would feel now, knowing his success. "He'd say, 'Whether you steal a buck or a million, you're still a thief.'" Recently, he said he loved his mother, but she was lost somewhere, subservient in the shadow of his Orthodox father and he "resented the way his mother was treated— the lack of respect."

"During pogroms, traits such as arguing were not negative," writes Dr. Myrna Hant. "Some [of these] look like pathology in this country. They became a negative, an embarrassment [for the children]. There is some disgrace and shame on the part of the writers. As a rationalization, the Jewish mother is a comedic device."

Of course, we can't eliminate anti-Semitism on the part of non-Jews as a possibility for the perpetuation of the image as well.

Scholarly pieces have been written about the assimilation and tug of war between the shtetl mother and her American child. Traits and values once revered in the Jewish mother now became a shameful embarrassment for some. This proved especially true for her sons since these traits were not only considered unnecessary now, but were also perceived as a noose, keeping them from being accepted and assimilated in the Gentile world. And they wanted to distance themselves from those characteristics. Jewish names were changed, while mockery and an alrightnik status became fodder for many comics.

"MR. POISSON," SAID THE SECRETARY, "YOUR
MOTHER, MRS. FISHMAN, IS CALLING."

"MAMA, ARE YOU OK? SOFIA AND I WERE
WORRIED WHEN YOU DIDN'T SHOW UP AT OUR
CONDO-WARMING PARTY LAST NIGHT."

"THE LOBBY'S GORGEOUS," SAID MRS. FISHMAN.
"I CAME, I SAW IT . . . THEN I WENT HOME."

"BUT MAMA, IF YOU WERE THERE, WHY DIDN'T
YOU COME UP?" ASKED POISSON, PUZZLED.

"I FORGOT YOUR NAME."

"The guilt induced by the Old World was not her siren song; rather she demanded loyalty to herself and her expectations in this New World. The Jewish mother, thus, can become a cultural construct of negative mothering, a form of backlash against powerful mother images," writes Dr. Myrna Hant.

"More, the womens' movement also created a backlash, by creating ambiguity toward motherhood. By ridiculing her we can laugh at all women's attempts at gaining power. We can laugh at her and keep her somewhat under control as she cleverly manipulates her own miniature environment. . . . The TV Jewish mother does represent a necessary but obnoxious 'object' in her children's lives who appears to exist only so that her offspring can either be better or achieve more."

The "Hover-Mother," who hangs on, is typical of the Jewish mother that is portrayed in the media and turns the legitimate behavior of the shtetl mother into a destructive and limiting force for her children who are desperately trying to break free. Without context and with exaggeration, the neurosis falls squarely on her, making her, at best, a comic character, or at worst, a mildly demented she-witch.

Notice that the majority of these shows and books are set in New York City, as a significant number of Jewish immigrants settled there and contributed to its character and culture. Perceived liberalism, cadences, style, vocal tones, fast wit, and what some consider "pushy" qualities lead many to equate New York with "Jewish." While the Atlanta Jewish mother, for example, behaves and sounds very different to the ear than the New York Jewish mother, Jewish mothers from all parts of the country, and most of the world, share similar beliefs and traits.

A second media problem is the fear or avoidance of creative material that appears "too Jewish."

A number of Jewish writers have complained that despite the fact that Hollywood film pioneers were Jewish, Jewish films (that aren't about dead Jews) aren't generally made. The term "too Jewish" is often used. Performers, until recently, changed their names, and especially females with exotic "Jewish" looks, such as Sarah Jessica Parker and Barbra Streisand, felt the sting of stereotyping early in their careers.

"Indy (Independent) films are more thoughtful," says Binyamin Jolkovsky. "You can't have *Touched by an Angel* Jewish-style. It's not going to be bought. Behind the scenes, there's a growing movement of Orthodox Jewish writers trying to right this wrong."

All in all, media affronts are especially painful to Jewish women today, who are educated, savvy, and often liberal in their thinking regarding social issues. While PC is extended to every group, we remain the sorry victims of exaggeration and portrayals without balance. Another part of the problem is our changing world that idealizes "youth."

"Parents are portrayed as cruel by young writers, even if unintentionally through dim-wittedness," says actress Joanna Gleason. "Now they're in their twenties and thirties. We've given adolescents power."

"Fifty years ago, there was respect for elders," says Mallory Lewis. "Now there's a general level of disrespect for anyone over twenty-eight."

A partial cause and consequence of the media stereotype, according to some scholars, is the "giving up" of a truly religious base on the part of many Jewish mothers who have traded Jewish spiritualism for materialism. Some are "Lite-Jews," who have identified "culturally," but have "negotiated" the actual practice of Jewish ritual, or have given it up altogether.

The late, great Wendy Wasserstein portrays this change in her famous 1993 play, *The Sisters Rosensweig*, which deals with three sisters, diverse in their assimilation yet bonded in love. Sara, the oldest, is the expatriate, atheistic banker in London. Then there is Gorgeous Teitelbaum, the observant housewife/advice maven from Newton, Massachussetts, who's president of her Sisterhood. Finally, there's Pfeni, the third-world socially conscious travel writer. When brittle Sara rebuffs the advances of Merv Kant, the visiting Jewish Brooklyn furrier . . . he challenges her by asserting their worlds aren't so very different. Yet Sara asks him to give up, explaining she has turned her back on her family, her religion, and her country. Bitter, cold, and guilty, she wonders if that isn't the old story of assimilation, suggesting he find someone who knows how to throw a good *Shabbes* and can carry off an orange crepe suit—something she cannot.

"Writers reflect what they've experienced . . . the majority are not traditionalists," says Binyamin Jolkovsky. "Hollywood does not reflect Jewishness or the Jewish mother. Jewish writers don't think spiritually. Mothers are portrayed as holding onto their child for their own aggrandizement. We have the mother who pushes for materialism instead of 'be the best person you can be, the mensch.' So we see the overbearing, distorted Yiddishe mama. A lot of Jewish males were affected and this has been self-perpetuating. Self-hatred is being fed."

"When you have the freedom to choose other than what you've been taught, mothers may be unable to adapt," says Rabbi Yocheved Mintz.

"The loss of this warm, giving anything of yourself for your children, is not used for the lens of tradition," says Binyamin Jolkovsky, editor in chief of the superb Jewishworldreview.com. "Instead it pushes materialism and power. There is a line . . . what becomes of selflessness, the consciousness of what is truly necessary and when you bring it into a culture that's material—it becomes nasty."

Along with the great liberties the Jewish mother and her family found in America, the price of assimilation has been costly. Human worth and success in the secular world began replacing Jewish values and traditions as a means of judgment, leaving some scholars and rabbis the Herculean task of holding their flocks together in an environment that no longer supports but, indeed, encourages a breakdown of our Jewishness.

In the extreme, the "alrightniks," the nouveau riche, who are more concerned with status than Jewish ritual, have provided fodder for media and comics. In fact, this ambivalence surfaces when even the "alrightnik" fails to recognize him or herself.

✡

MRS. LEVY FINALLY HIT UPON HOW TO CREATE THE MOST UNIQUE BAR MITZVAH FOR HER SON.

"A SAFARI!" SHE TOLD ALL. "THE CONGREGATION WILL FLY TO AFRICA AND NATIVES WILL CHANT AS MY SON RECITES IN HEBREW!"

ON THE APPOINTED DAY, FOUR HUNDRED JEWS WERE FLOWN TO AFRICA. WITH GUIDES SHLEPPING, THE GUESTS THREADED THEIR WAY THROUGH THE JUNGLE.

SUDDENLY, THE COLUMN WAS HALTED. "THERE WILL BE A DELAY OF ONE HOUR," SAID THE GUIDE.

"WHY?" DEMANDED MRS. LEVY INDIGNANTLY.

THE GUIDE REPLIED: "THERE'S ANOTHER BAR MITZVAH AHEAD OF US!"

✡
---

*N*o expense was spared at the Buchman bar mitzvah. Ice statues were flowing pink punch, and in the middle of the mammoth buffet was a huge, life-sized sculpture of the bar mitzvah boy in chopped liver. The proud mama turned to her unimpressed cousin.

"So, what do think of the gorgeous statue of my Brucie?"

"I've never seen anything like it," he said, unable to resist. "Who did it? Lipschitz or Rothenstyne?"

"Rothenstyne, of course," she sniffed. "Lipschitz only works in white fish."

On the other side of the equation, there are Jewish mothers who applaud assimilation and see it as not only inevitable but a wise course in human development.

"Change is occurring. We can't afford difference. In terms of values, religion . . . ultimately we have to be one," says Julie Cobb. "We have to see and hear audio news clips of Iraqi funeral homes. As mothers our first impulse is not to listen. It's too abrasive, too painful, like a . . . Greek chorus. I have purposely kept it on. Yet this is not a theater. This is the sound of all mothers. Personally, I think the separation has to stop."

"THEM" AND US

*I*s there really a difference between the Jewish and non-Jewish mother? After all, most mothers care deeply about their children, will sacrifice and yes, many within all groups and ethnicities will butt in and "give guilt." A small portion of those I interviewed felt there was no difference at all. A mother is a mother. It must also be said that just as not all Jewish mothers carry this ethno-type, there are many mothers within all groups, who, even without our unique history, share some of our ethno-typical behavior and beliefs. But many noted similarities among other ethnic mothers and Jewish mothers and held them out when compared to the so-called WASP mother.

"No. I don't see the Jewish mother as any different," says comedian Marty Allen.

"Women for whom children are the focus come in all ethnic groups [as do] women who live through their children," says Rabbi Shira Stern.

"Danish mothers love and care," says Jody Lopatin, "but the Jewish mother is more demonstrative, and as part of our tradition, encourages her children to be their best."

MARIA, AN ITALIAN, ATHENA, A GREEK, AND ESTHER, A JEW, ALL GRANDMAS, WERE SEATED ON A PARK BENCH DISCUSSING WHAT THEY WOULD DO IF THEIR DOCTOR GAVE THEM ONLY THREE MONTHS TO LIVE.

MARIA QUICKLY ANSWERED: "HMMM. I'D EAT MY WAY THROUGH ROME . . . EVERY CANNOLI WOULD BE IN MY MOUTH."

ATHENA SAID: "I'D CRUISE THE ISLANDS, AND BREAK DISHES WITH AS MANY TWENTY-FIVE-YEAR-OLD FISHERMEN I COULD FIND! AND YOU, ESTHER?"

"ME, DARLINGS? I'D CALL MY SON-IN-LAW AND GET A CONSULT WITH ANOTHER DOCTOR."

"I think the classic Jewish mother is just a more extreme version of what all mothers are about," says Amy Borkowsky. "Typically, there's a real lack of boundaries between herself and her child, so she worries excessively and can never really acknowledge the child is an adult. I get e-mails from people of all different backgrounds who sound like we have the same mother."

"ONE WOMAN WITH A HISPANIC NAME WROTE THAT HER MOTHER ALWAYS TELLS HER NOT TO STICK HER NOSE INTO FLOWERS WHEN SHE SMELLS THEM BECAUSE SHE ONCE HEARD OF A WOMAN WHO INHALED BUG EGGS AND THEY HATCHED IN HER SINUSES. APPARENTLY YOU DON'T EVEN HAVE TO BE JEWISH TO BE A JEWISH MOTHER."
—Amy Borkowsky

"The WASP mother feels her job is done when kids graduate high school," says Mallory Lewis. "The distinction is really between the ethnic mother and the WASP mother."

"I think the Jewish mother is more involved in different organizations and does more outside the home," says Melanie Strug.

"The WASP mothers are very different," says comedian/singer Marilyn Michaels. "They're cooler, less invasive."

"Jewish mothers are generally more interested in education," says Dr. Eileen Warshaw. "WASPs in suburbia tend to be more interested in making sure their child makes the football team. It's more about social status than grade level."

Iris Krasnow, author of *I Am My Mother's Daughter:*

*T*hree mothers, Peggy, a Catholic woman, Jane, a Protestant, and Molly, a Jew, were discussing when life begins.

Peggy said: "In our religion, life begins at conception."

Jane countered: "We disagree. We believe that life begins when the fetus is viable away from the mother's womb."

"You're both wrong," said Molly. "In our religion, life begins when the kids graduate college and the dog dies."

Making Peace with Mom Before It's too Late, reported that out of her 116 interviews, she could make no generalizations when comparing Catholic guilt and Jewish guilt.

I tend to agree. Among American "ethnic" moms, particularly Italian, many of these "characteristics" are similar; however, when I posed the question specifically, differences emerged.

"Doris Roberts as Marie Barone is completely family-oriented. She has to be in control. A Jewish mother has to be in control, but won't show it that way, it's more finessed."
—Zora Essman, mother of comic Susie Essman

"Jewish mothers, unlike Marie Barone, for example, don't show the same kind of favoritism—they try to hide it more. Our criticisms are less caustic and more manipulative. Jewish moms make *you* make their decision," says Judy Gold. "The Jewish mother fears more, which comes from what's happened to us as a people. [We not only have to deal with] how to protect ourselves, but also all of us, as a people."

"The Jewish mother pushes her kids to succeed, which creates a certain amount of anger. Children are their mirror," says Lainie Kazan, who, in her career, has played a multitude of mamas. "The Italian mother expects much less."

"I see very little difference," says Theodore Bikel. Then referring to other ethnic groups, "There's a preoccupation with food that is pathological in both Jews and Italians. One difference is Italian mothers are often devoutly Catholic, while Jewish mothers are often not religious. Jewish mothers have also had to survive in hostile environments."

Barry Levinson's film *Liberty Heights* (1999) deals with racism in the 1950s using a gentle comic and sentimental touch to expose attitudes. The film centers on the Kurtzman family, Jews from Baltimore. Ben, the younger son, describes a brush with "outsiders." In second grade, he thought the name Ping Dir was Jewish, and Min-Huey "definitely" sounded Jewish. His breakthrough occurred when he had lunch at Butch Johnson's house. His explanation to his mother is classic as he describes the "white bread and mayonnaise" meal. "Everything was white," he says, to which his mother replies, "Oh, they must not be Jewish. They're the 'other' kind."

These scenes could have taken place in my home in Flushing, New York. My own mother didn't keep kosher, but we did eat "Jewish-style," for example: chopped liver, matzo balls, and brisket. The idea of mixing milk with meat made us gag, as did the thought of "olive loaf," "pimento loaf," "headcheese," or dried beef. Large dinner sausages were never served. It was only when I was sixteen and went off to college that I learned, shocked, our "food" wasn't "American." I suggested we make *kasha varnishkes* (buckwheat groats with pasta bow ties) and my dorm mates looked at me as though I'd suggested chowing down on jellied eels.

"Religion aside, [Italian] mothers are not a lot different, but Jewish mothers place much more emphasis on tradition, compared to other ethnic groups," says Dr. Eileen Warshaw, executive director of the Jewish Heritage Center of the Southwest. "The Jewish mothers are thinking about their parents and grandparents . . . survival. There's an emphasis on remembering, history, where we came from. The thread we're holding onto the world with."

"THE POLL": NINETEEN NON-JEWISH PERCEPTIONS OF THE JEWISH MOTHER

*I*t occurred to me that "image" is often in the minds of the beholders. Any discussion, then would not be complete without sampling how we're viewed by "outsiders:"—non-Jewish women. After all, as with all groups we are not always able to see how *others* see us clearly or even accurately.

Having taken the odious statistics courses through college and graduate school, with an unflagging inability to figure out a chi square, I do know that nineteen people does not a sample make.

But these anecdotal responses give us an *indication*, an idea of how we're perceived. In fairness, while this sample of women represents different religions, regions, and ethnic groups, it is skewed. My criteria was to get feedback from people known to me to possess fairness and the ability to truth-tell without fear of insult. Some are well-known, others are in less visible pursuits.

In addition to basic demographic information, I asked each what they think of when they hear the term "Jewish mother," then let them expound.

The results are fascinating—and surprising.

1.   Kaye Ballard—*actress/singer, was born in Cleveland in the 1920s and raised Italian Catholic. Currently, though Catholic, she doesn't believe in any organized religion, but "honesty and kindness." She has no children.*

"A Jewish mother teaches her kids smarts. An Italian mother teaches you how to cook and get married. I always told people I was Jewish because I always thought they were the smartest people in the world—lawyers, doctors. Do you ever see a professional Jewish hockey player? The Jewish mother is most concerned about children. She wants her daughter to marry someone rich, and sons are everything to them. My mother was always competing with me. She would have liked me to have been married and have kids. I never involved her in my adult life. If I gave her an inch she'd take a yard. When I did the film *A House Is Not a Home* and she saw all these gorgeous hookers, her whole comment was 'Couldn't you dress like them?' She always expected more, and was disappointed I wasn't Ava Gardner. . . . If anyone called me a Jewish mother I'd be absolutely flattered because of their true love of family."

2. Michelle Patrick—*writer, including* All My Children, *was born in Detroit during the 1940s. She is African American and was raised Episcopalian. She has one sixteen-year-old son.*

"When I think of the Jewish mother, I think of Molly Goldberg— accessible, down-to-earth, practical, funny. *I'm* a Jewish mother. I'm involved, hands-on, protective, intense. The dean of my child's school called me a Mother Lioness. You know, 'Mess with my kid and I'll rip your eyes out.' My kid said, 'everybody knows that about you.' My own mother was like a Jewish mother. At nine, my son made it clear he preferred getting his own house, because his mother was too inquisitive. Well, I want to know where he is, what he's thinking, what's bothering him . . . and that includes inspecting his room. That's what I think the mother should be—advocate, protector, involved, engaged, committed. To me, the WASP mother is white bread, tidiness, with hidden, closeted feelings. A friend in college was a WASP. I was astonished by her mother, who ironed her scarfs, wrapped them in tissue paper, and put them in baggies. It has to do with the way people express their feelings. The ironing and rolling the scarf was probably her way of expressing affection."

> "My son said at fourteen, 'LEAVE ME ALONE,' and I said 'That will never ever happen!'"
> —Michelle Patrick, writer, African American, Episcopal

3. Shari Ritter—*former showgirl, was born in Manitowac, Wisconsin, in the 1930s. She is white and was raised Lutheran and is the mother of four grown children.*

"I was actually called a Jewish mother by my kids and their friends and I considered it a compliment. To me, that meant [I was] caring and concerned. You paid attention to your children. And . . . there was always food and food to share. I see it as a positive image of involvement, where you're a MOTHER and your primary career is your children and family—making sure everybody has everything they need from clean socks, to manners and respect."

4. Marta Sanders—*award-winning cabaret artist in the United States and around the world, was born in Houston, Texas, in the 1950s. Half Latin, half Texan, she was raised Quaker. She considers herself spiritual but ascribes to no particular religion or service. She is the mother of two daughters in their twenties.*

"When I hear the term 'Jewish mother,' I think of a mother who is very protective, sometimes overly vocal, opinionated, nurturing. The role she takes within the family is very strong, extremely child-first, and can be over the top. They're more verbal about the rules of the world, how the family will exist. They have an opinion right away, no hiding in the back . . . they're out there. Plus, I've never been offered so much food in my whole life. The non-Jew wants to please, the Jewish mother may impose pleasure. The WASP mother wants everything to be proper, but she won't impose or ask for any gratitude—the stiff upper lip. She has more ability to let her kids leave the nest faster. With ethnic mothers, their struggle has been constant and they're more in your face. The nonethnic mother has the freedom to relax. Her style is: Don't talk about money, be quiet, reserved, and don't show your cards. She wouldn't bond as quickly or share a problem about the kids. She'd talk more about: 'How are the curtains you were putting up?' WASPs struggle to stay in the right country clubs. If someone called me a Jewish mother, I would take it as a compliment. I'd look at the most positive image . . . somebody very loving, very protective."

> "WHEN OUR KIDS WERE YOUNG, WE WOULD
> HAVE PARTIES IN THE PARK. THE JEWISH
> MOTHER WOULD BEND OVER BACKWARD TO
> PLEASE, AND ASK 'DID I DO ENOUGH? DID
> MOMMY MAKE A NICE PARTY FOR YOU?'"
> —Marta Sanders, cabaret star

5. Mary Fischer—*yoga instructor, was born in Parkridge, Illinois, in the 1970s. She's Italian, and she was raised Catholic. She has one daughter, a toddler.*

"The Jewish mother is really into loving the kids, 'my kids are my whole life.' They'll do whatever they have to do to help them succeed. I think of both positives and negatives. The positives are the interest in their children, making them their centerpiece. The negative would be other people might see it as overbearing or overcontrolling. I see the Jewish and Italian mother as more similar than different. When my aunt wanted to go to college, my grandparents were pretty poor. Five hundred dollars was their life savings, yet they gave it to her. They, too, wanted their children to do well and were willing to do whatever they could to make it happen. I see the WASP as a colder mother. She'd give her child one hundred of the five hundred and say, 'Darling . . . this is our savings. You need to get a job.' She also let go earlier. I feel like my mother and my mother's mother, like Jewish moms, want to be mothers for life. The WASP mom wants to be a mother till the kids are grown, then she's onto her own thing."

6. Julie Gans—*"Domestic Goddess," the wife of international star Danny Gans, was born in Los Angeles in the 1950s. White, she was raised Presbyterian but is now part of the Foursquare, a Pentecostal denomination. She has*

three children, two girls and one boy, ranging from eleven to eighteen—and refers to herself as "Danny's Goddess."

"When I hear the term 'Jewish mother,' I immediately think of my husband's grandmother, who was Jewish. She knew how to pinch cheeks really great! When we were in Florida and just married, I got this phone call and I hadn't even met her: [In Yiddish accent] 'Hello, Julie? Dis is Grandma!' Any time we would ever talk, she'd pinch my cheeks and end every conversation with, 'So be good, be happy, make a lot of money, and be healthy.' She was extremely caring and loving but meddlesome. She was the Queen Bee. The Jewish mother tends to be more lenient and allows her child to get away with more. The WASP mother tends to call her kids on the carpet more. Personally, I'd like to be referred as one of the 'good' Jewish mothers . . . not whining . . . but very caring and loving."

"The flip side of unconditional loving and the desire for your child's happiness lends itself to indulgence."
—Julie Gans, Pentecostal, wife of international star Danny Gans

---

7. Frances Coyle Brennan—*social work administrator, was born in Philadelphia in the 1940s. She was raised Roman Catholic and is of Irish descent. She has two children, a son and daughter, both in their twenties.*

"I see the 'Jewish mother' image as loving, but also, overbearing, interfering, controlling. I wouldn't consider the term as either negative or positive. If someone called me a Jewish mother, I'd take it to mean that I was too overly involved. The Irish mother is a little more distant. She might use denial as a bit of defense. Don't ask, don't tell." [At which point her son, Tommy, took the phone and said:] "Jewish guilt is fast-acting and Irish guilt is long-lasting. It'll come up easier and later. There's open communication in Jewish homes, but many Irish never talk about anything problematic."

8. Name Withheld on Request—*actress/writer, was born in Boston in the 1940s. White, she was raised a Christian Scientist, but now considers herself a Unitarian or a spiritual agnostic and adheres to the principles of Al-Anon. She has one sixteen-year-old son.*

"My first mother-in-law was a Jewish mother. Her son was more important than her husband. She cooked exactly the meal he loved . . . tsimmes, brisket, and matzo ball soup . . . and it was very important to make him his pear, jam, and vanilla pudding. I saw her as dedicated to her child, protective, inflexible, wary of outsiders. Also, fiercely loyal. Once you were in the inner circle you were there. If I were called a Jewish mother, I'd view the term as a put-down. The comment would mean I was overcontrolling, living through my child, and interfering in his life. Taking it to an extreme, that loyalty may become suspicion, and dedication may become smothering. Guilt is a big issue. I realize, of course, this is more the "stereotype." The Italian mother is also feeding. They never sit down. Both mothers are very physical—in loving, anger, and frustration. Jewish guilt and manipulation seem less overt than in the Italian mother. For WASP mothers, food is not the center of their universe. They're about manners, thank-you notes, etc. They're equally dedicated, but much quieter. They show disapproval and expectations in a more passive-aggressive way. It's the unspoken, the unwritten rule. They'll raise an eyebrow, and silence is a big one."

9. Mary Keating—*songwriter/performer, was born in Rural County, Pennsylvania, in the 1940s. White, she was raised Catholic, but now considers herself "neutral." Married to actor Charles Keating, she has two grown sons and five grandchildren. NOTE: One of her daughters-in-law is Jewish.*

"I see the Jewish mother as someone who is a bit overprotective. She wants her child to succeed and preferably marry within the faith. I see these traits as positive, because they are so caring, they'll do everything they can for their children—and they do well. The Jewish mother cares what profession her children go into, for example, medicine, law, finance. I realize these are blanket statements, but it seems non-Jews are less intense and protective. You want them to do well but they don't have to be perfect. You often see parents who don't care what their kids are doing, or who they're hanging out with. When you find someone really focuses and is in touch—even if the kids appear not to like it—they have that sense of security and being cared for, which is much more positive."

> "AT MY STEPGRANDCHILD'S BAR MITZVAH, THERE WERE SO MANY PEOPLE, COUSINS, RELATIVES, THAT THE RABBI JOKED THEY COULD THEY LEND OUT A FEW. WHEN YOU HAVE SO MANY PEOPLE TO ANSWER TO, IT'S GOT TO BE A GOOD THING."
> —Mary Keating, songwriter/performer

10. Ginger Tafoya—*editor/writer, was born in Los Angeles in the 1940s. Latino [Mexican], she was raised Catholic. Today, she considers herself "a believer—spiritual." She has three grown children, two daughters and one son.*

"Some Jewish mothers are overinvolved. The negative is, overinvolvement may be putting too much pressure on the child to succeed and negative attention if they don't. The positive is, of course, they love their children, will nurture them, and make then number one. The Hispanic mother puts less pressure on children. Personally, I felt there wasn't enough caring about what the kid did or education. It was more about raising them and getting them out the door. There is also a definite preference for the male child. A Hispanic mother is often more nurturing and hovering toward the boy, so males are not really taught to respect women, as they become adults. In a sense, the son represents what her husband isn't, so she bonds with her male child."

"The only thing I know about the WASP mother is June Cleaver, who didn't visit El Barrio, in Los Angeles."

—Ginger Tafoya, editor/writer

11. Siofra Willer—*homemaker, was born in Long Beach, California, in the 1950s. White, she was raised Roman Catholic of Irish descent and is a strong believer today. She has two daughters, eleven and fourteen.*

"The Jewish mother, though occasionally overbearing, is, on the positive side, very caring. She's particularly aggressive in the arts and education, which is a good thing. Frankly, I don't see much difference from Christian mothers, except perhaps in the level of aggressiveness. The Jewish mother tends to be pushier and more aggressive with her children."

12. Allyson Rice—*former actress on* As the World Turns *(Connor Walsh, 1990–1996). She is now founder and director of the Total Human, which are life-changing retreats and workshops that include increasing creativity, ancient women's teaching, yoga, meditation, and unlocking potential in daily physical life. White, she was born in Huntington, West Virginia, in the 1960s and raised Presbyterian, but now draws from many different spiritual traditions. She has one eleven-year-old son.*

"The Jewish mother is very tightly family oriented, sometimes overprotective, and uses guilt. She's very different from the WASP mother. It has to do with their relationship to emotions. Any culture that has had to overcome adversity, a culture that's had to fight against being broken down, has a tighter feeling and stronger bond. The WASP mother is more emotionally reserved, often having lost her cultural roots, there's been a diffusing of family ties, lack of common history, lack of common reason to come together as a community."

> **"JEWISH MOTHER TRAITS OF A STRONG FAMILY IS A POSITIVE THAT REALLY BUILDS COMMUNITY AND FAMILY STRENGTH AROUND A COMMON HISTORY."**
> —Allyson Rice, founder and director of the Total Human life-changing workshops and retreats

13. Janel Bladow—*producer/writer, was born in Washington, D.C., in the 1940s. White, she was raised Catholic of Hungarian descent. She has no children.*

"When I think of the Jewish mother, I see a gray-haired elderly mom, with a big apron in the kitchen, making proper meals for her family, saying, 'My kid this, my kid that.' She's caring, loving, but competitive—about kids, money, possessions. But . . . she's compassionate and will be there and fight for her family. Mothers in general are getting a bad rep in sitcoms. In the fifties and sixties, they were idealized to a joke—the perfect pearl-wearing mother. In the seventies, we had the working, liberated mom. The career woman emerged. But in the nineties, they became overbearing or slightly crazy, as in *Malcolm in the Middle*. In my home, we weren't raised competitive, not pushed as much. Sometimes I wish we had been encouraged to be the best we could be—and gone to Harvard. I was raised to be fair, and nice, and not step on people. Money wasn't the big thing . . . compared to my Jewish friends. In Jewish families, there was more talking. I also laughed a lot in their homes and saw the warmth. The WASP house was much more restrained, reserved, and concerned about proper image, rather than expressing feelings. Their expectations and ambitions weren't so obvious. Of course, the upper-class WASP already had their 'connections' in place."

14. Jennifer Collet—*marketing director, was born in Jefferson City, Missouri, in the 1950s. White, she was raised Episcopal and has three children, ages eleven to seventeen.*

"Jewish mother. To me these are iconic words for 'the good mother,' who is the nurturer, solves problems, takes care of things. I don't see her as overbearing, but rather sometimes overfunctioning, but with good intent. If I was called a Jewish mother, I'd take it as a compliment."

15. Jeanne Bavaro—*personal manager for, among others, her husband, international singer/impressionist Bill Acosta, was born in Chicago, Illinois, in the 1950s. White, she was raised Catholic and isn't practicing now. She has one seventeen-year-old daughter and a twenty-two-year-old son.*

"When I hear the term Jewish mother, I think of myself, as I have more chutzpah than all of my friends. Family and food are two priorities in life—and financial successful is critical. On the negative side, Jewish moms don't let them cut the apron strings. They may be oversmothering, too into the details of their children's lives. Yet, I wouldn't have it any other way! The WASP mother has a certain lack of tradition. A lack of passion, which I consider middle-of-the-road mediocrity. And they bore the hell out of me."

"*I* don't think there's a kid in the world who is not Jewish who wouldn't relish the thought of having a Jewish mom. Everybody wants to be cared and fussed over."

—Jeanne Bavaro, entertainment manager

16. Pat Caso—*former producer, was born in Westport, Connecticut, in the 1950s. White, she was raised and remains Roman Catholic. She has two boys in their twenties.*

"My parents' best friends were the Goldens. Mrs. Golden was a very vivacious, honest, direct, bold person, who knew exactly what she wanted and always got it. I see the Jewish mother as very involved, proactive in the community, and service oriented. When you think typical Catholic, you think church, and church involvement. The female saints are role models. But the Jewish mother is active in the PTA. To me, a Jewish mother is a demonstrative, family-oriented, goal-oriented individual. She would be a strong leader and very educated. In celebration, for example, she's concerned that each person knows not only what is going on, but why."

17. Nancy Byrne—*producer/writer, was born in Atlanta, Georgia, in the 1960s. White, she was raised Catholic of Irish descent, and now considers herself "spiritual," but not religious. She has no children.*

"When I think of the Jewish mother, I see her as doting, loud, loving, demanding of her children to be the best they can be. Overall, I see this as a positive. *I perceive* the WASP mother as interested in blue-blood, society, doing little work outside the home, except for charity. She's very controlled and a little bit cold. I don't like perpetuating stereotypes but there is humor and truth in it. My own mother's intentions and efforts are always in the right place, though irritating from time to time because she won't let things go. I should hit the tape recorder when she calls because she repeats how I'm not married! I can tell my mother, 'I'm happy, I'm divorced. All is well'—and it's like talking to a brick wall. The reality is, it doesn't offend me. I don't take it seriously."

18. Eileen Fulton—*actress and star of* As the World Turns, *writer, and chanteuse, was born in Asheville, North Carolina, in the 1930s. White, she was raised Methodist, daughter of a minister. She has no children but three dogs and a truckload of friends, which she claims is "more than my share."*

"There was this Jewish lady who lived next door. She made the best matzo ball soup in the world. I remember the wonderful food, parties . . . laughter. . . . I just wanted to curl up on her couch. The Jewish, Italian, and Black mothers' homes represented hearth, food, and comfort. My mother was very loving, as are many Christian mothers, of course, but reserved. I've known so many uptight Christians."

19. Dr. Rena Nora—*former chief of psychiatry, preeminent expert on gambling rehabilitation, was born in the Philippines in the 1940s and was raised Catholic. She has three grown children: a production manager, a judge, and an oncology surgeon.*

"What comes to mind when I hear 'Jewish mother'? Me! I have been called a Jewish mother. It means a very doting, strong, opinionated, no-nonsense mom. I consider the term a positive. The Jewish mother is verbal, expressive, assertive, and courageous. If they are in a situation where they feel they're right, they won't hesitate to be creative and resourceful to get their point across, which is often in support of a family member, usually a child. The WASP mother is much more liberal and often gives her children more independence too soon. It's better for children to be nurtured longer. One of the higher suicide rates is in Scandinavia. One of the theories is it's due to early independence. In contrast, the Filipino, if they can keep their sons way past their forties they're happy, which is similar to the Jewish mother."

> "I would not hesitate to say, 'my son the surgeon.' It's not even bragging, because bragging is not true. It's more about being proud, stating the facts."
>
> —Dr. Rena Nora, psychiatrist

Overall, these non-Jewish women were generally positive regarding the Jewish mother and saw differences in mothering styles. The major distinction made was between the ethnic and the WASP mother. Despite concerns about overprotectiveness, many, especially ethnic mothers, not only identified, but defended traits that many Jewish children complain about.

A MOTHER IS A MOTHER IS A MOTHER? WHAT MAKES US DIFFERENT?

True, Jewish mothers share traits with mothers of other ethnic groups. Yet, we have a distinctive history, culture, and religion that derives from a unique place: Judaism. And it's our Jewishness that has informed our motives and intentions. Judaism itself, along with custom and tradition, lay out the role of Jewish mother along with the way she should be treated.

RELIGION

As this is not a course on Judaism, I'll attempt to provide the most basic explanations—and how these apply to the Jewish mother.

A basic precept is "Jewishness" comes from the mother. In Jewish law, if she is Jewish, the child is Jewish. This fact alone gives the female the ultimate role in "mothering" the future of Judaism and Jewish identity.

In the Jewish home, the mother is center stage with a holy mission—to keep the home as a dwelling for the presence of God, which can only and uniquely be achieved by following the directives of the Torah. The Torah is the "Constitution" of Judaism, given to the Jews by God at Mount Sinai about 3,300 years ago. In its simplest meaning, the Torah consists of the five books of Moses, but can also refer to the entire Jewish Bible. Along with Torah is the Talmud, which explains the meaning of the scriptures, how to interpret them, and how to apply the laws. *Acceptance of Talmudic authority is an essential difference between Jews and everyone else.*

The responsibility for doing so in the home is largely the Jewish mother's role. For example, she must ensure that kosher laws are observed. It is the mother who is given the privilege of welcoming the holy Sabbath by ritual candle lighting, along with separating challah (ritual bread) from the dough. (She also must follow sacrificial and purity laws.)

Though she may have a separate career, the Jewish mother is charged with creating the home atmosphere that is the cornerstone of Jewish life—bringing well-being, true happiness, and peace to the family. This will go on through each generation, through teaching children to make the Torah and Judaism their daily guide.

"Within Judaism, it is the woman's role to ensure that the tradition is carried through, which is highly specific in the Jewish tradition. Religiously, the Jewish mother is expected to instill the home with the rituals," says Rabbi Yocheved Mintz. "She must be knowledgeable about the laws of *kashrut* and purity, aware of the Jewish calendar, keep peace in the home (Shalom Bayit), and, in addition, in many cases, earn a sufficient living so the husband could pursue his studies."

"Ingrained in the Covenant, what we could not finish our children can continue on," says Blu Greenberg. "Barely below the surface, this is critical due to our historical vulnerability. We carry through our history, how to protect ourselves to make it to the next generation."

Specific and heavy involvement in all aspects of the home, the family, and especially the children—far from being a "neurotic" or nuisance trait—was and remains a religious commandment.

Therefore, Jewish women and mothers, despite early prohibitions against studying fully, were given adored status. For example:

- *Rahamanut* is the loftiest word in Hebrew. Literally "mother love," it means mercy and compassion.
- According to the Zohar (Book of Splendor, Kabbalistic movement) man is not man until united with woman.
- The Talmud instructs men to love their wives as themselves and honor them more.
- The absence of wife beating in times and places where the practice was customary—even admired.
- Legal protections in Jewish law, regarding improper sexual behavior, desertion, divorce, widowhood, property, financial independence, and control.

Long before New York and Beverly Hills attorneys were drawing up prenuptial agreements for the rich and famous, there was the *Ketubah*, the Jewish marriage contract, which came about in the second century BCE. Today, the Ketuba is still signed by two witnesses before the Jewish wedding ceremony and spells out what all husbands are obligated to give their wives, including food, clothing, and conjugal rights. It also includes his financial obligation in case of divorce or death. This contract is so binding that if it is lost the couple is technically forbidden to live together until a new one is written.

Style as well can be traced to the Talmud. Even actual rules of behavior can be extracted from the Torah's general directives, since the Talmud is filled with everything from stories, anecdotes, history, humor, and yes—debate—endless, detailed debate and argumentation over the smallest issue.

> ### "We do not argue for its own sake but to find the truth."
> —Binyamin Jolkovsky

For the Jewish family, and certainly the Jewish mother, family arguments are seen as not merely "normal," but constructive. Not only does questioning and disputation hone the mind, it releases emotions and also teaches that life is not a peaceful pursuit. And by the way, it kicks up excitement.

The Jewish mother ethno-type is no retiring flower. Whether she's been called verbal, opinionated, questioning, a fighter or yes, pushy, there's a direct correlation between Talmudic examination and argumentation and the domestic verbalization, analysis, and hair-splitting, which constitutes normal family interaction. The arguing and questioning about all details of life served as a survival mechanism—a way to actually protect the family from the far more destructive effects of "out there." So, is it any wonder we have moms today who *are* "out there." Storytelling, anecdotes, gossip, and humor are also part of our legacy.

There are 613 *mitzvahs*, or commandments, in the Torah that a Jew must obey, covering everything—from how a chicken was to be slaughtered to which shoes should be worn each day. According to Michael Wex in *Born to Kvetch*, there are 248 "thou shalts" and 365 "thou shalt nots." These do's and don't's are yet another critical difference between Jews and others. If we are the chosen people, we've been chosen *not* to do a whole lot of things that are acceptable for everyone else, such as chowing down on a grilled ham and cheese sandwich or having a malted with our burger.

Our life and language (Yiddish or *mama-loshen*) is rife with rules, discipline—and kvetches (complaints).

SHTETL LIFE

In the nineteenth century, half of all Jews lived in small towns known as shtetls. These shtetls, home to Eastern European Jews, were found in White Russia, the Ukraine, Slovakia, Bessarabia, Galicia, Lithuania, Poland, and in northeast Hungary.

These shtetls, portrayed as difficult and dangerous but also sentimentally in *Fiddler on the Roof*, were more often woeful. These desolate, squalid, isolated settlements for "outcasts" were filled with mud, poverty, and lack of food. Life was harsh and the people who lived there were constantly imperiled.

The Jewish mother was the valiant underpinning of the shtetl community. She not only sacrificed for her children, but, as scholarship was prized above all as the pathway to God, she frequently earned the living—while providing spiritual and psychological support—so the males in the family could pursue their studies. These communities were much like unofficial countries, connected by deeply religious and spiritual ties, language, and shared martyrdom. Their spirit would soar during the Sabbath—and this critical demarcation between themselves and the outside world was the Jewish mother's duty and privilege to make.

> "Suffering
> is part of greatness."
> —Dr. Howard Halpern

Yet, despite grueling hardship, the shtetl mother gave her children a daunting, enriching legacy. A determined survivalist, she and her daughters possessed uncommon spiritual energy, perseverance, protectiveness, courage—and the ability to sacrifice for children, family, and community. And the results

We took my late grandmother to see *Fiddler on the Roof*, thinking it would remind her of her childhood village. Afterward, she said, "Dis is a play? No. Dis vas my life, only it wasn't so good." She then explained how she made teeth for brides—from bread.

have been remarkable. Children of the shtetls have contributed mightily, not only to their own culture, but also to world culture: in literature, science, activism, medicine, entertainment, and law, among other fields. Surely, the inordinate success of many Jewish children—no matter how much they kvetch or joke—is due in large measure to these remarkable women, their shtetl mothers and grandmothers.

SISTERS?

When we add the remarkable findings of the Technion-Israel Institute of Technology in 2006, that about 40 percent of all Ashkenazi Jews today derive from four Jewish mothers, there may be yet another (small) factor that differentiates us. Sisterhood . . . literally.

We comprise one quarter of 1 percent of the world population, and about one half that if we only count females. Less, if we only count Jewish mothers. Yet what a cultural racket we've made virtually everywhere we've gone, which is . . . anywhere we were tolerated, until the establishment of the State of Israel.

Through a melding of our strict commandments, traditions, history, and perhaps DNA, along with tribalism and relatively little intermarriage, we have become a unique ethno-type. As the role of women in general became more assertive religiously, politically, and socially, we were set free to use our gifts not only to mother, but also to become scientists, artists, activists, and religious leaders with the same determination, wisdom, and courage.

CHAPTER 3

Jewish Mother Jokes:
INSULT, INSULATION, OR JUST PLAIN FUNNY

For those who say there's no such thing as "Jewish humor," the legendary *Seinfeld* first took on the matter in episode 152 in 1997, when Jerry suspects his dentist, Tim Whatley, converted to Judaism for—the Jokes.

I recently asked two Jewish comedians about Jewish humor. "I don't know what that is," they protested. One cited the definitely *not* Jewish Red Skelton, as being "no different" from himself. As talented as Skelton was, along with the magnificent Bob Hope, few would mistake them for a Jerry Lewis, Alan King, or Sid Caesar in style, cadence, material, or presentation.

Now, whether this comedian was trying to be politically correct, or, more likely, has a morbid fear that the taint of "Jewishness" might conjure images of Simon Says and borscht, there are many who would insist there is "no such thing" as "Jewish humor," or leap into deep offense, seeing all Jewish jokes as yet another form of stereotyping.

OK, yes. Not every Jewish comic "does" Jewish humor. And true, we share some of the traits labeled "Jewish" with other ethnic groups. Also true, some "jokes" about Jewish mothers are simply outmoded and insulting.

But to deny that Jewish humor exists and has value, to deny there is a sensibility that is specifically Jewish, would be like denying that Italians have a "knack" with opera.

Jewish humor not only exists, it has become universal, through our large contribution to humor. Most people today "get it," or Jerry Seinfeld, Judy Gold, Susie Essman, Roseanne, Elayne Boosler, Rita Rudner, Carol Leifer, Wendy Liebman, Robert Klein, Jeff Garlin, Jon Stewart, Richard Lewis, Gary Shandling, and older comics, such as Carl Reiner, Mel Brooks, Jerry Lewis, Jackie Mason, Freddie Roman, Shelley Berman, Norm Crosby, Shecky Greene, Marty Allen, and Don Rickles, would be playing Goldberg's deli in Brooklyn's Borough Park instead of the big rooms in clubs and casinos all over the world.

More, their TV work would be a summer replacement on cable 99 in Century Village instead of hits on HBO—even in the cornfields on Iowa. And what they're "getting" in those fields and in clubs ain't pastrami on white.

In his book, *Funny People* (1981) the late Steve Allen (who was not Jewish) estimated that about 80 percent of America's leading humorists over the preceding forty years (from 1940 through 1980) had been Jewish. (Today, the field has widened as other ethnic comics, notably Black, Hispanic, Asian, and gays and lesbians are mainstreaming using their own cultures to get a laugh and make a statement.) However, during a period when Jews comprised only 3.5 percent of the American population, there were more Jews flinging, flying, and always pushing the comic envelope, than even Good Humor trucks—whether on sound stages, in writers' rooms, nightclubs, or in front of dancing cigarette boxes during the early days of television.

Yes, it can be—because we're funny. Whether we're talking about Molly Goldberg's gentle meddling and malaprops, Joan Rivers's shtick on having a baby, Mel Brooks and Carl Reiner's kvetching masterpiece, the *2,000 Year Old Man*, Lenny Bruce's onstage smoke-screening Yiddish, Allen Sherman turning a banal French sibling (*Frère Jacques*) into "Sarah Jackman," Woody Allen's description of his mother's mah-jongg overdose, or Jerry Seinfeld's attempt to gift his folks with a Caddy (causing them to miss the early bird special and lose the condo presidency), we're not just funny—we're Jewish-funny.

More proof? Ask someone, "Quick! A Finnish joke!" and see how far you can milk a sauna. What . . . ? "Darling, watch . . . Your uncle Otto once sat too long and his kidneys dried like peas?" Oy!

The Jewish joke, and the Jewish mother joke, are distinctive and most simply wouldn't work (or be comprehensible) if attributed to another ethnic group.

Ruthie and Esther, both grandmas, were in deep conversation.

Ruthie said, "Listen . . . you're the up-to-date one. My son has a mobile phone. So how do they work?"

"Well," said Esther, "in the left hand you take the phone, and with the right, you push the buttons. A piece of cake."

But Ruthie wasn't satisfied. "*Nu?*" she asked, "and how can one talk with such busy hands?"

JEWISH JOKES: WHY AND WHAT ARE THEY?

*L*ike a good *tsibeleh* (onion) we Jews are a complex pastiche, layered with strands of oys running through the joys. Many studious pieces have been done analyzing Jewish humor, from Freud to rabbis to contemporary historians. Much like beautiful pieces of music, we analyze and philosophize, but it's often difficult to formulate the precise elements that make a joke (or comic) "Jewish"—at least without some annoying maven finding the exception. (Of course, that's *very* Jewish.) We do know that suffering is involved.

Author Tim Boxer reports on the time Alan Alda sat at a dinner with Simon Wiesenthal, the legendary Nazi hunter who died in 2005. Alda reported that Wiesenthal, who loved jokes, was right in the middle of a story, when a man came up to him and said, "Do you remember me?" Wiesenthal looked at him. And yes. He remembered him from the camps. Without saying a word, they just nodded, tears filling their eyes—and the man turned and walked away. "Wiesenthal then turned to me and finished the joke," said Alda. "This to me is the Jew's special relationship with humor and suffering."

> "You keep alive your
> own spirit through humor."
> —Theodore Bikel

"Humor is such a critical part of our heritage. If we haven't laughed we would have gone."
—Dr. Eileen Warshaw

Yes, Jewish humor is a powerful survival tool to manage pain by offering some relief, some point of view to get through, some liberation from torment and tormenters. And God knows, as Jews have known pain, we have been perfectly set up for being the purveyors of humor. Imagine for a moment Jews without humor. We'd have jumped off that roof with the Fiddler. Unlike some scholars who see Jewish humor as masochistic, I see our ability to use our comedic gifts as a testimony to our background, our will, and our strength.

The Jewish joke is (obviously) about something Jewish—with or without others involved. The topics can be anything: children, husbands and wives, money, survival, health, food, enemies, "types" (the *shadchen*, the *shnorrer*, the *Chelmites*) in the community—almost everything is fodder, which is a key aspect to the Jewish joke. It's democratic and yes, antiauthoritarian. Anyone, and anything, is treated with the same ironic wit and sarcasm.

> Jewish mother: "Hello, operator! Give me the manager from the fancy-dancy room service."
> Manager: "Room service."
> Jewish mother: "This is room 402, Mister Room Service. I vant to order breakfast."
> Manager: "Certainly, madam. What would you like?"
> Jewish mother: "For me, I vant a glass orange juice, but bitter with pits. The toast, should be burned, till black! For mine children, the milk should be curdled and—"
> Manager: "Madam, I can't fill an order like that!"
> Jewish mother: "Aha! You did yesterday!"

The first recorded scriptural laugh is in Genesis when the aged Sarah laughs at the prospect of her pregnancy. When the Lord asks, "Is anything too hard for the Lord?"—she lies, saying she didn't laugh, to which God replies, "You did laugh." While not a knee-slapper, the subversive aspect of Jewish mother humor was born.

Four rabbis engaged in theological arguments, and it was always three against one. Finally, the odd rabbi out appealed.

"God!" he cried. "I know I am right! Please, a sign to prove it to them!"

Suddenly, from a sunny day, it poured.

"A sign from God! See, I'm right!"

The other three disagreed, saying storms often cool hot days.

So again: "Please, God, a bigger sign!"

Lightning slammed a tree.

"Is that not a sign from God?" cried the rabbi.

"A sign of nature!" they insisted, again making it three to one.

Just as the rabbi is about to beg an even bigger sign, the sky blackened and a booming voice intoned: "HEEEEEEEE'S RIIIIIIGHT!"

The rabbi, hands on hips, said, "Well . . . ?"

The others shrugged, "So now it's three to two."

As we see, even God is not off-limits. Unlike many other religions, God is humanized, intimate, and social. God can be spoken to, included. Yet these jokes coexist with our deep love of God and our rituals. Hey, we're just kvetching.

Jewish jokes are almost always verbal. (OK, yes, there's Marcel Marceau, but he's one the few exceptions proving the rule.) They often involve a canny, even convoluted or loony use of logic, irony, and surprise or the quick turnaround.

Sophie demanded of Hannah a pot, which she claimed was never returned to her to make Sabbath dinner for her family.

"In the first place, I never took a pot from you!"

"In the second place, it was an old pot!"

"And in the third place, I gave it back to you in better condition than when I took it from you!"

Mr. and Mrs. Kornmell decided to go to the newest, fanciest Jewish fusion restaurant in New York to celebrate their twenty-fifth anniversary. They were served course after course of kasha with bananas, pupu poi and ying-yang tortillas. The owner himself brought over the anniversary cake of gefilte mousse.

"So *nu*," said the owner. "Did you enjoy your dinner?"

"Well," said Mrs. Kornmell, "to be perfectly frank with you, the food you serve here—*khaloshes*! Terrible! . . . And such small portions!"

They also make a point with punch.

David came home from work to total mayhem. His children were in the yard, playing in dirt. There was a sink full of dishes and there were toys a foot high in the children's room. Worried, he looked for his wife, Marcia . . . and found her curled up in bed with a book.

"Darling, how was your day?" she asked, smiling.

Bewildered, Irving asked, "Marcia! What happened here today!?"

"You know how every day you come home from work and ask me 'what in the world did you do today?'"

"Yeah," he replied.

"Well," she said, "today I didn't do it."

Our skepticism and kvetching about life and ourselves through jokes can be deprecating, self-deprecating, critical, or self-critical. And, they are often wise and philosophical, with a definite knack for putting down pretension.

> Lisa, unlike her immigrant mama, had the benefit of higher education, and was a regular "intellectual" at home, always spouting philosophy.
>
> "Mama, I accept the universe as it is," stated the "intellectual" pompously.
>
> Mama thought for a while. "*Nu*, darling," she countered, "and if you didn't?"

The jokes we tell offer insight into how we see ourselves in society and in the world. It's been suggested that as outsiders, better to give ourselves a *zetz* (punch) first. By jumping in, not only do we defuse pain, but come out with the edge. As outsiders, criticism of those in power, especially the pompously powerful, are ripe for put-down. (Some mavens have suggested that Yiddish itself and its "stepchild" Yinglish, with its wit and creativity, may be viewed as a satire when played against the rigid formality of German.) Jews are in the unique position of having been persecuted, *while feeling quite superior intellectually*, which leads to humor over what we consider to be absurdities, unfairness, and pomposity of life in general, and within ourselves.

> A rabbi in the hospital received a large vase of flowers with the following note: "The congregation wishes you a full and speedy recovery—by a vote of 212 to 74."

Often irreverent, we are defiant and laugh in the face of authority. We may have lost many a battle, but by using our wits to uncover prejudice, for example, we come out the winners.

> An anti-Semite declares without shame, "All our troubles come from the Jews!"

The Jew responds: "Absolutely! From the Jews—and the camels!"

"Camels? Why the camels?" asks the anti-Semite.

"Why the Jews?" asks the Jew.

ATTITUDES AND ATTITUDE

*J*ewish mothers have always been fodder for Jewish jokes. But, some feel that today, in the absence of a strong religious base, and with assimilation and media, we've *become* a Jewish joke. And no matter how much truth there is in the ethno-type, many are still offended.

A bus with thirty Hadassah ladies turned over and were dispatched to heaven. Unfortunately the computers were down, so God had to ask Satan to provide temporary housing. Soon after, He received an urgent telephone call from Satan telling Him to take the women off his hands.

"What's the problem?" asked God.

Satan replied, "Those Hadassah ladies are ruining my whole set-up. Only two hours and already they raised $100,000 for an air-conditioning system!"

Rabbi Shira Stern is one who considers the Jewish joke offensive, as does Dr. Myrna Hant. "They're every part of the stereotype, revealing strong Jewish frustration and anger."

"Perceptions creates reality," says Rabbi Yocheved Mintz. " If humor or exaggeration becomes the perception, it can be a detriment."

The majority of those I interviewed had varying points of view—but there are factors that make the Jewish mother joke more acceptable. Certainly taste was one. The quick stereotypical two or three-liners, for example, aren't particularly funny—or tasteful. Few would laugh at:

Q: What's the difference between a rottweiler
and a Jewish mother?
A: *Eventually, the rottweiler lets go.*

Most of us would find the above harsh, simplistic, and offensive.

> "If it's in good taste, I don't mind.
> They make jokes about everybody."
> —Melanie Strug

"I only find Jewish mother humor offensive if it's bad from a comedy perspective—you know, when it's something that's been done to death," says Amy Borkowsky. "I don't think I could take one more joke about Jewish moms giving us guilt, making chicken soup, or reminding us to put on a sweater. My mother was a little more original."

But the issue of stereotyping or, as I call it, ethno-typing was not held to be necessarily objectionable—as many claimed all humor involves some stereotyping. But more, for those comedians, like Amy Borkowsky and Judy Gold, who freely joke about their mothers, their humor, they say, involves truth—the truth that comes from personal experience.

"It would be hard to accuse me of stereotyping, because I present my mother as she actually was. My CDs, my act, and my book all have my mother's real messages," says Amy Borkowsky. "I think the best humor comes out of struggle, because there's nothing funny about everything going right. If you went to a comedy club and the comic opened with, 'So I just got a gorgeous new girlfriend, lost thirty pounds, and won the Publisher's Clearinghouse Sweepstakes,' they would get resentment, not laughs. Jews have been comedically blessed, because we've had plenty of struggles throughout our history. Prejudice and persecution have made Jewish mothers worry obsessively about their kids which then makes the Jewish mother herself one more issue to deal with. And it's a stroke of good fortune if her kid happens to be a comic."

"STEREOTYPES EXIST FOR A REASON. NO
ONE EVER WORRIES THEY'RE GOING TO BE
JUMPED BY A BUNCH OF YESHIVA STUDENTS.
ANYONE WHO SAYS HE OR SHE IS NOT
AFFECTED BY STEREOTYPES IS LYING."
—Mallory Lewis

"A lot of humor is based on stereotypes but obviously we're all individuals. [Jewish mother jokes] is a journey to determine issues with your own mother," says Judy Gold, the star of the critically acclaimed Off-Broadway show *Twenty-five Questions for a Jewish Mother* that earned her a Drama Desk nomination. "I find the people who live in a safety net are surrounded by numbness. They can criticize me all they want. [What they don't] realize is, I'm doing my mother. The basis of humor comes from looking at something in different ways, which is also the basis of Judaism—looking for interpretations. Jewish women are funny because they've been through hell, survived, learned, and we constantly challenge the system."

The Jewish female comedian, not unlike her male counterpart, sees humor as pushing the edge, even if it makes some uncomfortable. While the male has been generally able to get away with more direct language and bawdiness, attacking every arena, the female comic has often focused on those themes of special interest to women, such as family, romantic foibles, and feminism. But this turf is also being expanded as more and more females are pushing the envelope successfully.

Comedians have a responsibility to be subversive. It's social commentary, bringing awareness in a positive way. It's sad when we can't laugh at ourselves. When people take themselves so seriously it bugs the crap out of me."

—Judy Gold

"You fat •&%)#!" comes out of the mouth of Zora Essman's daughter Susie in her role as wife of the portly, wimpy agent, Jeff Greene, in *Curb Your Enthusiasm*. Mrs. Essman says: "A lot of my friends resent it . . . her language. It doesn't bother me. She's able to make the switch from the Jewish bitch to the nice woman. I say, 'Well that's the way Larry David thinks.'"

But then Zora Essman is a funny Jewish woman. "My children have a very different view of me. I don't think Susie thinks that of me, but I have great timing. My husband didn't have timing. He was an oncologist. I didn't talk as much when he was a alive."

A number of Jews, even those not in "the business," simply felt, "Why make a big deal?"

"Lighten up! Laughing at ourselves actually mocks the stereotype," says Binyamin Jolkovsky, editor in chief of Jewishworld review.com. "I think every stereotype is based on a bit of truth. It's very important that we laugh at ourselves. If we can't, it sends an alert that we should not engage in that behavior. If you don't acknowledge it, you can't eradicate it."

"Don't take yourself so seriously," says Orthodox feminist Blu Greenberg. And Dr. Ruth Gruber suggests, "If you find some jokes offensive . . . just leave them out."

"I'm not offended by the Jewish mother joke," says Dr. Eileen Warshaw, executive director of the Jewish Heritage Center of the Southwest. "Every group is stereotyped in this day and age. It's fun to make fun of ourselves and just stupid to be paranoid."

Who's doing the *telling* makes a large difference to Jewish mothers, indeed most Jews. If a fellow Jew is the "who," we trust motive. If a non-Jew tells the same story, we get a *shtikl* (little) anxious, even if we know and adore the teller. Mistrust flickers just behind our funny bone. "Why is he telling me this?" we wonder. "OK, it's because I'm Jewish and thought I'd find it funny, but where did he hear it? From some anti-Semitic friend? Why does he know it? Is this some veiled form of anti-Semitism, or at least stereotypical thinking if *he* finds it funny?"

"I'm not offended by Jewish mother jokes—if a Jew tells it, it's funny," says Mallory Lewis. "If a non-Jew tells it, it's not only not funny, but makes me uncomfortable."

"Jewish jokes told by Jews are not offensive," says Sig Liberman, descendant of pioneer Jews in America.

"Jewish humor is part of our history."

—Rabbi Felipe Goodman

"The essence of Jewish humor is making fun of ourselves. Fun makes events not so harsh. Talking at a Shiva, for example, mollifies the pain," says Harry Leichter, creator of the *Schmooze News*, www.schmoozenews.com. "As long as Jewish mother jokes are within the tribe, it's OK."

"When Chris Rock tells a joke, we laugh, but maybe a Black person laughs harder. It's the recognition factor," says Joanna Gleason.

Along with the fear of anti-Semitism, coveting is an issue, as in the *Seinfeld* episode of the dentist who converted "for the jokes." I see a more serious underpinning behind the kvetch.

Personally, I've known very few non-Jews who actually tell a good Jewish joke well. And why should they? True, Jewish humor has had a profound effect on American humor, but it comes from our thousands of years of experience. Basically, they lack the DNA to own it, tell it right, sell it, or even understand with their heart, because they lack a Yiddishe *kop* (Jewish mind). The telling of a Jewish joke is more than a setup and punch line. It's an experience!

The Jewish Mother Experience and Experienced:

A BISSEL OF INFORMATION, COMMENTARY, DEBATE, ANECDOTES, AND HUMOR

MANIFEST OF ALIEN PASSENGERS FOR THE UNITED STATES:

SS *Estonia*, sailing from Danzig 20.Nov.1926, arriving at Port of New York, 4 Dec. 1926

FAMILY NAME	GIVEN NAME	COUNTRY OF ORIGIN	SUBJECT RACE
Fertel	Sheva	Russian	Hebrew

ON COMING TO AMERICA

And so my mother was designated, and came to America. I recall my mother and grandmother talking about the "old country," but not often. When my grandmother who was Polish, married my grandfather, a Russian, they were always on the move, running from place to place with a young child, trying to get to America. They outwitted border guards, took work wherever they could find it, and wound up in Danzig, where they remained until they could get passage to the United States.

As an adult, I find their courage astonishing. In coming to America, they left behind parents, aunts, uncles, nieces, nephews, friends, and a way of life that included three languages, and tradition.

> "*I*n the evening…my mother would make me sit on her footstool…she would gaze into my eyes…to absorb enough of me to last her for the coming months of absence…. 'And if I should die when you are gone, you will remember me in your prayers'…When the train drew into the station…. There was a despair in her way of clinging to me, which I could not then understand. I understand it now. I never saw her again."
>
> —Marcus Ravage, *An American in the Making*, 1917, describing leaving for America

> "**I** have broken away from the Old World; I'm through with it…. I must face this loneliness till I get to the New World…. I must hope for no help from the outside. I'm alone; I'm alone till I get there…But am I really alone…I'm one of the millions of immigrant children, children of loneliness, wandering between worlds that are at once too old and too new to live in."
>
> —Anzia Yezierska, "Cinderella of the Sweatshops," *Children of Loneliness* (1923)

Leah Pearlstein Berkman left Testreny, Russia, in the fall of 1855, near Hanukkah. "We were on the sail ship eleven weeks. My mother asked for . . . food that she could make a soup. [They] gave her a grain that was prepared for rats. . . . My . . . sister cooked the broth. . . . She died that night lying next to me. . . . My mother never saw her again, though she . . . implored them to let her dress her as becomes . . . our kind. [But] the officers . . . threw her in the ocean. My younger sister died the next day. . . . My mother motioned [for all] to step back. . . . wrapped her in a clean white sheet. . . . Years after when I would see [her] weeping . . . her answer was, 'My dear child, haven't I got lots to cry for?'"

My own family's journey—to live in a tiny one-bedroom apartment in Ridgewood, New York, where my mother remained until she married—was to allow them to live freely in the Golden Land.

Their story is typical of many. By 1890, areas such as the Lower East Side of Manhattan were teeming with vast numbers of Jewish immigrants or "Greenhorns." From the Bowery on the west to Houston Street on the north, these Jews often lived in steaming tenements, literally on top of one another. The streets overflowed with immigrant life, including boisterous bearded men with pushcarts, screaming, in Yiddish: "Good fruit, bargains!" By 1900, there were more than seven hundred people per acre within this small enclave scrounging to find work, make homes—and keep tradition alive in a new land, separated from everything and often everyone they knew and loved.

In Neil Simon's *Broadway Bound,* Kate, the mother, describes arriving in America, with passengers wailing and shaking when they saw the Statue of Liberty. Not only because this was their dream, but after taking a look at the Statue . . . she didn't look Jewish. Oy, were they going to have problems again, she wonders.

Despite the hardship encountered in the New World, these streets were also humming with old-world values, customs, and the rich influence of Yiddishkeit. Between the late 1880s and 1914, there were more than 150 Yiddish magazines, newspapers, and periodicals in New York City. Every adult was literate and hungry for news and read a Yiddish newspaper. In the 1920s, it was estimated that there was a readership of over 2 million Jewish people. Many extraordinary people came out of these New York ghettos.

Eddie Cantor was one of them. Born Israel Iskowitz in 1892, the son of Russian Jewish immigrants, Meta and Mechel Iskowitz, he was left orphaned at age two. He was raised by his grandmother, Esther Kantrowitz. The two lived in poverty on Henry Street on the Lower East Side. His strongest memory was of the steaming heat. His *bubbe* (grandmother) barely got them by through selling candles and finding jobs for girls as maids. Cantor found his first audience singing and juggling in the crowded streets. Later on, he credited Grandma Esther and the Henry Street Settlement with keeping him on track, which ultimately made him a star and a renowned philanthropist. In honor of his grandma Kantrowitz, he took the name "Cantor"—a shortened version of hers.

An inveterate fund-raiser, Eddie Cantor was affectionately called the *shnorrer* (beggar) in the state of Israel for his tireless efforts on that country's behalf. In addition to Jewish causes, when President Franklin D. Roosevelt asked Cantor to organize a drive to raise funds to fight polio, the comic/singer suggested asking each donor for only ten cents—and coined the term, the March of Dimes that became the program's slogan.

Cantor dated a young girl named Kitty Brookman when she was fourteen. She later married someone else—and gave birth to Mel Brooks.

MAMA-LOSHEN: YIDDISH AND YINGLISH

I grew up in a home where Yiddish and Yinglish were often spoken. My late mother and grandmother would often talk in Yiddish, especially when someone said, "*Sha*. Not in front of the *kinder*!" (Which of course was us kids.) We knew the curses and bad words (of course), but were never fluent in the language. Most frustrating were the jokes. Picture it. Fifteen relatives around the table, listening to a joke—in broken English. Now, generally, these stories took, on average, fifteen minutes to set up. There we were, my brother and I, along with a myriad of young cousins, listening raptly, eager to hear the punch line already.

Then suddenly, after this interminable wait, the speaker would—at the precise moment of the punch line—switch to Yiddish! Oy. After sitting through farmers, *shlimazls*, *shadchens*, and a trainload of evil soldiers on their way to Pinsk, each "Yinglishly" and deliciously described, we'd finally hear: "And *then* he said . . . *A finstere cholem auf dein kopf und auf dein hent und fiss*." Wha? Here we were, sitting, like victims of an unfinished sexual experience (which of course, we actually knew nothing about). No question, when Yiddishe mamas came here, they maintained their inalienable right to say what they wanted, when they wanted in Yiddish—and scare us, but also fascinate us.

Even as a child, I understood the majesty and power of Yiddish and Yinglish (basically "Yiddishized English," which the great Leo Rosten made famous).

These are words and expressions that carry a strong underlying subtlety and nuance not found in most other languages. For example, the word "mensch" means "person." But when a Yiddishe mama uses it to describe someone, she means a *person*. A real doll, filled with humanity, integrity, and goodness. In fact there are some words, I simply can't say *without* Yiddish. "Chutzpah" means gall, or "some nerve." But way more. In humor or anger, English just doesn't quite do it.

A Yiddishe mama got on a hot, crowded bus and stood in front of a girl.

Mama said, "If you knew what I have, you'd give me your seat." The girl gave up her seat, then took out a fan.

"If you knew what I have, you'd give me that fan," said mama. The girl gave her the fan.

Minutes later, the woman yelled at the driver, "If you knew what I have, you'd let me out here!"

He swerved and opened the door. As she stepped out, he asked, "Madam, what is it you have?!"

"Chutzpah," she replied.

CHUTZPAH! WATCH . . .

"Mrs. Farber had the gall to bring her own turkey to our house for Thanksgiving."

"Mrs. Farber shlepped her own turkey to me on Thanksgiving! What chutzpah!"

The first is way too polite, and probably ends the issue.

The second is felt down to the spleen. "What an insult! Did that idiot think I wouldn't make enough? Was she just being a witch and showing off her hotsy totsy silver serving plate? Can you believe a normal human would do such a thing?! This, I'm getting to the bottom of!"

Then there's the reply:

"Mrs. Farber had the chutzpah to bring to you her own turkey on Thanksgiving?" you ask.

"Gall" would never even make it onto the runway. In this example, the speaker could be silently chuckling, thinking, "Way to go, Mrs. Farber! You risked wrath and possible banishment, but you had the chutzpah to finally bring a turkey that wouldn't send people to Mount Sinai hospital." See? And it all comes from the glorious—Yiddish.

As Yiddish and Yinglish are artfully used by many a Jewish mother, and language is a critical component of culture, here are some facts and examples, which gives us a sense of not merely a language, but a mindset. For a thorough examination of Yiddish, I recommend *Born to Kvetch*, by Michael Wex.

YIDDISH: WHAT IS IT?

Yiddish, not to be confused with Hebrew, the language of Eastern European Jews, is a hybrid of German, Polish, Russian, Romanian, Ukrainian, and other Slovene dialects. It is also known as *mama-loshen*, "mothers' language," since Jewish women, who were taught little Hebrew, spoke it to their children, who, as adults, spoke it to Jews from other Eastern European countries in shtetls—or on the run. Yiddish became the common denominator and contributed to its remarkable richness. My grandmother, for example, was Polish. My grandfather was Russian. Yet they communicated in Yiddish. It is doubtful there is another language that is quite so brave, anxious, hilarious, critical, bawdy, nuanced, passionate, hysterical, subversive, loving, irreverent, expressive, filled with majesty, and sentiment—and kvetching.

Yiddish began when Jews from the north of France

Timeline:

Initial Yiddish	1000–1250 AD
Old Yiddish	1250–1500 AD
Medieval Yiddish	1500–1750 AD
Modern Yiddish	1750–on

settled along the Rhine, adding Germanic dialects to their Hebrew and old French. The language flourished, beginning in 1179, as Jews, driven by pogroms into a variety of countries, brought their languages along.

AN OFTEN OVERLOOKED FACT: While the sacred books are in Hebrew and/or Aramaic, discussions in the shuls, yeshivas, and other Jewish institutions were and frequently still are conducted in Yiddish!

AS OF 2001:
- Harvard has the only endowed Yiddish chair.
- Only 0.5 percent of Yiddish literature has been translated into English.
- About a hundred books are printed in Yiddish annually.
- Apart from the Andrews Sisters record of "Bei Mir Bist du Schön," the only Yiddish song that mainstreamed was Joan Baez's 1960s version of "Dona, Dona."
- The *Oxford English Dictionary* contained 144 words of Yiddish origin.

Gertie and Betty were discussing Yiddish when Betty observed, "You know, there's no word for 'disappointed!'"

"I can't believe it. Wait, I'll call my mother."

To her mother, Gertie asked in Yiddish, "Mama, if I promised to bring the family to dinner, and you worked all day to make the finest meal—chopped liver, soup, chicken—then, two minutes before we're supposed to arrive, I telephone to say something important came up and I can't come. What would you say?"

"Hmmm," she sighed. "I'd say, '*Oy bin ich* (am I) . . . disappointed.'"

I can recall my own mother asking my *bubbe* (gram) how to say "Happy Birthday" in Yiddish. After mulling, she blurted: "Heppy Boyzday!"

As the language of the persecuted, along with our superstitions, much of Yiddish is euphemistic and critical. God forbid anyone should think something's going well, someone (or something, such as the evil eye) will make sure to snatch it. Many a Jewish mother felt it was better not to tempt fate by over-talking.

"So, how's your son Joel's practice?"

"Eh . . . it's there."

"I heard your daughter's engaged."

"Finally."

"I saw in the paper your grandchild was valedictorian and plans to go to Harvard."

"We'll see."

Better yet, the Jewish mother may pretend not to be too crazy about good fortune.

"Ma, don't worry. I'm sure the doctor will say it's nothing serious."

"I should be so lucky!"

"Eliot just got a promotion!"

"With any luck, he'll keep it."

"Mama, the new pool Dad put in is great."

"With his *mazel* (luck) he'll hurt his back with his swan dives."

Many Jewish mothers also *gestured* to ward off enemies, demons, and evil eyes when hoping or speaking well of something. One of our most popular, which many including myself use, is the ubiquitous, ever handy—spit. (And you thought it was only used by Jewish mothers to wipe a smudge.) Heaven forbid, you say, "I hope my son passed his entrance exams—spitspitspit," "Your baby? Gorgeous—and so healthy—spitspitspit," or "The buyers made a bid on our house—spitspitspit," those around you could water their lawns.

Less humid is the *keyn eynhore*, or "no evil eye." It's a magical phrase that when uttered has the power to ward off bad events. The Jewish mother has the option of saying: "My triplets—are now developing perfectly, *keyn eynhore*."

UNARGUABLY, A LANGUAGE OF ARGUMENT

The flip side of protecting our assets in a brutal world is complaining and arguing about it. And Jews, with a rich tradition of argumentation, have peppered Yiddish with *tsouris* (trouble) and kvetches. If we understand Yiddish and Yinglish in the context of our history, it may not take the sting out of the language, but makes it comprehensible—and today, often hysterical.

THE STORY OF OY

There has never been one word that constitutes a small vocabulary more than "oy." The ubiquitous kvetch, the Jewish mother uses it to register surprise, pain, relief, despair, or horror. The meaning varies from, "Oy, I gained five pounds" to "The IRS is auditing?! Oy vey!" (The "vey" adding more woe to the "oy.") Bigger than "too bad," it comes from the *kishkas* (guts) of Jewish trials.

A classic:

> "Oy . . . " said Mrs. Levy.
>
> "Oy-oy-oy," sighed Mrs. Stein
>
> "Oy vey, " answered Mrs. Cohen.
>
> Mrs. Fein folded her beach chair. "Bite your tongues! Didn't we agree not to discuss the children?!"

A first cousin is "*nu*"—registering any and all from a sigh, a grimace, a sneer, to a grunt, among more benign emotions.

> "Lisa, I saw you talking to that nogoodnik, *nu*?!" (What's the story!)
>
> "*Nu*, he stopped me on the street." (So what could I do?)
>
> "And the next time . . . *Nu*?" (Haven't you learned your lesson, with that *yutz*?)

Oy and *nu* together work like a dictionary!

> "*Nu*?" said Mrs. Frankel.
>
> "*Nu*," said Mrs. Greenbaum.
>
> "*Nu*!" said Mrs. Frankel.

"*Nu*??" said Mrs. Greenbaum.

"*Nu*?!!" said Mrs. Frankel.

"Oy! Alright, already!" said Mrs. Greenbaum. "This week I'll take carpool!"

In addition to the always handy "oy," the Yinglish-speaking mother can use a number of linguistic devices to register scorn and criticism. A few of these include: repetition, sarcasm, shifting emphasis or meaning, the afterthought, word additions—and of course, the *question*.

Repetition: This device simply requires answering a stupid question— with the question in declarative form.

"Mama, don't you want to me to be happy and fulfilled?"

"No, I don't want you to be happy and fulfilled."

(Did my daughter suddenly become a *shmegegge* [idiot] or what?)

Sarcasm: Also a handy device for the stupid comment. Exaggeration here makes the point beautifully.

"Mama, should I have a car pick you up?"

"Actually, I'd prefer shlepping on three buses."

(Did my son suddenly become a *shmegegge* or what?)

Shifting emphasis can turn "scorn" into art. Listen . . . "Is this a serious relationship?" Simple right? Not right.

Is this a serious relationship? (I'll believe that when elephants fly.)

Is *this* a serious relationship? (Finally, one before I die.)

Is this a *serious* relationship? (Or are you *futzing* around, as usual?)

Is this a serious *relationship*? (From what I saw between you, darling, I have more of a "relationship" with my butcher.)

"Lovely" is, by most people, a nice compliment. But when my mother or grandmother said it, it meant, "Oy, you could *plotz* from that!"

> "On you, it looks lovely." (Burn it.)
> "Your new girlfriend? Lovely, just lovely." (Bring me the Rolaids.)
> "Your son's studying flamenco. How lovely." (Oy . . . he needs therapy.)
> "It was a lovely thought." (Too bad you didn't have a better one.)

One of the linguistic traits my grandmother failed to pick up was the "white lie." No matter how many times we tried to tell her the absolute truth wasn't entirely necessary, she never quite got hold of the concept. Every time we saw disaster coming—like the time Mrs. Needleman insisted on showing photos of her grandson—my mother and I would clutch our hearts and say a little prayer. But there it was. Grandma would take one long look at the photos and say in her deeply Yiddish accent, "Hmmm, not very good-looking, *nebuch* (pity)." After losing four friends, we began mumbling something about "arterial flow-problem."

The afterthought: There is nothing like an "innocent" add-on of a word, or a partial word, to make a point when the listener is not doing his job. Expert Yinglish speakers can emphasize (OK, zing) with the afterthought, which, of course, is the whole point.

> "So, Molly," said Myrna, "have you made up your mind where to send your David for speech therapy?"
> "No . . . we're still considering the whole thing."
> "Don't rush. Sleep on it. Listen, by the time he's married, he'll probably talk right—*if there's still time.*"

More examples of the afterthought.

> "Yes, OK! I admit, a good cook she is, that witch."
> "Even so, he graduated medical school, that *nudnik.*"

"Yet she managed to snag a millionaire, that alrightnik."

New word additions, or partial word additions: A little inventive word play or exclamations can completely alter a sentence.

The poetic "shm" when added to a word can deflate faster than a dirigible on the Space Needle.

Rich-shmich: "Your boyfriend doesn't spend a nickel."

Fancy-shmancy: "Darling, it still looks like a *shmatte* (cheap rag)."

Dentist-shmentist: "He still spits when he talks."

Pate-shmate: "It can't touch my chopped liver."

And finally, the Queen of Yinglish—the Question! Whether this comes from thousands of years of debate and argumentation and/or reflects our precarious relationship with the world where a question is safer than making a definitive statement, answering a question with a question is at the very core of Yiddish and Yinglish.

"Ma, your soup was delicious."
"And the brisket you didn't like?"

"Ma, when's Passover this year?"
"What am I, a calendar?"

"Ma, I finally bought a new car."
"And who can afford the insurance?"

"Ma, I haven't called in a week. So what's new?"
"You didn't wonder if I was lying dead somewhere?"

> **S**ince many Jewish mothers answer a question—with a question—why not try it?
>
> **MOTHER:** "Esther told me a single doctor just joined the temple. Why don't you come with us this Friday?"
>
> **DAUGHTER:** "So how are things with Esther?"
>
> **MOTHER:** "Who knows? Would it kill you to come to temple this week?
>
> **DAUGHTER:** "Is Esther's arthritis still acting up?"
>
> **MOTHER:** "What am I, a rheumatologist?"
>
> **DAUGHTER:** "When you see her, will you ask her?"
>
> **MOTHER:** "What's with you and Esther? You know what? Forget I even asked!"

THE WORLD OF IDIOTS

Yiddish and Yinglish do not bear fools lightly—and neither do Jewish mothers. There are almost as many words for fools as the Iron Chef has recipes for rice. With the emphasis on learning, personal ethics, and common sense, it's not surprising the Jewish mother holds those "without" in contempt. Although, one theory sees the fool as the "anti-scholar," lightening the learning load in the shtetls. But more, in the small insular towns of Europe, where Jews held no status in the outside world, one's own psychological status within their community may be raised by recognizing yet, those who are deemed inferior.

Many have been elevated to first and last name status. Leo Rosten describes a few: Chaim Yankel, Joe Nebuch, Shmerl Narr, Moishe Kapoyr, Shimmel Shlemiel, Lester Lemish, Shimon Shmegegge, Moishe Pupik. These are all pathetic souls who blend in with the wallpaper—or rip it falling because someone stepped on them. And the outspoken Jewish mother was a master, given her gift for both the verbal and the psychological.

Here are a few more fools and their frailties:

nar	baffoonish fool
yold	naive fool
shmendrik	weak fool

bulvan	oafish fool
kuni lemmel	yokel fool
shmegegge	whining fool
shloomp	creepy fool
paskkudnyak	nasty fool

WHEN MAMA MEANS BUSINESS: CURSES!

Yiddish and Yinglish are delicious—in humor and hatred. Listen . . . *"Er zol vaksen vi a tsibeleh, mit dem kop in drerd."* No one would translate it for me until I was twenty-one, then solemnly, *"It means . . . 'He should grow like an onion with his head in the ground.'"*

Unlike English expletives that render a quick statement, the Yiddish curse, nuanced and tricky, is a juicy, literate, malediction that no mere obscene word could possibly convey. It may start with a positive wish or statement, then bite you in the tagline, inviting further debate. Indeed, the whole point of the curse is not to swear, but to . . . prophesize. As the proverb goes: "A curse is not a telegram: it doesn't arrive so fast." Like caviar, it must be savored.

- May the *mohel* circumcise your first son—and bless the wrong piece.
- May you eat chopped liver, pickled herring, gefilte fish, boiled beef, potato pancakes—and may you choke on every bite.
- May you turn into a blintz, and may your enemy turn into a cat, and may he eat you up and choke on you, so we can be rid of you both.
- May the lice in your shirt marry the bedbugs in your mattress and may their offspring set up residence in your underwear.
- May your blood turn to whiskey, so that one hundred bedbugs get drunk on it and dance the mazurka in your belly button.
- May you fall into the outhouse just as a regiment of Ukrainians is finishing a prune stew and twelve barrels of beer.

   OY!

THE WHOLE WORLD IS YINGLISH?

As a college student, I was the only Jew in my dorm. By summer, the others went home to places like Picawa, Wisconsin, saying, "Oy *vey*! I can't believe the shlepping I did!" But given the richness, the vastness, the chutzpah of Yiddish and Yinglish, it's not surprising that it's "catching."

Many Yiddish and Yinglish words today are in common use. English-speakers quickly picked up phrases, which are literal translations. Here are a few:

Go hit your head against the wall.

You should live so long.

I need (blank) like a hole in the head.

Alright already.

It shouldn't happen to a dog.

I should have such luck.

He knows from nothing.

And many in the mountains of Montana might utter: *bubbe,* bupkes, chutzpah, cockamayme, *emmes, farklempt, feh,* gelt, kibitz, klutz, knish, kvetch, maven, megillah, *meshugge, nakhes,* nosh, *plotz,* shlemiel, shlep, *shlimazl,* shmaltz, shmear, shmooze, shnook, *shnorrer, shpiel,* shtick, *shvitz,* yenta, *yutz,* and *zaftig.*

WILL THERE ALWAYS BE YIDDISH?

"I've always resembled my grandmother, from the curly hair to the ample bosom. But I never thought it possible that I would actually turn into her . . . once I became a mother. [My] Michaela's thighs were henceforth known as *pulkes.* . . . Her nickname . . . was *Mama Shayna, Ziskeit,* and *Shayna Maidel.* . . . I wasn't surprised that Yiddish came naturally to me; after all, I had heard it spoken all my life. But when I began to observe my friends and acquaintances whose forebearers were more American than mine, also using Yiddish with their young ones, I began to suspect a trend," writes Gabriella Burman in her marvelous article, "Savoring Yiddish."

"All of a sudden, I'm calling my kids *bubbeleh,* squeezing the *kishkas* out of them, and telling them to watch their *keppies* [heads]," said Amy Carson Schlussel, an attorney and mother of two, in the article.

Marc Miller, a professor of Yiddish at Emory University in Atlanta, said that he and his wife referred to their son as *sheyfel* (little sheep). "Yiddish today is so tied up with nostalgia, it comes to the surface."

Burman reported that Devorah Pinson, a mother of two who is prone to saying *gay shlufe* (go to sleep), finds her daughter Chaya, four, addressing Mendel, seven months, in Yiddish!

"Pinson," reports Burman, "says she hopes her children will continue speaking Yiddish into adulthood, especially when they become parents themselves. But do a few words preserve a language for eternity? My grandmother doesn't think so. It is, however, 'better than nothing,' she says, giving her typical glass half-full response. Such optimism, perhaps, is the greatest Yiddish lesson of all," ends Burman.

As long as there are Jewish mothers, Yiddish and Yinglish will prevail, I believe. After all, what other language can say "I love you," with quite the same nostalgia—and passion?

On Giving Birth . . . and a Little Sex

The Hebrew word for womb, [rehem], has the same root as the word compassion. The womb is the innermost area of the feminine part of ourselves, the place where life is created and formed.

Obviously, to give birth, sex is (usually) involved. We are a practical people; sex, in Judaism, rather than being seen as shameful, is considered a critical responsibility in the marital relationship. And there's much commentary on the husband's duty to satisfy his wife (which is, no doubt, why Viagra is considered kosher by some authorities).

The minimal frequency of marital relations legislated in the Talmud was based on a man's profession and time spent at home: "Every day for those who have no occupation (hmmm), twice a week for laborers, once a week for ass-drivers; once every thirty days for camel drivers; once every six months for sailors (*Mishna Ketubot* 5:6; *Ketubot* 62b)." Moreover, a husband cannot change professions without his wife's permission, for example, from ass-driver to camel driver, if her conjugal rights will be affected.

"Men are the ones responsible for having children. Men must sire," says Rabbi Shira Stern. "After ten years without children, the wife may seek a divorce."

Dr. Ruth has often said that a strong element in her being a sex therapist is that in the Jewish tradition sex has never been a sin, and that it has always been an obligation of the husband: providing sexual gratification for his wife.

"During the holiday, there were special delicacies," wrote Sam Levinson in *Meet the Folks*.

"Mama's home-baked challah, which was so arranged that you didn't have to slice it. There were bulges all around, which you just pulled out of their sockets . . . into nice, oily soup. The sought-after prize in the soup . . . was a small unhatched egg. There was one egg and eight children. What a strain on Mama's impartiality to choose the deserving child. [It] usually went to the girls because of some folk-theory about fertility."

Many Orthodox Jews believe God plans families; however, Jewish law clearly permits birth control in certain circumstances, for example, for nursing mothers, if a couple already has a child of each sex, or if pregnancy might be risky. Hormonal methods of birth control, such as pills, patches, injections, and implants, are generally acceptable. But, as Jewish law prohibits men from destroying or wasting seed, coitus interruptus, condoms, and vasectomy are forbidden by most Orthodox authorities. Condoms, however, may be acceptable to protect against the spread of an incurable sexually transmitted disease.

"NO SEX EDUCATION WAS GIVEN. SO, I GOT MARRIED AND KNEW BUBKES—NOTHING! I'M DRIVING WITH MOM; SHE'S CURIOUS TO KNOW HOW MUCH I LEARNED IN ONE MONTH OF MARRIED LIFE. SHE SAYS, 'TELL ME, MALKA, DO YOU KNOW WHAT A DIAGRAM IS?'"

—Marjorie Gottlieb Wolfe, writer

Years ago, a "*kimpertorn*," a woman in labor, lay in a "*kimper*" to protect the expectant mother from several problems, explains Michael Wex in *Born to Kvetch*. To protect the *kimpertorn* from miscarriage, she would wear an eaglestone. Sometimes a baker's shovel and bread loaves were hung over the bed to make the delivery as smooth as a bun slides out of an oven.

During labor, many mothers would agree there are better ways to use that baker's shovel!

According to ancient rabbis, (*Niddah* 30b), life begins with a push, hence the indentation between nose and mouth! During the nine months in the womb the baby studies the entire Torah with an angel. At the time of birth, the infant holds back, wishing to remain within the warmth of the womb. The angel presses upon the spot (between nose and mouth) to nudge the babe into the world. Once born, the child forgets all he's learned. Our lives on earth are spent rediscovering that which we have forgotten.

When my own son was born, I felt it was not only miraculous, but a renewal. Within the few years prior to his birth, my family suffered a spate of death and grave illness. He was named for my late mother, as is custom (to name for a deceased relative). His birth was a reaffirmation of life's circle, representing hope for the family, and for our continuing Jewish line. I was overwhelmed by his presence in a way I had never been before, or will be again. And the sheer power of that maternal love was so great, so strong, I could barely look it in the eye, for fear, much like staring at a solar eclipse, I'd be forever blinded.

While Jewish boys were traditionally welcomed into the world with a *brit milah* or circumcision ceremony on the eighth day of life, no parallel ceremony for baby girls had existed until American Jewish feminists invented them. On March 14, 1977, the *New York Times* reported that the new Reform Jewish prayer book, published in February 1977, included a ceremony for baby girls for the first time, and that Ezrat Nashim was also about to publish a booklet entitled *Blessing the Birth of a Daughter: Jewish Naming Ceremonies for Girls.* Generally called *simchat bat*, or rejoicing in a daughter, aided the process of egalitarianism for both the female child and the women around her, as mothers and grandmothers are prominent in these ceremonies. Rabbi Irving (Yitz) Greenberg, a well-known supporter of Jewish Orthodox feminism (and husband of feminist Orthodox pioneer Blu Greenberg), was supportive, expressing the feeling that Jewish feminists, rather than "turning their backs on religion, were demanding expression . . . within religious life." Today, girls' naming ceremonies are common within all branches of Judaism.

KIDFIRST—THE OYS AND JOYS

A Classic:
      Rachel and Esther met for the first time in fifty years. Rachel began to tell Esther about her children.
      "My son is a computer maven with four kids. My daughter has three. So Esther, tell me about yours?"
      Esther replied, "Unfortunately, we never had any children."
      "No children? No grandchildren? Tell me, Esther, what do you do for aggravation?"

And so the old joke goes. But most Jewish mothers would agree, during the best and worst of times, raising a child may be better termed "aggravating-ecstasy." As we become mothers, we also become the benefactors of instant emotional comprehension. All those "wait till you have your owns" we were treated to by our own mothers suddenly turn into a frightening and joyous reality.

Is there a mother who doesn't plan to be "perfect"? (A truly absurd goal.) Especially we "moderns" who are equipped with more self-help books than there are reruns of *The Brady Bunch*.

Fortunately, the Jewish mother also comes equipped with thousands of years of tradition!

VALUES

In our home, values—most of which came from Jewish thinking and sensibility—weren't some nebulous concept to be gleaned. Nor were they instilled exclusively in the synagogue.

Values were an intricate part of our daily lives and experience. They were discussed (OK, debated) at dinner, and raised when behavior (ours or someone else's) came into question.

"My mom insisted on buying one-day old meat and baked goods," says Michael Medved. "As a preteener, I was embarrassed, but she made the point that there's nothing embarrassing about being sensible. She'd say, 'People have better things in life to do than watch you.'" In his book, *Right Turns*, these thoughts were echoed in "Lessons: Never be Embarrassed." "My mother was sloppy. When I was applying to college, she cleaned up the living room for my interview with Harvard. I was scrubbed, and put on a skinny tie. This guy comes in, and my dad who happened to be home, says hello . . . in his underwear. She shrugged. [Regarding the interviewer] My mother took the point of view, 'Don't worry about this shmuck.' So I went to Yale."

"I brought my children up with all those values—honesty and integrity," says Zora Essman. "To me, that was part of being a Jewish mother. You have to model them."

Grounding is a critical value to Melanie Strug. "Kerry doesn't see herself as a star. She's very well grounded. She graduated a straight-A student, and continues to do charity events and works with kids. She does gymnastics clinics and works for the Department of Justice in Juvenile Justice. We instilled motivation. Our oldest daughter, before she became a mom, was a marketing executive for Coca-Cola. Our son has a high position doing computer audits for the Marriott Corporation. All our children are high-achievers. I was brought up the same way—and passed it on."

"She taught us to laugh but allowed us to cry. Laughter at the end of her life didn't heal her, but it gave her dignity and strength and helped us to find those same qualities in ourselves," wrote Lee M. Hendler, author of *The Year Mom Got Religion*, about her mother, Lenore (Lyn) Pancoe Meyerhoff, politician, activist, and philanthropist. "Mom's life was one long lesson in attention. Life matters, she taught. Pay attention. Do your best."

WORRY

All mothers worry. But, as we've seen, for the Jewish mother, optimism is often a long-range *plan*, but in the immediate, we're emotionally and traditionally a *bissel* (little) more pessimistic. These are our jewels, our children. And given our history, such concerns are not unnatural. Yes, we're out of the shtetls, but we carry a sense-memory of our forebearers. And world conditions, along with some local conditions, aren't reassuring.

"I had started earning enough money by writing *The Steve Allen Show* to get my own New York City pad," says writer, author, producer, and composer Bill Dana. "I called to tell my mother. 'Ma, wait till you see it! It's in a great neighborhood—Fifty-second and Second Avenue. You enter and there's a kitchen level and you take three steps down to a living room area, then you step up right to my nice-sized bedroom and bath. Then you step back down from the bedroom to the living room area, then two steps down to a den with steps up to a lovely garden behind glass!' Nothing. Then after a minute, she finally said . . . 'Don't fall.'"

> **B**ill Dana ("My name: José Jimenéz") wrote the multi-Emmy-winning *All in the Family* episode "Sammy Davis Visits Archie Bunker" that featured Sammy Davis Jr. kissing Archie. The episode is number twelve in the "*TV Guide* Best One Hundred Episodes" in the history of television.

Our legacy of worry, of course, came from our shtetl mothers, who, in addition to all the real stresses in the world, had demons to ward off, since the shtetls were hotbeds of superstition (for example, slapping a newborn if the baby laughed during the night so that the demonic Lilith would not kidnap the babe). By keeping vigilant, the Jewish mother could fight back the evil spirits with her *keyn eynhores* and spits. Active worry: The mother who would rather be sick or hungry than see her child suffer—while to many a child is a nuisance, is also seen by some as the height of mother love.

✡

LITTLE ISAAC HEARD A NEWS STORY ON
TELEVISION AND RUSHED INTO THE KITCHEN
WHERE HIS MOTHER WAS MAKING DINNER.

"MAMA! MAMA! THEY SAID ON TV THERE'S GOING
TO BE AN ECLIPSE! CAN I GO OUT AND WATCH?"

"GO, DARLING," SAID HIS MAMA. "ENJOY. BUT I'M
WARNING YOU . . . DON'T GET TOO CLOSE."

✡

The renowned rabbi and author, Joseph Telushkin, tells the story of Chaim Bermant, an English-Jewish writer, who, while a correspondent during the 1973 Yom Kippur War, was asked by soldiers to phone their parents and reassure them they were OK. His record of one of the conversations is almost a classic conversation of "worry," where the mama continues to question the harried reporter, disbelieving his reassurance. After all, if her son was OK, why wouldn't he call himself? There must be a way—even from a desert.

How many of us have a wafting sense we've done something like that ourselves—questioning like an attorney general to get the "real" scoop—only to find wormholes we can disbelieve? A show of hands, please. (Wait . . . I can't type with two hands up.)

CONTROL, INVOLVEMENT—AND ADVICE:
(BUT THEY WOULDN'T LISTEN ANYWAY!)

We Jewish mother-worriers, as active as we are, may at times turn to overprotection, interference, and yes, boundary busting—even when our children haven't been children for ten years, or forty.

"I do everything. You rule that roost," says Mallory Lewis. "We not only feed them, but know what's best for them. I do everything. The sadness is, nobody . . . listens (as far as the mother is concerned)."

> "**A** Jewish mother knows where her kid is until he's ninety-eight. She's calling: 'Did you eat yet? Did you sleep yet? Did you go to the toilet yet? Did you put on a sweater? Did you take the sweater to the toilet? . . .' A toilet to the sweater? . . . When a Jewish kid goes to an out-of-town college the whole family follows him . . . 3,000 relatives are running to give him extra jackets, coats, blankets, sandwiches . . . extra telephones in case the carpenters are fixing . . . two of everything just in case."
>
> —Jackie Mason

> "**H**i, Amila. I had something on my mind that I wanted to tell you, but I don't want you to get mad at me. I just wanna make sure if you get involved with someone, that you don't use lambskin condoms. Because if you're worried about AIDS, using lambskin is the same as if the guy had a totally naked *shmekel*. And y'know, they used to make graduation certificates out of sheepskin. So before you do anything foolish, you may wanna ask yourself, 'How safe would I feel with his shmekel wrapped in a diploma?'"
>
> —Mother of comedian Amy Borkowsky, creator of the hit comedy CDs and book, *Amy's Answering Machine: Messages from Mom*

OY!

"I found many a Jewish mother who's trying to take care of you, and control everything that goes on around them. No matter how old you get," says Harry Leichter, "she wants it her way."

"My *father* was the typical very controlling 'Jewish mother,'" quips Dr. Ruth Gruber. "In our household my mother and father were the odd couple."

"We talk about what should be, we'll think about it, then we warn each other to shut up," says Zora Essman. "We know she's [the daughter] not going to listen, but . . . we're still the mother."

"I've spoken many times about my mother, Jeanette Gottlieb, who passed away last year at age eighty-eight," says writer Marjorie

Gottlieb Wolfe, author of *Are Yentas, Kibitzers, and Tummlers Weapons of Mass Instruction? Yiddish Trivia*, who found her mother to be a source of both information and misinformation. "She told me that 'VD' (venereal disease) meant '*voden*' (Yiddish for 'what else'?). She said that 'debris' were leftovers at a circumcision!"

A forestry graduate received a five-year post in the middle of nowhere. In his survival gear, much to his surprise, he found a recipe for matzo balls. Confused, he asked his superior, Goldberg, about it.

"A few years from now, when you've had it already with the bears and trees and you're going a little meshugge from the solitude, you'll remember your matzo ball recipe. Get it out and start making some," said Goldberg.

"And what will that do?" asked the graduate.

"Before you know it, you'll have ten Jewish mothers looking over your shoulder, shouting, 'You think that's the right way to make a matzo ball?!'"

"My mother never got into the guilt. 'You never write, you never call,' wasn't her thing," says Amy Borkowsky. "But what she lacked in guilt she more than made up for with the advice-giving. There was the time I moved to an apartment on the twentieth floor, and she leaves me a message: 'Hi, Amila. I'm just thinking, if God forbid you needed to get out of your apartment real fast and the elevators weren't running, maybe you oughta get yourself a parachute.' Then there was the time she warned me not to wear my red bathrobe when I take out the garbage because her friend's grandson said that red is a 'gang color.'"

NO SACRIFICE IS TOO GREAT!

And why shouldn't the Jewish mother interfere? Get involved? After all . . . we would do anything for them. And they know it.

Consider this excerpt from *All Roads Lead to the Jewish Mother* by Stacey Marcus:

"Where's my pink shirt?" says the Jewish daughter.

"In the laundry," replies the Jewish mother.

"Oh my gawd, I planned to wear that to school today!" shouts the Jewish daughter.

"I found it rolled up in a ball near the trash can so I thought perhaps I'd wash it," says the Jewish mother.

"Can you stop yelling at the kids?" pipes in the Jewish husband from behind the shower door.

"Why are you so stressed out?" asks the other Jewish daughter.

I walk into the living room to reclaim my equilibrium and step directly into a dog poop.

"You really need to train me," says the Jewish dog's eyes.

Thus begins another day where I am blamed for everything from late laundry to puffy hair to the tsunami and Hurricane Katrina and the clock hasn't even struck eight. I have been held accountable for everything from the Gap not having the right color capris to the nimbus clouds on vacations. One of my favorites is the fate of the puffy un-Jennifer Aniston hair.

Deep in my heart, I understand that the reason they feel so comfortable dumping their worries and woes into my open arms is: 1.) I am the Jewish mother and my arms are open. 2.) There wasn't a long line of applicants who want to be responsible for everything under the sun including planning a vacation where there are no airline glitches or clouds in the sky.

It's like Charles Schulz said, "Sometimes I lie awake at night and ask why me? Then a voice answers nothing personal, your name just happened to come up." I am glad it did.

✡

NINETY-YEAR-OLD MRS. BRONSTEIN VISITED HER
LAWYER WITH A REQUEST.

"I WANT YOU SHOULD MAKE ME A DIVORCE."

"BUT MRS. BRONSTEIN," SAID THE LAWYER,
"YOU'VE BEEN MARRIED SEVENTY YEARS!"

"DAT'S IT. I WANT YOU SHOULD MAKE A DIVORCE
NOW. I'VE SECKRIFICED ENOUGH!"

"BUT WHY NOW?" PROTESTED THE LAWYER.

"I WANTED TO WAIT UNTIL THE CHILDREN WERE
OUT OF THE HOUSE."

✡

THE OTHER SIDES OF SACRIFICE: GUILT

We give and we give and what do we expect for our devotion?
Their happiness and success, naturally. But a *bissel nakhes* wouldn't
hurt, either. It's not only quid pro quo, but we see our children's
successes as the ultimate goodness life can offer us. The definition
of success has changed significantly since shtetl days, as we've
assimilated American values into our own belief system, but one
thing hasn't changed: Guilt.

"When control tends to hang on too long, the mother can
become the victim, the martyr," says the author of *Cutting Loose*,
Dr. Howard Halpern.

In *The 2,000 Year Old Man in the Year 2000*, Mel Brooks and
Carl Reiner discuss guilt. Despite the fact that the 2,000-year-
old man invites his parents—who have traveled in the rain to see
him—they refused to enter. They didn't want to be a "bother."
Besides, they ate squirrels and berries on the way. All they wanted
was for their son to think of himself, as they are "nothing." And
such may have started guilt.

"When my mother was in an old-age home and asked how I was, not a single time could I fall asleep again," says Theodore Bikel.

Men in Black director Barry Sonnenfeld recalled one of his most embarrassing moments. As a youngster, attending the first Earth Day concert in 1970, the event was interrupted by a call on the loudspeaker with an urgent announcement: "Barry Sonnenfeld, call your mother."

The only child of a Jewish family, Sonnenfeld went to NYU because his mother threatened to commit suicide if he went to a "sleepaway" school.

Sometimes guilt can backfire as our daughters learn the knack:

> One morning, as little Deborah was sitting at the kitchen table watching her mother wash the breakfast plates, she noticed that her mother had several strands of white hair mixed in with her dark hair.
>
> "Mommy, why have you got some white hairs?"
>
> "Well, *Mamala*, every time a daughter does something naughty to make her mother cry or unhappy, one of mama's hairs turns white."
>
> Deborah thought about this information for a few moments then said, "Is that why all of *bubbe*'s hairs are white?"

But another side of unerring devotion, unbridled love, and sacrifice can also be unequivocal acceptance—and more.

CAN DO NO WRONG

If, despite our adoration, suffering, advice, worry, and sacrifice, our child errs, is hurt, or doesn't always grab that brass ring, there are a few quite so supportive as the Jewish mother. I have no doubt we were the ones who developed "spin" and the ability to put "a good face" on almost everything involving our children.

> Haym turned red as he read a paper. On the front page was his son David running around with protesters.

"Why does he do these things?!" Haym barked to his wife.

"*Sha*," she said.

"Last week, he walked every street with a sign about taxes. Then, he picketed all over the university about pay cuts. Today, he's running to inspect every power line!"

"Look at it this way," urged the mama. "It's the only exercise he gets."

When actress Gina Gershon landed her role in *Showgirls*, she called her mother with the good news. When the actress slowly imparted she was dancing naked and kissing another woman, and maybe having sex with her, her mother wanted to know if she was a nice girl.

Two Jewish mothers, Beryl and Gert, were bragging about their sons, who just graduated college.

"My Joel," said Beryl, "landed a job, one-two-three with the top firm in Chicago, because he had one terrific résumé!"

"Very nice, very nice," said Gert. "But my boy, Mitchell, has had so many interviews, his résumé is now in its fifth printing!"

"My mother's best quality was that in her eyes I was perfect," says Mallory Lewis about her mother, Shari Lewis. "She was always on my side," adds Mallory, whose "sibling" was a puppet— Lamb Chop. Was she ever jealous of her "little sister" who, when Mal was young, got all the public attention? She laughed, "Not at all. I knew she was a sock. But Lamb Chop was a source of comfort. Today, my own son will tell Lamb Chop secrets which mom will never hear!"

Like her mother, Mallory is convinced her progeny is perfect. "Whenever we have a disagreement I convince him I know best because, I tell him, 'I made you in my tummy.' He's seven and he's already had a girlfriend. My son is going to be a wonderful hubby. Like my own mother, I support him totally."

I WAS ALWAYS THERE . . .

"When I had my first child, that was it, I was a mom and my husband would moonlight so I could stay home and give my children the very best," says Melanie Strug. "I think it mattered. I was always there."

Many of those children who have written about their shtetl moms, or the absolute devotion of the Jewish ethno-typical mom, have done so with great admiration, even adoration.

"Talk about outsiders . . . I'm a left-handed, gay Jew," Congressman Barney Frank (D-MA) told the *New York Times* in 1996. When Parents, Families, and Friends of Lesbians and Gays asked his mother to add to their cookbook, she e-mailed her recipe for mandel bread, he reported in *Stars of David*. She also made speeches on his behalf. In a 1982 campaign ad, she said: "How do I know he'll protect Social Security? Because I'm his mother."

"My mother thought everything I did was perfect," said legendary New York Congresswoman Bella Abzug. "And if I was scolded in school, she'd go to the school and scold the teacher. In fact when I was elected to Congress, election night, she said, 'I always knew Bella would make it. Because she always did her homework and practiced her violin without being asked to do so.' In addition to which [when asked] 'How do you account for Bella's success?' She answered: 'I was always there . . . I was there.' And indeed she was."

*M*rs. Rifkin was bragging to her neighbor, Mrs. Horowitz, about her son.

"My boy, David," she said, "graduated first in his class with degrees in philosophy, history, and social psychology."

"You must so proud!" said Mrs. Horowitz.

"I am," replied Mrs. Rifkin. "He can't get a job but, ai-ai-ai, does he know why!"

EVERYONE'S CHILD

The Jewish mother's largess is not only directed at our own children. With an abundance of adoration and experience, along with our strong belief in children as our hope for the future, we often expand our mothering through our work—and most definitely in our personal interactions. As Mallory Lewis, daughter of the late Shari Lewis, puts it: "You're not a mother just to who you gave birth to, but you're the universal mother to everyone you come in contact with."

A Classic:

A hysterical young mother sprang to the ringing phone.

"So, darling, how are you?" said the voice.

"Rotten, Mama!" she sobbed. "The baby won't eat, the washer's leaking, so I slipped and sprained my ankle. Worse, company's coming and I can't shop because the car's broken!"

"Darling, for you, I'll shop. Also, I'll send a repairman. Then I'll feed the baby and make a brisket."

"Mama...you're the best!"

"What are mothers for? Listen, if the car's broken, how did Harold get to work?"

"Harold?"

"Harold! Your husband!"

"...My husband's name is Norman."

"Norman...?!....Is this 555-2122?"

"This is 555-2212." Then, after a pause, "...Does this mean you're not coming...?"

Probably nowhere is this universal mothering more profoundly seen than in Israel, where the constant threat of violence requires an exquisite connection among all—and vigilance over all.

Devorah Talia Gordon described a trip to Israel when a woman approached, started speaking to her in urgent Hebrew, and gestured to her fourteen-month-old son who was sucking on a lollipop. It seems the woman was saying "no good"—that it was dangerous for a toddler. Ms. Gordon concluded that in Israel, a Jewish child belongs to everyone, as though all were part of a large extended family.

JEWISH MOTHERS AND DAUGHTERS

The intimacy between mother and daughter, much described in articles and books, is unique and dynamic. As we share the same gender, the relationship between us is a complex affair, made even more complicated when mother and daughter not only come from different generations, but different daily cultural experiences. As our first and usually primary nurturer, the bond between us is almost unshakeable, as is our early need for approval and love.

American sthetl-thinking, along with feminism, double whammied this tender relationship, making it very precarious at times. Loving daughters now found themselves at odds with the beliefs, roles, and behavior that our mothers thought were fitting.

During the 1950s and 1960s, the Jewish mother, along with many, expected her daughters to be virgins on the marriage bed, and to feather it, as her natural role in life. Careers, particularly teaching, were pushed, as they offered time with "the children." This, while the Gloria Steinems, Betty Friedans, and Helen Gurley Browns were not only telling us to break glass ceilings (and hymens) but showing us how to do so in columns, magazines, and books.

It's been said one has daughters for the rest of your life. Yet, these daughters of the '60s were moving out of range. While the bond still fiercely held, the boomer daughter and her mother were often caught in a critical philosophical quagmire. With mom's voice echoing, we daughters found ourselves emotionally divided.

We could have made life easier by keeping our own council and telling mom what she wished to hear. But many of us, like our own mothers, shared the tradition of emotional honesty, debate, and argumentation. More, we were still seeking mama's approval.

For mama's part of it, a great ambivalence existed. Yes, she wanted the best for us. But in this changing new world, did that still mean . . . "be a teacher and marry a doctor"? Especially when we wanted to *be* the doctor or even fly the space shuttle—or dated, slept with, or lived with a non-Jewish partner? By accepting or not accepting these changes, what then, was the Jewish mother saying about her own life? Her own values? Was she bending over so far backward she was abandoning her beliefs?

"*A* young mother is only half a mother. When the children are small, there is absolute protection of them, but as time passes, they grow with their right to 'say.' This other half, becoming a total mother, we're not ready for. There is no school for this, no teachers. During the building years there is no time to develop a shield for the shocks to come. One day the rooms are empty, the refrigerator less full. My daughter's independence came quickly and we said, 'this is as it should be.' The child will always be there to love. Now we have to make friends with the woman.

"'I love you, my child. Do you love me?' It's disquieting to have to wonder."—1975

—Shirley Miriam Winston (my mother),
born October 14, 1925, died September 16, 1977

Today, almost two generations removed from the advent of feminism, mothers and daughters can reach an easier rapprochement. As mothers move closer to new, broader conceptions and their daughters become mothers, they often develop a mutual understanding. But the "negotiations" still continue.

"Susie and I have had our mother/daughter problems. We remember things completely differently," says Zora Essman. "For example, she has this new boyfriend with children, in junior high and high school. Susie's never been married or had kids. All of a sudden she's soccer mom. She called me and said, 'Ma, you had no idea what I had to do. I had to take one to ballet . . . to soccer,' and on and on. Like she invented this."

In *Every Mother Is a Daughter*, by Perri Klass and her mother Sheila Solomon Klass, they describe this generational difference. Although both mother and daughter married academic men and had three children while working full time, they're markedly different. Sheila grew up during the Depression, and had to fight to get an education. Today, she still lives frugally, always taking subways instead of taxis. Despite her work schedule, a hot meal on the table was de rigeur, a sign of good parenting.

Daughter Perri, a pediatrician, raised in the privileged suburbs, spends money comfortably, thinks ordering take-out is fine, as is sending her children off with a handful of nuts, instead of a full breakfast.

MY JEWISH MOTHER

The late playwright Wendy Wasserstein's mother was given an award by NOW—for being her mother. Yet Wasserstein saw far better reasons.

Wasserstein referred to her mother's . . . verve . . . as "Lola-isms," because Lola Wasserstein was never like other mothers. (Once she arrived at Wendy's apartment dressed as Patty Hearst . . . with beret and toy gun.) No Donna Reed, her mother was more Carmen Miranda—and wore fruited hats . . . because she was all "go-go."

Lola Wasserstein would take the family to the great Christmas show at Radio City Music Hall every year—and bypass the impossible lines around the block by walking up to the

*I*t was Ira's third birthday party. Soon it was time to open his presents. The biggest was from his *bubbe* (grandma) Dora. To his delight it was a huge drum set. He jumped up and down with joy and started banging with the sticks, making a racket. His mother turned to her own mama with disbelief.

"Mama," she said. "I'm shocked you bought that! Don't you remember how we used to drive you meshugge with the noise, when we were young?!"

Bubbe Dora smirked, then replied. "Oh yes, *Mamala* . . . I remember it well."

head usher and saying they were visitors from Kansas, in the city for one day only (she chose Kansas because the day before they watched *The Wizard of Oz*).

When they dined at Luchows, the famous New York German restaurant, Lola decided Wendy was shy. So, once a month Lola would tell the oompah band it was Wendy's birthday . . . and Wendy had to sit through an accordion rendition of 'Happy Birthday.'"

Wendy never doubted her generosity . . . her love—even though separating herself from her children was impossible.

She recalled one Passover when her father sat on her mother's lap and, as she kissed him, rejoiced in the fact that they had "done it": nine grandchildren. Wasserstein wondered if she would ever accomplish something that would make her feel as fulfilled or whether she would be able to love as totally and selflessly as her mother.

One of Bella Abzug's two daughters, Liz, now head of her own consultant firm, says: "My mother was a great politician, a great mother—and a great friend. She was a mother who enlightened us. . . . She did say to us, 'It's great to marry a good Jewish man at the end of the day.'"

Although Liz was once engaged to a Jewish man, both of her daughters found great Jewish partners in women. "My mother knew, and was fine with it," says Liz.

> "Mama's philosophy and approach
> to life were succinct: If it's good it's
> not forever, and if it's bad it's not forever."
> —Molly Picon

"My mother was way ahead of her time," says Jody Lopatin. "She went to university. We girls were always encouraged as there were no boys! . . . My mother, who's almost eighty recently said, 'when you're calling someone an SOB . . . always remember to do it with a smile on your face.'"

"My mother sat on a myriad of boards," says Rabbi Shira Stern of her mother Vera Stern. "She did more than twelve people could. Her interests were many: the arts, Israel, indigent musicians. My father [Isaac Stern] couldn't have been who he was without her. She helped direct him into creative areas. She was a Holocaust survivor. She was incredibly strong. [She taught me] to be fierce and protect my family; to speak up, protect, and defend others. I was given an award, and [I realized] it was for what I learned from her. I am what I am because of my mother: We are all six degrees of separation—and one should always be cognizant of the connection."

"My mother, Lily, is a phenomenal parent," says actress/singer Tovah Feldshuh. "She was the connoisseur of tough love. She would say:
- 'Selfish people are the loneliest people in the world.
- 'Never beg a man for a hat . . . you buy your own.
- 'When you walk into a room, see what's wanted and needed in that space.
- 'Be ruthlessly honest.'"

Tovah, herself the mother two, has her own philosophy. "To be a good mother, Jewish or otherwise, you need to do two things: love your children unconditionally—and show up."

"My mother was twenty when I was born on the Lower East Side," says Congresswoman Shelley Berkley (D-NV) about her late mother, Estelle Auslander. "Three things were her life: her family, Israel, and the Democratic Party," describes the bright, earthy, and hysterically funny congresswoman. "Though she wasn't an activist, she was a major big shot in our house—and very opinionated. She'd yell at the Republicans on TV and was beside herself during the Clinton impeachment hearings.

"Eight years ago, when I was first running for Congress and dating my husband Larry (I finally met a doctor, she was thrilled), after a few dates, he told me he had a confession to make. Oy, I thought . . . another one. Then Larry admitted: 'I'm a Republican.' I was so relieved. But I told him, 'Don't tell my mother. If she brings up politics, here's what you say, no matter what she says or screams: 'Your daughter is wonderful. Your grandchildren are great.' That's it.

"So every time she expressed an opinion he'd say 'Your daughter is wonderful. Your grandchildren are great.' Finally, my mother turned to me and said, 'I've never seen a man more in love.'

"Anyway, we're all at the jewelers choosing an engagement ring. My mother was sitting in a chair reading a paper . . . and we hear a shriek: There it was, in the paper, 'Democratic Congressional Candidate Engaged to a Republican.'

"She rose up, 'HOW COME I DIDN'T KNOW?!' Then . . . she looks at the diamond, looks at Larry, looks at the diamond, looks at Larry . . . 'It's OK.'

"I am a Jewish mother, absolutely. I have two children and two stepchildren. . . . I always carry my cell phone set at ON, and if it's one of the children . . . I'd make a president hold."

"My mother said I drove her crazy. I did not drive my mother crazy. I flew her there. It was faster," says Robin Tyler, comic, event organizer, and creator of the comedy album *Always a Bridesmaid, Never a Groom.*

"When I told my mother that I was a lesbian, in 1959, she took it very well. She did not say 'Here, take a knife, stab me! Pour salt in the wound.' She picked up the knife and tried to stab herself! I stopped her, because why should I take that privilege away from my father?

"My mother used to introduce my brothers and I in the following way:

'Here is my son, the doctor.

Here is my son, the accountant.

Here is my daughter, the lesbian.'"

"Mom served as one of three presidentially appointed public delegates to the United Nations in 1983," wrote Lee M. Hendler, author of *The Year Mom Got Religion,* about her mother, Lenore (Lyn) Pancoe Meyerhoff, politician, activist, and philanthropist who died of cancer in 1988.

"Mom claimed that she was born defiant. . . . Alternately reckless, mischievous or courageous, Mom's defiance had a triple edge. At ten, she secretly smoked a corncob pipe stuffed with stolen tobacco. She was arrested at age fourteen for driving her Aunt Minnie's car at ninety miles an hour without a license. [Her adored maternal aunt, a nonconformist herself, was in the car at the time.]

"[Mom] confronted a prominent trial lawyer who imported illegal domestic help and paid them slave wages. He stopped. She helped women survive grueling and degrading divorces.

"Socially, she preferred men over women because she was attracted to power, but she was vigilant over its abuse by others and considered herself the champion of the powerless.

"[She] believed that children learn and grow best by taking physical and emotional risks. Her teaching may seem hard-hearted now, but we experienced it as liberating because she gave us the gift of confidence. When we were very little, she would perch us in trees and then walk away. If we whined, she'd tell us to stop whining and figure out how to get out of the tree if we wanted to get down so badly. Soon, we were tree monkeys. . . . Mom insisted that we take on teachers who were petty or unfair. She handled medical emergencies with the aplomb of a trained medic, teaching us that keeping our heads in a crisis was not only admirable, but lifesaving."

MY DAUGHTER, THE STAR

In Fred A. Bernstein's *The Jewish Mothers' Hall of Fame*, Estelle Bauer, mother of Dr. Joyce Brothers, described her famous daughter with her own brand of common sense:

"Joyce was bright from the start. She has a retentive mind. At fifteen, she went away to Cornell. But the courses weren't enough for her. She wrote home asking for more money so she could take more classes."

Mrs. Bauer also had thoughts about parents who can't let go:

"Selfish, selfish, selfish. They kill the child. Nature provides that when a child is old enough, it feels its wings. If you don't let it, you're destroying the child's character."

"You have to understand our household—there was always music," said Ruth Manchester, mother of singer/songwriter Melissa Manchester, in *The Jewish Mothers' Hall of Fame*. Ruth knew right from the start that her daughter was unusual, even by the standards of a family that revered music. "David, my husband, is a bassoonist. You'd play 'Greensleeves' and she'd [Melissa] go twirling around. And you would always hear her singing." Yet despite fame and star pals such as Burt Bacharach, Carol Bayer Sager, and Barry Manilow, Ruth said her daughter is still the Melissa who calls and says, "Ma, what are you cooking tonight?"

JEWISH MOTHERS AND SONS

"*J*ewish men make the best husbands." We've all heard, read, or thought it. Behind the compliment, I believe, there's an implication of docility or pliance in the Jewish male, who's been "house-broken" by his mother, even as he's conquering new fields in medicine or science. And, in truth, I've seen it: The guilty, ambivalent Jewish son (or husband), who will appease at any price, through clenched teeth. Certainly, not all fit this model, but enough do to make the argument that "the Jewish son"—even today—often has a highly complicated relationship with his mother that includes anything from resentment, to confusion, to adulation, or a combination of all three.

I have long argued that for a mother who feels powerless in her female role as a woman and wife, her son, then, is not only her child, but may become her vehicle into the world. Prior to feminism, mothers of all persuasions, particularly those that came from a strongly religious or cultural patriarchy, sometimes saw their sons as their private "chosen" ones, who would deliver "Mama," vicariously, all the power she herself was denied.

A Classic:

After leaving Brooklyn and shlepping on planes and donkeys, Mrs. Bloom arrived in India at the ashram of the guru, Baba Ganish.

"I gotta see him," she told an assistant.

"Nobody sees the Great Guru."

"Mistah—I gotta see him!" she insisted, but he was adamant.

So she sat at the doorstep until he reluctantly agreed.

"OK. But you may say no more than three words."

"Three words it is."

Mrs. Bloom was led to a marble room, where a young man was on a mat chanting, "*Om chanti*."

Stepping in front of him, she yelled, "Come home, Morris!"

Such a mother might alternatively treat her sons as gods on earth, showering them with unswerving adoration, or more negatively, she might use her *own* maternal power to manipulate them, especially, if she also feels powerless with her mate. Her son, then, instead of being treated as a child whose needs are supported toward independence, becomes a surrogate power force, or may be assigned the "husband" role, providing attention, affection, and protection.

Mr. Sheinbaum shlepped the half mile to Milsky's kosher bakery in a blinding snowstorm. He entered, soaking wet.

"Milsky . . . I'll take one bagel and one bialy."

"That's it?" asked Milsky, shocked to see Sheinbaum's condition.

"One bagel, one bialy," replied Sheinbaum.

"Sheinbaum, your wife sent you out on a night like this for one bagel and one bialy?"

"Who then?" said Sheinbaum, sighing. "My mother?"

The son, then, is not only the promise, but a male that she, as mother, could control and live through vicariously. For the son, this powerful love was a double-edged sword and could also lead to a strongly bonded connection with mom, or resentment and the need to break away—or most often ambivalence. The Jewish mother, already "kidfirst," who fell into this category, would, then, have a Herculean effect on her sons. And letting go, for these mothers, is difficult, if not impossible, as it means truly letting go of a significant part of herself and her own identity.

A Classic:

Three Jewish mamas in Miami were bragging about their devoted sons.

Mrs. Cohen said, "Mine son is so devoted he bought me a cruise around the world. First class."

Mrs. Lapidus counters: "Mine is more devoted. On my birthday, three hundred people he flew in from Brooklyn—and catered!"

Mrs. Fine sniffed, "You want to hear devoted? Three times a week my son goes to a psychiatrist. A $120 an hour he pays him. And what does he talk about the whole time? Me!"

On the other hand, the Jewish mother who gives her son unconditional love, a strong sense of himself, and supports his need to fly free has given many a Jewish male uncommon confidence and courage.

What does a Jewish mama do when her son is running for vice president? What the late Marcia "Baba" Lieberman, Senator Joseph Lieberman's mother did: play matchmaker for *machers* (bigshots) and send food. Following her son's acceptance speech for his party's nomination in 2000, "Baba" invited Al Gore over for a little cheesecake and coffee. She also sent reporters care packages that included Manischewitz bagel chips, postcards (to write their mothers)—and the following handwritten note: "Please be kind to my son! Enjoy. Marcia Lieberman (Joe's mom!)" When reporter Charlie Gibson asked her how the press responded to this "bribery," she quipped, "They love it."

For the immigrant in 1900, the kitchen, presided over by the Yiddishe mama, was at the heart of family life. As mothers cooked, fathers read, children did schoolwork, and boarders ate on a large wooden table covered with oilcloth. Cramming everyone in the kitchen also saved on gas and electricity. The kitchen was intimate, noisy, close, and communal. In a 1973 interview, Zero Mostel called it, "My own private Coney Island." The only avenue to privacy could be found in the toilet or the streets. (Mostel, the brilliant actor, intellect, and art collector, used to tell the story about his worried mother's insistence that he start a savings account. "Show me a bankbook with $10,000 and I'll be satisfied," she would say. Well, the day finally came when he proudly displayed his bankbook—with $10,000. Her response? "You call that a lot of money?")

In 1888 Leah and Moses Baline had one son, Irving. In 1888, when the Cossacks burned Jewish homes in Siberia, they left for New York where Moses worked as a cantor, gave Hebrew lessons, and toiled in a slaughterhouse. After Moses died of overwork, Irving (Izzy) quit school at age eight to peddle newspapers, hoping to get mom a rocking chair. Izzy also sang in saloons, playing only the black keys to accompany himself. A printing error on sheet music he wrote anointed him, "I. Berlin (Irving Berlin)." He created ragtime and composed "White Christmas" and "Easter Parade"—two of the most popular Christian songs ever written, got mom a new rocker—and a mansion!

> "IF YOU DO NOT LET YOUR SON GROW UP AS A JEW, YOU DEPRIVE HIM OF THOSE SOURCES OF ENERGY WHICH CANNOT BE REPLACED BY ANYTHING ELSE. HE WILL HAVE TO STRUGGLE AS A JEW. . . . DO NOT DEPRIVE HIM OF THAT ADVANTAGE."
> —Sigmund Freud

Throughout his career, Irving Berlin composed on the piano in only one key: F sharp. Later, he had a special piano built with a lever to transpose into any key he wanted while he continued to play only on the black keys. In addition to "God Bless America" and other legendary songs, the master also wrote a number of songs for "mama," including: "Next to Your Mother, Who Do You Love?," "Run Home and Tell Your Mother," "You've Got Your Mother's Big Blue Eyes!," and "If the Managers Only Thought the Same As Mother." Not bad for a poor Jewish immigrant who never learned to read or write music!

The phrase "God Bless America" was taken from Berlin's mother. While he was growing up on the Lower East Side, she would say "God bless America" often to indicate that without America, her rather large family would have had no place to go.

When the talented comic, impressionist, and singer Marilyn Michaels had a boy, she and I, also the mother of a son, discussed this monumental event.

"Oy, is he a going to be a Jewish prince," she quipped. "Forget 'prince,' I quipped back. "He's going to be the last emperor!"

MY JEWISH MOTHER

"My mother's love for me was so great I have worked hard to justify it," said artist Marc Chagall about his mother, Feija-Ida Chagall. Chagall's parents, cousins, were natives of Liozno, a village not far from Vitebsk, Russia (now in Belarus). Mrs. Chagall ran a shop, took care of the house, supervised his father, started their grocery trade, and got a whole wagon of goods on credit. The shop was so profitable, the Chagalls were able to raise eight children and build four houses. "Her life was hard and her hairs got gray very early. Her eyes were often full of tears," wrote her son. "All my talent was hidden in my mother and everything from her . . . was transferred to me."

Three sons left their homeland for America and prospered. Each sent Mama a gift, hoping to top his brothers.

Avram bragged, "I built a mansion for Mama."

Moishe said, "I sent her a Mercedes with a driver!"

David boasted, "You know how Mama loves the Bible. Now that she can't see very well, I sent her a remarkable parrot who can recite it all, chapter and verse!"

Soon after, mama wrote back.

"Avram," she said, "about that house, I live in only one room, now I have to clean thirty."

"Moishe," she said, "I'm too old to travel in that car, plus the driver is a *gonif* (thief)."

"But Davidela—the chicken, it was delicious!"

Oscar Goodman (D-NV), the tell-it-like-it-is flamboyant mayor of Las Vegas, once known as the mob lawyer for defending crime figures such as Meyer Lansky and Anthony "Tony the Ant" Spilatro, has enjoyed immense notoriety nationwide. He appeared in the film *Casino*, was the subject of a book, *Of Rats and Men*, and, in 2005, was a guest photographer for *Playboy*. Yet when it comes to his mother, his eyes well as he remembers the woman who died in 2004, "She was perfect."

Laura Goodman, a talented artist who studied with some of the greats and was gifted with a Modigliani, raised her brood in Philly. Although she wasn't a milk and cookies mama, she was always there, encouraging, supporting. "You're the handsomest, smartest person in the world. You can do no wrong. If anything bad happens, make it good." These were all her mantras, but mama also had a few tricks up her artistic sleeve. "There were six of us, so she bought seven lamb chops," says the mayor, laughing, implying there were lessons of negotiation to be learned. Little Oscar staked his claim—by licking the extra. Though his mama wasn't the greatest cook, the mayor, who has dined with more celebs than Robin Leach, had his best flounder ever when his mother forgot to take the flounder out of the oven, burned it to bits—and created a gastronomic masterpiece.

Strong, liberated, and fiercely independent, she expected the same from her children. Despite her constant stream of positives, mama did take a hand to Oscar once. "I got an unsatisfactory grade in music . . . so I tried to commit suicide—by swallowing a mothball." The mayor-to-be was eight at the time.

While she used unconditional encouragement with the family, this was not always the case with others. "Oh, she was opinionated and critical! But never about her family," says the mayor. When she finally moved to Las Vegas at ninety-one, instead of moving in with Oscar and his fabulous wife, Carolyn, she insisted on her own apartment. "We got a call from the manager. They wanted her out." It seemed the elder Mrs. Goodman was a rabble-rouser. Her objection? "No live food!" It all came from cans and boxes. "I hate it!" So, she took action—and got real potatoes. Without question, Laura Goodman's son is a true chip.

Jason Alexander, of *Seinfeld* fame, dropped out of college in 1980 to become an actor.

He left his New Jersey home for a studio apartment in Manhattan, which broke his mother's heart.

"She wept," he said. "That's what Jewish mothers do. I was throwing my life away," reported Tim Boxer in his book *Jewish Celebrity Anecdotes.*

He told her, "Mom, in ten years I'll be doing Tevye on Broadway."

He beat his own prediction and did Tevye nine years later in Jerome Robbins's *Broadway.*

His parents, Alex and Ruth Greenspan, attended the opening—and his mom wept throughout the show, which of course, is what Jewish mothers do.

MY SON, THE STAR

"When he was growing up, I didn't know he was a genius. Frankly, I didn't know what the hell he was," Leah Adler, mother of famed director Steven Spielberg said in Fred A. Bernstein's *The Jewish Mother's Hall of Fame*. "For one thing—he'll probably take away my charge accounts for this—Steven was never a good student."

Mother Leah, a former concert pianist, had four children with Arnold Spielberg (Steven is the oldest). After their divorce, she married Bernie Adler. Leah is the proud owner of a kosher dairy restaurant, the Milky Way, in Los Angeles—and is hands-on—and there for her customers.

Despite his classic films (*Jaws, E.T., Close Encounters of the Third Kind*), Spielberg didn't win his first Oscar until *Schindler's List* (1993). Mama Leah later said: "I think if he hadn't gotten it, you would have seen one irate Jewish mother storming that stage!"

The controversial Abbie Hoffman still had a Jewish mother, Florence. In an interview with Fred A. Bernstein she reported that while he was a fugitive, she managed to send him dental floss and toothbrushes through underground connections, along with notes reminding him of the importance of dental hygiene. No matter where he was going, or what he was doing, Florence always had the same advice: "Dress warmly." Abbie once said: "When I think of her, I think of the Merle Haggard song. You know, 'Mama Tried.'"

"ONCE, I WENT TO THE DRESSMAKER AND I SAID, 'I'M ROBERT KLEIN'S MOTHER,' AND SHE SAID, 'THAT'S NICE. I LIKE BUDDY HACKETT.' I NEVER WENT BACK TO HER."
—from *The Jewish Mothers' Hall of Fame*

"My husband and I were musically inclined. We would rather miss a meal than miss a concert. We couldn't afford the lower seats, so we would climb all the way to the roof. People would look askance when they saw my little son on my shoulders," said Marutha Menuhin in a 1991 interview about her son, Sir Yehudi Menuhin, virtuoso violinist and conductor. "He never cried," she added. "I popped a warm bottle of milk into his mouth to comfort him, but he popped it out just as quickly, because he wanted to listen intently."

The youngster was never without two sticks in his hands to simulate the playing of a violin until age three, when he received a toy violin. At age four and a half, he insisted upon being tutored by a first-chair violinist. After scrimping, Marutha arranged for the boy's first lessons with the violinist.

Sir Yehudi Menuhin, also a renowned humanitarian, attributed his career and philanthropy to Jewish tradition and his family's activism.

In Fred A. Bernstein's *The Jewish Mothers' Hall of Fame*, Jackie Fierstein, mother of Tony Award–winning playwright and actor, Harvey Fierstein, recalled when her son was a starving playwright: " . . . and I mean starving," said Jackie, who brought Harvey food in his Brooklyn basement apartment. Recently widowed at the time, she would say, "Your mother still doesn't know how to shop for one; you'll have to take some." Then she'd return home—and worry. Even though those days were over, she said her son would still ask his lawyer if he could afford to buy something, and the lawyer would reply, "Harvey, the sky's the limit." Fortunately, Harvey's lawyer was her other son, Ronald.

To Melvin Kaminsky (Mel Brooks), born in Brooklyn in 1926, his mother was a heroine. Widowed when Mel was two, Kitty worked days in the garment district, and nights making bathing suit sashes. She adored him. "I was always in the air . . . kissed and thrown in the air again. Until I was six, my feet didn't touch the ground." Brooks took his stage name from her maiden name, Brookman.

> SCIENCE FICTION LEGEND ISAAC ASIMOV RELATED
> THIS STORY ABOUT HIS JEWISH MOTHER.
> "MY MOTHER DECIDED TO GO TO NIGHT SCHOOL
> AND LEARN HOW TO WRITE ENGLISH. ONE OF THE
> TEACHERS FINALLY ASKED HER, 'PARDON ME,
> MRS. ASIMOV, ARE YOU BY ANY CHANCE A
> RELATION OF ISAAC ASIMOV?'"
>
> "MY MOTHER, WHO WAS FOUR FEET, TEN INCHES
> TALL, DREW HERSELF UP TO HER FULL HEIGHT
> AND SAID, PROUDLY, 'YES. HE IS MY DEAR SON.'"
>
> "'AHA,' SAID THE TEACHER, 'NO WONDER
> YOU ARE SUCH A GOOD WRITER.'"
>
> "'I BEG YOUR PARDON,' SAID MY MOTHER,
> FREEZINGLY. 'NO WONDER *HE* IS SUCH
> A GOOD WRITER.'"

If Freud was the Father of Psychoanalysis, his Yiddishe mama, Amalie Nathansohn Freud, was definitely the "mother." Freud, the first of eight children, was born on May 6, 1856 in Moravia to Amalie and Jakob Freud, a wool merchant. He was indulged and overly attached to mama, especially after he was spurned by a girl at age sixteen and showed no interest in women until he was twenty-six. Mama Freud became peculiar with age. Notably, she was tight-fisted and narcissistic about her appearance. At ninety-five, she complained that a photo taken of her made her look one hundred!

In Fred A. Bernstein's *The Jewish Mothers' Hall of Fame*, Eleanor Sedaka, mother of singer/songwriter Neil Sedaka, offered some memorable "quotables" about her son:

- "When he's on TV, I have to watch him all alone, so I can scream and cry without anybody thinking I'm crazy."

- "He's such a marvelous person. . . . He's like a piece of fresh rye bread."
- "I'll hear Neil singing and it's like he's singing to me. And on the outside, I'll stay calm, but inside, everything is jumping."
- "Long after he's gone, my son will be remembered. How many mothers can say that?"

"I grew up in New England with a mother who was not your typical Yiddishe mama," says rabbi and comedian Bob Alper. "My becoming a rabbi was a dream come true for her, as her brother was a rabbi who died young. She was skeptical but supportive when I turned to comedy. In fact, after my career took off, when she was eighty-five, our phone conversations inevitably began with her question, 'Any new gigs?' Around that same time, she attended one of my shows and I left out a joke about her for fear of offending her. She loved being the center of attention, and therefore was insulted: 'Why didn't you use that bit about me?'"

His mom, however, didn't always get his wacky humor. "I put a message on my answering machine: 'You reached 291-3664. As of next month, our number will be re-hyphenated, becoming 2913-664.' The first call? 'Hellooo. It's your mother . . . I don't get it.'"

"And as for my father, the day before he suddenly died, I got an agent. He and mom celebrated that major early career step—which was nice. For the next sixteen years, Mom attended my performances whenever she could, and kept scrapbooks."

THE MIGHTIEST SHOWBIZ MOMS

Few were more intense than Minnie Marx, matriarch of the Marx Brothers, and Sadie Berle, Milton's mom.

Minnie Marx, sister to vaudevillian Al Shean, started Groucho as a boy soprano. By 1912, all her boys were into the musical act, which turned to comedy, and Minnie kicked off a dynasty. In the early twentieth century, after New York, Chicago was the major vaudeville center—so Minnie the manager, shlepped the family there in 1909. Shortly after they arrived, Minnie Marx "became" theatrical entrepreneur "Minnie Palmer." At the time, there *was* a famous singer by that name but Mama Marx didn't seem to mind the confusion. This new "Minnie Palmer" billed herself as "Chicago's only woman producer," and produced several acts apart from her sons.

Minnie Marx offered a young Jack Benny a job as music director, but his mother wouldn't let him tour!

Groucho, a brilliant comedian, especially with the ad-lib, was a difficult curmudgeon in his personal life. He had troubled relationships with women, no doubt, due in part to his own troubled relationship with the aggressive Minnie. Her pet was her eldest son, Chico. She thought of Groucho as unattractive—and let him know it.

Minnie's influence was so enormous that in 1970, the story was brought to Broadway in *Minnie's Boys*.

> "My mother loved children—she would have given anything if I had been one."
> —Groucho Marx

When it came to "advice" (OK, pushing), few Jewish mamas could compare to Milton Berle's mother Sarah. "She wanted to be [in show business], but her parents wouldn't allow her because they thought it was too racy," Berle once recalled. Under the watchful eye of his mom (a former department store detective), young Milton modeled, was dragged to New Jersey's Edison Movie Studios in 1914 to do extra work, and was then finessed by her into supporting roles—including the part of a newsboy in the first-ever feature-length comedy, *Tillie's Punctured Romance* (1914). Under Sarah's mighty management, Berle moved into vaudeville, making his debut at the prestigious Palace Theatre in 1921.

When he became the first TV superstar in the forties, Sarah was his one woman band—which included paying people to sit in the audience and laugh at her sonny's jokes. Aspiring comic Henny Youngman once made fifty cents chuckling at Milty. She also warmed up the audience by laughing and applauding wildly. She adored being mom to the star and would literally say in public, "This is my son the star, *Milton Berle!*"

---

*F*lorence and Shirley were talking about their sons' future careers over tea and a little cake.

"You know, Shirley," said Florence. "I don't think I'll send my Bernard to medical school. Being a doctor these days isn't what it used to be, believe me. There are now many kinds of scientists around with much more prestige than doctors. Maybe you, too, should reconsider."

"You're wrong. I can't agree," replied Shirley.

"And why not?" asked Florence.

"Because, my dear Florence, it's much more difficult to say, 'My son, the nuclear physicist.'"

Sarah's influence extended to Milton Berle's personal life as well. In 1941, when he married a chorus girl (Joyce Matthews)—Mama Berle played the back room—on their honeymoon! (The couple divorced twice after two unsuccessful tries. Are we surprised?)

THE PARADOXICAL WORLD OF WOODY

Woody Allen is terrified of losing his trademark glasses, he has said, because he'd look like a clone of his mother.

Love or loathe him, if there's one comic, writer, and producer who has imprinted the Jewish mother image to the world, it would have to be Woody Allen (Konigsberg).

When Allan Stewart Konigsberg was born on December 1, 1935, he looked just like his mother—replete with carrot-red hair, big ears, and milky skin.

Nettie Cherry, Allen's mother, the daughter of an immigrant Austrian Jew, was born and raised on the Lower East Side of Manhattan. Yet, she embraced shtetl thinking. Yiddish and German were her first languages.

When she married Marty Konigsberg in 1930, the couple had trouble putting food on the table. Marty was a dreamer and a drifter. He told everyone that he was a butter-and-egg salesman, but went from job to job, while planning get-rich-quick schemes— and spending his days at Ebbets Field, pool halls, or buying new suits he couldn't afford.

The elder Konigsbergs had a rocky marriage. Because of Nettie's constant belittling and Marty's itinerant habits the two became angry antagonists—at least as depicted in Woody's later work.

> "I'm annoyed by the idea that Woody Allen is quintessentially Jewish when he is profoundly un-Jewish. I don't have a lot of sympathy for what he did (re: his affair and subsequent marriage to Mia Farrow's adopted daughter). He said, you have to follow your heart. There are two conflicting messages in all cultures: Follow your heart and do your duty. Well, you do your duty. Taking Woody Allen ... as the voice of Jewish authenticity is a terrible shame."
>
> —Michael Medved

During his childhood, Woody would witness the rancor and warfare between his parents. He, too, was not immune to hostility. According to reports, his mother had a hot temper and was always taking a whack at him, yet, he never cried. He had an amazing ability to restrain his emotions, but the experience left him believing he was truly unwanted.

Shortly after his first birthday, Nettie found work as a bookkeeper for a florist, leaving her son with a succession of ignorant caretakers. Woody claimed to remember one horrifying incident when one of them shoved a blanket over his face and almost suffocated him.

Even when Nettie returned from work, she wasn't exactly a "cuddler."

During the 1960s Woody used these childhood recollections in his routines. He'd say, for example, his mother left a live teddy bear in his crib, or, if anybody with candy beckoned him into a car, he was "advised" to hop right in.

Allen's parents recalled that, at age six, their son became "sour and depressed," setting the scene for his later films.

In *Annie Hall* (1977), for example, the protagonist, Alvy Singer, flashes back to his childhood to seek cosmic answers. In one scene, his panicked Jewish mother has brought her precocious, but dour, bespectacled nine-year-old son to a doctor. She explains his obsession with death and the doom of humankind because of the impending expansion of the universe. Alvy's mother, completely out of tune with her sensitive, neurotic child, tries to explain, "Brooklyn is not expanding."

Later, as she peels carrots at the camera, Alvy's mother still "hocks" her adult son, telling him he always only saw the worst in people. He never could get along with anyone in school and was always out of step with the world. Even when he became famous, he still mistrusted the world.

Over time, Allen mellowed and presented Nettie and Marty almost nostalgically in *Radio Days*.

Dr. Bruno Halioua, author of *Mères Juives des Hommes Célèbres* (*Jewish Mothers of Famous Men*), has sympathy for Nettie, writing that she bore the brunt of family responsibilities, morally, and often financially, for decades.

MARRIAGE AND MOTHERS-IN-LAW

*Y*es, true. Certainly a generation ago, the Jewish child was expected to marry. And not just marry, but marry "in." As a teenager, for example, I wasn't allowed to date a non-Jew.

"When they come to get us, on which side will your husband stand?" was the admonition from many Jewish mothers. Now there are those who would consider those words paranoiac and insular. Yet in the context of recent history, for these parents, the Holocaust wasn't merely a horrific memory, but an experience they lived through—that could happen again.

And marriage to a Jewish mate has long been a religious duty, a way to preserve and protect our faith and our heritage.

As we've become more secular, there are those who consider intermarriage an acceptable view.

In looking at the last few generations within my own family, all of my father's siblings married Jewish mates. Any other choice simply wasn't on their radar.

Among their children, some married non-Jews who converted.

Today, some of the grandchildren are marrying non-Jews who haven't converted. The change is clear and reflective of many assimilated Jewish families.

"When my mother [Shari Lewis] met my future husband, she was horrified!" says Mallory Lewis. "A *sheygets* (non-Jewish male) skydiver? Not the Jewish doctor she envisioned.

"When I had a small skin cancer on my lip, my mother and my future husband sat for two hours together while plastic surgery was being performed. After the surgery, the first thing she said was, 'He's a wonderful man,' to which I replied, 'Give me a mirror.' I knew even if he was the prince of England, I would have to look pretty bad for my mother to be sanguine about a non-Jewish guy. I looked so bad after surgery, she figured this is it. Ultimately, she did see what a wonderful man my husband is.

"Our kids will be raised Jewish. My husband said whatever it takes (maybe to sleep with me). I believe it's more important that our son is raised Jewish because he's half not-Jewish."

"In the 1960s I met a Danish man, a non-Jew," says Jody Lopatin. "We moved to Israel, as he was a student. He converted before we were married. Nevertheless, my grandparents said 'We'll stick our heads in the oven.'"

DEBBY CALLED HER MAMA WITH FANTASTIC NEWS.

"MAMA, I GOT MARRIED!"

"MAZEL TOV!" SCREAMED MAMA.

"BUT . . . HE'S NOT JEWISH. ALSO, HE'S A SOLDIER
OF FORTUNE.
HE TRAVELS THE WORLD HUNTING PEOPLE."

"FROM THIS HE MAKES A LIVING?" ASKED MAMA.

"UH . . . NOT REALLY. WE HAVE NO PLACE TO LIVE."

"OK, SO YOU'LL COME LIVE WITH ME."

"BUT MAMA, YOU ONLY HAVE ONE BEDROOM.
WHERE WILL YOU SLEEP?"

"DARLING, ABOUT ME, DON'T WORRY.
THE MINUTE I HANG UP, I'M DROPPING DEAD."

MARRIAGE AND THE DAUGHTER

When I was in my early twenties, I was hospitalized for a blood clot. By this stage, my grandmother was sitting *shiva* (the mourning ritual) for me already. One day she called and said, "So *nu*, you're in a hospital, just lying there. Did you meet a doctor yet?" Actually, I had. An ophthalmologist. "Oy," she moaned. "From *eyes*? Vat kind doctor is that?! No. You want a doctor from brains and hearts! Now dat's a doctor!"

"Oy" is right.

In the hysterical book and CDs, *Amy's Answering Machine* (SendAmy.com), Amy Borkowsky presents this message from her mom:

BEEP
(Singing) "Happy birthday to you,
Happy birthday to you,
Happy birthday dear Amila,
Happy birthday to you.
How old are you now,
How old are you now,
Better hurry and find a husband,
Before your ovaries shut down."

Referring to her single status, the late Wendy Wasserstein told the *Los Angeles Jewish Journal*, "I am a walking *shanda*—a disgrace."

Singer Julie Budd told Tim Boxer that her mother, who lived in Brooklyn, objected to her show business career. She wanted her daughter to fix her nose and marry a doctor.

And some Jewish mothers will help the process along.

A Classic:

A Jewish mother is sunning herself. It's 110 degrees. A pale, middle-aged man is walking toward her, dressed in a tie, shirt, and jacket.

She says, "Mister, take off the jacket, mit the tie and shoit, and go for a swim!"

"I can't. I'm just out of prison."

"For what?!" she says.

"I killed my wife. I cut her up into little pieces and I stomped her into the ground."

(Pause) "So . . . you're single?"

> WHEN I DISCOVERED A ZIT ON MY FACE A
> DAY BEFORE MY HIGH SCHOOL PROM,
> MOM SAID, "*DEIGEH NISHT*!
> (DON'T WORRY!) IT WILL HEAL IN
> TIME FOR THE VEDDING." I MET MY
> "*BASHERT*" (MEANT TO BE/SOULMATE) IN
> 1957 AND SHE WAS RIGHT; MY COMPLEXION
> WAS CLEAR FOR THE VEDDING!
> SHE ALSO ADVISED ME—SHORTLY BEFORE
> MY MARRIAGE—TO ALWAYS HAVE A
> "*KNIPPEL*" (MONEY TIED IN THE CORNER OF
> A HANDKERCHIEF). A SECRET STASH.
> BY THE TIME MY GRANDDAUGHTER
> GETS MARRIED, HER KNIPPEL WILL
> CONTAIN A VISA CREDIT CARD!
> —Marjorie Gottlieb Wolfe

AND WHAT'S HER NAME?

Many Jewish mothers can't wait for the time their son chooses a bride (I'm one of them—send names and addresses, please—to me), as in Judaism, this *shiddach* (match) is considered crucial, and the *chasseneh* (wedding) is a blessing— with the promise of Jewish grandchildren. Yet other mothers are ambivalent or less enthusiastic—even some who had no clue they might feel a bit outsourced when faced with an actual prospect.

Those who do share their *mishegoss* with other (primarily) ethnic mothers. Marie Barone in *Everybody Loves Raymond* is one example of this "mother-wife" mama, who wants her sons married (God forbid they should be gay. But if so . . . they'll support), yet the poor daughter-in-law becomes the rival, whether it's about attention—or cooking. This stereotype is creeping into the WASP mom, as we saw in *Monsters-in-Law*.

Author Tim Boxer tells the story of Broadway producer Arthur Cantor (*On Golden Pond, Private Lives, Gideon, Vivat! Vivat Regina!*) whose mama constantly *nudzhed* (bugged) him about getting married. Finally, he brought home a prospective bride. Mama remained unmoved.

"What's the matter, Ma?" Arthur asked. "She's nice, she's Jewish, and she doesn't smoke. You always wanted me to get married. What's wrong?"

"What's the hurry?" was his mama's reply.

Sheldon excitedly told his mother he'd fallen in love and was getting married.

"Mama, just for fun, I'll bring over three women and you guess which one she is." Mama shrugged—and agreed.

The next day Sheldon brought over three beauties who sat on the sofa and chatted with "Ma" over a little cake.

After they left, he said, "OK, Mama. Guess which one I'm going to marry?"

Without flinching, she replied: "The one in the middle with the red hair."

"You're right. But Mama . . . how did you know?" asked Sheldon, amazed.

"Because *her*, I don't like."

THE JEWISH MOTHER-IN-LAW

Jew or non-Jew, there are fewer images that have been as disparaged as "the mother-in-law." Much as the stepmother endures a legacy of horrific fairy tales where visions of evil apples and she-witches dance around the poor step-child, the mother-in-law—of any ethnicity—is assumed to be intrusive and demanding—a sandbagger who simply can't cut loose from her progeny. And, in fact, there are a number of winding roads down the in-law journey: competition from two different families, along with "how *we* do things," plus the intense connection between parent and child.

Then, of course, as in-laws, we're automatically supposed to love the arbor from which our mate has grown. Our partner's beneficence is attributed to ourselves, while shortcomings come from "his (or her) side of the family."

Joe Lieberman remembered when he was sworn in as senator from Connecticut in 1989. After the ceremony, Senator Paul Simon of Illinois told him, "I just had a conversation with your mother-in-law. She reminds me of what Senator Hubert Humphrey once said: 'Behind every successful man there is a surprised mother-in-law.'"

On the other hand, in-laws can embrace each other with adoration, wisdom, dignity, respect for new roles, and the promise of a lifetime of "family." Much depends upon the personalities, fears, and needs of all parties—and requires exquisite patience and acceptance of difference.

Judaism, however, prepares for this. When the families of the future bride and groom meet, some sign a contract, the *tenaim*, which are the conditions that define the obligations of each side regarding the wedding. After the witnessed signing and reading of the *tenaim*, a plate is smashed, traditionally by the future mothers-in-law, symbolizing the impending "breaks" in their relationships with their children, who will soon take responsibility for caring for each other.

As the female is often "the emotional voice" of the family, if a problem arises, she's usually—through clenched jaw— assigned the task of "fixing" it either aggressively, or passive-aggressively.

Like the little girl with the curl, when things are good between in-laws, they can be very, very good. A loving relationship between in-laws may even surpass the ones we have with our own parents. In-laws can be fountains of support, wisdom, and that extra set of hands we can depend on. They can also be an inspiration. But when they're bad . . . well, you fill in the rest.

A Jewish town had a shortage of men so they had to import them. One day a groom-to-be arrived by train and two prospective mothers-in-law, Bella and Dora, were waiting, each claiming ownership of him. The rabbi was called to solve the problem.

"There is only one solution," said the rabbi, "We shall divide him in two and give each of you a piece."

At this, Bella threw up her hands, screaming, "No! Give him to Dora!"

"Ah ha!" said the rabbi. "Done! The one willing to cut him in half is the real mother-in-law!"

Gerald came home from work. As usual, he dropped his jacket on the chair in the living room. And, as usual, his wife Bessy picked it up. As she's about to hang it up in the closet, she noticed something on the jacket.

"Gerald!" she yelled. "There's a long gray hair on your jacket. You've been to your mother's to get sympathy again, haven't you?"

INSPIRATIONS!

"My mother-in-law, Ida Mintz, was the world's oldest female marathoner!" says Rabbi Yocheved Mintz. "She started running at age seventy. She exercised, literally, in the closet by doing her sit-ups. This habit no doubt started because as a child, hidden in the attic in Poland . . . she wasn't allowed to run. She ran her last race at age eighty-five in Chicago, and holds the record for the oldest female marathoner.

"But more, she was a nurturer, a kind soul, who took care of people. She would sacrifice her own ambitions for the sake of helping the family. She always looked fastidious. And, as her record proves, she was very bright and focused."

When you hear the name Woodie Guthrie most of us think of "This Land is Our Land" and the dustbowl. What you *don't* think of is klezmer (an Hasidic and Ashkenazic secular musical tradition, developed around the fifteenth century, that drew on devotional traditions extending back into Biblical times. Klezmer continues to evolve today).

How can this be? Woody Guthrie wasn't Jewish. Ah ha! But he had a Jewish mother-in-law, extraordinaire—Yiddish poet Aliza Greenblatt. When Guthrie married Greenblatt's daughter, Marjorie Mazia, a dancer, he became a *landsman* (a fellow countryman). In 1942, Woody and Marjorie lived in Brooklyn, and through his mother-in-law, Guthrie and the Coney Island Jews found each other. During this period he wrote "Jewish" songs, with themes ranging from history, to holidays, to the Holocaust.

After his death in 1967 from Huntington's chorea, Guthrie's Jewish lyrics were lost in archives for nearly thirty years. In 1998, his daughter, Nora, found them and asked the Klezmatics, a seven-member band, to write new music for the lyrics, so they could be heard for the first time.

Aliza Greenblatt was more than an inspiration to and collaborator with her son-in-law. She also had a kinship with her grandson, musician Arlo Guthrie.

Doris Ruben, a New Yorker, didn't quite fit in with her middle-class Jewish family. She wanted to see the world and be a journalist. To her family's shock, she went overseas in 1938 and became a correspondent for UPI, covering China and the Philippines. During World War II, she was, perhaps, the only Jewess captured and imprisoned by the Japanese (for two years). She was released when General MacArthur was about to move in. In 1947, she wrote of her daunting experience in *Bread and Rice*, and married the publisher, Thurston Macauley. The pair spent the next fifty years traveling and writing until Thurston's death in 1997 at age ninety-seven. No matter where they were, Iceland, Turkey, Spain, or Okinawa, Doris Macauley, along with her non-Jewish husband, always celebrated Yom Kipper. Doris is now ninety-three and is still writing—an inspiration to me, her daughter-in-law.

The greatest mother and daughter-in-law ever told is the story of Ruth and Naomi. In order to escape famine, Naomi and Elimelech of Bethlehem, along with their sons, Mahlon and Chilion, moved to Moab, where both sons married Moabite women, Orpah and Ruth. After the men died, Naomi, having no blood relations, wanted to return to Bethlehem. Her two daughters-in-law, Orpah and Ruth, offered to accompany her to Judah. Naomi tried to dissuade them since she knew how hard life was for the Jewish people.

While Orpah was convinced to stay in Moab and remarry, Ruth refused. She wished to remain with Naomi and become Jewish, saying the immortal words, "Wherever you go, I will go; wherever you lodge, I will lodge; your people shall be my people, your God shall be my God" (1:16). With this statement, Ruth converted to Judaism.

Naomi sent her daughter-in-law to her deceased husband's family for protection, where Ruth married Boaz. Their son, Obed, begat Jesse, the father of King David, proving that true "Jewishness" is judged not by ancestry, but by acceptance of God and the mitzvoth. Indeed, it was from this convert's line that the savior of the Jewish people was born. Ruth, for whom an entire book is devoted in the Jewish Bible, considered a righteous convert and flawless heroine, is one of the most respected women in Judaism.

BUBBES (GRANDMAS)

The smell of her kitchen, anecdotes, or stories about the old country, and most of all, her preference for you—over your parents—are the hallmarks of the *bubbe*. After all, the Jewish *bubbe* has now seen the fruits of her efforts. The line will continue and flourish—plus, she can go home when the *kinder* starts kvetching.

In her new role, she can relax a bit, loosen up, and spoil her grandchildren. One of the great sadnesses is that today, the extended family has been eroded with frequent moves, isolating the grandchild from his or her roots, and that critical emotional backup. I've always argued that the relationship between grandparents and grandchildren can be magical. To grandma, they can talk. From grandma, they can get comfort, time, history, and unwavering support. And from this, "*bubbe*" legends are made.

> $\mathcal{M}$y grandmother used to call me "a *shaineh maidel*," which is a "beautiful girl." When she died, I knew there would be nobody in the world who would ever again call me a *shaineh maidel*.

"Momma and Poppa . . . raised us to the point where we could produce grandchildren," wrote the gentle humorist, Sam Levinson. "We were dopes. *They* are smart. Smart? GENIUSES. If we went to the park they called us loafers. The baby is . . . dragged because . . . it's good for him . . . . [He] can't walk yet but there's a bicycle waiting for him. We missed the best things in life. We should have been grandchildren."

According to author Tim Boxer, when the late great actress Shelley Winters's daughter "the doctor" (Vittoria Gassman), gave birth to son Ari Joseph, the seventy-year-old new *bubbe* said, "I never had such *nakhes*, such joy. I looked in his face and I saw me, I saw my mother, I saw my father. You feel safer when you know your grandchildren will know what it means to be a Jew. There is a kind of safety when you understand your covenant with God. That is immortality."

Many of my generation had *bubbes* who came from "the old country." They spoke broken English, or Yinglish, and despite assimilation, had a shtetl logic that was a *shtikl* strange, often unshakeable—and hysterical.

Dora, an elderly Yiddishe mama, was sitting at home one day when her phone rang.

She picked it up and said, "Hello."

A breathy male voice replied. "I can tell from your voice you'd love me to come to your house, throw you onto your bed, and make mad passionate love to you."

"Excuse me, mistah . . . but all this you got from one 'hello?'"

Milton attended a seance at Madame Frieda's to talk to his dear departed *bubbe*—for fifty dollars. He held hands around a table, humming. Suddenly Madame Frieda's eyes bobbed open.

"Is that . . . Milton's *bubbe*, I hear . . . ?"

"Milteleh . . . " a voice quavered.

"Yes! This is your Milty! *Bubbe*, are you happy?"

"With your grandpa here . . . bliss!"

After more questions, Madame Frieda said, "The angels are calling her. Only one more question."

"*Bubbe*," asked Milty, "when did you learn to speak English?"

Esther, an elderly *bubbe*, was on her way to Bloomingdale's on a snowy winter day, when she heard music coming from close by. On the corner, she saw a busker playing a violin. So she joined the small crowd listening to the music. Suddenly, a flasher walked by, opened his coat, and bared all.

Esther turned to the busker and asked: "Listen, darling . . . how much do you want for playing, 'Button Up Your Overcoat'"?

My own grandmother, Bella, didn't learn to drive until she was seventy-five. (OK, she bribed the inspector.) My father tried to teach her, but gave up, when, during every lesson, she'd take her hands off the steering wheel to "wave" to all her friends. Fortunately, she confined her driving to after dark. At 3:00 a.m., she became Mario Andretti. Eventually, she learned to step on the gas—but parking? Forget it. Once when I was with her, she parked on a corner, over both curbs. Literally. When we returned, there was a cop scratching his head. "Lady," he said in amazement, "I've just been standing here watching your car!" Her response?

"Oy . . . denks very much! Such a good boy, vatching mine car!" Then she drove off.

On her first visit home from college, Lynda felt like a bigshot academic. Arguing with great intensity, she discussed Darwin and the influence of heredity and environment. Finally, *bubbe* spoke up.

"Heredity . . . environment. Young girls, thinking about such things? *Feh!*"

"It's a very complicated issue, *Bubbe*," said Lynda, somewhat condescendingly.

"Complicated-shmomplicated! Please. Even sixty years ago in Russia, we knew the answer, 1-2-3. If the baby looks like his father, that's heredity. If he looks like the milkman, *that's* environment!"

> *"When my second grandson was born,*
> *his parents named him Connor. Mom instructed me*
> *NEVER to tell him that in Yiddish, a 'kaneh' is an enema."*
> —Marjorie Gottlieb Wolfe

One day, while attending a mock trial at her East Coast university [Harvard], Natalie Portman, the young Israeli actress, was approached by someone *else*'s Jewish grandmother. "You're Natalie Portman?" the woman asked. Natalie admitted that she was. "I just wanted to thank you," the woman declared, "for being so short."

✡

"TWO *BUBBES* IN THE BRONX
WERE HANGING CLOTHES TO DRY.

ONE ASKS, 'HAVE YOU SEEN WHAT'S
GOING ON IN POLAND?'

THE OTHER REPLIES, 'I LIVE IN THE BACK
—I DON'T SEE ANYTHING.'"

—Myron Cohen

✡

In *Modern Maturity*, Billy Crystal related that Louis Armstrong came to a seder at Crystal's childhood home. He was a guest of Crystal's uncle, the famous music producer Milt Gabel. Armstrong, of course, was noted for his very raspy voice. Crystal's grandmother came up to Armstrong and said, "Louis, have you ever tried just clearing your throat, just coughing it up?"

*B*ubbe was directing her granddaughter who was visiting her for the first time how to find her apartment in her new Florida condo.

"Darling, come to the front of the complex. There's a panel by the door. With your elbow, push 14T. I'll buzz you in. The elevator is on the right. With your elbow, hit 14. When you get out I'm on the left. With your elbow, hit my doorbell."

"No problem, *Bubbe* ... but why am I hitting all these buttons with my elbow?"

"What ... ? You're coming empty-handed?!"

In 1896, Nathan Birnbaum (George Burns) was the ninth of twelve children born to Polish immigrants on New York's Lower East Side. Burns wrote of his grandmother, who struggled to provide food for the family after the death of his father:

"She used to go around to all the weddings in the neighborhood whether she was invited or not. She wore a petticoat under her skirt that had a big, deep pocket on the right side. . . . When we'd see her coming home, if she tilted to the right, we knew we had something to eat."

"*Bubbe*," said Herschel, "do you realize it cost the United States $10 billion to put a man on the Moon?"

"Tchk, tchk—including meals?"

Joan Nathan, in her marvelous *Jewish Cooking in America*, recounts a first-hand description of a late nineteenth century San Francisco boarding house. J. Lloyd Conrich of San Francisco describes his grandma's strictly Jewish boarding house. As such, no food was served on Yom Kippur. It was here that he first learned, as a boy, about the glories of imported cheese both with and without holes, bagel and lox, herring in sour cream, gefilte fish, cheese blintzes with jelly, anchovies, King Oscar sardines, olives soaked in olive oil and garlic . . . good coffee and homemade pastry . . . plus other goodies, intended to make life less painful.

Of course, today, the Jewish grandma is often young, active, and "modern," enjoying her new freedom, and starting new ventures and adventures.

"I'm a modern *bubbe*," says Jody Lopatin. "I have a life of my own, as do my children. I want my children to respect my growth and development. I want nurturing in return. I'm still involved and very much in touch, but I closed up the kitchen, traded in the pots and pans for the yoga mat—and moved to Vegas!"

BUBBES PORTRAYED

The year is 1942. The family matriarch, shaped by hardship and driven by survival is forced to examine what she sacrificed when she takes in her two grandsons—love. Neil Simon's *Lost in Yonkers* won four Tonys and the 1991 Pulitzer Prize. Toward the end of the play, as the boys are leaving and thanking her, they realize they learned a great deal from the experience—some good and some bad. Most of all, they learned to speak the truth that everything hurts—whatever good life offers, you also lose something. Her truth? Even if they hate her, it's only important that they live.

> *Sometimes when my eyes hurt so bad, I close*
> *them and watch the images on the back of my*
> *eyelids, just enough light comes through and I can*
> *see everything . . . it's not so much my imagination as*
> *my memory:*
> *like the little brook*

in the back of our house
in the old country.
     ... When you're as old as I am ... you have a lot
of memories.
     ... Here, eat some liver, some challah, baked
fresh yesterday. How many matzo balls do you
want ... ? I can never remember who likes what
combination. But when you were younger, you
always wanted no soup, just matzo balls."
     —Abbe Don, *Bubbe's Back Porch*, "No Soup, Just Matzo Balls"

NAKHES (PRIDE)

Since family—especially children—are the center of Jewish life, should it not also follow that all those years of devotion reap rewards? Right? Of course, right. Pronounced *nockiss* (a little throat clearing on the "ck"), the word means pleasurable pride. Not just because Junior learned to tie his shoe. Big pride. So now you can die a happy person.

According to author Tim Boxer, when the late Brooklyn judge, Louis Heller, was a young lawyer, he and his mother went into a store where *The Jewish Hour* radio program was being broadcast. During a break, Heller's mother was asked to sample gefilte fish, then express her opinion on air. She did—and more.

"My grandmother couldn't make fish as good as this and, by the way, if you need a good lawyer, my son Louie just graduated Brooklyn Law School!"

"But Ma, you can't say that!" Louis cried, as lawyers couldn't advertise.

After his father deserted them, the late great Walter Matthau was raised by his mother. Years later, when Matthau had risen to the height of his film career, hoping he gave his mother a little *nakhes*, he asked her how she felt about his triumph. Her answer? "If you had had a decent father, you could have been a doctor."

"Why not, Louie?" she said. "About the gefilte fish I was lying. About you I was telling the truth."

It used to be that in the case of sons, *nakhes* was attained from their religious, then professional status, while for daughters, the word connoted a good *shiddach* (match) and becoming a good Jewish *baleboste* (homemaker).

✡

MRS. GOLD AND MRS. BLOOM RAN INTO EACH OTHER IN THE STREET AFTER TWENTY YEARS.

"HOW'S YOUR DAUGHTER," INQUIRED MRS. GOLD, "THE ONE WHO MARRIED THE SURGEON?"

"DIVORCED," ANSWERED MRS. BLOOM.

"OY."

"AH, BUT THEN SHE MARRIED A BRILLIANT ATTORNEY."

"MAZEL TOV!"

"AH, THEY WERE ALSO DIVORCED. BUT . . . SHE'S NOW ENGAGED TO A MILLIONAIRE DEVELOPER."

MRS. GOLD SHOOK HER HEAD FROM SIDE TO SIDE: "AI AI AI! SO MUCH *NAKHES* FROM ONE DAUGHTER."

✡

Naturally today, pride in daughters has expanded to include their accomplishments outside the home—especially when mama feels part of it.

According to Zora Essman, her daughter Susie doesn't like her mother to see her shows, since she talks a lot about her, but

Mrs. Essman is still extremely proud of her daughter's success. "It feels good [to be the mother of a star]," says Mrs. Essman, who then quips. "Though I have to hold my tongue and not say she got it all from me."

"*Nakhes* is the goal, not *kvelling* [to brag or gush]," says businesswoman and Connecticut politico, Rona Ginott. "If you honor your child, with luck, you get the honor. The child should be happy is the underlining issue."

Melanie Strug's greatest *nakhes* comes from her daughter Kerri's grounding. "I went with her, traveling first class," she says. "People are very surprised at how humble and down-to-earth she is."

"I had a famous mother," says Mallory Lewis. "It was wonderful—the vacations, the VIP treatment. And [Shari Lewis] had a famous father, Abraham Hurwitz, who was the official magician for New York. Now, I'm thrilled to give my son the same pleasure."

Then, of course, there's reality.
One day, Miriam met her old friend Lilith in a dairy restaurant.
"So how's your son the lawyer?" asked Lilith.
"David's fine. Please God every lawyer should be as clever as he is. Soon his practice should take off."
"And your daughter Rebecca?"
"She's so talented, she could play piano in every major concert hall around the world."
"And what about your youngest son?"
"Oh, Mordecai? OK, I suppose. He's selling *shmattes* [cheap clothes] to all the street markets in the Lower East Side, denks God. If it wasn't for my Morty, we'd all be starving."

HOW ARE YOU? DON'T ASK—
CLEANLINESS AND HEALTH

$\mathcal{M}$y own late mother ran her home like an operating room. The Mayo Clinic had shoddier standards. She even sent bath towels to the Chinese laundry. They came back perfectly folded, with a width of one-half an inch. Her towel strategy developed so she could fit them into the closet neatly—even though it was like drying yourself with a loofa. My dear cousin, friend, and best-selling author, Stephanie Winston, the organizing guru, swears that those of us who live in a sty are rebelling against our surgical nurse mothers. (Which of course, wouldn't account for my son, but that's another story.)

It was not only *schmutz* (dirt) that offended, but clutter. A friend recently heard a Howard Stern show where he was complaining that once, when as a youngster, he returned home, he found all his comic books gone. Now, these were particularly valuable, having covers drawn by his cousin, Jack Adler. His mother's response (I'm paraphrasing) was, "I don't like clutter." His protests that he owned them didn't register. She thought he was "too old" for them, so she gave them to a neighbor.

Oy.

What I wouldn't give for my "clutter," which included the very first line of Barbie with that striped bathing suit and little see-through high heels. If my mother hadn't been so "tidy," I'd be writing this from a beach in Barbados, with two native lads cooling me with palm fronds.

But again, to the Jewish *baleboste* (homemaker), cleanliness and order was a duty. And a spotless home where anyone could drop in (for an operation, maybe) elevated the status of the Jewish mother. In fact, many a Jewish daughter, Sandra Bernhardt included, recalls her mother cleaning up for the maid.

The next time your Jewish mama tells you to wash your hands after leaving the washroom, it's more than just cleanliness (though not a bad reason). There's also a religious basis. After using the bathroom, Jewish law requires the washing of hands and reciting (excerpted/adapted): "Blessed are You, O Lord, who formed man in wisdom and created within him various openings and orifices. Should one that should be closed, open, or one open, close, one could not remain alive before You for an instant." This blessing not only thanks God for creating a well-functioning body—but made Jews less vulnerable to disease during the Middle Ages.

And cleanliness itself should lead to health. Right? Of course.

Health is not merely a Jewish obsession, it's a religious obligation. One verse in Deuteronomy begins, *v'nishmartem m'od l'nafshoteichem*, "carefully guard your lives."

Indeed, Judaism teaches that health care is the responsibility of our entire society. Maimonides listed medical care first on his list of the ten most important communal services that a city is required to provide to its residents. In the Mishnah Torah, Maimonides quotes the famous passage from Leviticus: "You shall not stand idly by while your neighbor bleeds."

Which no doubt explains the reverence many Jews feel toward the medical profession.

But there's more. In returning to the shtetl Jewish mother, where conditions were harsh, food was scarce, and worrying about the children (and no evil eye) paramount, health was of primary concern—and remains so today.

So, How are you? Don't ask . . .

Greeting: "How are you?"
Answer (non-Jewish): "Fine."
Answer (Jewish): "How should I be?"

For many Jews, including me, it's quite normal to assume that a splinter of the toe could be (*shhh*) an *early warning sign*. Whether this is because "Guess who died last night?" often follows "Hello," or we have a morbid fear of the evil eye smiting us, there are many who have some difficulty, especially over fifty, admitting they feel good. Optimists, we're not.

Rebecca, in Los Angeles, called her great aunt Rivka in the Bronx.

"So, *Tante* [aunt], how are you feeling?" she asked.

"Don't ask. Terrible!"

"Oy . . . and how long has this been going on?"

"In three weeks it'll be a month."

"Give him some chicken soup!" cried the *bubbe* when an actor died onstage. "It wouldn't hurt." So goes the Jewish joke. But Jewish mamas have "the gift" (however odd).

> "MY DOCTOR SAYS FEED HIM WHEN HE'S HUNGRY.
> HOW DO YOU KNOW? . . . JUST KEEP ON FEEDING."
>
> "I HAVE TWO THERMOMETERS, ONE ON THE
> WINDOW, AND ONE IN THE BABY."
>
> "MY BABY DOESN'T SIT UP. . . . HE'S ONLY THREE
> MONTHS OLD! MAYBE HE'S A CRIPPLE?"
> —Sam Levinson in *Meet the Folks*, who added . . .
> "By this time, it's the mother who is ready for the psychiatrist."

Seymour (Sy) Kleinman, lawyer and raconteur, recalls Mama Kleinman on illness. According to author Tim Boxer, when Sy was sick, she'd say, "Pull your eyelids three times and spit." No good? OK, they needed a consult—with Mrs. Moskowitz, whose credentials was a husband who washed windows at Mount Sinai Hospital. When Sy's brother Ira took a bunch of aspirin, the maven suggested, "Tell your mother to give Ira a headache."

> "Hi, Amila. It's me, honey. If you haven't already left to go to the motor vehicle bureau, keep in mind that the wait is very long. So before you get in line, you may want to empty your bladder. Alright, honey, that's all for now. Bye-bye."
> —Amy Borkowsky, *Amy's Answering Machine/*
> *Volume One: Messages from Mom* and *Volume Two:*
> *More Messages from Mom* (SendAmy.com)

But mama wasn't finished and had other important advisories.

"Hi, Amila. There was just one of those health watch stories, and they were saying how the bacteria that causes gum disease can be transmitted through saliva. So if you're gonna plan on kissing any new guys, you should just casually ask them if they have gingivitis. Ok, honey? Give me a call. Bye-bye."

But sometimes, mama is very right. "My appendix was rupturing," says Joanna Gleason. "It was my mother who came and got me to the hospital. She knew not to let it go."

Given our penchant for bucking authority, even doctors are not immune to our critical humor.

A Jewish *bubbe* called Mount Sinai and got the receptionist.

"I vant who gives the information about the patients, because I need the whole story, soup to nuts."

"Well, madam, that's an unusual request, but I'll see what I can do."

An authoritative voice came on. "Are you the woman who is calling about a patient?"

"Yes, darling! I'd like to know all the information about Sylvia Fleigel. Everything. A to Z. She's in room 408."

"Hmmm. Fein, Fingle, Fleigel—oh yes, Mrs. Fleigel. Here it is. She's doing very well. Her tests are normal, her blood pressure is down, and she'll be discharged Tuesday."

"Tuesday! Oy! Denks God! Such vonderful vonderful news!"

"From your enthusiasm I take it you're close to the patient," said the man.

"Close! Vat close? I *am* the patient! My doctor don't tell me nothing!"

> **"L**isten, sonny," said Mrs. Goldberg, who had an appointment with a gynecologist. "I can ask you a question?"
>
> "Certainly," the doctor replied.
>
> "Tell me," she said. "Your mother knows that from this you make a living?"

"Every Jewish mother knows the best doctor in her hometown, like my mother who lives in Winnipeg, yet," says Lorrie Cohen, editor with the *Tucson Citizen* and stand-up comic. "Her child could be seeing DeBakey, but the doctor has to be a Jew—and in Winnipeg—where she knows someone better.

"My brother in San Francisco had a minor heart problem. This is the conversation I had with my mother:

"'I feel so much better,' my mother said. 'I called Irving Kornmel here in Winnipeg . . . you know Kornmel . . . you may not know who he is but . . . you know *of* him. So I asked him, . . . who's the best cardiologist in San Francisco? Of course I didn't tell him why . . . but anyway, so Irving says he'll get me the name as soon as he gets back from his bridge game. I feel so much better now.'

"Meanwhile, my brother was already taken care of," says Lorrie.

Sheva was kvetching to her son, Myron, the doctor, about feeling out of shape.

> **S**eventy-year-old Devorah went to a psychiatrist.
>
> "When I get into bed, I'm afraid there's somebody under it. All night I spend looking. I'm going crazy!"
>
> "Come three times a week." said the shrink.
>
> "How much?"
>
> "A hundred dollars a session."
>
> "I'll think on it," said Devorah.
>
> Three weeks later, the doctor ran into Devorah and asked, "Why didn't you come back?"
>
> "My son cured me for free."
>
> "Really? How did he do that?"
>
> "He cut the legs off the bed!"

"Mama . . . go get some exercise at the health club." So, Sheva joined and went.

"So how was it?" asked Myron.

"Darling, for thirty minutes I sweated, I bent, I twisted, I pulled, and I pushed."

"Terrific, Mama!"

"Not so terrific. By the time I got my leotards on, the class was over."

But what of the "truly" unusual?

Mrs. Friedman, lying on Dr. Shlockman's couch, was sent for psychoanalysis.

"My husband insisted I come here. God only knows where he got such a meshugge idea! My only son is married. And his in-laws? The best. His wife? A doll. And . . . they've decided to move to Sweden with my darling grandchildren. I'm feeling A-1, tip top, in the pink . . . !"

"Stop!" said Dr. Shlockman, in horror. *"How long has this been going on?!"*

If all fails, there's always plans to be made—and hope.

Sophie: "Let's go to a movie Sunday—if, *halevai* (I wish, if only)—we're alive."

Doris: "OK. And if not? We'll go Wednesday."

ESSEN (**FOOD**)

Food! For the Jewish mother, could there be a sweeter-sounding word? One of the strongest (and strangest) memories I have of my grandmother, Bella, was her "*setchel*" (satchel). People thought the immense bag with the brass lock was just an old lady's purse, but we knew better. It was gram's magical microuniverse. All we had to do was conjure up a culinary thought and Poof! food jumped out from grandma's "satchel." It hung from her arm like a third appendage. No mere pocketbook, she shlepped a bag that would be considered "cargo" on the *QE2*. Like Felix's magic bag of tricks, it both delighted and frightened with its ability to refill itself with all sorts edible goodies: Cheesecake, chicken, Borscht, noodle pudding, kishke, oranges were all neatly wrapped in a hanky—dipped in My Sin perfume. To this day, I can't eat chocolate cream pie without a little cologne chaser.

Even then we knew that "setchel" was security. It held rations for a Jewish family on the run. The satchel, with its old, odd cache—was, and always would be . . . *safety*.

The importance of food to the Jewish mother has been honed by thousands of years, and for many reasons.

Who among us boomers didn't hear, "Eat! Finish your plate! Children are starving in Europe." For the shtetl mother who was starving in Europe, on the run, or . . . in the Camps, food came at a premium, and what little there was was often given to the *kinder* first.

I would argue that hunger, as a core need, is one of our strongest and longest-held memories—and deep, abiding hunger, the basis of some of our greatest fears. The desire to feed and keep feeding our children remains with ethno-typical Jewish mothers.

The taking of food, so connected with family and socializing, when put together with argumentation can make a Jewish meal with family and friends a noisy affair.

Food, then, was synonymous with love. The ethno-typical Jewish mother who feeds everyone—OK, overfeeds—is also offering up a huge side dish of love that fills mama with satisfaction. When not taken, it can upset, or even offend.

> "WHEN MY SON WAS FIVE AND DIDN'T WANT HIS VEGETABLES, MY WIFE PULLED OUT A TODDLER SWEATER AND SAID, 'YOU'RE GOING TO SHRINK BACK TO THIS SWEATER!'"
> —Rabbi Felipe Goodman

Five-year-old Sheldon gave his parents Leona and Morris much *nakhes*—except, he hadn't spoken a word since he was born, which worried them immensely. One day, at breakfast, Leona, who ran out of Frosted Flakes, gave Sheldon grapefruit segments. After the first spoonful he spit it out.

"Yuck!" he shouted. "It's terrible! Starting the day with such bitter fruit!"

"Sheldon, darling," cried Leona, "You just said your very first words."

Overjoyed, Morris asked: "Why so long to speak? You're already quite articulate."

"Because," answered Sheldon, "up until now the food has always been excellent."

Many a Jewish child, even at the youngest ages, has figured this out—and used it as a manipulative ploy. Acceptance of mama's food is love; rejection is, well, rejection of more than strained peas. But many a mother will also see this as a "health" issue.

"You're not sick," is many a Jewish mother's diagnosis. "You're hungry. Eat!"

"Tell me what you eat, and I shall tell you who you are."
—Jean Anthelme Brillat-Savarin's famous maxim

Our kosher commandments have been a critical element in separating Jews from the rest of the world and establishing a unique group identity. The primary responsibility for keeping a kosher home rests with the mama. Not only can Jewish mothers pass on their cultural and religious heritage, but also, while doing so, history, anecdotes, and other prized remembrances are shared, as mother bonds with daughter—over making chicken soup.

$\mathcal{M}$arcia watched her mother prepare corned beef by carefully slicing off both ends.

"Mama, why did you cut both ends?"

"Well . . . It's what my mother always did and I do the same. It must be a ritual. Let's ask *bubbe*."

They phoned *bubbe*. *Bubbe* replied, "Darlings, that's the way my mama made it. It must be a ritual."

Very curious, they visited greatgrandma, and in solemn voices, asked: "Why do we slice off the ends before cooking corned beef?"

To which the ancient *bubbe* shrugged: "In Russia, who had a pan big enough?"

ON KEEPING KOSHER

Kosher means "that which is fit." *Kashrut* is the method—the hows—to live fittingly and righteously. Simply, the foods affected are those derived from animals. Land animals must chew their cud and have cloven hooves. So, cows are kosher, while pigs are not. Birds can't be scavengers or birds of prey, making chickens OK, and vultures *treyf* (non-kosher). Sea animals must have scales and fins, ruling out all shellfish.

Eggs, milk, and vegetables are all kosher.

Kosher *preparation* of acceptable animals is crucial and strict. They must be killed with a stroke of a sharp, nickless knife across the throat, which is supposedly painless. This is performed by a Jewish butcher, or *shochet*, under the supervision and scrutiny of rabbis. The blood of the animal must be drained, and the carcass inspected for illness.

Another set of rules involve which foods may or may not be consumed together. There are three categories: milk, meat, and pareve. Pareve foods, which include vegetables, fruits, fish, and eggs, are neutral and may be eaten with anything. Meat and dairy must never be mixed. A truly kosher Jewish mother keeps separate dishes to ensure against any contamination by mixing them.

One of the most persistent myths pervading Jewish culture to this day is the notion that kosher dietary laws (Leviticus 11:44–45) were created for health reasons. Many of these laws did prevent disease, but they are observed because they are mandatory statutes (*chukkim*) for the purpose of purifying our instincts, leading to holiness and self-control, both of which lead to discipline, critical in character development. As it is said, "You should observe the words of this covenant, *Lema'an Taskil*" in order that you should act intelligently in all that you do.

Yet there was true merit in the healthful aspects of keeping kosher for the Israelites.

Removing the blood from animals, for example, kept disease within the Jewish community lower than their non-Jewish counterparts. In 1348, the Jews were less affected by the Black Death because of superior hygienic standards—this was another condition of *kashrut.*

UNUSUAL FACTS FOR THE KOSHER JEWISH MOTHER

You may be surprised to learn that giraffes, gazelles, and certain species of grasshoppers and yes . . . locusts all pass kosher muster. However, better to leave the locusts off the bar mitzvah buffet—unless they're covered in bittersweet chocolate.

The Talmud makes reference to foods that excite and delight—and those that dampen and "limpen." Yes, we're talking aphrodisiacs, the edible kind. According to the great scholars . . . well, grab a pencil.

Uplifting: Eggs, fish, garlic, wine, milk, cheese, and fatty meat were judged to increase sexual potency.

Feh!: Salt and egg barley *only* to be consumed in great quantities during SATs.

ℋosher Steam?

THE ISSUE: You're at a Jewish resort lining up for the "so goood" brisket—and creamed potato soup—on the steam tables, when oy-oy-oy! The Orthodox rabbi next to you screams: "The steam passing from meat to dairy has compromised the food! It's no longer kosher."

MORE COMPLICATION: Since only food can taint food, is steam a food? The test? It is not "food" if a dog won't eat it. Hmmmm. Dogs drink water.

SOLUTION: Israeli engineer Dov Zioni. Zioni determined that pine oil added to water to make steam is spurned by dogs! Such steam, then, is not food and hence, we have kosher steam!

The Talmud studiously recommends some veggies over others, detailing the rewards—and punishments. Cabbages and beets made the preferred list. Here are others:

Lentils: If eaten once in thirty days, protect from respiratory problems.

White olives: Cause forgetfulness, but olive oil is prescribed for old men.

Garlic: The chicken soup of herbs, it does everything from increase seminal fluid to curing tapeworm.

Speaking of garlic, Eliezar Segal, professor of religious studies at the University of Calgary, and author of *Why Didn't I Learn This in Hebrew School*, discusses this mighty herb.

"Rabbinic literature is full of praises for this common herb. It satisfies hunger, it warms the body, it illuminates one's face, it increases seed, and it destroys intestinal parasites," writes Professor Segal.

While modern-day herbalists agree, and make even more claims for garlic, from curing skin diseases to cancer, Segal refers back to an ordinance ascribed to Ezra during the Second Commonwealth that required "Jews to eat garlic on Friday nights. The reason for this, as understood by the Talmud, is because garlic serves as an effective aid to ardor and fertility, and enhances the marital lovemaking that is an essential component of Jewish Sabbath observance." (Of course, getting near your loved one might have posed a few problems!)

> Vaudeville and Clifford Odets' plays portrayed the Jewish woman as fruit-giver.

How do we know Eve was Jewish? Who else would say, "Here, have a piece fruit" goes the old joke. In Eastern Europe, fruit was a luxury. When Jewish women saw the availability of this precious commodity in America—given her duty to provide hospitality—she reveled in her ability to say, "Have a piece fruit." I heard my own grandmother say it often when I was a child.

> **S**halom Airlines hired a wonderful Yiddishe mama to handle their public relations. Her first assignment was to write the cabin notices, which she did:
> FASTEN YOUR SEAT BELTS
> NO SMOKING
> EAT A PIECE FRUIT

"[On the boat to America a lady] offered me an orange," wrote Yuri Suhl, in *One Foot in America.*

"I refused . . . saying that I was not ill. 'But you don't have to be ill to eat an orange,' she said, as she pushed the fruit into my hand. I was puzzled. The painful memory of my mother's dying came back to my mind.

"The barber of my Polish hometown was also the town's 'doctor.' When he had prescribed an orange for my mother, everyone knew she was gravely ill. Oranges were not available in our small town, so that day my father hired a carriage and set out for the neighboring town, which was much bigger. He returned late that night and the whole family crowded around him to see the fruit with their own eyes. We watched him lift the orange carefully out of a straw basket of the kind which peasants used for carrying eggs in. I had seen an orange for the first time."

AMERICA GOES "KOSHER"

In response to the burgeoning Jewish community in the early 1900s, a number of manufacturers, Jewish and non-Jewish, realized there was an untapped market and began providing for the Jewish mother *balebostes* (housewives).

Take ketchup, for example. This ubiquitous food was served by immigrants and first generation Jewish Americans with *everything* as a replacement for tomato sauce—which might be contaminated by cheese or meat. It "saved" all manner of food for the mother who wasn't such a terrific cook.

"Without ketchup Jews would starve to death. You needed ketchup not just for the taste but for the lubrication. . . . If Vaseline tasted, you'd have that on your steak," comedian Shelley Berman told author Tim Boxer.

And this obsession with ketchup continued. In my home, ketchup was a "gravy" served with fish—and naturally, spaghetti.

In 1923, the Heinz Company, with the Orthodox Union, developed the use of the "Circle U" symbol, making Heinz the first brand of processed foods to carry the "kosher" symbol.

One of the most important prepared products for the Jewish housewife was the invention of Crisco in 1910. Three years after the product was on the market, Procter and Gamble advertised this new totally vegetable shortening as a product for which the "Hebrew Race had been waiting 4,000 years."

They advertised in the Jewish press claiming how inexpensive and kosher Crisco was.

The company's ads in the Yiddish press showed Brooklyn and Bronx housewives making potato pancakes and strudel with Crisco. In 1933, the company published a bilingual booklet, *Crisco Recipes for the Jewish Housewife*, in Yiddish and English, which included about sixty dishes such as baked gefilte fish, brown potato soup, kipfel, and mandlach.

And many a greenhorn Jewish mothers were and had to be thrifty.

Mrs. Steinberg made a trip to the bakery for her son.

"So, how much are the bagels?" she asked.

"One dollar for two," said the baker.

"How much for one?"

"Seventy-five cents."

"Vonderful!" she replied. "Then I'll take the other one."

Mrs. Goldfarb asked the deli man for corned beef for her family's dinner.

"How much?" he asked.

She pointed to a huge slab. "Cut. I'll tell when to stop."

When the pile was high, he asked, "Enough, lady?"

"Cut. I'll tell you when."

Twice more he asked if she had enough. Twice more she said, "Cut!" Finally over a mountain of slices, she asked, "Have you reached the middle yet?"

"Just about."

"Good! Now, from the middle cut me a quarter pound."

KOSHER "LITE" AND KOSHER ADAPTED: ASSIMILATION

Keeping kosher in this multicultural land was difficult and tested. And many a Jewish mother, over time, moved toward assimilating new foods, adapting them, or abandoning *kashrut* altogether.

We all know Jewish mothers who will keep kosher at home, then pig out on—well, pig—with rationalizations that would stun even the greatest Talmudic scholars. I know one woman, for example, who won't touch pork—unless it's called a "sparerib."

By following *kashrut*, a solid wall is established against assimilation, and mixed marriage, as well. Yet, social contact with Gentiles is often through dining. Breaking with this law, many feel, has been a critical factor in Jewish "disaffiliation."

> "*I* hereby affirm my own right as a Jewish American feminist to make chicken soup, even though I sometimes take it out of a can."
>
> —Betty Friedan

In fairness, not all Jewish mothers are terrific cooks. "My mother doesn't really cook. One night she was having people over for dinner and needed to poach a salmon," says Joanna Gleason. "She called me for the recipe, which she was writing down. I got a call from her later, and everyone around me heard me say, 'Mom, the water *covers* the fish!'"

Even among some of those who could cook well, the fare didn't necessarily include "Gentile-style" food.

My own mother always made brisket. I never tasted English-style roast beef till I was a young adult. It was a proud moment when she called me for the recipe.

Little Hymie and his family were having dinner at his *bubbe*'s house. When everyone was seated, the food was served. As soon as little Hymie got his plate, he dug in right away.

"Hymie, please wait until we say our prayer," said his mother.

"I don't have to," Hymie replied.

"Darling, of course you have to. Don't we always say a prayer before eating at our house?"

"Yeah," Hymie explained, "but this is *Bubbe*'s house and she knows how to cook."

Donald Siegel, author of *From Lokshen to Lo Mein: The Jewish Love Affair with Chinese Food*, cites sociologists who claim the connection began in New York City during the early 1900s. Proximity was one reason, as Jewish immigrants in the Lower East Side of Manhattan were next to Chinatown. Also, Chinese and Eastern European Jewish foods have some common ingredients, such as chicken, fish, cabbage, celery, garlic, and onions.

As Chinese chefs rarely use milk products, the likelihood of mixing kosher and non-kosher foods was diminished, so Jews often felt that Chinese food was "safe *treyf*."

ASHKENAZI (EASTERN EUROPEAN) COOKING

Chopped liver, gefilte fish, chopped herring, potato latkes, and pickled cucumber are the dishes of Russian, Polish, and Eastern European shtetl Jews. Whether kosher or non-kosher, these Jewish mothers took their style of cooking with them to their new lands. As Jewish mothers came to America from all over the world, we brought our recipes, as well as our dreams.

"Chicken any which way, gefilte fish, chopped liver—we created all that," said actor Fyvush Finkel. "Don't let the French tell you about pâté! They got the pâté from us! We made the pâté. They got their pâté but we had our pâté. And our pâté was even better than their pâté! . . . My grandmother—she rest in peace—never knew . . . about recipes. They did it all by heart, they never measured. They did it all with their fingertips and it was delicious—delicious! I still can't get the boiled beef like she used to make. There's an art to that. We created boiled beef. . . . There was a lot of fat involved. So from that we used to get the gout. We created the gout. That's our disease."

Recipes! While many have been handed down from generation to generation, and can be found in the marvelous books by Joan Nathan, among others, some just "felt" their way to the promised food.

My grandmother was one of them. To this day, I've never tasted either chicken soup or gefilte fish the way she made it. But if my late mother or I asked for a recipe? Forget it. "A little this, a little that" (I'm cleaning it up). And, to be honest, while her food was always outstanding, each time she made a dish, it was a little different if "the this and that" changed.

And we're solid in our adoration for these delicacies—even if it causes heartburn like you wouldn't believe.

Neil Simon's *Brighton Beach Memoirs* (1986), set in 1937, is a memoir of Eugene, a Jewish teenager, going through puberty, while living with his overburdened, overcrowded, and underfinanced family in Brooklyn. In one scene much is made of . . . liver. Yes, liver was often served in Jewish households. But according to Eugene, it was a Jewish medieval torture. And cooked cabbage, another "favorite," could be smelled "farther than sound traveling for seven minutes."

The place? The MGM private dining room. The food? Chicken soup. Not just any chicken soup. Mayer's Mama's! Louis B. Mayer insisted chicken-matzo ball soup—supposedly a duplication of his mom's—was served daily. In Joan Nathan's *Jewish Cooking in America*, Daniel Selznick, Mayer's grandson, explains his grandfather would send back the soup if it didn't include fresh-killed chicken. He had a very developed palate because his father-in-law was a kosher butcher.

BAGELMANIA

Many Jewish mamas remain serious about our bagels. I'm one of them. Not too long ago, I had (non-Jewish) guests over for brunch. I served a variety of bagels, cream cheese, and lox. Much to my horror, one of them grabbed a cherry bagel, upon which he shmeared blueberry cream cheese. Yecch!

As our foods have become Americanized for all palates, we've seen a metamorphosis that would make a purist gag. A jalapeño bagel, for example. Oy! Then there's a certain deli chain that serves kosher-style corned beef and pastrami. Double oy! Those Jewish moms who have moved away from large Jewish population centers would give an eyetooth for "the real thing." Oh, and good Chinese food.

KVETCHING

OK, true, the Jewish mother "food-kvetcher" is not what I would consider part of the ethno-type, and certainly other ethnic groups, particularly Italians, share this peculiarity, but so many adult Jewish sons and daughters have mentioned it that I'll give it a little shrift.

Some Jewish mothers have been known to be—a little picky.

My brother, Joshua, a veterinarian and stand-up comic, tells the story of one Jewish mother he knew who was never satisfied.

"She'd order a chef's salad and here's what she'd say: 'Listen . . . I want a chef's salad. BUT . . . leave out the tomatoes, I hate chicken, no cheese. I'm allergic. Also forget the ham. And also, include croutons and Caesar salad dressing.' I'd say to her, 'Why don't you just order a Caesar salad? Her answer? 'Because I want a chef's salad!'"

As the old joke goes:

Q: What did the waiter ask the group of dining Jewish mothers?

A: *Is ANYTHING all right?*

I, too, have seen my share of Jewish mothers who spend a meal kvetching, "It's too cold (about iced tea), it's too hot, *I'm* too hot, it's too rare, it's too well-done, it's stringy, it's lunghy. Why did we come here? Let's move to another table," and on and on. One mother in particular could drive more waiters into rest homes than (God forbid) TB.

THE MODERN FOOD PARADOX

On coming to America, many a shtetl mom took on American values that simply couldn't work with shtetl food values. In a word: "weight."

Once a zaftig (plump) child meant health and prosperity. But then she grows up. And in America, never more than today, should a female fail to resemble a Q-Tip, she's "fat." And "fat" doesn't make for a good image, or marriage prospect.

Oy, what to do . . . what to do?

In 1972, Gail Parent wrote the funny, poignant classic humor novel, *Sheila Levine Is Dead and Living in New York*, of an overweight Jewish girl in New York who can't find a husband. When her mother questions whether she'll get enough to eat after Sheila announces she's going on a diet, Sheila reassures her that in her life, she's eaten enough for the whole city of Trenton. In fact, if she stopped eating for one day, one could feed all the starving people in India.

Social worker Karen L. Smith in her article, "Jewish Women and Eating Disorders," believes that the Jewish female body is rarely genetically predisposed to fit the current beauty ideal. The Yiddish word "*zaftig*," once a complimentary reference, is now associated with the overbearing Jewish mother forcing unwanted nourishment/advice/love into her children. She goes on to describe the dilemma of Jewish mothers wanting to "feed" their children the richness of their heritage, yet also wanting to help them fit into the mainstream culture. So, many straightened their daughter's "kinky" hair, or allowed their sixteen-year-old daughter to get a nose job, or even encouraged endless dieting.

"My mother's tall and skinny—an ex-runway model—size two. The only thing on me that's size two is my navel," quips editor and comic Lorrie Cohen. "Obviously, my mother had a one-nighter with Danny Devito. She expected a daughter who looked like Uma Thurman, and I expected a mother who looked like Estelle Constanza.

"On the *phone* she'll say, Lorrie, you *sound* like you've gained a few pounds. She visited Australia for awhile. All I know is, 'the women are so thin there, you can't find a Sweet 'N Low anywhere.' I have no idea about Australia—except for their calorie intake. That was my mother's *cultural* intake.

"Then there's the birthday countdown: 'Only sixty-seven days to lose weight!' And the promises. Like an anorexic Bob Barker, Mom promised, if I lose, I can 'come on down' and get a whole new wardrobe and a trip!' I shoved a cheesecake down my throat.

"Should I ever get down to a pencil—and die—she'll put on my tombstone: 'OK LORRIE'S DEAD, BUT WAS SHE *THIN*.'"

Feeding vs. fat was a lifelong issue in my house. I've now defined this food *mishegoss* as a two-stage process. I was born a mere five pounds and lost weight at home. Oh, the hysteria. From that point on, my childhood was one of stuffing myself. Clap clap, hears the child. "Look, her cheeks are so chubby!" Chubby cheeks are cute—under age twelve. Then stage two kicked in. No longer "adorable" at 175 pounds, the next goal was to make me marriageable. My late mother was always overweight—and worried that I should face the same fate. After all, how long could she get away with calling it "baby fat"? (I was fourteen.) One summer at camp (which I detested) took care of that. I'd gone, without knowing, from "Chubbist" (my nickname) to Marna-bones. Of course, I also developed athlete's foot. Today, I call those extra pounds "bloat."

THE HOLIDAYS

Cooking kosher, or at least obeying some laws and traditions pertaining to food, are still practiced by many Jewish mothers, even those who are "lite-Jews," and reserve custom primarily for holidays.

"I suppose it would be nearly impossible to go through an entire week of Passover for Reconstructionist and Reform Jews, not to mention eight days for the rest of you, without the profound experience in practically every pore of your body that Jewish identity is inextricably bound up with food," said Dr. Steven Carr Reuben, Senior Rabbi of Kehillat Israel, the Reconstructionist Congregation of Pacific Palisades, California, in a sermon entitled "Jews, Food, and Holiness."

"This past week of Passover . . . has reminded me that when it comes to Jews and food, it's really no laughing matter. Judaism and food—a contemporary reinvention of food as a vehicle for holiness in everyday life. What is now called 'eco-kosher' represents what Rabbi Mordecai Kaplan would have called 'transvaluing,' the powerful notion . . . that the food we eat provides a daily opportunity to experience the holiness inherent in our relationship with sustenance. . . .

"Each time we make conscious choices of what we eat based on Jewish values, we elevate food and the act of eating to the level of holiness.

"Some of us will choose to follow the laws of *kashrut* as they are written in the Torah. Others follow the later rabbinic interpretations of the biblical laws. Still others see ourselves as partners in the evolution of Jewish civilization and make dietary choices designed to sanctify our lives and the spiritual consciousness with which we eat every day."

The Sabbath prohibits lighting a fire. So how do you prepare hot food? The solution? In advance. And so *cholent*— a slow-cooked stew of beef, vegetables, beans and barley—became a Sabbath specialty!

"Ma would peel six pounds of potatoes, then leave them in cold water overnight to prepare for the cholent . . . *served to the menfolk when they come home from synagogue. . . . Ma and the other women on our block would blend and season their* cholent . . . *and let it cook all night on a low fire. . . ."*
—Barney Ross, U.S. boxing champ (1909–1967)

In Fred A. Bernstein's *The Jewish Mothers' Hall of Fame*, Florence, a Holocaust survivor and mother of rock star Gene Simmons, shared her Yiddishkeit with Gene's pop-star pals:

One year Gene brought Cher and her family to his mom's home for a Passover Seder. Mom was thrilled. "I said, 'Gene, you're bringing Cher? She's such a fancy, schmancy lady.' And Gene said, 'No, she's just an ordinary, nice person.' And Gene was right." All wore yarmulkes for the services, led by Gene. Gene's chauffeur also attended. "I always invite him in," said Florence. "What's another plate?"

Joan Nathan, the preeminent expert on Jewish cookery and its historic roots in an article entitled, "Family Treasures Hold Kosher America's Roots," describes a wooden bookcase in a West Side apartment where a box is filled with recipes and handwritten cookbooks. The oldest, covered in fabric and handwritten in ornate script, dates from 1879, just eight years after the first kosher cookbook was published in America. Its author, whose initials appear on the title page, was Justina Hendricks Henry, a New York homemaker and the daughter of one of the founders of Jews' Hospital, now Mount Sinai. Mrs. Henry's great-granddaughter, Ruth Hendricks Schulson, is legally blind, but she has memorized the recipes. Stuck in one of the cookbooks [is] a list for Passover, written in 1963 by Rosalie Nathan Hendricks, Mrs. Schulson's mother. Like Sephardic Jews throughout history, Mrs. Hendricks made her Passover and Sabbath wine from raisins. She also jotted down five boxes of raisins for charoset. Mrs. Schulson still makes the charoset balls with her daughter and grandchildren.

Ms. Nathan also describes a suitcase in a closet in Marion Mendel's house in Savannah, Georgia, equipped with a fork and knife belonging to her eighteenth-century ancestor, the famous Mordechai Sheftall.

HOLIDAY FAMILY WARMTH

While Christian families, for example, may often serve turkey or ham for Christmas and Easter, our choices, in the blending of religious readings and their relationship to specific foods (the seder plate, for example), tend to follow tradition, even in assimilated homes.

Warmth, togetherness, and the knowledge that Jews around the world, and over thousands of years, have said the same or similar words over similar symbolic dishes, is a continuing source of pride, strength, and continuity for Jewish families. The Jewish mother was, and remains, in the center of it, as matriarch, fulfilling her duty to light up the house with joy—and legacy.

"We do the holidays together," says Melanie Strug. And she adds her "children are passing these holiday traditions onto their own children."

The recollection of a young pioneering Jewish boy in Arizona reveals the earnestness with which Jewish pioneers observed Passover.

Linda Mack Seldoff, author of *Prairie Dogs Weren't Kosher* (1977), describes a scene in preparation of Passover. "Before the holiday, his mother, my sister, and he would get the house ready, which included whitewashing the walls and scouring the floors. His mother made the utensils kosher for Passover with scalding hot water. The furniture was carried down to the [slough] and scrubbed and allowed to dry."

The holidays made remaining a practicing Jew in the old Southwest difficult. The lack of Jewish synagogues in the region forced families to depend on each other to maintain tradition and share observances.

In *Keeping Passover* (1995), Ira Steingroot describes how Jewish families would come together and celebrate the sacred observance in one house in Nogales, Arizona. All holidays were celebrated at home, where the baked goods were made. Families went to Sonora, Mexico, to buy the fish for the gefilte fish for Passover. The matzo were bought in Tucson.

Faye Moskowitz, author of the *And the Bridge Is Love* and *Her Face in the Mirror: Jewish Women on Mothers and Daughters* described closing her eyes and thinking of her grandmother tasting a bit of her childhood each Hanukkah when she prepared the latkes as her mother had made them before her. The memories of her family—mother, grandmothers, aunts—floated back to her, young and vibrant once more, making days holy in the sanctuaries of their kitchens. These rituals connect her to the intricately plaited braid of their past, and looking down the corridor of what's to come. She sees herself join them as they open their arms wide to enfold her children and grandchildren in their embrace.

> **A LITTLE JOY: . . . "CAN YOU GUESS, CHILDREN, WHICH IS THE BEST OF ALL HOLIDAYS? HANUKKAH, OF COURSE. . . . MOTHER IS IN THE KITCHEN RENDERING GOOSE FAT AND FRYING PANCAKES. . . . YOU EAT PANCAKES EVERY DAY."**
> —Sholom Aleichem

"The Irish and Italian boys had Christmas once a year; we had exultation every Friday," wrote Hutchins Hapgood in *The Spirit of the Ghetto.*

"In the . . . neighborhood . . . rent by the shouts of peddlers and the myriad noises of the city, there was every Friday evening a wondrous stillness. . . . From the synagogue you could hear . . . the murmured prayers of the congregation. Once the service was over, you came home to find your mother dressed in her wedding dress with a white silk scarf around her head. And your father told you all the sufferings throughout the centuries were dedicated for this moment, the celebration of the Sabbath."

In *The Jewish Festival Cook Book*, Fannie Engle and Gertrude Blair beautifully describe the Sabbath evening. There's a holiday air about the house when the mother spreads the dinner cloth. Two loaves of challah have been placed at the head of the table (representing the twelve tribes of Israel). The Sabbath candlesticks have been placed in the center of the table. The mother lights each candle, while the children watch silently. She stands, hands spread toward the flames, then places them over her eyes. Silently she recites a benediction, looks at the candles and adds a prayer. For centuries Jewish mothers have reverently observed this ceremony. "*Gut Shabbas!*" The greeting breaks the quiet as mother and children greet each other after the lighting of the candles.

> "SABBATH! THAT IS THE WORD WHICH WE, AS MOTHERS IN ISRAEL, MUST BRAVE AGAIN. OURS IT IS TO BE THE SAVIORS OF OUR PEOPLE. OURS IT IS TO AROUSE COURAGE AND HOPE IN THE LEADERS OF THE NATION'S DESTINY."
>
> —Rebekah Bettelhiem Kohot, "Welcoming Address"
> National Council of Jewish Women Proceedings, 1896

CHAPTER 5

Yes, They, Too, Are Jewish Mothers

Rebels, groundbreakers, and greatness. Some of these Jewish mothers and their stories are well-known. But too often our history and lives are given short-shrift, or ignored in popular media, yet many of these Jewish mothers shaped and literally changed the world we live in.

PIONEER AND COLONIAL JEWISH MOTHERS

Jewish pioneer men have been well documented. However, the struggles and hardships that Jewish pioneer mothers faced, as they brought their menorahs from Europe to the frontiers of America, have been far less recorded and remembered.

Keeping a Jewish home only added to the difficulties that these women faced. Yet they did it with great dedication, strength, and dignity, often contributing mightily to the growth and development of what was then the far outreaches of the American West.

Women, in particular, through determination and activism, created many cultural institutions. They were central in organizing schools and building the first synagogues on the frontier—starting the grassroots of Jewish life in the Southwest and other parts of the country.

In the nineteenth century, most Jews who lived west of the Mississippi River came from Germany, Austria, Poland, France, and Russia. Some also migrated from the East to the West. A small number of Jewish merchants and traders settled in Texas in the 1820s and 1830s and in New Mexico in the 1840s when these territories were still part of Mexico. After the discovery of gold in California in 1848 and the completion of the transcontinental railroads in the late 1800s, Jews, as well as others, moved West in search of greater freedom and opportunities.

In particular, Jewish pioneers found open societies in the far West with few restrictions.

Some observances became difficult to exercise in the wilderness for Jewish mothers, and enormous resourcefulness was required to remain kosher. Many would, for example, grow their own vegetables or raise cows and other livestock.

Keeping two sets of dishes and cookware to separate meat from dairy was not an easy task for the kosher pioneer Jewish mother, yet many packed the necessary items in advance of their westward journey. Still, holidays, such as Passover, proved a problem.

"When we got ready for Passover, we even scrubbed the door knobs. We had a library with books in it. For Passover, my mother made me go through every one of those books, shake them out, God forbid someone would be reading a book a crumb would fall out," reported Seymour Siegel in 1959, when he quoted from the journal of a young Jewish girl in Mesa.

Jewish roots are deeply embedded in the history of the Arizona Territory. These mothers not only kept Jewish homes, but they also aided their husbands in business, mining, ranching, banking, and trade.

Clara Ferrin-Bloom was born in Tucson on July 26, 1881. She graduated from the University of Arizona in 1901, became a teacher, and married merchant David Bloom in 1912. They had three sons and two daughters. Clara was a member of the university's Alumni Association, a founder of the board of the Tucson Women's Symphony Association, as well as a member of the National Council of Jewish Women, and the Tucson Festival Society. She was the oldest member of Temple Emanu-El when she died.

The Clara-Ferrin Bloom Elementary School was established in 1973. Her son David and his wife created the superb Bloom Southwest Jewish Archives at the University of Arizona.

In 1996, the Bloom Southwest Jewish Archives acquired a set of ten dolls honoring Jewish women who contributed to the development of Jewish life and culture. The dolls include models of Clara Ferrin-Bloom, Dora Loon-Capin, Jennie Migel-Drachman, Rosa Katzenstein-Drachman, Josephine Sarah Marcus-Earp, Terese Marx-Ferrin, Anna Freudenthal-Solomon, Bettina Donau-Steinfeld, Julia Kaufman-Strauss, and Julia Frank-Zeckendorf. They were anonymously donated with the intention of sharing these remarkable images and stories with the public. These dolls were originally a bat mitvah project of thirteen-year-old Gerri Pozez, as a way of linking Jewish women from one generation to the next. The *Tucson Citizen* carried a story about the dolls in the July 16, 1996 edition.

Rosa Katzenstein was born in Baltimore on January 6, 1848 and married Philip Drachman in New York in 1868. "There they were, these Jewish women in the middle of nowhere," says Dr. Eileen Warshaw, executive director of the Jewish Heritage Center of the Southwest. "It took them three months to prepare to go into the wilderness. They finally departed for Tucson on October 21, 1868, after the Holy days, traveling 'in style,' by hitching a four-horse ambulance. It took them forever, what with camping across the desert among the Indians. They traveled twenty-five miles per day, finally arriving in Tucson on November 15, 1868.

"There were Anglo men, but only one other white woman. Rosa was so excited that she named her first child Harry Arizona Drachman, the first Anglo child born in the area. She subsequently had ten children.

"She had a hard, hard life. Her husband, Philip, owned a saloon and cigar store. He died leaving her with the kids. So . . . this Yiddishe mama ran a saloon and cigar store with her kids."

Rosa became the confidante of the new influx of women. Jewish men, who had married Mexican women, asked her to teach them how to make challah, light the candles, and teach their children Judaism. Rosa died on July 25, 1918. Her tombstone reads: "Mother Drachman," for the matriarch who helped build Tucson's community. The Tucson branch of Drachmans continued to be involved in community and business ventures in the area.

Rosa's sister-in-law, Jennie Migel-Drachman, was born in 1859 in Russia, and was the daughter of a California Jewish merchant. At seventeen, she married Samuel Drachman, of Tucson. The couple remained there for thirty-seven years, raising four children. They both held very strong religious beliefs.

"Sam Drachman took the role of acting rabbi, although he didn't have the education or certifications," says Dr. Warshaw. "So he married and buried people—with no authority. In 1887, their son was the first male child in Tucson whose circumcision was performed by a *mohel*. Where would you find one in those days? California!"

However, according to Jewish law, the circumcision must take place on the eighth day after birth. Oy. Getting to California was a seven-day trip.

"Jennie gives birth at noon. The next morning, Sam puts her on a stage to California. Remember, in those days there were no paved roads, just rutted paths . . . Indians. This woman was on the stage with her baby . . . *feeding* him on the stage," describes Dr. Warshaw.

> **"We didn't walk in those moccasins."**
> —Dr. Eileen Warshaw

"Jennie would meet the new stages, welcome, and help newcomers. She would care for the children, and was very helpful in the smallpox epidemic (1877–1878).

"Though there wasn't much money, Jenny loved society and music, organizing the first Purim Ball in Tucson," says Dr. Warshaw.

In 1886, the *Tucson Citizen* described the first Purim Ball Jennie helped plan as: "The most brilliant social event in the history of Tucson." While Jennie was active in the Hebrew Ladies Benevolent Society, her husband was the first president of Temple Emanu-El. Today the Drachman name appears on a street, a school, and the Drachman Institute at the University of Arizona.

Jennie died in 1927 at the age of sixty-eight. This couple was instrumental in keeping Judaism alive in the desert Southwest.

According to Harold I. Sharfman, there were three Jewish households who lived in Nogales, Arizona. The wives would often lend food or other necessities to their Jewish neighbors. They helped each other when in need and celebrated the holidays together. It was this strong Jewish bond that allowed these families to hold onto their heritage, which was critical in maintaining a vibrant Jewish community.

Sophie Kaufman (Cohen) was an early Jewish Arizona settler and a force to be reckoned with, says her son-in-law Sig Liberman, president of the League of Arizona Cities and Towns, who was the only Jewish council mayor in Arizona (1968–1972).

Sig's wife, Rose Lee Liberman, one of two daughters of Charles and Sophie Kaufman Cohen, was born in Tucson in 1926 and grew up in the Wild West. "My wife's family, the Kaufmans," says Sig, now retired in Texas, "was born in Russia. After coming to America, they eventually moved to Arizona." It was love at first sight between his wife's parents, Sophie Kaufman and Charles Cohen. After the couple married, they both worked with her father, Mr. Kaufman.

"But Sophie was the big *macher* (big shot) who learned Spanish and two Indian dialects to help her Dad run the store. Sophie, the first female graduate of the University of Arizona's School of Business in Tucson, was family-first business-oriented, loving, witty, protective, and into everything. She started the Rainbow Girls, a group that was involved with education and entertainment for both the Jewish and non-Jewish population," says Sig.

The small store expanded into the famous Kaufman's Department Store. The family prospered with the Kaufman's Spanish movie theater and became very successful in real estate. They also contributed property and helped develop the local synagogue.

In 1929, the Cohens moved to Coolidge, Arizona, where they opened another store. They were the first Jews in the area and closed their stores on Jewish holidays.

> "ONCE WHEN OUR SON WAS CALLED A DIRTY JEW, HE HIT THE OFFENDER. ROSE LEE AND I SAW THE PRINCIPAL AND SAID WE EXPECTED AN APOLOGY, AND ANY TIME OUR CHILD WAS CALLED SUCH A THING . . . HE HAD HER PERMISSION TO DEFEND HIMSELF."
> —Sig and Rose Lee Liberman

"Every once in a while there was trouble with red necks. But the Indians loved my mother-in-law, Sophie, and were eager to trade with her. During the holidays, they returned to Tucson to be with family and other Jews," he says.

Solomonville, located in the Gila Valley in Graham County northeast of Tucson, Arizona, owes a great debt to Anna and her husband Isidor Solomon.

Anna Freudenthal was born in Poland in 1845 and was "one tough lady," says Dr. Warshaw. She had survived cholera and smallpox. When her father left for America, thirteen-year-old Anna assumed his duties in Poland: She ran his store and took care of five siblings, and her mother, who never recovered from smallpox. She married Isidor Solomon and then immigrated to Pennsylvania with their three small children. In 1876, Isidor sold his assets to seek freighting opportunities in the West. Since traveling with three very young children in a crowded stagecoach was daunting, Isidor left his family in Las Cruces while he found a place for them to settle in Pueblo Viejo (later Solomonville in what would become the Arizona Territory). They headed to their new home in a two-seat buckboard hearing coyote calls or Indians on the warpath at night. Anna doubted they'd make it to their destination alive.

What greeted them in Pueblo Viejo, in the upper Gila Valley, was "a raw little place in the middle of nowhere," says Dr. Warshaw. "There was no law, no refinement. When Anna arrived in 1876, she was an oddity, as there were so few females out there."

Anna later recalled, "We had some very dark and sad times." But their future brightened. Anna's family owned the Clifton Mining Company, and contracted with Solomon to deliver charcoal. Anna attended to the store they purchased, which had the only safe in the area. Farmers and miners stored their money there, and eventually, banking became the Solomons' business as well. (Their Valley National Bank was later taken over by Bank One, now Arizona's largest financial institution.)

Over time, they ran a merchandising and real estate empire, and built the Solomon Hotel. "Anna added that touch of class, insisting on the cowboys having manners," says Warshaw. "She held dances, Christmas parties, but she stayed a Jew. Her husband was timid and withdrawn, so she stuck a foot up his butt and urged him to form a community." As their businesses thrived, so did the area, and Anna became known as the Mother of Solomonville. In 1878, mail carrier William H. Kirkland suggested renaming the community Solomonville (today known as Solomon), which was the Graham County seat from 1883 to 1915.

Anna made sure her children married Jews, and the great clan spread to Holbrook, Globe, Phoenix, and Tucson. The Solomons are one of the great Jewish pioneering families of the Southwest, and their legacy still endures in Arizona today.

"*M*rs. Mansfeld and Mrs. Bettina Steinfeld had their first meeting at the home of Mrs. Terese Marx Ferrin, to start the first temple in Tucson, on March 20, 1910. (Temple Emmanuel—now The Jewish Heritage Center). To raise money for the temple, Mrs. Mansfeld sold toys to Gentiles for Christmas."

—Dr. Eileen Warshaw

Julia Frank was born in Germany in 1840 and immigrated as a youngster to New York. At eighteen, she married William Zeckendorf, who was also from Germany. When William went to work with his brothers in New Mexico, then Arizona, the couple honeymooned by train across country. When Julia left San Diego, she was shocked to see her new husband in Western garb—pistols on hips and rifle in hand. The couple relocated to Tucson and had four children. Julia entertained elegantly for the Jewish community. Eventually, they returned to New York, but the Zeckendorf name became part of the historical records of Arizona and New Mexico because of the family's involvement in merchandising, mining, cattle raising, and farming. Generations of Zeckendorfs then built a real estate empire in New York, and Julia's grandson, William II, put together the land parcel that John D. Rockefeller donated to the United Nations.

When Jewish pioneers Alec and Bella's bull died, Bella went to an auction, while her husband, Alec, tended their struggling ranch. If she bought, she'd wire Alec to bring a wagon to shlep the bull.

The bidding was high, but Bella bid on the last bull, leaving her with ten cents. She hurried to the telegraph office.

"Mistah clerk, how many vords can I send to mine husband for a dime?"

"Five cents a word."

Bella pondered her dilemma, then said, "OK, here's mine message: 'COMFORTABLE.'"

Bettina Donau was born on June 2, 1861. She married Albert Steinfeld in Denver in 1883 and settled in Tucson, where her husband had a small business. The couple had four children. As their fortunes grew, they eventually built a mansion but never failed to respond to a community need. They also had a large cattle operation, and were one of the first families in Tucson to own an automobile, a Pierce-Arrow. The *Tucson Citizen* ran this headline: "FIRST ARREST FOR SPEEDING IN THIS CITY." Their chauffeur was fined $25 for exceeding the twenty-mile per hour speed limit!

In the early twentieth century, Annie Rochlin, who lived in Nogales, Arizona, had the sole responsibility of running her huge estate during her marriage and after her husband's death. Her daughter-in-law Harriet writes: "With the Sonoran women who worked for her, my mother-in-law was just and straightforward. Having been a seamstress in a sweatshop she was a sympathetic employer, but everyone worked, and no one longer or harder than she. She knew their origins, vital statistics, and current concerns. Asked or unasked, she offered advice but didn't expect them to alter their ingrained ways."

Terese Marx was born in Germany in 1846 and immigrated to San Francisco with her family. She married Joseph Ferrin there and the newlyweds soon relocated to Tucson.

Terese raised three children, while engaging in philanthropic work. In 1890, she was president of the Hebrew Ladies Benevolent Association, and was instrumental in planning Temple Emanu-El. In 1910, she was present for the laying of the cornerstone of the first synagogue in the territory of Arizona.

Terese, known as "The Angel of Tucson," often accompanied one of the town's doctors on emergencies. She was a self-trained holistic practitioner and herbologist, and it was said her remedies never failed.

Julia Kaufman was born on July 14, 1850, in Tennessee and married Charles Strauss in 1868. The couple had four children, including one who died from diphtheria. They moved to Tucson in 1880 because of Charles's poor health and then became extremely active in their new community. Julia made her home a cultural center, often played piano, and hosted the first meeting of the Lotus Club, which included many prominent Jewish area women. Charles ran for mayor in the 1880s, and despite anti-Semitism from his opponent, he became Tucson's first Jewish mayor—thanks to his wife's encouragement.

"*It* was usually the women who retained and passed down old-world Jewish traditions. They never forgot where they came from. It was the women who, in the 1920s, made sure the rabbi they hired was also a kosher butcher. It was the women who acquired a Torah. Jewish Tucson women started the Temple of Music and Art in the early 1900s. It was the women who retained Hebrew and Yiddish—the culture that their mothers had given them. In your experience, if any event or writings are attributed to 'Anonymous,' it was probably a woman."

—Dr. Eileen Warshaw

Jewish mothers and early settlers contributed to their communities all over America. Talk about Jewish mothers! The following is an account of a mother of twenty-one.

"Rebecca Machado was born into an eminent Jewish family of Portuguese descent," reports Dr. Yitzchok Levine, professor at the Stevens Institute of Technology, in his column, "Glimpses into American Jewish History" that appears in the *Jewish Press* each month.

A secret or crypto-Jew, Rebecca's family had lived a double life for years. Even after their move to America, they recited Hebrew prayers—with a Catholic rosary.

Crypto-Jews are Jews of Hispanic descent who were forced to convert to Catholicism during the Spanish Inquisition in the fifteenth century. They secretly performed Jewish rituals in the home and some mothers revealed their identity to their children near the end of their lives—to make peace with God and pass along their Jewish legacy.

In 1762, at the age of sixteen, Rebecca married Jonas Phillips, who had been trained as a *shochet*. Within a year, she gave birth to the *first of their twenty-one children* in New York. When her husband's business failed, Jonas secured a position as a *shochet* and *bodek* (one who performs the ritual slaughterer and examiner of meat). Tragedy followed the young couple from 1763 to 1772, when four of their children died before reaching their first birthday.

In addition to raising her growing family, Rebecca, like most eighteenth-century women, manufactured cloth, and prepared processed comestibles to keep them through the winter.

In 1769, when Jonas went into business again, this time in Philadelphia, their fortunes turned. They became quite wealthy and contributed generously to Congregation Mikveh Israel. Rebecca took an active part in communal affairs and fund-raising, and at age fifty-five, she was one of the founding members of the Female Association for the Relief of Women and Children in Reduced Circumstances, to help the sick and indigent. She was widowed two years later, leaving her a single mother of her huge brood.

Yet, at age 74, Rebecca served as first directress on the board of the Female Hebrew Benevolent Society of Philadelphia.

This uncommon colonial mother of twenty-one children was a tireless community activist and philanthropist—roles that Jewish mothers would continue to embrace in this new land.

Bilhah Abigaill Levy Franks (1696–1756) was a born letter writer. Her letters to her son Naphtali (edited by Isidore Mayer and Leo Hershkowitz) are housed in the archives of the American Jewish Historical Society.

She was born in London in 1696, the eldest of Moses Raphael and Richea Asher Levy's five children. She dropped the name Bilhah when she came to New York City with her family around 1703. In 1712, when Abigaill was sixteen, she married Jacob Franks. Her husband grew to be a primary supplier of food, clothing, and ammunition to Britain's colonial forces.

Abigaill had nine children. When her eldest, Naphtali, moved to London to represent the family business, her letters to him revealed the life of a colonial Jewish matriarch.

While in New York, Abigaill organized the ladies of the Spanish-Portuguese Congregation into a fund-raising unit to help build a new synagogue. Every single Jewish woman in New York contributed, and Abigaill was considered the spiritual mother of all synagogue sisterhoods.

Her childrens' education, both Jewish and secular, was her priority and she sent them to a *melamed* (teacher) and to a Protestant educator. The girls were sent to Mrs. Brownell's, a finishing school, and Abigaill's letters speak of their fine progress.

Finding a suitable match for her daughters was no easy matter, since New York's Sephardic society looked to the Caribbean for brides. On June 7, 1743, Abigaill, heartbroken, wrote Naphtali that his sister, Phila, secretly married Oliver Delancey, a prominent Huguenot. This was the first (known) case of an American Jewess marrying out of the faith.

Despite her teachings, not one of her family passed on Judaism, a story that is relevant to Jews today—the conundrum of maintaining Judaism in an assimilated society.

JEWISH MOTHER PIONEERS, EARLY SETTLERS: FEMINISM AND ACTIVISM

In 1874, the highly educated and outspoken seventeen-year-old Flora Langerman married Willi Spiegelberg, in what was the first wedding in the new Reform Temple in Nuremberg, Germany.

After an elegant European honeymoon, the couple set out for Santa Fe, New Mexico, where Flora endured a grueling trip over rough country with the cuisine consisting of dried buffalo, bear meat, buffalo tongue, buffalo steaks, beans, and chiles—not exactly haute cuisine.

The bumpy stagecoach ride caused Flora to miscarry, as she was "terribly frightened" when she saw Indians for the first time. When the couple finally stopped at a hotel in Las Animas, Colorado, she was the first woman the men had seen in months. Under the gaze of cowboys at the ramshackle hotel, she had to climb a ladder to her bed while the men looked on. Flora was so anxious and uncomfortable that she slept clothed.

When the couple finally arrived in Santa Fe, they were greeted by the Spiegelberg brothers and their families, while a band played Lohengrin's "Wedding March." The local people cheered Willi and his tenderfoot bride.

Instead of going into culture shock, Flora devoted herself to improving her new community. She organized literary and dramatic clubs and in 1879, she helped establish the first nonsectarian school and the first children's playground and garden in Santa Fe.

Flora conducted two religious schools herself, one a Sabbath school on Saturdays for Jewish children and the other, a Sunday school for Catholic children. Among her Jewish students were Hyman Lowitzy, who became a member of Teddy Roosevelt's Rough Riders, and Arthur Seligman, who went on to become governor of New Mexico in 1930.

Flora also had her share of decidedly "frontier" experiences. One night in 1887, an angry mob insisted that her husband join in lynching two Mexicans who allegedly murdered an Anglo physician—but she convinced the mob to leave. On another occasion, she met the infamous Billy the Kid when he came to the Spiegelbergs' store in 1876 to buy new duds.

In the late 1880s she insisted that her family join the other Spiegelbergs in New York City so their daughters, Betty and Rose, could eventually marry Jewish men.

She became a social activist in New York, organizing the Boys Vocational Club and, in 1889, the first Jewish Working Girls Club. Flora was the leading force behind the creation of a modern system of garbage collection in the city and Thomas Edison even made a film about her plan. She was dubbed "The Old Garbage Woman of New York."

Although criticized at times for her "unladylike" concerns with garbage, Flora explained that health and cleanliness was "quite within the province of women." She also served on the New York City Health Commission, the Street Cleaning Department, the Public Water Commission, and the Daylight Savings Commission, and even had a moderately successful career as a writer. In 1937, Flora published some of the stories from her own life in "Reminiscences of a Jewish Bride on the Santa Fe Trail," which appeared in the *Jewish Spectator*.

Despite her remarkable achievements, the name Flora Langerman Spiegelberg has remained largely unknown.

Florence Prag Kahn was born November 9, 1866, to Polish Jews who were early settlers in California. In the mid-1860s, the family moved to Salt Lake City, Utah, where her father became friendly with Brigham Young. Her mother was an educator and early "feminist" who wrote *My Life Among the Mormons.*

Florence was a teacher when she married Julius Kahn in 1899. They later moved from California to Washington, D.C., when her husband was elected to Congress.

When Florence and her husband were invited to dine with President McKinley, they walked to the White House, as a carriage cost one dollar to hire. "In what country," asked Julius Kahn, "could two poor Jews be on their way to dine with the head of state?"

The Kahns, Republicans, were dedicated to Judaism and their two sons were bar mitzvahed at Temple Emanuel. Florence, known as a brilliant, take-charge woman with great humor, was once asked "Would you favor a birth control law?" She replied: "I will if you make it retroactive."

In 1924, after her husband's death, a special election was held and Florence took his seat, making her the first Jewish woman to serve in the United States Congress. She completed five congressional terms and was also the first woman to serve on the Military Affairs Committee. Florence traveled throughout California encouraging women to become involved in national politics.

She remained dedicated to Judaism and was in involved in numerous Jewish organizations. Florence Prag Kahn died on November 16, 1948, of heart disease.

Rebecca Gratz was born in Philadelphia on March 4, 1781 into a wealthy Jewish family. She was a very beautiful and religious woman who gave up the love of her life because he wasn't Jewish. She had no children of her own, but after her parents' early deaths she raised her siblings and then was mother to her late sister's children.

At twenty, she organized the Female Association for the Relief of Women and Children of Reduced Circumstances in Philadelphia, serving as its first secretary and fund-raiser. Rebecca was also one of the founders of the Philadelphia Orphan Asylum. In 1819, she founded the Female Hebrew Benevolent Society, and then in 1855, she created the Jewish Foster Home and Orphan Asylum.

> **R**ebecca Gratz no doubt inherited her spirit from her mother, Miriam Gratz, whose home in Lancaster, Pennsylvania, was a gathering place for traders, Indians, soldiers, and trappers. Miriam was a canny trader and administrator, keeping her firm's agents— from Canada to the Ohio River—in touch with one another by post.

In addition to her groundbreaking work on behalf of orphans, Rebecca presided over the establishment of the first Jewish Sunday School, on February 4, 1838.

The Philadelphia Hebrew Sunday School Society was based on the Christian Sunday school and offered free weekly classes to children from early childhood to the early teens. It also gave Jewish women an unprecedented role in the education of Jewish children, with its teacher training program. Rebecca was the school's superintendent for over twenty-five years.

The school was an immediate success and branches were opened all over Philadelphia and the country. Her 1838 design for supplemental Jewish education is still used in the United States today.

> ratz, one of the most famous women of her time, had friends which included Henry Clay and Washington Irving. Irving told Sir Walter Scott about the extraordinary Rebecca Gratz, who, then, it is believed, became his role model for the heroine in *Ivanhoe.*

THIS LAND IS OUR LAND

Since the very start of United States history, Jewish mothers, as all mothers, felt pride and also suffered grievous loss when their children went to war, or fought within our own country for justice. What many may not know is that Jewish mothers also courageously participated far more directly in the war effort.

REVOLUTIONARY WAR

During the Revolutionary War, Mordecai Sheftall became the highest-ranking Jewish officer of the American Revolutionary forces. He attained the rank of Deputy Commissary General to the Continental Troops in South Carolina and Georgia. Sheftall and his son were captured by British forces and imprisoned in Antigua but eventually traded for two captured British officers.

Mardecai was such a militant rebel during the American Revolution that the British put a price on the head of his wife, Frances "Fannie" Sheftall. Just before the British arrived—when her husband and son were captured and imprisoned—Mrs. Sheftall fled to Charleston, South Carolina, home to the largest Jewish community in America at the time. Despite the danger, Frances not only nursed the American troops, but also took care of those affected by a smallpox epidemic.

Esther Hays of Westchester, New York, was one of the most courageous mothers of the American Revolution. Her village was burned by the British, yet she refused to disclose the whereabouts of patriots—including her seven-year-old son, Jacob—who were driving a herd of cattle through British lines. Both Jacob and her other son Benjamin grew up to be celebrated members of their communities. Arthur Hays Sulzberger, Benjamin's grandson, was the late publisher of the *New York Times*.

Abigail Minis, her husband Abraham, and their daughters Leah and Esther left Europe and arrived in Savannah, Georgia, on July 10, 1733. She eventually gave birth to three more daughters, Judith, Hannah, and Sarah, and four sons, Phillip, Minis, Joseph, and Samuel.

Her husband, an influential farmer and businessman, died in 1757, appointing Abigail as the executrix of his estate—an unusual vote of confidence for an eighteenth-century woman. The horses and mares went to his surviving sons, and his cattle to his daughters. All other possessions went to Abigail to " . . . enable her (Abigail) to maintain, educate, and bring up our children."

Abigail was allowed to start the Minis Tavern in her name, which proved highly successful.

When the American Revolution came to Savannah, her son Phillip (the first white male child born in the settlement of Georgia on July 7, 1734), and her friend Mordecai Sheftall were firm patriots, although her loyalties were unclear at the time.

Mrs. Minis, as she was always referred to, was one of Savannah's great matriarchs. She owned property in three different Georgia counties when she died.

CIVIL WAR: DIVIDE HOUSES

Eleanor Cohen Seixas, a Southern patriot in South Carolina, kept a diary for ten years, from age sixteen to twenty-six. The following are excerpts from the last year of her diary (from February 2, 1865, to January 1, 1866)—as she discusses her transition to womanhood against the backdrop of the Civil War.

Entry: February 28, 1865: I am the eldest of three daughters, much petted and indulged. My first recollection is of a sufficiency, every comfort. But the wheels turned, and we were poor, very poor. A revulsion came, the Union was destroyed, the Confederacy formed, and grim-visaged war, with all attendant horrors, desolated our land. The war brought money to father's coffers, and soon he became a rich man, rich, alas, only in Confederate money.

"Dear Journal, I suppose you think, as I am still Miss Cohen and twenty-six, that I am an old maid. No, for next month was to have smiled on my wedding, now indefinitely postponed. But I am betrothed. I have been engaged six months to Mr. B. M. Seixas.

"We are now in the fourth year of the fearful war that is now ravaging our land. . . . The vile Yankees . . . left us in a deplorable condition after stealing from us, and oh, saddest of all, I know not where my precious love is or if he is a prisoner, wounded, or dead.

"April was to have been our bridal; now, alas, it is indefinitely postponed. I feel truly as if my fate was a hard one. From the pinnacle of happiness, I have reached the lowest depths of despair.

"April 16: Joy is mine, dear Journal. I have had a letter from my most precious love. He is well and . . . doing business in Charleston. Oh, happy I am to be reassured of his love. And yet there is a sad struggle in my heart, if to leave my dear parents in their time of trouble I have to do.

"April 21: A sad record today of crushed hopes, wasted life, and fruitless exertion. Our noble General Lee with 30,000 men were surrounded by 200,000 men, and were compelled to surrender.

"June 2: "Peace has come, but, oh, God, what a different peace to the one we prayed for! . . . Slavery is done away with. Our noble Jeff Davis . . . are prisoners. . . . Columbia and all the principal cities are garrisoned by Yankees. How it makes my Southern blood boil to see them in our streets!

"Another source of trouble to me is that Mr. S. wants to go North. . . . Although I long to know his family, yet I feel too bitter toward them to desire to go North.

"August 2, 1865: My wedding day, can it be, long thought of, long hoped for, here at last? . . . The wedding will be quiet, at two o'clock. If I can be loved by my new master, as by my family, all well be well. I can write no more; this is the last, dying effort of Eleanor H. Cohen, spinster.

"Entry number one of Mrs. B. M. Seixas. Richmond, August 6th, 1865: Yes, I am a bride, a wife, four days married. All passed off well. The glass broke; the ring was on my finger, and from every side I received kisses and congratulations. We arrived . . . in New York City. We met Mr. Seixas's father at the wharf. . . . His mother wept over us, and all greeted me with affection.

"Dear old Journal, let me whisper to you that a woman's crowning glory will, with God's blessing, be mine this year. I will become a mother. Oh, how my heart thrills at the word! Yes, please God, in May I will have a pledge of love given me in our baby. The blessed assurance of my husband's love. I can hardly believe it, that I will be a mother."

Eugenia Levy Phillips was an educated and determined woman, and an important figure in Alabama history. She was also a staunch supporter of the Confederacy.

Eugenia was born in 1820 in Charleston, South Carolina. She was one of six daughters born to Jacob C. Levy and Fannie Yates Levy. At sixteen, she married Philip Phillips, a prominent Mobile lawyer and businessman, and had nine children.

Her husband served two terms in the Alabama State Legislature. When Philip was elected to Congress in 1853, the family moved to Washington, D.C.

Although her husband was opposed to secession, Eugenia was a firm supporter of the South, and aided Rose O'Neal Greenhow, the famed rebel spy. Eugenia's family shared her views, and her sister, Phoebe Yates Pember (widow of Thomas Pember) was one of the South's most dedicated nurses.

Her support of the Confederate cause wasn't without consequences, however. When the Phillips' home was ransacked by Union troops, Eugenia managed to "destroy" incriminating papers: The maid hid them in her bodice.

Although taunts were the only evidence of her treason, Eugenia and two of her daughters were imprisoned in the attic of Mrs. Greenhow's home. It wasn't until Edwin M. Stanton, later Secretary of War, intervened that they were released, forcing the Phillips family to move to New Orleans.

However, when New Orleans fell to General Benjamin F. Butler, Eugenia became Butler's nemesis. In May 1862, shortly after he assumed control of New Orleans he issued his infamous Order #28 condemning the women for their insults, which enraged the entire South. Yet, Eugenia's defiance continued, as she threw a party for her children and laughed during a funeral procession for a deceased Union soldier. This so enraged Butler that he sentenced Eugenia to Ship Island, Mississippi, for the duration of the war—without judge or jury.

Although the conditions were horrific on Ship Island, and Eugenia's health declined, she never asked for special favors and continued her campaign for the South.

She was so frail when she was released that a servant slammed the door in her face, thinking she was a stranger. Her husband and children, having been given little information about Eugenia's status, were both shocked and overjoyed at their reunion. The famous battle between Eugenia Phillips and General "Beast" Butler that had drawn international attention was finally over.

The family then moved to LaGrange, Georgia, where Eugenia devoted the rest of her life and fortune to supporting and clothing the poor and ill soldiers of the South.

> "TO MY SIX NOBLE BOYS THERE WILL BE BEQUEATHED A LESSON IN THEIR MOTHER'S SUFFERINGS, WHICH WILL TEACH THEM JEALOUS WATCHFULNESS OF POWER AND A TIMELY RESISTANCE TO DESPOTISM IN WHATEVER SHAPE IT MAY ASSUME."
> —Eugenia Levy Phillips

WORLD WAR II

Matilda Blaustine and her daughter, Bernice, both served in the WAAC (Women's Auxiliary Army Corps) during World War II. Prior to the war, Matilda Blaustine was district deputy of New York in the Masonic Order, the highest position a Jewish woman could hold in that organization. In 1942, she was inducted as a staff sergeant into the first contingent of the WAAC and served as a radar spotter for U.S. Naval Intelligence in the First Fighter Command in New York until her discharge in 1945.

After the war, Matilda was an ardent fund-raiser for the Hebrew Immigrant Aid Society. She worked for the release of refugee families from the Displacement Camps and their subsequent resettlement.

Her daughter, Bernice Blaustein, joined the WAACs in 1943 and received basic training at Fort Bliss, Texas. She also served until 1945.

TODAY

"What is a nice Jewish girl from Brooklyn doing in the Marine Corps?" In a lecture in 2000, sponsored by the JWV Department of Florida, Col. Wendy Fontela, USMC, and Maj. Debra Powell, USAF, both Jewish mothers, provided answers.

Col. Fontela has been in the corps for over twenty-eight years and was mobilized for Desert Storm. As of 2000, she was serving as legislative affairs officer at the Southern Command. She and her husband have two sons.

"The saying was, 'If you were supposed to have a spouse, we would have issued you one.'"
—Col. Wendy Fontela, USMC

"It's a challenge and a career for anyone to be in the military," she said, and then discussed how the military has changed over time. "When I entered the service, a girdle was a required uniform item. I was in an organization that had little use for mothers. In 1977, you still needed permission to get married. Today women serve in all fields except those that are direct ground combat. We are no longer women marines. We are marines!"

At the time of the lecture, Maj. Debra Powell was head of the Requirement Section for Reserve Affairs for the Southern Command. The military had provided her with the opportunity to go to college, and after graduating from high school, she entered the University of Florida's Air Force Officer Reserve Training Corps. Her friends thought she was crazy for enlisting.

Debra is married to Maj. Shawn Powell and is mother of two sons. She has said: "Being Jewish, in my experience, hasn't affected my career. It is a great career and has opened opportunities that I don't think I would have had." But more, "I will do what it takes to secure our country for my children and grandchildren."

"I'm an American and very proud to serve my country and to help protect everyone's right to freedom. It's important to teach the value of service before self."
—Maj. Debra Powell, USAF

In a 2004 e-mail, Diane F. Godorov, D.O. CPT MC, U.S. Army, wrote about her experience in Iraq.

" . . . I have continued to be busy with doctoring our troops and humanitarian missions. . . .

"Many here go out of their way to help others and that is passed along from soldier to soldier. . . . Like any Jewish mother I have to mention my children Wolf-Ekkehard [eighteen] and Sieglinde [fifteen].

"They are both wonderful students with challenging classes and magnificent grades. Wolf will be entering West Point, class of 2008. I am very proud of both of my children. . . . I am known to the Iraqis as 'Doctora Diana' and to the soldiers as 'Doc Combat.' I have cared for camel herders and ridden their camels, been to the tank graveyard of the former Republican Guard base in Tikrit, been invited into homes for tea and flat round bread, seen the Tigress River from a village that has a sheik with seven wives and over 120 children! I have even seen the inside of a mosque. Oh, the stories I can now tell. . . . Thanks to Wolf, I was able to bring my favorite movie of all time with me, *Auntie Mame*. . . . In the movie Mame declares, 'All of life is a banquet, and most poor suckers are starving to death!' Not me!"

Barbara Diamond Goldin puts white socks, an alarm clock, and a hairbrush with some of the things she sends to her daughter, Josee, and son-in-law, Phillip Radzikowski, both stationed in Iraq.

"It's something I can do," says Goldin, "it makes me feel better," reports Rahel Musleah, an award-winning journalist, author, singer, speaker, and storyteller, in an article in the winter issue, 2003, of *Jewish Woman*.

"Other than one phone call in the middle of the night, Mrs. Goldin communicates with her daughter by short and sometimes infrequent e-mail. "I think about her and her husband every day. I say the traveler's prayer and a personal prayer for them every day," said Mrs. Goldin, a children's book writer who has become a news junkie. "When I tell people my daughter is in Iraq, they give me a blank look," she said in the article.

Angry about media coverage, she's a volunteer with an organization called Media Reform. But, she says, "I don't mention politics with Josee. I am in support mode. Few members of the Jewish community know much about Jewish women in the military beyond what they saw in *Private Benjamin*."

Political activism motivated Josee at an early age. She was alarmed at the genocide in Bosnia-Herzegovina and circulated petitions and lobbied her legislators. Following a physics degree from George Washington University, she attended Airborne School at Fort Benning, Georgia. Commissioned in 2001, she married Phillip Radzikowski, a captain, who was deployed in Iraq. Her first assignment in South Korea was a grueling year spent ten miles from the demilitarized zone. Sent to Iraq in 2003, the couple, stationed one hundred miles apart, saw each other when on supply missions.

Though Radzikowski did not disclose her religion to Iraqis, maintaining her identity as "a Jew, a woman, and an American" is critical, she said, adding, "I'd be lost without my faith, especially in the circumstances I find myself in."

"*J*ewish women have contributed to the U.S. military since the Civil War, when Phoebe Yates Levy offered her nursing skills and became one of the first women to break into the previously all-male field of nursing. [Women] have since [served] in every branch of the armed services. Of the 24.3 million veterans in 2000, 1.2 million were women, according to the Department of Veteran Affairs."
—Rahel Musleah, award-winning journalist

Lt. Col. Susan Rena Yanoff, an army veterinarian, says one of her most moving experiences was escorting a group of veterans from the 120th Evacuation Hospital on their visit to Buchenwald: They had been the first medical personnel there when the camp was liberated.

JEWISH MOTHER CHAPLAINS

Chaplain Bonnie Koppell grew up in Brooklyn, New York, near the army chaplain school. This piqued her curiosity and interest in military service and she joined the Army Reserves in 1978 while a rabbinical student at the Reconstructionist Rabbincal College in Philadelphia, Pennsylvania. She was ordained in 1981 and *became the first female rabbi ever to serve in the United States military.*

In 1991, during Operation Desert Storm Rabbi Koppell was ordered to report to the Academy of Health Sciences, a unit of the 5th Army Headquarters at Fort Sam Houston, Texas. There, preparations were underway to medevac an anticipated "massive" amount of American casualties, which would result from a planned major ground offensive against Iraq. As the only rabbi on staff, Bonnie was to provide for the spiritual needs of the sick and wounded.

Following her release from active duty, she was assigned to the 164th Corps Support Group in Mesa, Arizona.

After 9/11, she was again called to active duty in Fort Huachuca, Arizona, leaving her husband, David Rubenstein, a professional astrologer, and two daughters, Jessie, now twenty, and Sarah, seventeen.

Currently, she works with three congregations in and around Phoenix and is a chaplain for Tucson's Jewish Family and Children's Services.

In 2005, she was in Bagdad for Passover and in Afghanistan and Kuwait for Hanukkah, and then in April of 2006, she was in the northwestern region in Iraq for Passover.

Rabbi Koppell, now a full colonel, possesses not only a dedication to Judaism and America, but is also a marvelously caring and hysterically funny woman—who easily shares her extraordinary skills with all she encounters.

> According to the Jewish Chaplains Association, there are only twenty-eight active-duty Jewish chaplains and fifty-seven reservists.

"I AM PROUD TO CONSIDER AMONG MY MANY IDENTITIES AS WIFE, AS MOTHER, AS RABBI, AS TEACHER, AS FRIEND, YET ANOTHER—AS AN AMERICAN SOLDIER. GOD FORBID THE NEED SHOULD ARISE, OUR JEWISH SOLDIERS DESERVE TO HAVE RABBIS WHO ARE TRAINED AND READY TO DEPLOY ALONGSIDE THEM, TO BE THERE TO OFFER ALL THE SUPPORT THEY WILL NEED. I AM PROUD TO BE AMONG THOSE WHO STAND READY TO GO WITH THEM."
—Rabbi Bonnie Koppell

Rabbi Chana Timoner, who became the first Jewish *full-time* army chaplain, came from a military tradition. The *New York Times* reported that her mother joined the Canadian Army in 1940, in order to fight the Nazis.

Timoner was born in the early 1950s. She married at eighteen and then graduated from Southern Connecticut State University, while raising two children, who were teenagers when she enrolled in rabbinical school.

She commuted to New York City to attend the Academy for Jewish Religion, where she was ordained in 1989, and then spent another two years at the New York Theological Seminary, studying for her doctorate.

She was thirty-nine when she began her army career at Fort Bragg, North Carolina. Timoner officiated at all life-cycle events, organized donations to agencies and those in need on the base, ran the army's largest Jewish religious school, and was also active in counseling gay soldiers. She served in Korea, where she was stationed with an aviation attack regiment near the demilitarized zone, and was there when she was diagnosed with the Epstein-Barr virus.

She died in 1998 at forty-six shortly after her honorable discharge for medical reasons, leaving her husband, Dr. Julian Timoner, and two children, Samson and Aviva.

There was an empty seat at MIT in the 2003 commencement ceremonies when Samson J. Timoner received his PhD in electrical engineering and computer science. His mother, Rabbi Chana Timoner, had died in 1998, but the family still felt her loving presence: "We know she's here in spirit."

The year was 1964 when young Andrew Goodman said, "Mom . . . I have to go." She recalled, "It wasn't easy for us. But we couldn't talk out of both sides of our mouths. So I had to let him go."

On June 21, 1964, one day after Goodman arrived in Mississippi, Andrew, along with James Chaney and Michael Schwerner, who were all participating in an intensive voter-registration drive, were beaten and shot by a gang of Klansmen. Their bodies were found in a clay dam forty-four days later in Neshoba.

In 1967, Killen was tried on federal charges for violating the victims' civil rights, but the all-white jury was deadlocked, with one juror saying she could not convict a preacher. Seven others were convicted, but none served more than six years. The case received nationwide attention and hastened the passage of the landmark Civil Rights Act of 1964.

However, it took exactly forty-one years to bring the eighty-year-old Killen to justice. Witnesses said Killen rounded up carloads of Klansmen to intercept the three men and helped arrange for a bulldozer to bury the bodies. On June 21, 2005, he was found guilty of three counts of manslaughter and sentenced to three consecutive twenty-year prison terms.

The horror these young men endured has been memorialized in books and films, including *Mississippi Burning*. A new film about the event, *Neshoba* (working title), is currently near completion.

"It took so long," says Dr. Goodman, "because there was a lot of evidence to sift through. The DA and attorney general were terrific."

Speaking of her family—and her son, she adds, "My son was raised in our family to be the kind of person who believed we are a country of laws. His grandfather, a lawyer, was a man who felt if you believe in something, do it. Being a DOER requires that if you believe something is wrong and you have values, you do the right thing. I was told by my parents to, 'Make your own decision.' My mother was a community person. And then my husband and I taught each other." And they taught Andrew.

Our priority is "To work for freedom, which is what we did in the 1950s—and today."

> "The verdict was about justice. I don't believe in capital pun-
> ishment. I believe in justice and my wonderful son would have
> agreed. He was raised by our family to be the kind of person who
> believed we are a country of laws . . . and to do the right thing."
>
> —Dr. Carolyn Goodman, speaking with me after the conviction,
> forty years later, of Edgar Ray Killen for the murder of her
> twenty-year-old son, civil rights worker Andrew Goodman

YENTLS! SCHOLARS, RABBIS— AND JEWISH MOTHERS

Despite the fact that, for centuries, Jewish females did not participate in most aspects of religious life, many were far more emancipated than their country "women."

BIBLICAL JEWISH MOTHERS

We start with Eve.

The first mention of Eve (Genesis 3:20) calls her *ishah*, or "woman" (from *ish* meaning "man"). Adam called her woman or wife. The rabbis had no doctrine of Original Sin regarding Eve in the Garden, since it was removed by the Israelites.

Each and every Jewish woman is a descendant of the matriarchs: Sarah (wife of Abraham, the first Jewess, who gave birth to the Jewish people), Rivkah/Rebekah (wife of Isaac and mother of Jacob and Esau), Rachel (daughter of Laban, favorite wife of patriarch Jacob, and mother of Joseph and Benjamin), and Leah (wife of Jacob and mother of six of the twelve tribes). NOTE: More information about these women can be found in countless biblical resources and articles. I recommend the Dawn R. Schuman Institute for Jewish Learning.

It is incumbent upon every Jewish woman to remember her roots. Each of these builders of the House of Israel contributed a distinctive quality, which together produced the unique character of our Jewish people. The role of the Jewish woman is of crucial importance since she is the *akeret habayit*, the foundation of the home, who determines the character and atmosphere of the household, and the future of the children. This is considered the true work of Jewish mothers.

There can be no greater fulfillment for a Jewish female than to be a worthy descendant of the matriarchs. The process is achieved by actively pursuing one's own development while simultaneously working for the preservation and growth of our people.

An interesting aspect of the matriarchs is their imperfection. Sarah, Rebekah, and Rachel were initially barren, which was considered a serious imperfection in Jewish tradition at that time. And it is also noted that Leah had a visual disability.

In "The Women's Torah Commentary," Rabbi Lori Forman challenges traditional notions with a feminist perspective. Eve is often portrayed as an empty-headed wife who seduced Adam into sin. Rabbi Forman feels this paved the way for the religious denigration of women, because she sees Eve as a model of adventure and curiosity, rather than disobedience. She believes Eve should be recast as the woman who reached for "what was good, pleasant, and intellectually empowering."

Miriam was at least seven years older than her brother Moses. Some sources indicate that she was one of the midwives who rescued Hebrew babies from Pharaoh's edict (Exodus 1:15-19).

Miriam was the first woman described in scripture as a prophetess (Exodus 15:20), and is said to have prophesied that her parents would give birth to one who would bring about the redemption of their people.

Yocheved, the mother of Moses, saved her child by putting him in a basket in the Nile, to be found by Pharaoh's daughter. But it was Miriam who waited among the bulrushes while Moses's ark was in the river, watching over him to make sure he was safe (Exodus 2:4). When Pharaoh's daughter drew Moses out of the water, Miriam arranged for their mother, Yocheved, to nurse Moses and raise him until he was weaned (Exodus 2:7–9).

Miriam died in the desert like her brothers, before our people reached the Promised Land.

EARLY YENTLS

Rashi, the great twelfth-century French rabbi, had three daughters believed to be named Yocheved, Miriam, and Rachel. They were highly educated, assisted in the publication of their father's works, and it is also believed they rendered legal decisions in his absence. They gave birth to some of the leading Jewish scholars (male) of their time. In the sixteenth century, Miriam, a descendent of Rashi, and the mother of Rabbi Solomon Luria, lectured at a seminary from behind an opaque screen.

Although most think Jewish women entered the professions in the late nineteenth century, they were medical practitioners during medieval days. Hava (or Hana) was a surgeon who came from a prominent medical family, and there are reports of her rescuing a male, Poncius Procelli, who was attacked in his most "intimate" organ. When asked if she had palpated the wound, she replied that her son Bonafos did the actual "handling," while she instructed and prescribed the required medications.

At the turn of the seventeenth century, Rivkah bat Meir Tiktiner of Poland and Prague wrote an early ethical book in Yiddish, *Mekenet Rivkah*, which, in part, advises mothers " . . . about the education of daughters. Our sages said, 'If a daughter comes first, it is a good sign for sons. . . . she will be able to help the mother in the education of children who come afterward. Thus, every woman should try to educate her daughter to good deeds.'"

*L*ouise Scodie wrote an article about Regina Jones titled "A Forgotten Pioneer of Faith." Regina was born in 1902 in Berlin, and attended the city's center for Jewish studies (*Hochschule fur die Wissenschaft des Judentums*). This qualified her as a religion teacher but she was determined to become a rabbi. She encountered the predictable opposition until Rabbi Max Dienemann in Offenbach ordained her on December 27, 1935 and thus made the thirty-three-year-old the first female rabbi in history. Jones gave sermons and performed pastoral duties working among Berlin's Jewish community—a role she continued after she was deported to the Czech Ghetto Theriesenstadt in November 1942. She was murdered at forty-two in Auschwitz on December 12, 1944. Though Regina never stopped fighting or challenging the rabbinical patriarchy, her place in Judaic history was largely swept aside.

WE'RE MOVING ON UP!

On December 12, 1950, Paula Ackerman became the interim "spiritual leader" of Temple Beth Israel in Meridian, Mississippi, after her husband (the congregation's rabbi) passed away. Although she lacked official ordination, the state of Mississippi permitted her to perform marriages. She was allowed to *act* as a rabbi because of a result of a ruling in Reform Judaism.

She was born Paula Herskovitz and married Rabbi William Ackerman in 1919. As a *rebbitzin* (rabbi's wife), she taught in the Hebrew school, helped out with the sisterhood, and even took her husband's place on the pulpit whenever he was absent or ill.

After her husband died, fifty-seven-year-old Paula was asked to temporarily fill in until the synagogue could get another rabbi. Ackerman saw the challenge as giving her life meaning by opening doors for women to train for congregational leadership.

She steered Beth Israel for the next three years, leading services, officiating at events, and participating in meetings of Mississippi rabbis. In 1962, however, when the rabbi of Ackerman's childhood synagogue, in Pensacola, Florida, suddenly quit she agreed to return temporarily to hold that congregation together as well.

> **I**n 1946, Helen Levinthal Lyons, although not ordained, was the first woman to graduate from a recognized rabbinical school—now known as the Hebrew Union College-Jewish Institute of Religion.

Twelve-year-old Judith Kaplan Eisenstein (1909–1996) became the first American female to celebrate a bat mitzvah. Known as "Daughter of the Bat Mitzvah," she was the eldest daughter of German-born Lena (Rubin) and Lithuanian-born Rabbi Mordecai Kaplan, the founder of Reconstructionist Judaism. The rabbi believed that girls should have the same religious opportunities as their brothers, and arranged for his daughter to read Torah on a Shabbat morning, March 18, 1922, at his synagogue, the Society for the Advancement of Judaism. Although she was not allowed to read from the Torah scroll as modern bat mitzvah celebrants do, she read a passage in Hebrew and English from a printed *Chumash* (first five books of the Bible) after the regular Torah service.

Judith, a musical prodigy, married Ira Eisenstein (Kaplan's successor in the Reconstructionist movement) and then went on to a successful career in Jewish music. After studying at the Institute of Musical Art (now the Julliard School), she attended the Jewish Theological Seminary (JTS) Teachers Institute and Columbia University's Teachers College, where she earned an MA in music education in 1932. In 1996, she earned a PhD from the School of Sacred Music at Hebrew Union College-Jewish Institute of

Religion (HUC-JIR). She wrote many Jewish songs (on her own and with her husband), published the first Jewish songbook for children, and taught at the Jewish Theological Seminary Teachers Institute and the Reconstructionist Rabbinical College. She and her husband had four children. In 1992, eighty-two-year-old Kaplan Eisenstein celebrated a second bat mitzvah, surrounded by leaders of the modern Jewish feminist movement. This time, she read from a Torah scroll. She died on February 14, 1996.

By 1948, about a third of Conservative congregations held bat mitzvah ceremonies. By the 1960s, the bat mitzvah was a regular feature of Conservative congregational life. Today, it is a mainstay in synagogues from Reform to Modern Orthodox.

THE MODERN FEMALE RABBINATE

In 1972, Sally Priesand became the first ordained female rabbi in the United States. (Currently, there are over two hundred female Reform rabbis and fifty-five female Reconstructionist rabbis.)

ℊroundbreakers:

SALLY PRIESAND, AMERICA'S FIRST FEMALE RABBI

"Say little, Do much." —Rabbi Sally J. Priesand

On October 23, 1973, at the invitation of Congresswoman Bella Abzug, Rabbi Sally J. Priesand offered the opening prayer in the United States House of Representatives. According to Abzug, Priesand was not only the first Jewish woman, but the first woman to be accorded this honor.

Sally Priesand was born on June 27, 1946, into a Conservative Jewish family in Cleveland, Ohio. She had a burning desire to teach Judaism, and on June 3, 1972, she became America's first female rabbi. Since 1981, she has served as the rabbi of Monmouth Reform Temple and is a leader of the Reform Movement.

Rabbi Priesand shared the following letter she wrote to her mother on March 9, 2000.

"Dear Mom: ... On public occasions, I have often thanked you and Dad for giving me what I consider one of the greatest gifts any parent can give a child: the courage to dare and to dream. Your love and support enabled me to accomplish my goal and become a rabbi at a time when there were no women rabbis. I have neglected to tell you, however, what a wonderful role model you have been for me. You are always willing to help others, and watching you has made me a more compassionate person. Whenever people compliment me on my sensitivity, I always give you the credit. The Talmud teaches that in each and every generation there are thirty-six righteous people (*lamed vavniks*) for whose sake the world continues to exist. ... I truly believe that you are one of the thirty-six! ... know how proud I am of you! Much love, Sally"

On the occasion of her ordination, she said, " ... Even in Reform Judaism, [women] were not permitted to participate fully in the life of the synagogue. With my ordination all that was going to change; one more barrier was about to be broken. ... I decided to do this so that I would be the first woman rabbi to carry a torch for the feminist movement."

Although the Reform movement began ordaining women in 1972, the Conservative movement took another decade to do so. Amy Eilberg was enrolled at the Jewish Theological Seminary (JTS) when the school's faculty voted, on October 24, 1983, to admit women to the rabbinical program. Eilberg enrolled as a rabbinical student in 1984. When the JTS decided to ordain women the following year, Amy—after a long struggle within the Conservative movement—was the first to be ordained.

In the twenty years since her ordination, she has been passionately involved in health care and is a national leader in the Jewish healing movement. She was a cofounder of the Bay Area Jewish Healing Center and directed the Center's Jewish Hospice Care program.

In 1988, she contributed new rituals for women and couples grieving after a miscarriage or an abortion to an updated edition of the Conservative movement's rabbinic manual, Moreh Derekh, as well as creating a ritual for women healing from sexual violence.

Rabbi Eilberg is married to Dr. Louis Newman and is the mother of a daughter, Penina Tova, and two stepsons, Etan and Jonah Newman.

JEWISH MOTHER RABBIS—A DIFFERENCE

Just as women bring their own special contributions and experience to the world, female rabbis, and those with children, also bring a unique point of view to the rabbinate. They often offer a closer, more intimate relationship with their congregants than many of their male counterparts.

Along with their strength, women are good and caring listeners and able to relate spiritually to feminine issues, such as child-rearing, domestic violence, and menopause. Furthermore, female congregants are also more comfortable discussing these issues with another female: The woman-to-woman connection can be a powerful support.

Many female Reform rabbis, instead of wanting to shed ritual, want to make more ritual—but new ones. And so they have.

Women in the rabbinate have made it possible for women to mark the milestones in their lives in Jewish ways. They've created rituals for menarche, menopause, weaning, miscarriage, and abortion and they are responsible for making the ceremony for bringing a new daughter into the covenant as prominent in rabbis' manuals as *brit milah*. This contribution goes beyond women's ceremonies. There are now new rituals for men as well as women: rituals for retirement, new rituals for divorce, gay and lesbian commitment ceremonies, and rituals for becoming a grandparent.

THE MOMMY TRACK

In a 2003 article in the *Jewish Journal*, Ellen Jaffe-Gill reports on the special challenges and reach of the female rabbi. Gill noted that many rabbis are finding that the pulpit rabbinate is incompatible with being a mom—especially when their children are young–and therefore don't opt for congregational leadership.

Many choose administrative, communal, teaching, officiating at special life events, or part-time work as alternatives. Of course, "part-time" for a rabbi is often forty hours a week, and the "usual" days off for most are days "on"—Friday nights and Saturday. While other moms are doing "family stuff," these moms are working.

Invariably, female rabbis often face the "Whose mother are you?" queries from their children. These can be even more torturous for rabbis, whose role is to provide learning and spiritual guidance. Reconciling the time spent with congregants vs. their own families becomes not merely a scheduling dilemma, but a moral and spiritual one.

And, like other working moms, they must evaluate and self-actualization with traditional roles.

Among the 15 percent of women in the rabbinate who remain in full-time posts at congregations, some passionately voice the benefits of parenting from the pulpit and the congregation wraps its warm embrace around the rabbi's children.

Mothers who are rabbis raise the congregations' consciousness that all rabbis must set limits on the time they give their synagogues. Men as well are evaluating their competing demands. In looking for solutions, some lay people are taking on greater support roles, and in so doing, are developing greater knowledge of ritual as well as the necessary organizational skills.

Women Reform rabbis also are beginning to lead large congregations; for example, ten women currently lead congregations of 1,000 families or more.

RABBI SCHARFMAN, AN ORGANIZING MAVEN,
BROUGHT HER SKILLS TO HER NEW POSITION AS
THE FIRST ORDAINED FEMALE RABBI
IN HER COMMUNITY.

HYMIE, THE PRESIDENT OF THE SYNAGOGUE, VISITED
AND SAW SHE HAD THREE BASKETS ON HER DESK.

"WHAT'S THIS?" HE ASKED, PUZZLED.

"I'M ORGANIZING MY PAPERWORK IN ORDER OF
SUBJECT," SHE REPLIED, CHEERFULLY. "THE FIRST
IS 'TOP SACRED,' THE SECOND IS 'SACRED.'"

"AND THE THIRD . . . ?" ASKED HYMIE.

"I CALL IT, 'OY, DON'T ASK!'"

Yocheved Mintz, wife, mother, grandmother, teacher, is now the only female rabbi in Las Vegas, Nevada, and is following her family tradition. She comes from generations of rabbis, but she is the only female.

"My grandfather was head of the Orthodox community in Cleveland, so there was concern he would disapprove. I asked a family member how grandfather, who we called 'Abba' (patriarch), might have felt about my ordination. I was told that when my uncle, who was head of a synagogue in Buffalo, asked Abba how he would feel if he were to become head of a Reform Temple, Abba's reply was, 'Who better?' The day I was ordained, May 31, 2004, I viscerally felt the presence of Abba, my parents, in-laws, and all of the past generations approving. There were lots of tears. My husband felt it too.

"My mother and mother-in-law were born in Europe," she says. "My mother was a wonderful storyteller, writer, and linguist. She suffered a massive stroke six years before she died—she lost her language sense. She was a very brave woman, who let me go away to school. She provided a home where my brothers and I were Jewish down to our corpuscles." Their home was filled with Jewish books, and Friday night Shabbat was filled with *guests.* "We were very close to our grandparents . . . and were active in the synagogue. I developed a strong sense of Zionism."

"Keeping kosher was just a part of who you were," says Rabbi Mintz, who added supporting Jewish philanthropies was also important.

"The Jewish mother has a strong sense of heritage and she also has a very strong responsibility to Judaism."

Rabbi Mintz, a pulpit rabbi, also spends a good deal of her time working toward helping the burgeoning Jewish community in Las Vegas. She also uses her role as a director of the Las Vegas Jewish Center for Education, Media, and the Arts (LVJ-CEMA) to assist the community in various creative endeavors.

REBBETZINS (MATES OF RABBIS)

The wife of the rabbi has always had a critical role to play in the community, and many were revered as leaders themselves.

She shared communal leadership as well as led prayers. The Talmud discussions mention Beruria, the wife of Rabbi Meir, who was an expert in Jewish law and lore in the rabbinic era.

Rabbi Eleazar of Worms (1165–1230) praised his wife for her active religious and cultural life in the community.

In the biographies of Rabbi Judah Loew (1525–1609), the Maharal of Prague, we learn that when he and his wife, Pearl Loew, were promised at age six, she studied secretly, and was, in her own right, a Torah scholar and Talmudist.

Many rebbetzins had their own following. Sarale (1838–1937), wife of Reb Hayyim Shmuel Horowitz-Sternfeld, acted as a rabbi, as did her daughter, Hannah, who was the wife of Reb Elimelekh of Grodzisk (1892).

Rabbis' wives, despite their enormous contributions to their mates and congregations, have been given short-shrift in history. We do know that among the East European shtetl Jews, the rabbi's wife was quite often also the bread winner. A role model, she was expected to be a superb wife and mother, while exhibiting piety and learning. But her priority was maintaining her husband's standing in the community.

Perhaps one of the most fascinating rebbetzins (and God knows, patient) was the beloved Ruth Cohen Frisch, daughter of Galveston's popular Rabbi Henry Cohen.

Oy, did she get her "spirited" husband, radical Rabbi Ephraim Frisch, out of *tsouris* (trouble) and controversy more than once after he took the pulpit at San Antonio's Temple Beth-El in 1923. The rabbi was an avid New Dealer and friend of Clarence Darrow and Diego Rivera; sometimes he went . . . a *bissel* overboard, for example, when he blessed the hogs at the Stock Show on radio.

Rabbi Frisch's controversial views also got him into hot water when he chastised San Antonio's wealthy for ignoring poverty and disease in the Mexican barrio; criticized congregants who fought unionization of their factories; and ridiculed legislators who sought to ban evolution from being taught in the schools. He also angered a number of people when he backed pecan shellers in their strike against employers that included some of his congregants.

Yet his rebbetzin, wife Ruth, while also progressive, used her wit, warmth, and persuasiveness to smooth her husband's rough and tumble edges.

In addition to motherhood, Ruth held classes for youngsters, steering a number of children into the arts. At a later time in history, she might have been a writer, a pianist, or even a rabbi. In 1942, when she died from Hodgkins disease, her husband sunk into depression and "retired"—with the help of his congregation.

What do you call the husband of a rabbi? Why "hubbitzen," of course, quips Rabbi Yocheved Mintz, or adds . . . "or lucky . . . or doctors!"

FEMINISM AND ACTIVISM

With our commandment to "heal the world," plus our verbal acuity, not to mention our chutzpah, it's not surprising that Jewish women and Jewish mothers have been intricately involved in activism and feminism. In fact, given our significant social role, we may indeed have been the "first feminists."

NOTE: In scouring the contributions of the Jewish mother and activism, the list is no less than encyclopedic. The women I've chosen to highlight are not only formidable, but are meant to be representative of the vast numbers who have contributed mightily: to their religion, to all women, and in doing so, to the world. Many of those I couldn't include are noted in the appendix in "From These Roots: Jewish Mothers to Us All."

> "To be seen and not heard is not a role, and not who we are."
> —Rabbi Shira Stern

"Many people will say that women in the Bible are subservient, silent, not leaders," says Rabbi Shira Stern, who feels this is not an accurate picture. "Miriam was as important on the Exodus Journey and was seen as leader among the people. Deborah was a prophet [and strategist]. There have been a variety of ways in which women were instrumental in changing the course of Jewish history. Jewish women do stand out and influence even when they live traditionally."

In the morning blessings, traditionally men and boys recite the following: "Blessed are You, HaShem, our God, King of the universe, for not having made me a woman."

"When men thank God for making them men, it is really a recognition of the overwhelming responsibility of the female who has the weight of everything on her shoulders," says Rabbi Felipe Goodman.

The Recording Angel needed a new Executive in Heaven.

The first applicant arrived. "I was a lawyer."

"Excellent," said the Angel, "but I give a quiz to all applicants. Spell 'God.'"

"G—O—D."

The second applicant arrived. "I was a CEO."

"Impressive! First, a quiz. Spell 'God.'"

"G—O—D."

A woman approached. "I worked for a powerful man. I did everything and he got the credit." "Sure," said the Angel, "but there's a little quiz. . . ."

"Oy! Because I'm a woman I was harassed by chauvinists. I thought it would be different here."

"It is!" said the Angel. "I give this quiz to all applicants. Spell . . . 'Antidisestablishmentarianism.'"

Rabbi Yocheved Mintz has a slightly different take. "The *Artscroll Siddur* (an Orthodox prayer book) comments: The Torah assigns missions to respective groups of people. . . . Male, free Jews have responsibilities and duties not shared by others. For this, they express gratitude that, unlike women, they were not freed from the obligation to perform the time-related commandments. The topic is an interesting one," she says, "and the above explanation works within a traditional setting. However, in contemporary times, more liberal Jews have taken offense to the wording, as it seems to come across as sexist and somewhat demeaning to women. That particular part of the morning blessings is totally absent in the Reconstructionist siddur, and the modern Conservative prayer book says 'for making me in the divine image.'

"*M*other was an activist. A public speaker on Jewish subjects. She won many awards from the Jewish community. She was the first woman professional in Denmark in an executive position with JCC. Yet, she loved tradition and did keep Shabbat. Shabbat was her day of rest—from the Jewish community."

—Jody Lopatin

TZEDAKAH AND SOCIAL SERVICE

In Hebrew, there is no special word for "charity," as the Hebrew prophets held that social injustice is the cause of poverty. The word, "*tzedakah*," then means "justice"—that which is right, in the sense of piety. According to the Talmud, donors are given the opportunity to perform a mitzvah or commandment, based on the belief that all earthly possessions belong to God and that one's worth is measured in good *deeds*, not in material goods.

One can't be considered pious unless one lives a righteous and just life, and that requires devotion to helping the needy. The poor, both Jew and non-Jew, shall not be denied the feelings of joy and self-esteem that derive from performing the mitzvah of *tzedakah*. As the Talmud teaches: "When a person gives even a *perutah* (the smallest coin) he or she is privileged to sense God's presence."

The most famous formulation of laws concerning the relationship of donor to recipient is Maimonides' Eight Degrees of Charity.

From the lowest to the highest level they are to give
1. but sadly
2. less than is fitting, but in good humor
3. only after having been asked
4. before being asked
5. so that the donor doesn't know who the recipient is

6. so that the recipient doesn't know who the donor is
7. so that neither knows the identity of the other
8. in a manner so that the recipient becomes self-sufficient, thus avoiding the loss of self-respect that may result from receiving the lower degrees.

Seeing the enormous needs that arose in industrial America, *tzedakah* took on an American character and Jewish women acted.

"My mother taught me to sew at seven. Idle hands were sinful. I'm still that way," says Dr. Ruth Gruber. "She would invite the old ladies from the Menorah Home in Brooklyn to our yard for tea and mandelbrot. My grandmother ran a place where relatives stayed. An old man would come around and ask for money—there was always *tzedakah*."

"My mom was someone who taught me a lot about Israel," said the late mogul producer, Aaron Spelling, during a 1993 dinner of the American Friends of the Hebrew University, when he announced his family's Foundation for the Performing Arts (Jerusalem campus). "She had a little blue and white tin can with a slit on top, which she called her *pushke*. Every night, when my dad went to sleep, she would go through his trousers and gather up the change and put it in the pushke. And when I got paid for my paper route on Thursday afternoon, I would have to put a dime in the pushke."

$\mathcal{G}$roundbreakers:
HANNAH GREENEBAUM SOLOMON,
NATIONAL COUNCIL OF JEWISH WOMEN

In her autobiography, Hannah dotes on her children's crayon portraits, her son Herbert's chemistry experiments, and cooking her famous sweet and sour gefilte fish more so than her illustrious career in social service, and founding the National Council of Jewish Women.

Hannah was born in 1858, the fourth of ten children, to Sarah and Michael Greenebaum, German emigres. Her mother organized Chicago's first Jewish Ladies Sewing Society to make clothes for the needy, and during the great Chicago Fire of 1871, their home became a refuge for survivors. The family also helped found Chicago's first Reformed Temple.

At twenty-one, Hannah married kindred spirit Henry Solomon, and they raised three children together. Hannah along with her sister, Henriette Frank, became disturbed over the status of Jewish Women; she became a dynamo for change, and created many social organizations.

In 1890, Hannah organized a national Jewish Women's Congress for the World Columbian Exposition Parliament of Religions. The group became a permanent organization, and the National Council of Jewish Women was born. Hannah was elected its first president and served until 1905 when she was then made honorary president for life. Local chapters were formed in America and Europe. Her involvement in women's issues were widespread, from helping Russian-Jewish immigrants to founding the Chicago Juvenile Court.

Throughout her life, she was dedicated to her twin commitments—family life and civic responsibility.

"Even in our formative years," she wrote, "we children of Sarah and Michael Greenebaum were unconsciously affected by their spirit of joyous citizenship in a beloved country whose reverse side, our parents never forgot, imposed civic obligation."

Hannah Greenebaum Solomon died on December 7, 1942.

At a Jewish National Fund briefing at his Manhattan law firm, Mayor Michael Wildes of Englewood, New Jersey, mentioned the blue and white *pushke* (*tzedakah* box) his mom kept in the kitchen, reported Tim Boxer.

"Excuse me," said Hal Linden, "it's *pishkeh*."

TV's Barney Miller recalled how his mom used to lift him up so he could drop a coin in the *pishkeh*, on the butcher's block. The kids would cry that their nickel was gone and mom would say, "It's alright, they're building a country for the Jews."

ACTIVISM IN POLITICS AND GOVERNMENT

> **D**orothy Jacobs, fifteen, who had spent two years as a three-dollar-a-week buttonhole maker, organized the women in her men's coat shop into a local of the United Garment Workers of America.

As Jewish mothers came to the United States, we brought with us our passion, experience, and fervent belief in righteousness—doing for the community and world—which we viewed as a mitzvah. "Healing" the world was a matter of hard work, strategy, and a "mouth" that was not afraid to tackle the very things we believed in.

Groundbreakers:
DR. RUTH GRUBER, "MOTHER RUTH"

Reader's Digest saluted her as "America's Schindler." During World War II when much of the world turned its back on the Jews of Eastern Europe, the Brooklyn-born Ruth Gruber fought to make a difference and did. Gruber was born in 1911 and earned her PhD at age twenty. In 1944, while she was working for the secretary of the interior, Harold L. Ickes, President Roosevelt sent Gruber on a covert mission to escort 1,000 World War II refugees to America. During the mission, she was hunted by the Nazis as a spy. Afterward, she wrote her book *Haven*, about the experiences—which became a television movie in 2000. Dr. Alex Margulies, who helped develop the CAT-scan and the MRI, was among those rescued. The refugees were given sanctuary on an old army base in Oswego, New York.

In recounting the voyage, Gruber recalls a rabbi conducting a service as the boat passed the Statue of Liberty, and her pride in telling the refugees that the poem on the base was written by Emma Lazarus, an American Jew. President Roosevelt's intent was to see the refugees as "guests" to be sent back to their homelands after the war, although Gruber succeeded in her efforts to allow them to remain. As the quotas remained unchanged, the refugees were just subtracted from that year's quota.

Following the war, Gruber shined global attention on Jewish migration to Palestine and the growth of Israel. She continues to write and advocate for Jews, and is herself a worldwide symbol of Jewish rescue from oppression. When asked of her motivation, the Pulitzer Prize–winning mother of two and grandmother of four says, "I had to do it. FDR was born anti-Semitic. Policy had to be changed." She also says: "All of us must look inside our souls and find the tools to fight injustice wherever it exists. What I wish for the Jewish people is security and peace—and for the Land of Israel to continue to bloom."

One of the most interesting politicos was New Yorker Belle Moskowitz, who was born in 1877. This mother of three used her natural savvy to move in heavy political arenas. A devout social reformer, she cleaned up the "dancing academies"—places poor girls frequented, which were liquor-filled halls with side rooms for rent. The savvy Belle used her knowledge of Tammany Hall involvement to coerce legislation. After her second marriage to social worker and community leader, Henry Moskowitz, the couple arbitrated strikes in the garment industry. Belle also held high positions on the governor's Labor Board and the New York Port Authority, but her most famous role was that of left and right hand to New York governor, Al Smith. Smith rarely made an important decision or appointment without "Mrs. M's" advice, recommendation, or approval. He later wrote: "She had the greatest brain of anybody I ever knew."

"As a feminist, an immigrant, and a Jew, I was perhaps too different from the average Vermont voter, yet it was this identity that inspired me to enter public life and shaped my values," wrote Madeleine Kunin, who was elected the first Jewish and first

Groundbreakers:
BETTY FRIEDAN, BREAKING THROUGH

Betty Friedan, mother of three and journalist, became a revolutionary. When she surveyed two hundred of her college classmates, she learned that many, despite marriage, children, and affluence were depressed and disappointed, as a gap existed between their education and professional accomplishments. So, in 1963 she wrote *The Feminine Mystique*. It became an instant bestseller and spurred women to pursue their own interests. Friedan became a leading advocate for women's rights. The National Organization for Women (NOW) was founded in her hotel room on June 30, 1966, during the Third National Conference of Commissions on the Status of Women. Friedan and twenty-six other women discussed the formation of NOW as a separate civil rights organization dedicated to advancing gender equality. NOW was incorporated on February 10, 1967, with Friedan as its first president and works on critical issues, including economic equality, abortion rights, opposing racism, and ending violence against women.

female governor of Vermont on November 7, 1984. She served until 1991. In 1940, when the Swiss-born governor was six, she and her widowed mother escaped the Nazis threat and sailed to the United States on the last ship leaving Italy.

Kunin grew up in Pittsfield, Massachusetts, and attended the University of Massachusetts, Amherst, on a scholarship. She received a master's degree from the Columbia School of Journalism in 1957. When she moved to Burlington, Vermont, to work for the *Burlington Free Press*, she met and married Dr. Arthur Kunin. The couple had four children but divorced in 1995. While devoting herself to her family, she became an active community organizer, focusing on health care legislation and community safety. She was elected to the state legislature in 1972. Here, she gathered support for the ERA, and worked on the environment, education, and the welfare of families and children. In 1984, she was elected governor, and served three terms. Among her many achievements was the creation of a family court. In 1993, she became the U.S. deputy secretary of education, and in 1996, President Clinton appointed her U.S. ambassador to Switzerland. In February of 2006, at seventy-two, she married John W. Hennessey Jr., a fellow trustee of the University of Vermont. *Both* describe themselves as feminists. Mr. Hennessey said feminism is "in my genes," adding that his mother marched in the suffragist movement as a student at Vassar College in 1916.

In 1988, the day after Lenore (Lyn) Pancoe Meyerhoff's death from stomach cancer at age sixty, the lead editorial in the *Baltimore Sun* began: "Just the other day, Lyn Meyerhoff strolled into one of Baltimore's fancier eateries. . . . Hatless, wigless. . . . 'I'm fighting this monster,' she remarked, and then quickly launched into an electric conversation about the Baltimore Symphony's tour of the Soviet Union (her idea), Jeane Kirkpatrick's prospects for the presidency (her idea), and the work of a think tank in Israel. . . . (her idea)."

⚬ Groundbreakers:

BELLA ABZUG, FIRST WOMAN ELECTED TO U.S. CONGRESS ON A WOMEN'S RIGHTS/PEACE PLATFORM

Bella Abzug was born July 24, 1920 in the Bronx, and elected to Congress at fifty. As daughter Eve proclaimed: "We got her out of our house and into your House"—and with her famous hat in place she didn't merely rip the glass ceiling, she shattered it.

Bella's Hebrew schoolteacher recruited her to a labor Zionist group, Hashomer Hatzair (the young guard), and by age eleven, she was giving impassioned speeches.

Her mother, Esther Savitzky, encouraged her daughter when she was thirteen by allowing her to say the Mourner's Prayer for her father, Manny, traditionally done by males.

"Battling Bella" won a scholarship to Columbia University Law School, where she developed two additional passions: poker and

Martin Abzug. They married in 1944. "While I was at Columbia," Bella said, "he typed my term papers. Before we married it was agreed that I would work at my legal career even after we had children." Over the years, Bella pointed repeatedly to Martin's support as her crucial foundation. The couple had two daughters—Eve Gail (Elgee) born in 1949, and Isobel Jo (Liz) born in 1952.

During the 1950s, Bella defended victims of the McCarthy witch hunt. A strong activist, she helped create Women Strike for Peace, and became a prominent spokesperson against poverty, racism, and violence. In 1970 at age fifty, she agreed to run for Congress from New York City and was reelected for three terms. Abzug, called the hardest working member of Congress, was acknowledged by *U.S. News and World Report* as the "third most influential" House member.

Her numerous accomplishments include: sponsoring the Equal Rights Amendment, organizing the National Women's Political Caucus, serving as chief strategist for the Democratic Women's Committee, coauthoring the Freedom of Information Act, the Government in the Sunshine Act, the Right to Privacy Act, introducing the first federal bill to support gay and lesbian civil rights, cofounding the Women's Environment and Development Organization (WEDO), and being an influential leader at UN conferences to empower women around the globe. Despite breast cancer and heart disease, Abzug continued to confront the global problems of poverty and discrimination. Her daughter Liz called Bella "a great politician, a great friend, a great and enlightened mother."

> *"You try to adjust the family situation to the realities of your life. You don't put one ahead of the other. There is a balance, and you strive to keep that balance. The family grows with it. And the kids also know that the mother I am woman, wife, and lawyer. A total person. It makes them better people."*
>
> —Bella Abzug

Bella Abzug's dedication has fortified a global sisterhood never before imagined. At her funeral in 1998, Geraldine Ferraro said: "She didn't knock politely on the door. ... She took it off the hinges forever."

She grew up in the 1930s in one of the few Jewish families on Chicago's North Shore. She was the fifth child of a Jewish family in Wilmette, Illinois. Lyn Meyerhoff was a major figure in Maryland Republican politics, and blended her amazing skills as politician, networker, fund-raiser—and most important to her, mother. She served in President Ford's administration on the Council of International Economic Policy and worked with the Reagan administration while continuing to support Planned Parenthood and oppose efforts to reinstitute public school prayer.

"Most of what Mom stood for has a corollary in the Eyshet Hayil. 'The Woman of Valor,'" wrote her daughter, Lee M. Hendler. Meyerhoff believed it was her duty to confront injustice head on. "We are what we do, not what we say," was a favorite maxim. She was a vociferous advocate for the Jewish State from her very first federation visit to Israel in the 1950s. She was a member of Hadassah's Society of Major Donors, a charter member of Israel Bonds' president's and prime minister's clubs, and on a first-name basis with many of Israel's leaders, from Golda Meir to Bibi Netanyahu. She also founded the Jeane Kirkpatrick Forum at Tel Aviv University to encourage American/Israeli dialogue. In 1993, she served as one of three presidentially appointed public delegates to the United Nations. This amazing activist was committed to her role as wife and mother—and her vibrant, nonconformist personality and humor shined through.

Her daughter, Lee, wrote: "She hated to cook, preferred puppies to babies, refused to sew, and sent us to school pageants dressed in the wrong outfits, saying 'I'll be able to see you better!'" She could drive a farm tractor, tame a wild raccoon, raise chickens (that she gave away as party favors), catch fish, "woman" a truck, and captain a boat. Oh, and she was known to drop to the floor in full evening dress to challenge a fellow partygoer to one-armed push-ups. But she also lit candles on Shabbat and grew weepy at flag raisings. Her most ardent acts, apart from her response to the Holocaust, could be found in her leadership and philanthropy.

She was ashamed by Roosevelt's cowardice and horrified by how little America had done to combat the Holocaust, and was one of the first to articulate an American vision and rationale for the United States Holocaust Memorial Museum—for which she raised $1 million in just one morning from fifty non-Jewish business leaders.

She let her children "laugh but allowed us to cry. . . . Mom's life was one long lesson in attention. Life matters, she taught. Pay attention. Do your best."

$\mathcal{G}$roundbreakers:
RUTH BADER GINSBURG, FIRST FEMALE JEWISH SUPREME COURT JUSTICE

Ruth Bader Ginsburg was known as a "centrist" when she was sworn in as the 107th justice to the United States Supreme Court. On August 10, 1993, she became the second woman to sit on the court and the first Jewish justice since 1969.

She was born on March 15, 1933, the daughter of Celia and Nathan Bader of Brooklyn, New York. Her mother had a strong passion for reading, language, and a love of books, putting Jewish tradition in the context more of doing justice than of observance and pushed her daughter hard to succeed. Having felt the sting of discrimination, Ginsburg became the first woman to be tenured on the Columbia University law faculty—her mission to open up doors for everyone. She was also codirector of the ACLU's Women's Rights Project, working extensively on sex-discrimination cases, arguing and establishing that constitutional protections should apply to women—thereby establishing that differential treatment based on gender was unconstitutional.

In 1954, she married Martin Ginsburg, a well-known tax lawyer and professor. They have two children, one of whom is a law professor at Columbia.

Ginsburg was often referred to as the Thurgood Marshall of the women's rights movement and has a reputation for logic, reason, and realistic pragmatism.

Justice Ginsburg has pointed proudly to Judaism's eternal pursuit of justice, the promise of America, and the accomplishments of Jewish women who have preceded her.

Cohen, mayor of an Israeli town, passed a construction site with his wife. A construction worker called out to the woman.

"Sara . . . how are you?"

"Avi! Nice to see you again," she replied. Then she introduced her husband. After a short chat, they continued on.

"How do you know such a man?" asked the mayor.

"We were sweethearts in school. I almost married him."

He laughed. "See how lucky you are? If I hadn't married you, today you would be married to a construction worker!"

"If I had married him," said his wife, "so now *he'd* be the mayor."

ACTIVISM IN THE WRITING AND MEDIA

Minna Kleeberg received an excellent education in Germany and by the time she arrived in the United States in 1866, she was a well-regarded poet, known for her passion for social justice and her faith.

After her marriage to Rabbi L. Kleeberg, her poetry turned to liturgical creations, while continuing to serve as a vehicle for social expression. Her poetry was also feminist—before the word existed—and called for democracy and the emancipation of women. She also wrote verses on the joys and sorrows of domestic life, addressing these to her children.

A collection of her poems, *Gedichte*, was published in 1877 in Louisville, Kentucky, where her husband was serving as rabbi.

Groundbreakers:
BARBARA WALTERS, FIRST LADY OF NEWS

Barbara Walters was born into show business in Massachussetts, on September 25, 1931. She is the daughter of Dena and Lou Walters, a nightclub owner. Walter's mentally challenged sister no doubt honed her ability to create a special intimacy with her subjects.

After receiving her degree from Sarah Lawrence College, Barbara was hired by RCA-TV, NBC's local affiliate in New York City. Dave Garaway recognized her talent and made her a staff writer. She was soon doing on-air stories and became the first female cohost of the *Today Show*, a post she held for fifteen years. In 1976, she became the first female coanchor in prime-time network news at ABC, and she coanchored *20/20* from 1984 until 2004. Walters, who has one daughter, Jacqueline, holds the distinction of interviewing every U.S. president and first lady since the Nixons. Although her notable interviews include every "who's who" in the world, a special groundbreaking moment occurred in 1977 when she arranged the first joint interview between Menachem Begin and Anwar el-Sádát. Another "first" was her prime-time interview with Fidel Castro, which received worldwide attention.

Now creator, co-owner, coexecutive producer, and cohost of *The View*, this legendary lady has all but turned the glass ceiling in the newsroom to sand.

Dialoguing has long been a passion of Blu Greenberg, Orthodox feminist, author, and lecturer. Her books include *On Women and Judaism: A View from Tradition*; *How to Run a Traditional Jewish Household*; *Black Bread: Poems After the Holocaust*; and a children's book coauthored with Reverend Linda Tarry, *King Solomon and the Queen of Sheba*.

Since 1973, she has been active in the movement to bridge feminism and Orthodox Judaism. Amoong her many remarkable achievements, she is a founding president of JOFA, the Jewish Orthodox Feminist Alliance and cofounder of Women of Faith. She has been an active participant in the Dialogue Project and the Multi-Religious Women's Network (2000). In 1997 and 1998, she chaired the International Conference(s) on Feminism and Orthodoxy.

Blu has an abiding belief in interfaith and interethnic issues. She was first chair of the Federation Task Force on Jewish women.

She attended, among other conferences, the Jewish Tibetan encounter in Dharmasala in 1990 and the World Conference of Religious Leaders in Bangkok in 2002.

She is past chair or president of the Jewish Book Council and the Federation Commission on Synagogue Relations, and she serves on the editorial board of *Hadassah* magazine and the advisory board of *Lilith* magazine.

Blu Greenberg received a bachelor's degree from Brooklyn College in political science, a master's degree from the City University in clinical psychology, and a master's from Yeshiva University in Jewish history. She taught religious studies at the College of Mount St. Vincent from 1965 to 1973, and during a sabbatical, lectured at Pardes Institute in Jerusalem.

She is a deeply caring and accessible woman, a great pioneer, and an inspiration to her readers, the Jewish community, and to her beloved family.

Blu Greenberg is listed in *Who's Who in America* and *Who's Who in World Jewry*. Her papers were recently archived at the Schlesinger Library in Cambridge, Massachusetts.

This remarkable woman is married to Rabbi Irving Greenberg, who is a firm supporter of his wife's work. They have five children and nineteen grandchildren.

Letty Cottin Pogrebin is a premier journalist and author, and is a critical voice who combines feminist ideas with Jewish values.

She was born on June 9, 1939, to Cyral and Jacob Cottin. Her father was an attorney and her mother a designer. She was raised in an observant Conservative household in Queens, New York. In 1955, when she wasn't allowed to participate in the *kaddish minyan* following her mother's death, she rejected the patriarchal rituals of Judaism. She didn't rejoin organized Judaism until 1975, when the United Nations International Women's Decade Conference passed a resolution equating Zionism with racism. In 1959, after receiving her BA from Brandeis University, she became active in the American feminist movement, and in 1971, she was one of the founding editors of *Ms.* magazine, where she worked for seventeen years. Her name continues to appear on the masthead.

In 1970, Pogrebin published *How to Make It in a Man's World*, and the following year, she was one of the founders of the National Women's Political Caucus. She also consulted with Marlo Thomas on the breakthrough album *Free to Be You and Me*.

She has been influential in MAZON: A Jewish Response to Hunger, the Jewish Fund for Justice, the New Israel Fund, and the American Jewish Congress Commission on Women's Equality. She is a past president of Americans for Peace Now, spent five years in a Jewish-Palestinian dialogue project, and has also been active in dialogue efforts between Blacks and Jews.

Her memoir, *Deborah, Golda, and Me: Being Female and Jewish in America* (1991), delves into her own work, merging Judaism and feminism. *Getting Over Getting Older* (1996), deals frankly with the struggles and joys of aging.

She is still active in progressive and feminist politics, lectures frequently, and is also a regular contributor to *Moment* magazine.

Susan Weidman Schneider's *Jewish and Female: Choices and Changes in Our Lives Today* (1984) codifies two decades of Jewish feminist thinking. She was poised to write the book, as she was a "founding mother," and since 1976 has been the editor in chief of *Lilith*, an independent Jewish Women's Magazine. *Lilith* has now chronicled nearly three decades of Jewish feminism for its estimated readership of 25,000.

In addition to an active lecture schedule, she has regularly been invited to address the General Assembly of the Council of Jewish Federations and Welfare Funds. She has also published *Intermarriage: The Challenge of Living with Differences between Christians and Jews* (1990), and in 1991, she coauthored (with Arthur B. C. Drache) *Head and Heart: A Woman's Guide to Financial Independence*.

Susan was born in Winnipeg, Manitoba, in a tightly knit Jewish community. Her studies at Brandeis University during the 1960s helped hone her social consciousness and exposed her to the burgeoning feminist movement.

When she made a trip to Israel with her husband, Bruce Schneider, a physician, and their two-year-old, she was very impressed with the acceptance of working mothers and the accessibility of child care in that country. When she returned to the United States, she wrote and lectured about women's issues and the difficulty in realizing meaningful lives as both Jews and women.

In 1973, when Jewish magazines were edited by men, she knew it was time for a Jewish feminist magazine: *Lilith* was born and has advocated for women in all aspects of religious, spiritual, and philanthropic life.

Weidman Schneider is the mother of three grown children: Benjamin, Rachel, and Yael.

On January 3, 2006, fifty-five-year-old Wendy Wasserstein died of lymphoma and many of us felt as if they had lost a friend, besides a great writer and playwright. Her poignant, funny, and wry books and plays touched the souls of both Jews and non-Jews everywhere.

Born and raised in New York City, she was educated at Mount Holyoke College and the Yale School of Drama. When Wendy won the Tony Award for best play for *The Heidi Chronicles* in 1989, she was the first woman ever to do so. The play also garnered a Pulitzer Prize for drama, the New York Drama Critics Circle Award, the Drama Desk Award, and the Susan Blackburn Prize.

Wasserstein explored the females of our time through her writing and plays. *Chronicles* and *The Sisters Rosensweig* (1992), for example, examine the modern woman, and the issues of sexism, marriage, and careers.

Hit by the "too Jewish" criticism by some, her response has been: "When your name is Wendy Wasserstein and you're from New York, you are the walking embodiment of 'too Jewish.'"

The feminist writer became a Jewish mother in 1999.

ACTIVISM IN THE ARTS AND ENTERTAINMENT

Sophie Tucker (Sophia Kalish), the "Last of the Red Hot Mamas," was born "on the road" in the 1880s while her mother was fleeing Poland to join her husband. Her observant family settled in Hartford and ran a kosher diner and rooming house. Tucker, who was surrounded by theater performers, began singing for the customers.

Sophie's short-lived marriage to Louis Tuck at age sixteen produced one son. But Sophie still had plans to move on. However, she was so overweight that her early managers insisted she hide behind black face. In 1908, she lost the detested makeup. By 1909, her career skyrocketed with the Ziegfeld follies and grew for sixty years with her signature song, "Some of These Days" (1911), written by African American songwriter Shelton Brooks, and of course, "My Yiddishe Mama," written in 1925 by Jack Yellen and Lew Pollack, which she sang in both Yiddish and English. In 1931, the gutsy Tucker broadcast "My Yiddishe Mama" over Berlin radio. During Hitler's reign, her records were smashed in Germany, and in 1932 the song nearly set off an anti-Semitic riot during a performance in France.

Starting in 1922, the *3-D Mama with the Big Wide Screen* toured England, giving command performances in 1934 and 1962, but her proudest moment was when London's Jews gave her an ovation at Whitechapel's Rivoli Theatre.

Tucker headlined at Manhattan's Latin Quarter in 1966, just before she died at eighty-two.

Her philanthropy included contributions to actors guilds, Jewish and Zionist causes, synagogues, and hospitals.

She was big, brassy, and talented, and her "hot" songs were done with humor and a sense of her own power. Tucker's work challenged stereotypes of age, size, gender, and Jewish women's sexuality.

$\mathcal{G}$roundbreakers:

GERTRUDE BERG, "YOO-HOO, MRS. BLOOM?"

Molly Goldberg, played by the magnificent writer/producer/actor Gertrude Berg, was the quintessential Jewish mother both on radio and on TV in *The Goldbergs*.

She was born in the Jewish Harlem section of New York City in 1899 and was the only child of Dinah and Jacob Edelstein. The Edelsteins operated a boarding house in Fleischmanns, New York, and Gertrude entertained guests by writing and performing skits. It was also where she met her future husband, Lewis Berg, a chemical engineer.

In 1929, she submitted her script for a daily radio show called *The Rise of the Goldbergs*, which began one of the longest and most successful runs on radio and TV. In transitioning *The Goldbergs* from radio to television, she made "Yoo-hoo, Mrs. Bloom," a national buzz-phrase. The character of Molly, written and created by Gertrude Berg, was the problem-solver for her husband Jake, the children, and Uncle David. Her presentation of Jewish life brought pride to its Jewish audience for almost thirty years on radio, then until 1955 on TV. Her Yinglish "Mollypropisms" were legend. "Come sit on the table, dinner is ready," "You'll swallow a cup, darling," "Throw an eye into the icebox and give me an accounting."

The versatile Berg not only created the first sitcom, but long before the Roseannes and Streisands—she was the first female "hyphenate" as both writer-dash-creator. In 1951, she courageously took a stand against the blacklist by refusing to fire costar Philip Loeb—and won. She was concerned about Fascism and the welfare of European Jews and was active in many Jewish groups, which continued during World War II.

Gertrude Berg had two children, Cherney Robert in 1922, and Harriet in 1926. She lived a life of humanity, love, and respect for others—both personally and professionally.

Fanny Brice, born Fania Borach in 1891, the third of four children of immigrant saloon owners, knew her destiny early. At one point, her mother, Rosie Stern, struggled to make a living in the garment center in New York. Years later, Fanny sang "The Song of the Sewing Machine," honoring her mother and others who suffered a similar plight.

Although relegated to "Jewish" roles, she catapulted to fame through the Ziegfeld Follies in 1916, where her timing, accents, and poses often contained social commentary. She was not fluent in Yiddish, but her repertory included brilliant lampoons, wild vamps, Yinglish songs, and comic dances.

She said, "I never did a Jewish routine that would offend my race. . . . I wasn't standing apart making fun. I was the race. . . . They identified with me, which made it all right to get a laugh, because they were laughing at me as much as at themselves."

Brice's personal life was equally filled with drama. In 1918, she married Jules "Nicky" Arnstein, a handsome, sophisticated, but unfaithful and ineffective con. While her husband was in Sing Sing, Brice supported him and their two children by constantly working. Arnstein did give Brice her rare nonethnic hit—a straight performance of "My Man," in 1921, which filled Ziegfeld's audience with tears.

When he was convicted of bond theft and sent to Leavenworth in 1924, Brice stood firmly by "her" man, funding his expensive defense, and waiting for his discharge. When Arnstein was released in 1927, however, he disappeared out of her life. The indomitable Brice had another failed marriage, this time to Billy Rose, but then found her niche in radio in 1938 with the bratty, precocious Baby Snooks character, whose popularity lasted until her death in 1951.

Brice was multitalented: an art expert, costume designer, interior decorator for stars like Eddie Cantor, Danny Kaye, and Dinah Shore—and a minor hypnotist.

Her life became fascinating fodder for film producers. Ray Stark, producer of *Funny Girl* (1968) and *Funny Lady*, succeeded in making the Brice story film legend—for creative and no doubt personal reasons, as his wife was Brice's daughter Fran.

Fanny Brice was truly a comic pioneer, proving that women could create hilarious comedy without relying on blatant sexuality or domestic situations.

Louise Nevelson, one of America's most innovative sculptors, was born in Kiev on September 23, 1899. She was the daughter of Mina Sadie and Isaac Berliawsky and was raised in Rockland, Maine. Louise was influenced by her mother, who was a free thinker, and she knew that her destiny was to be an artist, despite being stigmatized as a Jew. In 1918, after high school, she met and married Charles Nevelson and in 1922, she gave birth to her only child, Myron, who also became a famous sculptor. The marriage failed because her husband expected her to play the role of the affluent Jewish wife. When they separated in 1931, true to her convictions, she never asked for support. She left her son with her parents and continued her art studies in Munich, Germany until the Nazis shut the school down. The first public showing of her sculpture was in 1933 and two years later, her work was part of an exhibit at the Brooklyn Museum. In 1964, Nevelson created *Homage to 6,000,000*, a memorial to Jews of the Holocaust that is in the Israeli Museum. Her huge breakthrough came in 1967, with a show at the Whitney Museum.

She virtually created environmental sculpture as an artist with large box-shaped pieces made from wood fragments. Among her most important works are *Dawn's Wedding Feast* (1959) and *Atmosphere and Environment XIII: Windows to the West* (1973).

Nevelson was also active on behalf of artists, as president and vice president of various artists' associations. In 1979, she was elected to the American Academy of Arts and Letters. She died in 1988. Today, her works can be found in art museums across the world and are showcased in prominent New York plazas. The largest collection is at the Whitney Museum in New York City. In 2000, the U.S. government issued special Louise Nevelson commemorative stamps in recognition of one of the most important American sculptors of the twentieth century.

$\mathcal{G}$roundbreakers:
BEVERLY SILLS, "BUBBLES"

Beverly Sills, "Bubbles," was born Belle Miriam Silverman Sills, in 1929 in Brooklyn, to Shirley and Morris Silverman, of Russian Jewish descent—and was a true child prodigy.

In 1949, after her father's death, Beverly and her mother lived in a one-bedroom apartment where she sang in a private club to help support them. Her ambition to sing with the New York City Opera Company became reality when she debuted in 1955 and drew critical reviews as Rosalinde in *Die Fledermaus*. By 1958, she was a leading coloratura soprano. The following year she married Peter Buckley Greenough, an Episcopalian with two children, whose family owned the *Cleveland Plain Dealer*.

Despite her loving marriage, she encountered enormous grief when her children, Meredith (Muffy) and Peter Jr., were born with severe birth defects. Sills felt her children represented a turning point, saying, "If I could survive this, I could survive anything." She took time off to devote to them, and then in 1964 resumed her operatic career.

Her mother was a pillar of strength and action. When Muffy went to the Boston School for the Deaf, run by the Sisters of Saint Joseph, grandma Shirley was adamant, despite Catholic ritual. "We've got to get Muffy using a hearing aid and . . . get this child educated."

In 1975, Sills debuted at the Metropolitan Opera in *The Siege of Corinth* and received an eighteen-minute ovation. After retiring from the stage in 1979, she became general director of the New York City Opera, and in 1994, was elected chairman of Lincoln Center for the Performing Arts, a post she held until she retired in 2002. Now, she serves on prestigious boards for the arts in New York and nationally. She's quick to share the credit for her success in juggling career and motherhood with her husband and her mother.

On mothering, Sills has said, "There's only one leader in the house, and she's it. . . . I raised my children that way. . . . I don't give an inch, and I never did. They tell me I was a very demanding stepmother, and I say, 'That's why you're such nice people today.'"

Sills, who has won the Presidential Medal of Freedom and Kennedy Center Awards, is one of the few women who has been immensely successful as an opera manager, world-renowned coloratura, and humanitarian.

"I love being Jewish. . . .
When I did my first Hanukkah special
with Lamb Chop, I felt I was really putting my
menorah in the window for the first time."

—Shari Lewis

According to author Tim Boxer, when the late great Shari Lewis aired her 1995 PBS special, *Lamb Chop's Special Chanukah*, she was eager to "put [her] menorah in the window" to "enrich the lives of non-Jewish viewers." The creative Lewis invited Pat Morita, the Japanese actor and martial arts expert, to participate. "Why not?" he said. "After all, I'm half ju and half jitsue!"

Lewis, a multiple award winner, was a puppeteer, ventriloquist, producer, author, and a pioneer in children's programming. She used "tough love" on her puppet progenies, Lamb Chop, Charley Horse, and Hush Puppy, and taught values through entertainment. But her most beloved "creation" was her daughter, Mallory, who joined her mom as writer and producer. Since her mother's death in 1998, Mallory has performed with Lamb Chop, and has a very special fan: her son.

Anna Sokolow (1910–2000) was part of the radical dance movement, which fused left-wing politics, Judaic themes, and dance. As a dancer and choreographer, she "felt a deep social sense about what I wanted to express." Her mother, Sarah, was

"*All* the girls hated me because I had such big boobs," Bette Midler told *Rolling Stone* magazine in 1973. "My parents just must have come from really tough stock," she has said. "My mother . . . was really feisty and really speedy, she could get to the store in a minute and a half. . . . She had some energy on her, and I guess I just inherited it." Bette Midler, a divine show business legend and Jewish mother, has spent a lifetime daring to be different. Her talent and moxie have made her dreams a reality.

Bette was born in Hawaii on December 1, 1945, into the only Jewish family in the neighborhood. She got her first big break in *Fiddler on the Roof*, and then became the flamboyant Golden Girl of the gay community. Midler soon reached stellar heights on all fronts: in sold-out concerts, recordings, TV, and in films like *The Rose*, *Down and Out in Beverly Hills*, *Ruthless People*, *Beaches*, and *The First Wives Club*.

both an inspiration and a possible detriment to her career. In 1910, when Sarah Sokolow came to this country, she was quickly forced to take the financial reins when her husband Samuel was diagnosed with Parkinson's disease.

"Eventually my mother, with her great energy, stepped in and took over," Anna later said. The Sokolows had four children and moved to New York City, where Sarah worked in the garment industry. She remained spirited and determined and became an activist: attending trade unions meetings, joining the International Ladies Garment Workers' Union, and participating in union solidarity marches, sometimes even bringing her daughters. She also took her children to Workman's Circle dances and the Yiddish theater.

When Anna told her mother she wanted to be a dancer, she was thrown out of the house. Sarah was convinced that Jewish women should work as teachers or secretaries until they married.

The two eventually reconciled, as Anna continued to pursue the dance, becoming world famous. Her work has reflected the horrors of the Holocaust and her early life in the tenements.

Profiles in Greatness:
BARBRA STREISAND, HEY GORGEOUS!

Barbra Joan Streisand, singer, actor, director, producer, philanthropist, and activist, was born on April 24, 1942, in Brooklyn, and was the second child of Emmanuel and Diana Rosen. Her father died of a cerebral hemorrhage before she turned two, and her mother worked as a bookkeeper to support her daughter and son, Sheldon. In 1949, Diana entered an ill-fated marriage to Louis Kind—she had a daughter, Rosalind (later changed to Roslyn—who also became a singer).

Her mother maintained a kosher home and Barbra went to a Jewish religious school. After graduating from Erasmus High School in 1959 with an A average and a passion for theater, she headed for Manhattan over her mother's protests. She got her start at the famous gay Lion Club, and quickly became a gay icon.

But, at nineteen, it was as Miss Marmelstein in Broadway's *I Can Get It for You Wholesale* that launched her stellar career. In 1963, she married costar Elliott Gould and in 1966, gave birth to Jason Emmanuel. Despite their divorce, they hosted Jason's bar mitzvah together.

From the start, Streisand had to fight the "too Jewish, too New York" image.

Her Oscar-winning role in *Funny Girl* (1968) sent her career into orbit and *The Way We Were* (1973) kept it there. The movie's theme then became her first number-one hit song.

In 1983, she produced and directed *Yentl*, an adaptation of Isaac Bashevis Singer's story, which was clearly a project of meaning for her. Since the 1960s, she has won more varied awards (Emmy, Grammy, Oscar, special Tony) than anyone else in show business, and has sold more records than any singer(s) except the Beatles. She has starred in sixteen major movies, three of which she directed, and her concerts remain huge events.

Streisand's a champion of humane and political causes and has raised a fortune for Democratic candidates, Jewish charities in the United States and Israel, and environmental and AIDS projects. The AIDS Project Los Angeles gave her its Commitment to Life Award (1992), the ACLU, its Bill of Rights Award and, in 2004, she received the Humanitarian Award from the Human Rights Campaign.

Barbra Streisand has bucked the system by insisting on control of her projects, and assiduously maintaining her "too Jewish" identity and sensibility. By doing so, she has shattered Hollywood stereotypes, conquering virtually every area of show business—and she has done it in her own, uncompromising style. In her sixties now, and for all time, she will be hailed: "Hey Gorgeous!"

ACTIVISM IN ACADEMIA

"The Germans had to be educated in violent anti-Semitism; the Austrians erupted with it spontaneously," wrote Dr. Gerda Lerner, a Jew, of her countrymen and women. "Within weeks of the Anschluss, the situation of Jews in Austria was far worse than that of Jews in Germany five years after the Nazi takeover."

Dr. Lerner was well aware of the horrors she wrote about and eventually became the godmother of women's history.

Her commitment to political struggle undoubtedly began in Vienna in 1934, when she heard the sounds of war from her family's darkened apartment. "I said to myself, this I can't live with."

She was born Gerda Kronstein, the first child of an affluent Jewish couple, Ilona and Robert Kronstein. Her father was a pharmacist, and her mother was a frustrated artist.

Dr. Lerner has written at length about her difficult relationship with her mother, who survived a concentration camp, but died in Europe far from her daughter and her estranged husband. In her 2003 memoir, *Fireweed: A Political Autobiography*, her personal history is inexorably tied to major world events—her family's flight to Liechtenstein, her six weeks in a Nazi prison, and her complicated relationship with her mother, artist Ilona (Ili) Kronstein. Although Lerner managed to get a U.S. visa, her family remained in Europe. Her parents and sister fled throughout Europe while many perished in concentration camps. Ili wrote to her daughter begging her to get her to America, which was impossible given the rigid quotas on immigrants. Yet her mother's letters also described her artistic breakthroughs, while Ili was away from her husband and social constraints. Ili died of multiple sclerosis in Switzerland after the war. Their failure to connect has been a lifelong pain for Dr. Lerner.

When a gaunt and exhausted Dr. Lerner arrived in the United States, she made an unfortunate first marriage just to stay here. Her second marriage to filmmaker Carl Lerner produced a son, a daughter—and a strong political agenda. The couple struggled to unionize the film industry, resisted the Hollywood blacklist, and became active in the civil rights movement.

Dr. Lerner also become a key player in the women's movement, and, at thirty-eight, she began her academic career—pioneering the field of women's history. In 1963, at the New School for Social Research, she taught what may have been the first postwar college course in women's history. In 1972, she established the first graduate program in the field at Sarah Lawrence College, and in 1981, she created a doctoral program at the University of Wisconsin-Madison. She then went on to become the Robinson-Edwards professor of history, emeritae, at the University of Wisconsin-Madison and a Fellow of the Wisconsin Academy of Sciences.

She is the author of eleven history books, has edited the groundbreaking *Black Women in White America: A Documentary History*, one of the first books detailing the contributions of Black women, and released a two-volume study titled *Women and History*, in 1986 and 1993.

Dr. Lerner was the first woman to receive the Bruce Catton Prize for Lifetime Achievement in Historical Writing from the Society of American Historians.

Annie Nathan Meyer, writer, and a founder of Barnard College, was born in New York on February 19, 1867, to Robert Weeks and Annie Florence Nathan, members of the upper-crust Sephardic community. She had a difficult childhood: Her father was a philanderer, his business failed, and her mother descended into depression. Annie prepared herself for college with special tutoring and enrolled in Columbia College. After a year, she married Alfred Meyer, a cousin and prominent physician. The couple had one daughter.

Annie was politically savvy and turned her attention to creating a women's college at Columbia. When she named the college for the institution's recently deceased president, F. A. P. Barnard, she won the support of his widow, and in September 1889, Barnard College was founded. She remained involved with Barnard throughout her life. Meyer wrote twenty-six plays, three novels, an autobiography, and two books of nonfiction. Most of her themes involved career vs. marriage for women.

JEWISH MOTHERS IN SCIENCE

"*M*edical policy on estrogen has been to 'shoot first and apologize later.' . . . Over the years, hundreds of millions, possibly billions of women, have been lab animals in this unofficial trial. They were not volunteers. They were given no consent forms. And they were put at serious, often devastating risk."

—Barbara Seaman

"Don't worry your pretty little head about it," or "It's all in your mind," were typical medical responses to women's concerns until fairly recently. Then there was Barbara Seaman.

Since 1969, Seaman, a medical journalist, has doggedly taken on not only the medical establishment but also the powerful pharmaceutical companies. She exposed their drive for profit at the expense of women's health—notably, slipping drugs to women without their knowing the consequences—and is a leading U.S. advocate for women's health.

In 1959, she watched her forty-nine-year-old aunt succumb to cancer. Her doctor then told her not to take the estrogen-based drug Premarin, as she might have the same susceptibilities. That conversation inspired Seaman to write *The Doctors' Case against the Pill* (1969), which shook up the medical establishment by showing the Pill posed risks of cancer, heart disease, diabetes, and stroke. The book also revealed how very poor women in Puerto Rico were used in the Pill's early testing at very high doses without thorough study. Several died of apparent heart attacks, with little medical attention and no autopsies.

Her book led to Congressional hearings in 1970, but the Senate barred women harmed by the Pill from testifying. These women, however, interrupted the hearings. As a result, birth control pills carry warning labels and for the first time the Federal Drug Administration allowed input from patients.

Seaman has also written *The Greatest Experiment Ever Performed on Women: Exploding the Estrogen Myth* (2003), cofounded the National Women's Health Network, and has published numerous articles and books on women's health and patients' rights. Her work triggered a revolution encouraging women to take their health into their own hands.

In 1947, Dr. Gerty Theresa Radnitz Cori, along with husband Carl F. Cori, and Dr. B. A. Houssay of Argentina, shared the Nobel Prize for Medicine and Physiology.

Gerty, the eldest of three daughters, was born on August 15, 1896, in Prague to Martha and Otto Radnitz. Her uncle, a doctor, urged her to study medicine at the German University of Prague's medical school where she graduated in 1920. She met her husband, Carl Ferdinand Cori, a fellow student there, and the two later accepted research positions at the University of Vienna. The couple had one son, Carl Thomas.

They came to the United States in 1922 and joined the staff of Buffalo's New York Institute of Malignant Diseases. Her husband became an assistant pathologist and she was appointed assistant biochemist. They studied sugar in animals and the effects of insulin and epinephrine.

The Coris then accepted positions at the Washington University School of Medicine in St. Louis. They were interested in the action of hormones and carried out studies on the pituitary gland. Their work on carbohydrate metabolism eventually focused on tissue extracts and isolated enzymes. In 1936, they isolated and tracked glucose-1-phosphate, which was called the Cori ester. This discovery made possible the enzymatic synthesis of glycogen and starch in vitro. Subsequently, other enzymes were crystallized.

Dr. Gerty Cori was the third woman to receive the Nobel prize and the first Jewish American woman to do so. She also received many other honors and honorary degrees before she died on October 26, 1957, from kidney failure. Newscaster Edward R. Murrow eulogized her dedication, intellectual integrity, courage, and professionalism in her pursuit of answers in biochemistry.

Groundbreakers:
ROSALYN SUSSMAN YALOW,
FIRST U.S.-BORN FEMALE NOBEL LAUREATE IN MEDICINE

Rosalyn Sussman Yalow was born in the Bronx on July 19, 1921, to Clara and Simon Sussman, German and American Jews. After graduating from Hunter College, she accepted a teaching fellowship in physics at the University of Illinois. She became the only female in the College of Engineering, and in 1945, she became the second woman to receive a PhD in physics.

She met A. Aaron Yalow, a fellow physics student and the son of a rabbi. They married in 1943 and then returned to New York where she accepted a lecturer's post in physics, which she held until 1950. During this period, they had two children, Benjamin and Elanna.

After World War II, the Veterans Administration began research into radioactive substances in treatment and disease. In 1950, Rosalyn was named assistant chief of the Bronx V.A. Hospital's radioisotope service. In 1977, she became the first American woman (and the second woman in the world) to receive the sole Nobel Prize in Medicine for development of radioimmunoassay (RIA). This allowed doctors, to diagnose conditions caused by minute changes in hormone levels, was useful in diabetes, in screening for hepatitis in blood banks, and also in determining effective dosages of antibiotics. Rosalyn has also received numerous other awards.

When the *Ladies' Home Journal* offered her a special woman's award, she politely refused—since the citation marked her as a brilliant woman, rather than a scientist.

Despite her busy schedule, she cooked kosher meals in her home and never lost her passion for both career and family.

In Fred A. Bernstein's *The Jewish Mothers' Hall of Fame*, Clara Sussman relates her pride in her daughter.

"[Rosalyn] wanted me to go [to the Nobel ceremony] in the worst way, but I was ninety-two. I didn't want to spoil her fun. I was at my doctor's and he said to everyone, 'This is the Nobel Prize winner's mother,' and they all applauded."

> When Clara was informed by a teacher that her daughter was a genius, she thought, "Genius? I don't want a genius. I want a normal child. I was thinking of Albert Einstein.... I had heard he was a little peculiar."

She's the Jewish mother of sex but known to millions as Dr. Ruth. Karola Ruth Siegal was born on June 4, 1928, in Frankfurt, Germany. She escaped death during the Holocaust when her family sent her to a school in Switzerland. Ruth never saw her parents again and assumed they perished in Auschwitz. She remained at the Swiss school, which became an orphanage, until after the war. In 1948, she joined the Haganah, the Jewish underground movement, and received training as a sniper. She has a daughter, Miriam, and a son, Joel.

She received her PhD in 1970 from Columbia University in family counseling, and trained at New York Hospital–Cornell University Medical Center, with noted sex therapist Helen Singer Kaplan.

After an academic stint, the diminutive lady with the laughing eyes and distinctive accent managed the improbable. She made her mark in radio, virtually initiating media psychology in 1980, with her radio program *Sexually Speaking*. Dr. Ruth's expertise can be found on television, in books, newspapers, video, and software. *The Dr. Ruth Show* aired on Lifetime and has been syndicated nationally and internationally. Ruth has been a pioneer in spreading what she has labeled "sexual literacy," and she advises in a straightforward, motherly, and even humorous fashion that promotes safe sex and contraception.

She was twice named "College Lecturer of the Year" by the National Mother's Day Committee, which has also honored Dr. Ruth as Mother of the Year.

She has said that her ability to talk about sexuality "has to do with my being Jewish. . . . For us Jews . . . sex is a mitzvah and an obligation." In 1995, she published *Heavenly Sex: Sexuality in the Jewish Tradition*, coauthored with Jonathan Mark, tying together Orthodox Judaism and her views of sex.

Westheimer credits her escape from Nazi Germany with giving her a certain amount of chutzpah. Her collection of toy turtles provides an apt analogy: "If a turtle stays in one place, he is very safe. But if he wants to move, he has to stick his neck out. You have to take a risk if you believe in something."

As early as 1981, Dr. Mathilde Krim knew that AIDS not only raised critical medical and scientific issues but that its sociopolitical impact would have grave consequences. She determined to dedicate herself to AIDS research and activism.

But then Krim had always been determined to fight the good and fair fight. Born Mathilde Galland, in Como, Italy, on July 9, 1926, and raised Protestant in Geneva, "I was the subject of taunts and ridicule starting at the age of six." After seeing a newsreel about the liberation of the concentration camps during World War II, she was so outraged and impassioned about these inhuman atrocities that she sought out Jews, and joined the Irgun (the militant commando group), then led by Menachem Begin. The blue-eyed blond would often ride her bicycle into France to smuggle messages for the Irgun.

Mathilde fell in love with fellow medical student, David Danon, also a member of the Irgun. When she married him and converted to Judaism, her father fainted.

The couple had a daughter, Daphna, and in 1953, they went to Israel, where Mathilde worked at the Weizmann Institute, and contributed to studies that laid the foundation for amniocentesis. She became one of the first experts in culturing cells, and studied the viruses thought to cause some forms of cancer.

After her marriage fell apart, the chancellor of the institute introduced the thirty-year-old biologist to his friend Arthur Krim, a forty-seven-year-old American, a governor of the Weizmann Institute and a film mogul.

They married in 1958 and settled in New York where Mathilde joined the research faculty at Cornell Weill Medical College and later, the Sloan-Kettering Institute for cancer research. But her concern for AIDS with all its ramifications at a time when it was considered a "shameful" or "gay" problem was still uppermost.

Krim eventually left full-time research, and became involved in AIDS treatment, and in 1985, she founded the AIDS Medical Foundation (AMF). In 1990, AMF merged with a California-based group. With the incomparable Elizabeth Taylor, the American Foundation for AIDS Research (amfAR) became the preeminent organization devoted to raising funds for research, prevention, and the development of AIDS-related public policies.

Dr. Krim holds fifteen doctorates *honoris causa* and, in August 2000, she was awarded the Presidential Medal of Freedom, the highest civilian honor in the United States.

JEWISH MOTHERS IN BUSINESS: FORCES TO BE RECKONED WITH

*J*ewish mothers and business have a long tradition in Jewish history, as many of these women worked so that their husbands could study.

At the beginning of the twentieth century in America, women from Eastern Europe often worked in factories and sweatshops. It's not surprising then, that as feminism progressed—although slowly—these women used their skills to seize any opportunity afforded . . . Some even grabbed hold of the golden ring in the Golden Land.

Today, a number of entrepreneurs are Jewish mothers who have achieved enormous success in all aspects of business—from Donna Karan to Linda Kaplan Thaler. The bios that follow celebrate some of these moms who cracked through the ceiling and paved the road, with brains, talent, and often, sheer chutzpah.

According to Howard M. Sachar's book *A History of the Jews in America,* at the turn of the century Jewish women constituted 70 percent of the workforce in the shirtwaist, or women's blouse, factories. Typically they'd work sixty-five to seventy-five hours a week in horrid and unsafe conditions. On November 22, 1909, the International Ladies' Garment Workers' Union—composed primarily of Jewish women—revolted against their sweatshop employers in a famous strike that became known as the "Uprising of 20,000."

These Jewish mothers who believed in economic equality and worked avidly for the labor movement were poised for feminism.

Ida Cohen Rosenthal was born on January 9, 1886, near Minsk in Russia. She was the daughter of a Hebrew scholar, while her mother ran a small general store.

At seventeen, Ida immigrated to New Jersey to join her boyfriend, William Rosenthal, who had come to America a few months earlier. They married in 1907 and had a daughter and a son, Lewis.

Ida was a dressmaker and, with her husband, and their business partner Enid Bisset, they formed their own clothing business. But . . . they were never satisfied with the way a dress fitted around the bosom. In the 1920s, women wore a towel-like brassiere with hooks in the back. Despite the popularity of the "flat-chested" look, Ida believed a natural bust line would enhance appearance. So she set about to design a brassiere—two cups, separated by a piece of elastic. It was a hit, and the Maidenform company was born.

She was a marketing genius and began a media campaign, making Maidenform the first intimate apparel company to advertise. By the end of the 1930s, department stores across the world were selling Maidenform bras. In 1949 the slogan, "I dreamed that I went shopping in my Maidenform bra" was one of the most recognized in the ad business.

Ida stayed on as honorary chairman of the board until her death in 1973 at eighty-seven. Her daughter, Beatrice, inherited the family company, and then her granddaughter, Elizabeth Coleman, took over.

Ida was an ardent philanthropist and served on many boards, including the Bronx Lebanon Medical Center. She and her husband also created the Ida and William Rosenthal Fellowship in Judaica and Hebraic studies at New York University.

> "NO ONE CAN HOPE TO BE ELECTED TO
> PUBLIC OFFICE IN NEW YORK WITHOUT
> HAVING HIS PICTURE TAKEN EATING A
> HOT DOG AT NATHAN'S."
> —Nelson A. Rockefeller

In 1916, when Ida and Nathan Handwerker founded Nathan's Famous—a Coney Island hot dog stand—little did they know it would grow into an institution. They used a special hot dog recipe developed by Ida's grandmother.

To keep the formula secret, Nathan hired two spice providers, with each developing half of the famous recipe. Through a series of ingenious marketing ploys, long workdays, and strong celebrity endorsements, the Handwerkers catapulted the hot dog into popularity.

By 1939, Nathan's was so popular, Mrs. Handwerker boasted that President and Mrs. Roosevelt served them to King George VI and Queen Elizabeth at a picnic at Hyde Park.

Ida had two sons, Murray and Sol, and a daughter, Leah. Her son Murray was a former president of the chain.

The woman with the exotic name, Estée Lauder, was born Josephine Esther Mentzer in 1908 in Corona, Queens, to Max and Rose Schotz Mentzer. Estée was the daughter of a French Catholic mother and a Hungarian Jewish father and was raised Jewish.

She honed her skills early, with the help of her uncle, John Shotz, a chemist, who specialized in skin-care preparations. Her cosmetics business was first launched in New York during the Depression, and later in Miami Beach, Florida.

At nineteen, she met Joseph Lauter (later changed to Lauder), the son of immigrants from Galicia. They were married on January 15, 1930, and their son Leonard Allen was born in 1933.

Estée improved upon her uncle's product, and developed an exclusive clientele. A large order from Saks Fifth Avenue advanced her business.

In 1985 she said, "I did not know how to be Mrs. Joseph Lauder and Estée Lauder at the same time." The couple divorced in 1939, then remarried three years later, and had a second child, Ronald, in February 1944. The second time around "took." Estée and Joseph maintained a lifelong personal and professional bond.

She had a genius for promotion, which included innovative free samples and a hands-on approach with clients. Much of her initial success came from word-of-mouth advertising, a strategy she called "Tell-a-Woman" marketing. Eventually, she invested in larger marketing concepts, using specially chosen models to sell her products. As upscale stores began to sell Estée Lauder cosmetics, she went to each store herself and individually trained the sales personnel who were demonstrating her products.

Her son Leonard became chairman of the board, while her other son Ronald became a businessman, civic leader, philanthropist, and art collector.

Estée Lauder was an ardent philanthropist during her lifetime and contributed to National Cancer Care, the Manhattan League, and various Jewish causes.

In addition to numerous awards from the cosmetics and fashion industries, she received the Albert Einstein College of Medicine Spirit of Achievement Award in 1968, was recognized by business and financial editors as one of Ten Outstanding Women in Business in 1970, was given the French government's Insignia of Chevalier of the Legion of Honor in 1978, and in 1984, she and seven others were chosen as Outstanding Mother of the Year.

In 1968, Governor Nelson Rockefeller designated June 16, Jennie Grossinger's birthday, as Jennie Grossinger Day in New York State. It was the first time such an honor had ever been bestowed on a living woman.

Jennie Grossinger, the veritable mother of the Catskills, turned a modest, run-down Catskill Mountain farm into an American resort icon.

Jennie was born on June 16, 1892, in Galicia, Austria, to Malka and Asher Selig Grossinger. Her parents came to America in search of a new and better life.

In 1912, she wed a cousin, Harry Grossinger, and became a waitress in her father's dairy restaurant. When her father's health started failing in 1914, they moved to a farm in Ferndale, New York, in the Catskill Mountains, where they housed summer boarders. At that time, Jews looked forward to escaping the city, and the Grossingers provided an inexpensive respite that also had kosher food.

Jennie's mother, Malka, cooked, while Jennie was chambermaid, bookkeeper, and hostess. The first year, they charged $9 a week and cleared a net profit of $81. Word of their economical rates and good food quickly spread.

In 1919, to accommodate their growing number of guests, they sold the farm and bought a large piece of property with a hotel, in Liberty, New York. Although Jennie had two children, Paul, born in 1915, and Elaine Joy, in 1927, she still managed the hotel while raising her family.

As Jews became more affluent, and were too often rejected by "No Jews Allowed" policies of some other hotels, Jennie expanded Grossinger's services, adding tennis courts, bridle paths, a children's camp, a social director, and a residential theater group.

In the 1920s, Grossinger's became a five-star destination for the upwardly mobile East Coast Jews. Many famous celebrities got their start or vacationed at the posh resort. The list is huge and includes Chaim Weismann, Vice President Alben W. Barkley, and Mrs. Eleanor Roosevelt.

Jennie raised so much money in World War II war bonds that an army airplane was named "Grossinger's" in her honor. A clinic and convalescent home in Israel also bears her name. She received a trove of honorary degrees and awards for her philanthropy.

Although she turned over the administration of Grossinger's to her children in 1964, Jennie was still the guiding spirit. The resort was then situated on 1,200 acres with thirty-five buildings and served 50,000 people a year. She died of a stroke November 20, 1972, in her cottage at Grossinger's.

"MY WHOLE PHILOSOPHY OF BARBIE WAS
THAT THROUGH THE DOLL, THE LITTLE GIRL
COULD BE ANYTHING SHE WANTED TO BE.
BARBIE ALWAYS REPRESENTED THE FACT
THAT A WOMAN HAS CHOICES."
—Ruth Handler in her 1994 autobiography

On March 9, 1959, inventor Ruth Mosko Handler unveiled what was to become a toy icon at the American Toy Fair in New York: the Barbie doll, named after Handler's fifteen-year-old daughter, rocketed the Mattel company to nearly overnight success.

"Barbie Teenage Fashion Model" had a long ponytail, a black-and-white striped bathing suit, and teeny feet that fit into open-toed heels. Mattel sold more than 350,000 three-dollar Barbies the first year.

Ruth Mosko was born in 1916, the youngest of ten children of Polish immigrants who settled in Denver. At nineteen, she vacationed in Hollywood and wound up staying. Her high-school beau, Elliot Handler, also relocated to California and they married in 1938.

The Handlers started a giftware business in their garage, with sales reaching $2 million within a few years. In 1942, they partnered with industrial designer Harold "Matt" Mattson. Eventually they specialized in toys, calling the company "Mattel"—a combination of "Matt" in Mattson and "El" in Elliot.

Earlier, the company marketed Chatty Cathy, a talking doll. But when Ruth noticed her daughter Barbara's fascination with paper dolls of teenagers or career women, she fashioned a lifelike doll—with breasts. Despite condemnation from feminists who claimed Barbie promoted an unrealistic body image, Hendler believed it was "important to a little girl's self-esteem to play with a doll that has breasts."

Barbie had friends: Ken (1961), named for the Handlers' son, then Midge in 1963, Skipper in 1965, and Christie, Barbie's first ethnic friend, in 1969. The first Barbie of color came out in 1981. Other dolls were later named for Mrs. Handler's grandchildren.

In keeping with the changing times, Barbie evolved from fashion model to career woman.

Sadly, the woman who became famous by giving breasts to a doll underwent a mastectomy in 1970—but this didn't stop Ruth Hendler. She then blazed another career by manufacturing and marketing the Nearly Me prosthetic breast for women who had undergone mastectomies. She was determined to make an artificial breast so real "that a woman could wear a regular brassiere and blouse, stick her chest out, and be proud."

In the 1970s, she personally fit former first lady Betty Ford, appeared on talk shows, wrote to breast-cancer patients, and spoke around the country about early detection of the disease that was then a taboo subject.

Ruth Handler has received numerous awards. The *Los Angeles Times* named her Woman of the Year in Business in 1967, the United Jewish Appeal named her its first Woman of Distinction, and in 1985, she was inducted into the Toy Industry Hall of Fame.

Forbes magazine has cited Lillian Vernon as one of the twenty-five most fascinating people, and she is. Vernon parlayed her modest wedding gift money into a multimillion dollar company—the first to be listed on the American Stock Exchange by a woman, and she did all this while raising two sons.

Lilly Menasche was born in Leipzig, Germany, on March 18, 1927. She and her family fled the growing Nazi threat, first going to Amsterdam, and then to New York City.

In America, her father manufactured leather goods, which would become Vernon's first foray into the mail-order business. "In 1951, there weren't many opportunities to launch a small business as there are in today's marketplace," Vernon said. "What inspired me and caught my attention was the advertising I saw for small businesses."

Lillian was four months pregnant when she started her mail order business. Her instinct was to advertise to young women who loved accessories that made them feel unique. She took out a $495 ad in *Seventeen* magazine for a personalized leather handbag and matching belt she designed. That small investment returned $32,000 in orders.

And Lillian Vernon was, as they say, in business. Her novel marketing concept was monogramming.

In 1956, the first Lillian Vernon catalog was mailed to 125,000 customers who had responded to her ads. In 1965, the Lillian Vernon Corporation was formed and by 1970, her sales had passed $1 million. Lillian had hit on an ingenious concept at just the right time, as women were entering the workforce and looking for a convenient way to shop.

In 1956, she opened her first manufacturing plant. By 1990, sales had risen to $238 million, and the mailing list had grown to 17 million. Lillian Vernon has kept up with technology by offering her catalogs online at www.lillianvernon.com and www.ruedefrance.com. There are also fourteen outlet stores around the country. The company now produces special lines for children, teens, and gardening, as well as products for the home. She still travels around the world searching for new products.

Vernon has two sons, Fred and David Hochberg. David is vice president of public relations, while Fred works for several nonprofit and political causes.

She also serves on the boards of prestigious nonprofit organizations and her company supports over five hundred charities.

In recognition of her civic contributions, she has received many awards, including the Ellis Island Medal of Honor and the Gannett Newspapers Business Leadership Award, and she has been inducted into the Direct Marketing Association Hall of Fame.

"Successful entrepreneurs think, dream, and live for their business. But as much as you have a desire to fulfill yourself and become an entrepreneur, you must balance your career with your personal life."

—Lillian Vernon

JEWISH MOTHERS AND SPORTS

There's an old joke that Jews don't play sports, they own sports teams. It's interesting to note that when Jews *do* play . . . oy, are they good. (If not, they *quick*! change careers.)

OLYMPIANS

At the 1996 Olympic Games, a four foot nine, eighty-eight pound Jewish athlete literally made viewers around the world hold their collective breath. The only way the U.S. Women's Gymnastics team could win their first-ever gold medal depended upon seventeen-year-old Kerri Strug's final vault. But could she? She fell in her first vault, tearing ligaments and spraining her left ankle. Kerri was worried, in acute pain, and barely able to walk, but she composed herself, readied . . . then sprinted toward the vault! She nailed an almost perfect landing and the gold for the team.

"It never occurred to me she would be a star," says her mother, Melanie Strug. "She sacrificed immensely. But she was a perfectionist.

"By age five or six we knew she 'had' it. The gymnastic coaches knew it." They also knew her daughter could only get so much training in Arizona and needed to move on. "I thought they were crazy," says Mrs. Strug, referring to local coaches.

"When she moved away from home to study gymnastics in Houston with Bela [Bela Karolyi, famed coach] when she was thirteen, we were devastated. Before we made the decision to let her go, we went to Houston to check this out.

"We didn't want her to do it. To be honest, we thought she'd come home in a week or two. But then Karolyi wanted to coach her personally," says Mrs. Strug, who loved the ballet, although her kids wanted gymnastics.

"A lot of the kids let school slide. School was always number one with us. Gymnastics was not going to be her future. Six months later she made the world champion team, and a year later, the Olympic Team. Yet she also graduated a straight A student from a good private school."

Of the fateful 1996 games, she says, "Initially we didn't know she was hurt. Then, after the first vault, when she landed on the one foot, we knew . . . and we were very worried, not knowing the extent of her injuries."

"*I*t was the Agony and the Ecstasy. A great moment, but we were worried and upset that Kerri would be upset. She wanted an individual gold medal. We got her to the hospital and learned she'd torn several ligaments. We were both crying. This was not how she envisioned winning. She knew something was wrong before that jump, but . . . you were there for your country."

—Melanie Strug

The first time women's gymnastics was on the program was at the 1928 Amsterdam Games. The team from the Netherlands won the gold medal. The Dutch team was about half Jewish, and all but one Jewish teammate, Elka de Levie, was killed during the Holocaust. The Jewish members of the Netherlands team were inducted into the International Jewish Sports Hall of Fame.

Jewish Mothers and Olympians in Memoriam

Lea Kloot-Nordheim was born in 1903. She was killed in the gas chambers at Sobibor on July 2, 1943. Her husband and their ten-year-old daughter, Rebecca, were also killed.

Stella Blits-Agsteribbe was born in 1910. She was killed at Auschwitz on September 17, 1943. Her two-year-old son Alfred and six-year-old daughter Nanny were also killed.

Anna Dresden-Polak was born in 1908. She was killed at Sobibor on July 23, 1943. Her six-year-old daughter Eva and her husband, Barend, were killed at Auschwitz in 1944.

Syd Koff was born Sybil Tabachnikoff in 1912 on the Lower East Side. She beat legends Babe Didrickson, Lillian Copeland, and Stella Walsh in amateur track and field events when she was only a teen. In 1932, she represented America at the first Maccabean Games in Tel Aviv and emerged as the games' greatest star. Koff qualified for the 1936 Olympic Team in the broad and high jumps, but boycotted the Games in Berlin, protesting the Nazi regime. She married, had children, and though she never got the chance to win Olympic gold, she played in the masters' division, and competed from the 1960s until 1972.

During the 1940s and 1950s, Hungarian-born Agnes Keleti was the winner of eleven Olympic medals, including five gold, and ranks as one of the world's all-time greatest gymnasts—earning more medals than any other Jewish female. Keleti was born on January 9, 1921. She overcame an early lung problem, and she suffered greatly when the Nazis moved into Hungary. Her other relatives were sent to Auschwitz, where her father was killed. Her mother and sister survived, due to the intervention of famed Swedish diplomat Raoul Wallenberg. In 1957, Keleti immigrated to Israel, married a Hungarian physical education teacher, and had two sons. She became a college physical education teacher and coached national teams. In 1991, Keleti was inducted into the Hungarian Sports Hall of Fame. She has also been recognized by the Jewish Sports Hall of Fame in Israel.

Irena Kirszenstein-Szewinska was born May 24, 1945, in Russia. She moved to Poland, was the first woman to hold simultaneous world records in the 100-, 200-, and 400-meter race, and, at age nineteen, she was Poland's Athlete of the Year. In 1967, she married photographer Junusz Szewinska and gave birth to son, Andrzej, in 1970. She felt the birth of her child boosted her ability in sports. In 1974, she was the first woman to break 50 seconds in the 400 meter and was named Woman Athlete of the Year by *Track and Field News*. Ultimately she did win seven Olympic medals, including three gold. Yet she maintained that no medals gave her as much pleasure as the birth of her son. She went on to become an economist with the Transportation Research Center in Warsaw. Regarding her life, she has said: "[Sports], together with my family, has brought me all the joys of the world."

When one of the greatest swimmers marries one of the greatest water polo players—what can they expect? A prodigy!

Eva Szekely competed in three Olympiads for Hungary (1948, 1952, 1956), bringing home gold and silver. In 1956, she and her husband Deszo Gyarmati arrived at the Melbourne Games at the start of the Hungarian revolt against Communism. Said Eva: "the Russians had come into power . . . we had no word of our two-year old daughter. I didn't get any real sleep for a week and lost over twelve pounds." Despite everything, she took home a silver medal in the 200-meter breaststroke.

At age fourteen, her daughter, Andrea Gyarmati, became an Olympic swimmer and, at the 1968 Mexico City games, she took home silver, and bronze in the 1972 Munich games.

In 2002, after an unprecedented dazzling final performance featuring two triple-triple combinations, figure skater Sarah Hughes took home the gold in Salt Lake City. Sarah, like many other Jewish competitors, passed up lucrative touring offers to get an Ivy League education.

She was born May 2, 1985, in Great Neck, New York. Her mother was Jewish and her non-Jewish father was an athlete. In a 2005 interview with *Lifestyles* magazine, Sarah said she and her brother received private tutoring in Hebrew at home. Rosh Hashanah dinner, Passover seders, and Hanukkah candles were all a part of her family tradition.

Sarah, like Kerri Strug, is competitive and a bit of a perfectionist. "I was always very competitive, regardless of what it was. When we were younger, we had a little rink in the back. I tried to skate faster than them [her five siblings]. I always wanted to be the first to do everything. . . . It wasn't so important for me to tie my skates first. It was because I was the only one who could do it right, how I liked it," she told the *New York Times* in 2002.

She credits her indefatigable spirit to her mother, Amy, who survived breast cancer several years ago. Hughes became an inspiration for her mother when she won the junior national championships in Philadelphia while her mother was undergoing treatment.

Figure skater Sasha Cohen was born Alexandra Pauline "Sasha" Cohen on October 26, 1984. She is the current U.S. National Champion and was silver medalist at the 2006 Winter Olympics in Turin, Italy. (Shizuka Arakawa of Japan received the gold and won by 7.98 points over Cohen.)

> Sasha Cohen finished fourth at the 2002 Games in Salt Lake City behind Michelle Kwan—bronze, Irina Slutskaya— silver, and Sarah Hughes—gold.

Cohen was born in Westwood, California. Her mother, Galina Feldman, is an immigrant from the Ukraine and a former ballet dancer. Her father, Roger Cohen, is a business consultant who used to practice law. Cohen, a gymnast from an early age, switched to figure skating when she was seven years old.

In April 2006, she joined the Champions on Ice tour, participated in the second annual Skating with the Stars, Under the Stars gala in Central Park, and performed in the Marshalls U.S. Figure Skating International Showcase. She also announced her intention to compete at the 2010 Winter Olympics in Vancouver.

"One of the greatest names in American swimming history—Dara Torres—received a new name last week: Mom!" reported Philip Whitten, on April 24, 2006, in SwimmingWorld Magazine.com.

Dara, now thirty-nine, was the first American woman to compete in four Olympic Games (1984, 1988, 1992, and 2000). She picked up nine medals, four of them gold. On April 18, 2006, she gave birth to Tessa Grace Torres-Hoffman. Tessa's already showing Olympic promise, as she weighed in at 8.1 pounds and stretches a lanky twenty-one-and-a-half inches in length. "We don't know who she looks like [Dara or husband, Dr. David Hoffman], but she definitely has my big feet and hands, and long toes and fingers," said the new mom.

Charlee Minkin was born November 13, 1981. She comes from Half Moon Bay, California. But don't mess with her. Charlee, like her family, started judo at five, following the path blazed by her brother, Benzam, and sisters Zesa and Davina.

They're tough like their mother, Carolyn Minkin, and their late father, Stephen Minkin, a Vietnam vet and Alaskan bush pilot. The family had planned to settle in Alaska, until his tragic death in a 1987 plane crash.

Mama Carolyn eventually became a black belt and the kids became judo champions. Davina trained in Israel for a year and worked with Yael Arad, an Israeli woman who won her country's first Olympic silver medal in judo in 1992.

"That's how we communicate—with touching and throwing and tripping and choking," a laughing Carolyn Minkin told reporter Joe Eskenazi of the *Jewish News Weekly* of northern California.

Charlee has endured several surgeries on her knee and trained at the U.S. Olympic Training Center in Colorado Springs while attending the University of Colorado. She won gold medals at several important 2003 tournaments and represented the United States in the Athens Olympics. She was, however, eliminated after she lost a match by the smallest of margins to Raffaella Imbriani of Germany.

As a youngster, Charlee lost herself in the sport after three years of watching her mother and her siblings. Two days after she took her first official lesson, she won her first tournament. Carolyn, a huge supporter of her children, was always on the job: carting them from Brandeis Hillel Day School in San Francisco, to judo training, to weekend tournaments, and to Sunday school, while holding down a teaching job.

JEWISH MOTHERS AND OTHER SPORTS

Table tennis was organized as a modern sport in the 1920s. It proved very popular with Jews. Lady Swaythling (1879–1965), president of the English Table Tennis Federation, donated the men's world team cup (1926), which bears her name. Her son, Ivor Montagu, was the first chairman of the Table Tennis International Federation, and held the post for over forty years.

Considered the world's greatest table tennis champion, Angelica Rozeanu won seventeen world titles. Rozeanu was born in Bucharest on October 15, 1921. She won her first international competition in 1938 at the Hungarian Open. Although her career was interrupted when the Nazis took over Romania, she kept training after the war, and married Hungarian Lou Rozeanu. During the 1950s she continued to win and served as a sports reporter for *Romania Libera*. She also received many sports honors by her government. In 1960, she and her fourteen-year-old daughter, Michaela, moved to Israel, where she then became a coach. Rozeanu is a member of both the Jewish Sports Hall of Fame and the Table Tennis Hall of Fame. In 1998, she was cited in the *Guinness Book of World Records*, for holding the most women's singles World Champion wins (six). Her daughter Michaela became a computer engineer in Haifa.

Activist and tennis enthusiast Gladys Heldman released the first issue of *World Tennis* magazine on May 13, 1953. A tennis player herself, she got into the sport in 1954 and went on to play at Wimbledon after giving birth to her two daughters.

Gladys Medalie Heldman was born May 13, 1922, in New York City. She was a Phi Beta Kappa graduate of Stanford University, and in 1942 married Julius Heldman, a former United States junior tennis champion. Her daughters, Carrie and Julie, were also accomplished players—Julie was ranked number five in the world in 1969 and in 1974.

During the 1950s and 1960s her magazine's goal was to develop equality for women in tennis. Heldman was concerned over the disparity in prize money between men and women, and in 1970, she competed with the U.S. Open by organizing independent tournaments. She created the Virginia Slims Tour for female pros, but after the women who competed in her events were met with reprisals, three years of lawsuits and negotiations followed. Finally, the Virginia Slims Tour merged with the United States Lawn Tennis Association and in 1973, both sexes finally played in the same events for equal prizes.

In the mid-1970s, Heldman sold the *World Tennis* magazine to CBS. In 1958, her achievements were recognized with the J. P. Allen Memorial Award of the Lawn Tennis Writers' Association of America. She was inducted into the International Tennis Hall of Fame in 1979, as well as the National Tennis Hall of Fame. Heldman died in 2003 in Santa Fe.

Grandmaster Susan Polgar earned her first checkmate when she was only four and a half and has since taken on the likes of Bobby Fischer, Boris Spassky, Garry Kasparov, and Anatoly Karpov.

> "Chess is in many ways like life itself. It's all condensed in a playful manner in a game format and it's extremely fascinating because first of all I'm in control of my own destiny, I'm in charge. Chess teaches discipline from a very early age—to have a plan and to plan ahead. If you do that, you'll be rewarded; if you break the rules, you will get punished—in life and in chess. You need to learn the rules to break the rules."
> —Susan Polgar

She believes that chess is the game of life and has devoted herself to being an ambassador for the game. She established the Polgar Chess Center in Forest Hills, New York, where she teaches students and hosts major chess events. She has also established the Susan Polgar Foundation to introduce the social, educational, and competitive benefits of chess to American children, in particular, girls.

The preference to educate females about the games no doubt dates back to her experience as a Jewish woman chess player in her birthplace in Budapest, Hungary. Although chess was a man's game, she was the first to break through, but even though she won awards (in Hungary), acceptance was not forthcoming. Polgar, born April 19, 1969, whose grandparents were Holocaust survivors, felt the subtle sting of anti-Semitism early in her life.

Opposition to breaking the gender barrier was more open. At age fifteen, she was the top-ranked female in the world, but acceptance didn't come until 1988 when she, and her sisters, Sofia and Judit, won the gold medal in the World Chess Olympiad for Hungary—a first victory over the Soviets. Then the government turned them into heroes. Polgar won nine other Olympic medals and was Women's World Champion four times.

Although the birth of her sons Tom and Leeam led Polgar to focus more on promotion, in July 2005, she broke four international records at a single match in Palm Beach, Florida.

In October 2005, she joined former Russian President Mikhail Gorbachev and seven-time World Champion Anatoly Karpov in Lindsborg, Kansas, to promote "Chess for Peace." Polgar also participated in the second Clash of the Titans—Battle of the Genders match against Karpov, with Gorbachev making the first move for Karpov.

The woman whose name is a household word in Hungary and among chess enthusiasts everywhere is also one of the best-selling chess authors in the world. She has also released DVDs, is a columnist, and is a three-time winner of the Chess Oscar.

Some Jews favored more "exotic" fare. In which sport do Jews comprise a quarter of the top-ranked? Sumo wrestling? Feh! More guts are needed for *this* sport—competitive eating—which is growing fast thanks to ESPN's coverage of Nathan's hot dog-eating contest and the [chicken] Wing Bowl. A top competitor is Don Lerman. Often attending these events dressed as Moses, he's downed twelve matzo balls in two minutes and fifty seconds, breaking the world record.

Eating . . . a sport? According to Leon Feingold, ranked nineteenth in the world, pro eating requires competitiveness, capacity, speed, and technique. "Jews are very competitive. They are intelligent, which makes them approach . . . technique . . . intelligently. *And they have Jewish mothers, which means they can't leave the table until they're done eating. This takes care of speed and capacity.*"

In 1975, Larissa Gurvich (USSR) won the European and world skeet championships.

On September 28, 1980, Ida Mintz, seventy-four, became the oldest woman to finish a marathon! Coached by her son, Dr. Alan Mintz, she joined over 4,600 runners in Chicago. A family affair, Ida raced with her son, daughter-in-law, and grandson—the first three-generation family to run a marathon. She then went on to run more marathons until she was eighty-five, when she was diagnosed with pancreatic cancer. Though ill, she gathered the strength to rise from her wheelchair to dance with her grandson at his wedding. She passed away on the eve of her eighty-sixth birthday. The last fifteen years of her life were filled with remarkable achievements and good health right up until her fatal illness.

JEWISH MOTHERS EVERYWHERE

*I*n 1914, Claude Israel, sixteen, went to the Fiji Islands from Australia to join his uncle, Henry Marks, one of a group of successful Jewish importers and exporters. In 1914, he returned to Sydney to marry his bride, Doris Abraham, and brought her back to Fiji, where she raised two children in a country where cannibalism existed. During World War II, Doris, who was keenly interested in politics, ran a canteen for the 50,000 American soldiers stationed in the Fiji Islands—which included marines training for their landing in Guadalcanal.

Dr. Fanny Reading was born in Russia into a family tormented by pogroms. Fanny's father left for London and then Australia. When Fanny was three, her mother took the courageous and difficult journey to Australia, surprising her husband, who was thrilled by the reunion. She gave birth to three sons "down under" and despite financial hardship, Fanny received her medical degree in 1922 and joined her brother's practice. Within a year, she became the force behind creating the National Council of Jewish Women of Australia. She was also dedicated to social welfare, and in 1961, Dr. Reading received an MBE [Member of the British Empire], an honor conferred by Queen Elizabeth II.

Dr. Aviva Gileadi, renowned nuclear physicist, spent years teaching at the Technion, Israel's famed institution of higher learning. She was born in Hungary during the reign of Nazi Germany. When Aviva was handed a shovel and told to dig, a former classmate warned her that she was digging her own grave—so she ran to the forest and remained in hiding. When Israel gained independence, she was determined to help. She completed her education in the United States, taught at Technion, married, and had two children. Soon after, the government of Puerto Rico asked her to establish a nuclear physics department in Santurce. She accepted, knowing she'd one day return to Israel, where her children would continue their studies.

In 1947, as a young woman, Shamsi Moradpour Hekmat, along with a small group of other women in Tehran, Iran, vowed to "to wash off the rust of ignorance, disease, and poverty from the innocent faces of the children of the *mahalleh* (ghetto)." They organized the Jewish Ladies' Organization of Iran. She and her cofounders set up daycare centers for children of needy families, started training classes for nurses and nursery school teachers, and organized literacy classes for women. Hekmat also engaged in the fight for women's rights, in particular the right to inherit from a male. This fight was won in 1966, when Israeli Sephardi Chief Rabbi Nissim came to Iran.

In 2005, for the first time the 77th Academy Awards honored a Jewish person of color. Sophie Okonedo was nominated for her work in *The Hotel Rwanda*, an acclaimed low-budget film about a hotel manager and his wife who housed 1,200 Tutsi refugees during the Rwanda genocide. Okonedo, a graduate of the Royal Academy of Dramatic Arts, was born in 1969 and raised by her British Jewish mother (she wore the Star of David during a Letterman appearance), and has a Nigerian father. She saw similarities in the film with the Jewish Holocaust and researched her role at the Belgian Shoah Museum. In 2005, Natalie Portman was the only other Jewish actor nominated and competing with Okanedo. (However, Cate Blanchett won for *The Aviator*.) Okonedo has one daughter, Aoife, whose father is Irish film editor Eoin Martin.

> "PEOPLE DON'T REALIZE THERE ARE COMEDIANS IN RUSSIA. IN RUSSIA, YOU HAVE TO CHOOSE YOUR MATERIAL CAREFULLY. . . . IF SOMEONE HECKLES YOU IN RUSSIA, IT DOESN'T WORK TO YELL, 'YOUR MOTHER WEARS ARMY BOOTS,' BECAUSE SHE PROBABLY DOES."
>
> —Yakov Smirnoff

On December 15, 1997, Janet Rosenberg from Chicago was elected president of Guyana.

She was born in 1920 and married Cheddi Jagan, a Guyanese, in 1943. In 1950, the couple founded the People's Progressive Party. Her husband was elected prime minister, but was deposed by Churchill. Husband and wife were jailed and placed under house arrest several times. In 1992, Cheddi Jagan was again elected prime minister when fair elections were held. Five years later, after his death, Rosenberg was elected to the post but then resigned for health reasons in 1999. A biographical film was made about Rosenberg, titled *Thunder in Guyana*. Her son Joey is also in politics in Guyana. The Guyanese consider this Jewish mama the mother of their nation.

CHAPTER 6

Jewish Mothers—
Did Jew Know?

We are all unique beings within our ethno-types. However, some have said and done the unusual, in achievement, comment, events—or just how they've chosen to live their lives. The following are surprising, fascinating, and at times remarkable facts that involve Jews and mothers and Jewish mothers.

Most of us know (and tell our children) that **ALBERT EINSTEIN** was no prize in school.

Albert was born in 1879, in Ulm Donnau, Germany. He was so backward in speech and math that he needed remedial study. Naturally this worried his parents, Hermann and Pauline Einstein. Einstein's grandmother thought her grandson's head was "Much too fat!" while his mother, Pauline, worried that baby Albert's head was lopsided. "Alright, OK, so he'll take violin lessons," must have run through *her* head when she insisted her child, the "*nebekhl,*" study the instrument. Although young Albert initially hated the lessons, he grew to love music.

"Now I know there is a God in heaven," said Albert Einstein upon hearing twelve-year-old Jewish violin prodigy, Yehudi Menuhin, play in Berlin in 1928, and recognizing a fellow genius.

In 1916, the world recognized Einstein's genius, when his Theory of Relativity was published, which he had worked on for ten years. Ironically, while he was a professor at Princeton, he often got lost and was baffled by tax forms, but was still asked to be president of Israel.

According to Bruno Halious's book, *Meres Juives des Hommes Célèbres (Jewish Mothers of Famous Men)*, when Albert Einstein won the Nobel Prize in 1921, he sent a telegram to his mother which read:
"Mother—WE won the Nobel Prize."

In 1955, when Einstein died, Dr. Thomas Harvey removed his brain without permission: The genius's brain, however, looked much like any other, gray, crinkly, and, if anything, a trifle smaller than average.

When she was pregnant with her first child, **QUEEN VICTORIA** and her husband, Prince Albert, vacationed in Hanover, Germany. The queen went into labor two months early and the famous Jewish philanthropist and British advisor **MOSHE MONTEFIORE** sought the counsel of **RABBI NATHAN ADLER**. If the child was born in Germany, its succession to the British throne might be challenged. The ingenious rabbi suggested the queen give birth on an English ship in international waters! She was quickly "delivered" to the British warship *Arc Royal*. That night, future King Edward VII was born. Years later, when the Dukes Place synagogue in London was seeking a rabbi, the queen wrote on behalf of Rabbi Adler. She supported the creation of the

*W*ho can forget the classic deli scene in *When Harry Met Sally*, when Sally (Meg Ryan) simulated a loud, moaning, mind-blowing sexual response to prove a point to Harry (Billy Crystal). And who can forget the older female diner who uttered, "I'll have what she's having." While working with Ryan on the scene, director Rob Reiner demonstrated the fake reaction, pounding away, when suddenly he realized the actress portraying the older female diner was—his mother, Estelle Reiner. Oy!

post of Chief Rabbi of the British Empire, which Adler filled with distinction for forty-five years. During Victoria's reign, her Jewish subjects had more rights than in any other European country.

The famous pirate **JEAN LAFETTE**, a free-thinking Jew, was many things: buccaneer, alchemist, communist, a frequenter of cabarets and balls—but still a loyal family man. This, no doubt, was greatly due to his *bubbe*, Zora Nadrimal, who raised him. According to his diary, Lafette was born in Port-au-Prince in 1782. His mother, Maria Zora Nadrimal, died soon after, and the young Jean was raised by his Jewish grandmother, Zora. His grandfather, Abhorad Nadrimal, was jailed, tortured, and died in prison in Spain. Since Jean was raised on stories of his grandfather's suffering, he developed a hatred of all things Spanish. He described his grandmother as training him "in the habits necessary to the development of a strong personality, prepared to face the vicissitudes of life with a firm and determined will and capable of ignoring all obstacles that would retard the development of my mind."

> **"I** had a great uncle in the Czech Republic," says Harry Leichter, recalling a most bizarre (OK, and funny) story. Before the Nazi takeover, his uncle's sister in Jamaica, Queens, invited his great uncle and his family to immigrate to America. But what did Harry's uncle do? He went to Jamaica, *in the West Indies,* while his wife, Frimscha, wound up going with the Russian troops to Siberia with her children—as a woodcutter. "Meanwhile, **'Wrongway' uncle** wound up in Bolivia, and lost track of his family. Auntie, the woodcutter, would leave food for her toddlers while she went off into the woods every two weeks," Harry explained. Miraculously, her husband tracked her down, brought them to Bolivia, and finally they all got to the right Jamaica—in Queens, New York. "When I met her," recalls Leichter, "she was solid muscle. Iron. Without one fat cell. If that doesn't demonstrate the strength of the Jewish mother to survive, nothing will."

According to Bruno Halioua's book, *Meres Juives des Hommes Célèbres (Jewish Mothers of Famous Men)*, **SARAH BERNHARDT**, known as the Divine Sarah, had an uneven relationship with her mother Judith, a Berlin-born courtesan. Judith was mistress to upper-class men during the mid-nineteenth century, when Jewish women, newly freed from the ghettos but still in poverty, were considered exotic to the gentleman of Western Europe. Consequently, Judith Bernhardt had little time to take care of her daughter and Sarah spent the early years of her life with foster parents (her father's identity is still unclear). When young Sarah returned home, she jumped from a window to attract her mother's attention, breaking an arm and leg. Later on, her mother did help her career by persuading the Duke of Morny, a family "friend," to intervene. Sarah was hired by the prestigious Comedie Francaise Theater Troupe even though the young thespian had yet to prove her talent.

LORNE GREENE became an icon in the long-running hit, *Bonanza*, in part thanks to his Jewish mama. According to author Tim Boxer, after Lorne did the pilot in 1959, he spoke with his mom in Florida, who told him a friend had died in Hollywood, and he should "run, pay a shiva call that night." (Shiva is a seven-day period of mourning, where the bereaved customarily stay at home and receive visitors.) Lorne told her he'd go the following evening, but mama insisted he go immediately. He listened to mama, and at the shiva home that night was an NBC executive who saw the rough cut. Lorne was signed to star in the series, which aired for fourteen years and was seen in sixty-one countries.

NOTE: *Bonanza* featured a number of Jewish story lines that weaved history with fiction. Adah Issacs Menken, whose story follows, was the subject of an episode.

ADAH ISAACS MENKEN was born in 1835 in Louisiana. Her mother was probably a beautiful French Creole woman, and Auguste Theodore, a respected "free" Negro, was her likely father. But the four-times married actress, poet, and literary figure kept her first husband's name—and religion. Adah was stunning, educated, and wild, and her dream was to perform. In

1855, when her stagecoach broke down in Texas, she met her first husband, Alexander Isaac Menken. The match instilled in Adah a lifelong adherence to Judaism, and she began to write poetry, using Hebraic illusions. The couple adored each other, but Menken wanted a traditional wife, whereas Adah preferred the adulation she received on stage.

In New York she met the Benicia Boy, Johnnie Heenan, who was a fighter. Adah was fascinated with his strength and married him. After a month, Heenan began beating her and they divorced. She did give birth to a son, but the child died at birth. Then Adah met Blondin—a daredevil who crossed Niagara Falls on a tightrope. She bargained that "perhaps" she would marry him if he'd let her dance on the tightrope above Niagara with him. He refused, afraid Adah's beauty would distract him and he'd plunge into the Falls.

Her career soared, however, when her manager encouraged her to do *Mazeppa*, a play based on Lord Byron's poem—that was popular on Broadway—with one significant change. At the climax of the play, the Tartar boy, stripped of his clothes by his captors and bound to the back of a wild horse, was "played" by a stuffed dummy. In Adah's version, however, she rode the horse in nude tights. This was a shocking sight for the day and gave her instant, intense notoriety.

Her flamboyance put her in the company of the likes of Whitman, Dickens, and Twain. Adah then married American humorist Robert Newell, divorced him, and married James Barkley. They had a son, Louis Dudevant Victor Emanuel Barkley, who died in infancy. (George Sand was godmother.) Although *Mazeppa* made her famous, Adah's deepest desire was to be considered a serious poet. She clung to her Judaism and continued to write and in the 1850s she published poems in the *Israelite*.

Charles Dickens quipped about Adah,

"She is a sensitive poet who, unfortunately, cannot write."

In 1868, although treated by Napoleon III's personal doctor, she died in Paris at thirty-three—apparently from peritonitis and tuberculosis. A rabbi kept a bedside vigil. Menken was buried in the Jewish section of Montparnasse Cemetery.

Fagin, the Jewish character in *Oliver Twist*, left some Jews believing **CHARLES DICKENS** was anti-Semitic. In 1863, **MRS. ELIZA DAVIS** began writing letters to Dickens to educate him about the Jewish people. Not only did Dickens donate to a Jewish cause after reading her letters, but he listened to Mrs. Davis's criticisms of his portrayal of Jews and included her suggestions in his subsequent works. Mrs. Davis, gratified by his response, sent him Scriptures in Hebrew, adding: "Presented to Charles Dickens Esq., in grateful . . . recognition of . . . having . . . the noblest quality . . . that of atoning for an injury as soon as conscious of having inflicted it, by a Jewess."

HEDY LAMARR, once known as the world's most beautiful woman, was also an accomplished inventor.

She was born Hedwig Eva Marie Kiesler in 1913, in Vienna, Austria, the daughter of a wealthy Jewish banker and his wife. She longed to become an actress. Her fifth film, *Extase* (*Ecstacy*, 1932), in which she appeared nude, made her a sensation, but it was banned in Nazi Germany.

When she married Nazi sympathizer, Fritz Mandl, he tried to buy back all the copies of the film. Supposedly, even Benito Mussolini had a copy that he refused to sell. Lamarr, unable to tolerate Mandl's jealousy, drugged a guard, escaped, and divorced him in 1937.

Louis B. Mayer signed her, insisting she change her name and make less sensational films. In 1838, she appeared in *Algiers*, followed by *Lady of the Tropics* and *White Cargo*.

When her career went into decline in the 1950s, she turned to science. Despite no formal training, she had an exceptional scientific mind, and with her coinventor George Antheil, the two developed a system for radio communication that is still at the core of many communications systems—including the GSM cell phone system, which is used by over 1.2 billion subscribers worldwide.

The basic idea was a radio control mechanism for torpedoes that would prevent jamming by using a frequency hopping mechanism.

Lamarr worked with Antheil for several months before sending a synopsis of the concept to the National Inventions Council. The director of the council suggested that they further develop the concept for patenting. They made their system operational with the help of an electrical engineer. Patent number 2,292,387 was granted on August 11, 1941, to Hedy Kiesler Markey and George Antheil, as a Secret Communication System. (Markey was the second of six of Hedy Lamarr's husbands.)

The patent also specified that a high-altitude observation plane could be used to steer a torpedo. Antheil lobbied for support with the navy, but they declined, not wanting to put up precious resources for the development process.

In 1957, engineers at Sylvania took hold of the basic idea with electronic circuitry and in 1962, the system was used in the blockade of Cuba—three years after the patent had expired.

Though Lamarr and Antheil didn't receive a penny for their idea, subsequent patent holders have usually referred to the Lamarr-Antheil patent as the basis of their work.

Today, the concept is used in cellular systems as well as in the basis of many military communications schemes where hopping is used to prevent jamming.

Hedy Lamarr died in January 2000 at eighty-six in a modest home in Florida. She had three children, James, Denise, and Anthony.

During her life she was quoted as saying "Any girl can be glamorous. All you have to do is stand still and look stupid." While she was certainly glamorous, as proven by her invention, she was most certainly not stupid.

When **VÉRA** Slonim was asked how she met her husband of fifty-two years, Vladimir **NABOKOV**, she somehow "couldn't remember." Yet, her biographer, Stacy Schiff, who won the 2000 Pulitzer Prize for *Véra: Mrs. Vladimir Nabokov*, describes the marriage between Vera and Vladimir as one of the most enduring and important partnerships in literary history.

We do know a mask was involved in their initial meeting and that Véra made a dramatic entrance into Vladimir's life on a bridge over a canal one spring evening in Berlin.

Although the young novelist was still grieving over his broken engagement to Svetlana Siewert, he corresponded with Véra when he went to France. Eventually Véra's supportive letters, plus the hint that this relationship may have been destined, brought the couple together.

They married in 1925 and had a son, Dmitri, in 1934. Véra was Nabokov's "everything": muse, editor, researcher, driver, typist, agent, and more. Despite her modesty, even their son referred to her as his father's full creative partner who typed his words, suggested alternative phrasing, contributed her observations, and later researched his lectures. Véra also played bodyguard and driver. When she accompanied him on his beloved forays into butterflying, she was the one who carried a gun for protection.

His sexually explicit novel, *Lolita*, was surprisingly considered a work of genius by Véra, who refused to let their son read Mark Twain when he was little. It was Vera who pursued publication—after fishing it out of the garbage where Vladimir threw the manuscript. It was published in 1955.

After her husband's death in 1977, Véra continued his work, checking new editions, performing translations (for example, the difficult *Hell Fire*, into Russian), and managing all legal affairs until her death in 1991.

In 1988, according to author Tim Boxer, after doing a radio show on his eighteenth birthday, **RIVER PHOENIX** and his mama, Arlyn, asked the host where they could find a vegetarian restaurant. Steve North, their Jewish host, suggested the kosher Greener Pastures on the East Side. "What's kosher?" River asked. Arlyn explained and North learned she was a Jewish woman from the Bronx. This made River a Jew according to *halacha* (literally, "the way" guidelines to insure the continuance of Judaism as a unified way of life. These guidelines provide the basis for the system of Torah law known as *halacha*).

She might well be the most famous Jewish bride who ever sat for a portrait. Dona Abigail Levy de Barrios was most likely the plump young lady seated alongside her stylishly dressed husband, in Rembrandt's famous portrait that has come to be known as ***THE JEWISH BRIDE*** (now in Amsterdam's National Museum). Some scholars claim the groom was one of the more colorful individuals in the eccentric Jewish community of seventeenth-century Amsterdam. Don Miguel de Barrios was born in Andalusia and, while living the life of a Spanish military officer in Brussels, also acquired success as a poet. Like many conversos, he led parallel lives. In Amsterdam, however, he practiced Judaism openly, under his Jewish name of David Levi de Barrios.

Don Miguel's second marriage in August 1662 was to Abigail de Pina, who was descended from a prominent Moroccan rabbinic family, and whose father owned a sugar refinery in Amsterdam.

Although they were still poor, they had two children and remained married until Abigail's death in 1686. It's been suggested that when the aged Rembrandt painted the picture, he was at a low point in his life, and derived tremendous inspiration from the idyllic image of this loving and stable Jewish family.

Her name? Jeanne Abel. Her game, willing "accomplice" to husband, Alan Abel, legendary hoaxster. Among their many pranks, the Abels created a character named **MRS. YETTA BRONSTEIN**, a Jewish homemaker who ran for president against Lyndon Johnson in 1964, and against George Herbert Walker Bush in 1986. Jeanne, who has a gift for character voices and dialects, played Mrs. Bronstein. Her motto? "Put a mother in the White House," and her campaign slogan "Vote for Yetta and things will get Betta," appeared in headlines worldwide. She also wrote a tongue-in-cheek book, *The President I Almost Was*. In the early seventies the pair produced two satires: *Is There Sex After Death?* and *The Faking of the President*. In 2005, their daughter, Jenny Abel, coproduced a documentary about her parents, *Abel Raises Cain*.

In 1894, **ANNIE COHEN KOPCHOVSKY** made a bet with a Boston gentleman and set out to be the first female to circumnavigate the world—by bicycle. The mother of three, whose cycling experience was limited to days before her historic ride, was charged to begin without funds, earn $5,000 above expenses, and complete the task in fifteen months. This resourceful lady picked up endorsements, and made speeches along the way. Not only did she complete her trip in ten months—she proved that a woman could make her own way in a man's world. She also helped popularize changes in women's garb, from full skirts to bloomers. Since she made the trip solo, she provided for herself, survived physical injury and mechanical problems with her bicycle—and the press took attention. Kopchovsky collected her $10,000 prize in Chicago and then rejoined her family. She died in 1947.

Is this a job for a Jewish daughter? **JULIA QUERY**, comic, exotic dancer, stripper—and award-winning filmmaker—thinks so. Julia, the daughter of Dr. Joyce Wallace, who is an activist and celebrated for her work with prostitutes, carries her mother's social conscience, but in a less traditional way. In 1997, Query was the guiding force in unionizing exotic dancers in San Francisco's Lusty Lady strip club and immortalized in an award-winning documentary, *Live Nude Girls Unite!* (2000). She hails her mother a hero: "A fabulous thing about my mother is that she knows I poured my entire inheritance from my grandmother into the film, and she never once said that was a mistake . . . Jews [women] have a strong history of being social activists . . . from Emma Goldman on down."

It's kosher! And it's country. And it's written and recorded by perhaps the only rabbi to do so—**BRUCE ADLER, THE BLUEGRASS RABBI**, with help from his wife, **DONNA**, who is also a rabbi. Their albums, *I Choose Torah*, *Walk Humbly with Thy God*, *If It Be Thy Will*, and *Eternally Hopeful*, have been called Jewish gospel. When asked how he became interested in country music, Rabbi Adler claimed he's been a mountain man ever since the Israelites stood at Mount Sinai 3,000 years ago! He says, "I'm ordained Reconstructionist, my congregation of eleven years is Conservative (Beth Israel). Donna is a Reform rabbi serving as Hillel Director of Miami University, in Oxford. We live with our son, Aaron, in Cincinnati, Ohio, who is starting to show an interest in singing and playing an instrument." He knows a lot of his parents' songs and sings along, but as far as becoming a rabbi like Mom and Dad, he's not quite sure about that just yet. Their songs are recorded and performed by folk, bluegrass, and gospel artists throughout the United States and available from Maplestaff Music.

Talk about odd alliances. Hitler was helped by Jews, notably his mother's doctor, **EDUARD BLOCH**. In two articles Dr. Bloch wrote for *Colliers* magazine, March 15 and March 22, 1941, entitled, "My Patient, Hitler," Bloch described how he treated Hitler's beloved mother when she was dying of cancer. Hitler and his sisters visited Bloch to thank him. He also received two hand-painted postcards of appreciation signed, "The Hitler family sends you the best wishes for a Happy New Year. In everlasting thankfulness, Adolph Hitler." In 1937, a number of local Nazis attended the party conference at Nirnber. After the conference Hitler invited several of these people to come with him to his mountain villa at Berchtesgaden. The fuehrer asked for news of Bloch. Was he still alive, still practicing? Then he made a statement, which irritated the local Nazis: "Dr. Bloch," Hitler said, "is an Edaljude—a noble Jew. If all Jews were like him, there would be no Jewish question." In March 1938, after Hitler annexed Austria, Hitler helped Dr. Bloch immigrate to the United States. The doctor was allowed to leave for America at sixty-nine—with sixteen marks instead of the customary ten—but he got out with his life.

Everybody who works in intelligence calls her Rita. **RITA KATZ** sometimes telephones people she hasn't met—important people in the government—to tell them things that she thinks they ought to know. She keeps copies of letters from officials whose investigations into terrorism she has assisted.

Katz, who was born in Iraq and speaks fluent Arabic, spends hours each day monitoring password-protected online chat rooms where Islamic terrorists discuss politics and trade tips, such as how to disperse botulinum toxin or transfer funds.

Traditionally, intelligence has been gathered by government agencies, such as the CIA and the NSA. But Katz, who heads Search for International Terrorist Entities, or SITE, has upset that monopoly. She and her researchers mine online sources for intelligence, which her staff then translates and e-mails to her hundred or so subscribers. Her client list includes officials in government, corporate security, and the media.

She has worked with prosecutors on terrorism investigations, and her work has been cited as often as twice a month in major news media. But her relationship with the government is "testy," since she is viewed as both consultant and sometimes antagonist.

Her tactics are aggressive. For example, a SITE staffer, under an alias, managed to join an exclusive jihadist message board for months that, among other things, served as a debarkation point for many would-be suicide bombers. He gained access to their true e-mail addresses and other initial information about them.

Rita Katz was born in Basra, Iraq, in 1963. She was one of four children of a wealthy Jewish businessman. In the wake of the Six-Day War in 1958, Saddam Hussein encouraged attacks against Iraqi Jews. Her father was arrested and charged with spying for Israel while his wife and children were transported to Baghdad and kept under house arrest in a stone hut. Katz's father was convicted in a military tribunal and executed in 1969. Rita Katz was six years old.

After living in the hut for months, Katz's mother drugged the guards and escaped with the children. She impersonated the wife of a well-known Iraqi general, whom she faintly resembled, and managed to get the family to Israel.

Katz did her military service in the Israel Defense Forces and studied politics and history at Tel Aviv University. In 1997, her husband won a fellowship to do research in endocrinology at the National Institute of Health, and they moved to Washington with their three children. (They later had a fourth.)

When she saw an ad for an Arabic-speaking research assistant, she applied for it and got the job. Her employer was the

Investigative Project, run by Steven Emerson, a former reporter with an interest in terror networks.

The Investigative Project did undercover work at Islamic fund-raisers and rallies. When she participated in particularly radical fund-raisers and conferences, she wore a burka, spoke a deferential Iraqi-accented Arabic, and sat apart from the men, eyes averted. She figured out which organizations were funneling money to the suicide bombers by volunteering to send their families cash.

On December 14, 1999, an Algerian named Ahmed Ressam was arrested as he tried to cross the border from Canada with a trunk full of explosive materials that he intended to detonate at Los Angeles International Airport. Richard A. Clarke, President Clinton's counterterrorism adviser, called Emerson and asked the Investigative Project for a report on militant Islamic cells in North America. There was concern that Ressam was part of a larger plot, and Katz became convinced there was a single global terror network.

By June of 2001, Katz set up her own office, taking staff members from the Investigative Project. She got by on small government contracts. Some of that work, which was done for the Treasury Department, involved identifying Islamic groups that might be sending money to terrorist organizations. She also had a contract with the Swiss government and with a group of relatives of 9/11 victims who were suing Saudi Arabian officials, businesses, and charities.

Detractors have questioned SITE's translations, claiming they always pick the most violent translation, which Katz denies. Rita believes that it's far better to overestimate rather than underestimate the threat.

Award-winning newsman **JOHN STOSSEL**, anchor of ABC's *20/20* specials and best-selling author of *Myths, Lies and Downright Stupidity Get out the Shovel—Why Everything You Know Is Wrong*, has focused much of his energy on exposing everything from pop culture to government regulations on his "Give Me a Break" segments. This is one newsperson who has an ardent dislike for frauds, myths, and nonsense.

His dedication to exposing untruths may resonate personally. His mother, who he describes as "alive and articulate," raised her sons as Protestants. "She claimed she wanted to assimilate and had no interest in religion," says the acclaimed newsman, who was a member of the Congregational Church.

Then, as a teen, "I made a remark about a Jewish boy picking his nose—and my brother said, 'what the heck do you think you are?'" He doesn't recall his mother telling him of their family heritage. He embraced Judaism at about age thirty. He also married "in."

"My brother-in-law is a Jewish activist," he says. Today, he and his family observe the Sabbath and do the blessings.

CHAPTER 7

Jewish Mothers—Courage Between the Tears

Some Jewish mothers, like those of all religions, races, and ethnicities, have had to endure unimaginable loss—the loss of a child. Pain and grief is a unique experience for everyone. Most never truly recover, but some turn their energies into even greater activism, much like Carolyn Goodman, when her son Andrew was murdered over forty years ago by the Klan.

Mothers, particularly those from ethnic and religious groups that have been persecuted, carry the burden of more than their share of suffering, tragedy, and overwhelming loss. Jewish mothers have been shedding tears for thousands of years, as time and time again, Jews have been singled out for annihilation. Our protectiveness, sacrifice, and raw courage in the face of this is, without question, rooted in our ethno-type. It provides an understanding of who we are, and deserves enormous respect when pitted against the comic images we're fed.

During the Holocaust, or Shoah, millions of Jewish mothers and their daughters were called upon to exhibit sacrifice and courage, the extent of which is simply unimaginable. But then, the deliberate brutality and organized murder of an entire group in those numbers was virtually unparalleled in recent history.

Regardless of the nature of the loss, Jewish mothers who are child-first have suffered incomprehensibly. And there have also been extraordinary non-Jews throughout history who risked their own lives to spare the lives of Jewish families. These stories are deeply agonizing but also uplifting, because courage and sacrifice under the most extreme conditions remains one of our most enduring lessons and legacies.

I hope you read between the tears. For it is in courage that we see the character of people when their most precious beliefs—and love—are tested beyond comprehension.

They embody the simple word: "hero."

Is the Jewish mother different in her acceptance of loss and sacrifice in the face of impending loss?

According to Jonathan Singer, in *Cultural Differences Among Elderly Women in Coping with the Death of an Adult Child*, Jewish mothers often meld personal boundaries, viewing themselves as more mothers than wives. When we lose a loved one, we confront the pain and expect help from others to cope. Non-Jews are more stoic and less likely to share their pain.

Singer found that while the Jewish mothers maintained their attachments, even after death, non-Jews were more able to stop mothering the dead child. Jewish mothers were also more depressed, lonely, and felt less in control of their lives.

Culture and religious ideology was one explanation for this difference. While Christianity believes that this life is a preparation for death and that resurrection brings eternal life, Judaism often focuses on the here and now of this life. More, Jews are culturally more likely to verbalize heightened emotions, whereas non-Jews are more likely to minimize them.

THE INQUISITION

$\mathcal{G}$racia Nasi, a converso (a secret Jew), whose Christian name was Doña Beatrice de Luna, was born in Lisbon in 1510. She spent her life helping her fellow Jews escape Christian persecution in sixteenth-century Portugal.

Gracia was born into a wealthy and prominent Jewish family. In 1528 she married Francisco Mendes, also a secret Jew, and they had one child, Rayna. The couple amassed great wealth and then used their network to provide escape routes for Jews that were victimized by the Inquisition.

After her husband's death, Gracia joined her brother-in-law,

Diego, in a highly successful business partnership in Antwerp. When Diego died in 1542, he left her his estate. She was eager to practice Judaism openly, and she did so when she reached Turkey, taking the name Gracia Hannah Nasi.

She created an underground railroad from Portugal allowing hundreds of conversos to leave. When she settled with her daughter in Constantinople, she actively provided for the Jewish community by funding hospitals, synagogues, schools, Hebrew-language printers, and even Jewish scholars and writers. She also confronted Pope Paul IV about his anti-Semitic policies. In 1558, she arranged with the Turkish sultan to buy the city of Tiberias with the intention of making it an independent Jewish city-state. This courageous activist died in 1569.

THE HOLOCAUST

The Nazis publicly hanged a mother and her five-year-old daughter. The mother's crime: She illegally bought an egg for her starving child. The child's crime: She ate the egg.

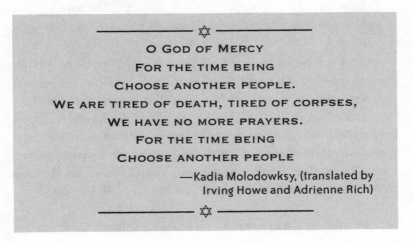

O GOD OF MERCY
FOR THE TIME BEING
CHOOSE ANOTHER PEOPLE.
WE ARE TIRED OF DEATH, TIRED OF CORPSES,
WE HAVE NO MORE PRAYERS.
FOR THE TIME BEING
CHOOSE ANOTHER PEOPLE

—Kadia Molodowksy, (translated by
Irving Howe and Adrienne Rich)

COURAGE AND SACRIFICE UNBRIDLED

Hannah Szenes was a paratrooper, poet, and hero. During World War II, the twenty-three-year-old parachuted behind enemy lines to warn Hungarian Jews of the Nazi scourge. She followed her mother's courageous example. As a child, she attended a Protestant girls' high school. Her mother challenged the discrimination of school tuitions, which were three times higher for Jewish students—and won. Hannah, an ardent Zionist, moved to Palestine. She wrote to her mother, "I am home. . . . This is where my life's ambition . . . binds me. . . . I am fulfilling a mission."

In 1943, she enlisted in the British Army and trained in Egypt as a paratrooper—the first woman to do so. When she was captured by the Germans and sent to Budapest, she was tortured. Her mother, also imprisoned, was threatened with torture if Hannah failed to reveal her radio code. Szenes refused. Although her mother was later released, Hannah was executed by firing squad on November 7, 1944, at age twenty-three. She was buried in the military cemetery on Mount Herzl in Jerusalem.

> "My God, My God, may these things never end: the sand and the sea, the rush of the waves, the lightning of the sky, the prayers of humankind."
>
> —Hannah Szenes

When the Nazis rounded up the Jews of Piotrekow for deportation to the concentration camps, four-year-old Yisroel was slated to go with his mother to Ravensbruck—and probably perish. According to author Tim Boxer, the boy's mother, Chaya, pushed him away, allowing his older brother to stash him in a duffel bag to Buchenwald where he would have a chance of survival. His mother didn't, but her son, Yisrael Meir Lau, grew up to become Israel's Ashkenazi chief rabbi from 1993 to 2003.

The following was written by a Jewish mother who was about to be taken to a concentration camp:

September 23, 1943

Bronia . . . I beg you: take care of my son. Be a mother to him. I am afraid he will catch cold:

He is so weak and sickly. He is very intelligent and has a very good heart. I am sure he will love you. Bronia, this letter is a cry from the heart. Michael must eat, become strong, be able to withstand sufferings. Please, it is necessary to dress him in warm clothes, that he wear socks. I cannot go on writing. Even my tears have dried up. May God protect you both.—Genya

Eventually he was captured. Both mother and son died in the camps.

1932: EG, Testimony 4 "Jewish Responses to Nazi Persecution" describes a tragic scene, as a neighbor, Froh Golde Graucher, burst into his home crying. Although she had gotten a pass to Palestine, two of her children were taken away. His own mother cried, knowing their days were numbered, and then begged her neighbor to save her youngest child, registering him as her own. The two mothers sobbed in each other's arms. His mother tried to make him believe she would follow. When the train finally starting moving, he had to force himself to call Froh Graucher "mameh"—and fought back tears as he saw his mother, wondering if he would ever see her again.

During August and September of 1942, the Jews of Kowel, Poland, were imprisoned in the synagogue and then 18,000 were executed. They knew they were slated for death and many wrote on the walls in Hebrew, Yiddish, and Polish, using anything . . . even their fingernails. Two read:

Reuven Atlas, know that your wife Gina and your son Imush perished here. Our child wept bitterly. He did not want to die. Go to war and avenge the blood of your wife and your only son. We are dying although we did no wrong.

Forgive me! Mother, I want you to know that they caught me when I went to bring water. If you come here, remember your daughter, Yente Sofer, who was murdered on 14.9.1942.

"My dear sister, today is the anniversary of dear mother's death. She was killed by Nazi criminals on November 14, 1941. On that day, at five o'clock in the morning, they began massacring the Jews in our town. By nightfall, 9,000 people had been killed—men, women, children. My dear mother's image is engraved in my mind. She thought of her children till the bitter end. A family friend, who was taken to the pit with our mother, later escaped and told us that our mother had talked about us all the way. Her last words were, 'Thank God, my children are alive. They are not here.'"

—Vladimir Shteinberg, November 14, 1944

In studies done on women of the Holocaust, critical differences were found that reflect *gender* differences, biologically and socially.

Rapes, sexual torture, and medical mutilation were performed routinely on women. The Nazis turned the mothers of newborns in the camps into murderers, forcing them to kill their own children, or be killed with them in the ovens.

Women, with traditionally feminine values of cooperating and caring, were more used to social interaction than their male counterparts and formed powerful sisterhoods with their fellow prisoners. They found strength, comfort, support, spiritual sustenance, and solidarity from these relationships. Judy Cohen, who, in her superb 2001 work, *Lessons Learned from Gentle Heroism: Women's Holocaust Narratives*, details these sisterhoods. While women nurtured, the men were more demoralized, continuing their "lone wolf" behavior.

The women, in their prewar roles as homemakers, were also superior organizers and this helped them survive. Whether it was sewing, cleaning, or exchanging recipes to make food stretch, they felt some degree of control and responsibility—even if it was an illusion.

In one example, Judy Cohen describes a group of Belgian women prisoners at Auschwitz that formed an ad hoc insurrectionist organization. Through "connections," they became attached to the Schuh-Kommando, sorting the shoes of prisoners, a job that allowed them to "organize" shoes for themselves and their friends. These activities, she notes, not only gave them purpose, but also contributed to their sisterhood and bonding, which made their daily lives bearable and helped them survive. In this horrific environment, the simple act of caring required a courage that can only be considered heroic.

In the *Scrolls of Auschwitz*, a manuscript found in the ashes of Auschwitz written by a member of the Sondercommando, surrogate "motherhood" and solidarity is described. One woman would give her bread to her starving friend or do her sick friend's work.

"While I had typhus, I was bordering on madness," said one woman. "I was delirious from fever. I once asked for an apple. My friends went and exchanged their bread rations for an apple. Thus, solidarity saved my life—and the lives of other women comrades."

Rudolf Hoess, Auschwitz commandant, noted in his autobiography where "time and time again" he "witnessed mothers with laughing or crying children [who] went to the gas chambers." He recalled a young woman who, as she stood at the gas chamber, said: "I deliberately avoided being chosen for labor because I wanted to take care of my children and go through this in full awareness of what was happening. I hope it won't take long."

Another tragic scene, described in 1943, tells of the children who were undressing in the anteroom of the gas chamber. When guards tried to hurry them, one eight-year-old girl resisted, crying: "Go away, you Jewish murderer! Don't put your hand, covered in Jewish blood, on my sweet brother. I am his good mother now and he will die in my arms."

CHILDREN OF THE HOLOCAUST

> "'FATHER, WHY IS THE WORD
> AUSCHWITZ SO FRIGHTENING?' . . .
> I . . . IMMEDIATELY SENSED THAT I HAD
> MADE A MISTAKE. I HURT MY MOTHER, AND
> SHE DOESN'T HAVE THE POWER TO HELP.
> WHY DID I HURT HER? . . .
> I FEEL THE TEARS RUNNING FROM HER
> EYES ON TO MY ARM, ON TO MY HAIR. . . . "
> —Cila Liberman

Today, we mothers worry about the effects a wrong word, a short separation, a TV show, or a rebuke may have on our children. For adults, the atrocities Holocaust survivors witnessed and suffered are incomprehensible . . . but for children . . . ?

In testimony after testimony, children of the Holocaust describe the gnawing hunger, families screaming and separated, orders to dig graves—for themselves . . . and seeing their mothers shot right before their eyes.

> I've turned thirteen,
> I was born on Friday the thirteenth.
> —*The Diary of Eva Heyman, Child of the Holocaust*

Eva Heyman was captured and sent to Auschwitz with her grandparents. They were murdered there. This is an excerpt from her diary:

April 5, 1944: . . . I met some yellow-starred people. They were so gloomy, walking with their heads lowered. . . . Still, I noticed Pista Vadas. He didn't see me, so I said hello to him. I know it isn't proper for a girl to be the first to greet a boy, but it really doesn't matter whether a yellow-starred girl is proper or not . . . [Grandma Lujza] says she doesn't care if she dies. But she is seventy-two, and I'm only thirteen. And now that Pista Vadas spoke so nicely to me I certainly don't want to die!

April 7, 1944: Today they came for my bicycle. . . . I threw myself on the ground, held onto the back wheel . . . and shouted all sorts of things at the policemen. . . . One of the policemen was very annoyed and said: " . . . No Jewkid is entitled to keep a bicycle anymore. The Jews aren't entitled to bread, either." . . . Imagine, dear diary, how I felt when they were saying this to my face.

May 30, 1944: . . . We can take along one knapsack for every two persons. . . . Rumor has it that food is allowed, but who has any food left? . . . It is so quiet you can hear a fly buzz. . . . Dear diary, I don't want to die; I want to live. . . . I would wait for the end of the war in some cellar, or on the roof, or in some secret cranny. I would even let the crossed-eyed gendarme, the one who took our flour away from us, kiss me, just as long as they didn't kill me, only that they should let me live. . . . I can't write anymore, dear diary, the tears run from my eyes.

"I think they heard the baby crying, and that brought them as far as our hiding place. Let the child go, he hasn't done anything, he's only a baby! . . . But the murderer's heart of stone was not moved. He replied: 'He's a baby now, but he'll grow up to be a Jewish man. That's why we have to kill him.'"

—From the diary of Donia Rosen, Polish, who was twelve when she hid in the forest after the murder of her family

Don't They Know the World Stopped Breathing?

And once,
there was a garden,
and a child
and a tree.

And once,
there was a father,
and a mother,
and a dog.

And once,
there was a house,
and a sister,
and a grandma.

And once,
there was a life.

—Anonymous

Donia Rosen survived and immigrated to Israel. In *Forest, My Friend*, she wrote:

"Words fail me, but I must write, I must. I ask you not to forget the deceased. ... to build a memorial in our names, a monument reaching up to the heavens, that the entire world might see. Not a monument of marble or stone, but one of good deeds, for I believe with full and perfect faith that only such a monument can promise you and your children a better future."

In 1940, Sala Garncarz, a sixteen-year-old Jewish girl who lived with her family in Sosnowiec, near Krakow, volunteered to take her sister Raizel's place when the Nazis ordered her to report to a labor camp for what was to have been a six-week period. The weeks stretched into five years that she spent in seven different camps in Germany, Poland, and Czechoslovakia. The letters she exchanged with friends and family members became Sala's lifeline. She collected and saved more than three hundred of these cards and letters, which were on exhibition at the New York Public Library through June 2006. After liberation Sala married American GI Sidney Kirschner and raised a family. The library has published *Letters to Sala*, a companion book to *Letters to Sala: A Young Woman's Life in Nazi Slave Labor Camps*. The companion book was written by Sala Garncarz's daughter, Ann Kirschner.

In her book *From Thessaloniki to Auschwitz and Back*, Erika Amariglio from Salonika wrote: "It was pitch dark and huge spotlights pierced the darkness, blinding us. '*Steigt schnell aus!*' [Climb out at once!], they were blinding us. '*Schnell! Schnell!*' [Faster! Faster!]—but nobody understood. Stunned by the long journey, stiff, hungry, frightened, desperate, everyone tried to jump out of the railroad cars. . . .

"The cold was terrible, it froze our faces, hands, and feet. We were chilled to the bone. Mothers held their babies tightly in their arms, and the older children clung to their skirts.

"Father, confused and frightened like the rest of us, pushed us to one side. . . . The Germans shouted out orders: 'All the children, the elderly, the ill, and the women go to this side.' That side? There were trucks waiting there. They stopped my father, who was about to push us toward the crowds going to the trucks. The SS-man asked him, 'Are you and your wife the ones who speak German?' 'Yes,' answered father and added, 'My children also speak very good German!'

"The SS-man sized us up and asked sullenly, 'How old are they?' This time father made us two or three years older. . . . 'Wait here until I come back,' the SS-man told us. People continued to get into the trucks, which, as soon as they were full, drove off. Where were they going? We had no idea!

"How many tragic scenes remain unforgettable in my mind. Mothers whose children were taken away—running after them so that they wouldn't be separated. Old people calling to children who remained behind. They snatched a young woman's baby by force and pushed her to the other side. Screams, sobs, farewells. And the smartly dressed SS-men shouting and raging in their midst.

"Suddenly all was silent. Nearly all the people were gone, only a few men and women remained. The SS-men formed them into columns, five abreast, men and women separated. They ordered them, to march: '*Vorwärts! marsch! schneller! Los!*' [Forward! March! Faster! Get moving!] We heard them shouting until we lost sight of them.

"Only the four of us remained. . . . There was just us and some SS-men. The silence was overwhelming in the dark night. The spotlights that had turned night into day were switched off."

Erika Amariglio and her mother survived various camps, and after the Holocaust they managed to find her brother and father, also survivers.

"Today I have seven grandchildren. . . . For my grandchildren and all the children of the world of any religion, I have written my testimony fifty years later so that they will be able to reply to anyone who dares to deny there was a Holocaust and so that they will always be on guard to make sure that there will never again be another Holocaust: NEVER AGAIN."

SURVIVORS AND THEIR CHILDREN

ADELE'S STORY: "'Are you my mother?' I asked the stranger that tried to hug and kiss me. In 1945, at the age of nine, I was a suspicious and mistrustful survivor of three concentration camps. When the woman came closer, I saw in her eyes the inexplicable mixture of sadness, fear, and love. I recognized those eyes. They belonged to my mother. Suddenly, I was flooded with memories of my sad childhood.

"I remembered how . . . we boarded the train to Auschwitz. We were saved when the German soldier could not find our names on the list and asked us to leave the train.

"I remembered how the Germans scheduled the resettlement of the men, and my father cut a hole in the ceiling of the barrack and hid for weeks in confined space, on top of the beams.

"I remembered how with trembling hands my mother buttoned my coat and pushed me out of the camp, for my escape to Switzerland. I was six years old at that time. I remembered and cried. But those were tears of joy. I felt like a child again. A normal child with my own mother."

Yet this was not the end, but another beginning. One that created between mother and child a unique and often painful experience.

"*I* always felt like my parents didn't really want to tell me everything. And sometimes I would read things or look at some pictures from Auschwitz. . . . I couldn't look for too long. Sometimes I would go and ask them about what happened. And I would wonder why didn't they tell me before I asked. I felt like they were keeping things a secret from me."

—Child of a survivor

An old Jewish woman pushed her daughter-in-law under the bed, saying: "You hide, I want to have grandchildren." She walked out to face the Germans.

Eighteen months later a miracle happened. The formerly barren woman conceived, and entombed in a bunker, gave birth to a baby girl—and they all survived.

We can only imagine that survivors of the Holocaust carry core wounds that never heal. While many have turned their rage into activism and great success, many found that coming back from deliberate madness is something that can't be completely understood by "outsiders." When they did "come back," married, and had children, how could they explain it? Should they explain it? How to relive the horror, the humiliation, to a child with no reference? How to mother—when one's soul and trust in the world has been shattered?

As a teenager, I became friends with Lily, a new girl in the neighborhood, who was the child of survivors. She was, we believed, a distant cousin. I remember her parents—quiet, afraid. Her mother, in particular, seemed nervous, abrupt, even "unwelcoming." I was deeply curious, and asked Lily about their experience. All she knew were two things:

First, that her parents escaped from the camps—and now they couldn't even abide looking at a German shepherd, the dogs used to find escapees. And the second, how her father and other camp survivors continued to support one male, an old man, who consistently said Hebrew prayers.

Beyond that, all I saw was the sadness—and loneliness.

I made a connection with my own grandmother and mother. Though they "got out" before the escalation of the Holocaust, they, too, left their families, ran in fear, and were detained in Danzig before getting passage to the United States. My grandmother rarely spoke about the details of their sacrifice or struggle—except for a few anecdotes about the old country, and mention of relatives as I pointed them out in scrap books. It was just too painful, and evoked too many memories of loss.

The horrors these survivors suffered have not only affected their lives but also the lives of their children. However, as with all human experience, some of these children, despite the pain and their own outrage over what their parents endured, have also made remarkable contributions.

Scholars who have studied children of survivors have written that many lived around secrets, partial communication, or silence. Even if the silences were motivated by protection, a lot of children were fearful and anxious, not truly "knowing." In a sense, they too, I believe, felt like outsiders in their own homes.

Witnessing deeply painful feelings and behavior in our parents—without fully knowing what happened—can cause horrific and frightening feelings in a child. Fantasy and speculation about the experience can run amok. "What did my parents do? What did they resort to, in order to survive?" are common questions. And yet, these children were often reluctant to push their parents, feeling both ambivalent and fearful of evoking strong reactions of sadness or depression.

> **CHILD OF SURVIVOR:** "I remember my mother telling me that she worked sorting dead people's clothes, and that this was a good job because many people brought food to the camp, and also you could exchange the shoes . . . for food. But . . . from her

reaction I felt that she almost felt like it was a crime to have worked there. . . . She was able to survive because she had access to dead peoples' things. I got sort of afraid to ask her more questions about it."

Yet, these children wanted and needed to make sense of what happened to their parents and to the world. It was important to help them develop a personal identity, even if that included a profound sense of personal and social injustice.

CHILD OF SURVIVOR (CRYING): "When I first realized what my mother went through . . . the horror of it, the pain, the suffering she experienced, I felt guilty almost. It sort of evoked these maternal feelings in me for my own mother. Even though I wasn't born yet I felt like I wished I could have protected her, shielded her. Also, I had this feeling of how unfair it was. She was only seventeen years old. I would look at pictures of her brother. He was only twelve years old and he was killed in Treblinka. I never could understand how another human being could do that. And it left me with this feeling of outrage."

Some children took on the outrage of their parents, but were disappointed they (the parents) weren't Simon Wiesenthals. Many took on the battle themselves, trying to right this horrific wrong, and some passed the need for retribution onto their own children and grandchildren.

Post-traumatic stress disorder (PTSD) and depression were higher among offspring of survivors during periods of severe stress. In 1996 Bruce Bower's article "Trauma Syndrome Transverses Generations" (*Science News*) studied eighty Jewish adults who were born to Holocaust survivors and twenty Jewish adults whose parents had not faced Nazi persecution. Twenty-nine percent of the offspring of Holocaust survivors had experienced symptoms of depression and PTSD, as opposed to 0 percent of the control group.

Other studies have found that children of survivors evidenced problems with communication, identity conflicts, and suffer a higher frequency of separation anxiety and guilt.

Those who were children in the camps were often too traumatized, having lost their own parents, to parent their own children without passing along survivor guilt. Some withdrew from their children or deprived themselves to provide everything for them.

Yet . . . the reverse was also true. Data suggests that some survivors not only managed to resume their lives but were also more successful than other American-born Jews of comparable age. In these survivors, adaptability, initiative, tenacity, along with luck may have accounted for their later success (Dr. Ruth, for example), and these traits may also have been passed on to their children.

In My Grandmother's Kitchen
by Jackie Ruben

I am in my grandmother's kitchen, in apartment 8B on Avenida del Libertador, Buenos Aires. It's the late 1970s. I'm a child and I sit on that old blue table where my own mom once must have sat at my age to eat, as I will, a feast of "chicken paprikash" with "tarhonya" noodles . . .

"Mami, where are your parents?"

Something changes . . . Can my little child memories crystallize?

"They're dead. . . ." A whisper, ". . . they were killed. . . ."

She sets her wooden spoon down and stares out the window, her left hand touching her cheek and covering her mouth, as I've often seen her do since that first memory, so many years ago.

"Were they killed with a sword?"

No answer . . . What's happened here? I've never seen my grandmother cry . . . her bright green-gray eyes become water as I approach her . . . fearing whatever it is, what the shadow, the terrible thing is . . .

And she hugs me and whispers in my ear, "No, my '*muggetcita*,' my little flower, no . . . "

Holocaust . . . The word that symbolized my family's taboo subject. To me, it is a word that encompasses it all, yet will never be enough. It is a word that has followed me throughout my life. It is also the wound of my heart that will never heal. It is, in short, my family legacy—one that, I have sworn to myself, I will pass down to the generations—the most important lesson to teach my kids.

STRANGE AND WONDERFUL BEDFELLOWS: NON-JEWS

"*W*hosoever preserves one life—it is as though he has preserved the entire world."

Yad Vashem (from the words of Isaiah, means Eternal memorial) is located on Har Hazikaron (the Mount of Remembrance) in Jerusalem, Israel. It was established in 1953 by the Israeli Knesset. Today, its forty-five acres is a complex of monuments, museums, resource centers, and teaching facilities.

Yad Vashem honors the righteous non-Jews who helped Jews in the hour of our greatest need—on behalf of the Jewish people. Their deeds prove that it *was* possible not to "stand by" or "take orders"—that one can and should oppose evil.

Those so honored serve as role models for future generations and as a beacon for ethical conduct—even when faced with grave physical and psychological danger.

Oscar Schindler has been immortalized in books and on the screen, but relatively little is known about his wife, Emilie. In 2001, a book was published in German, *Ich, Emilie Schindler* by the Argentinian author Erika Rosenberg, which examines Emilie Schindler's great contribution in saving Jews during the Holocaust.

She was born Emilie Pelzl on October 22, 1907, in the village of Alt Moletein, in the German-populated border region of what was then the republic of Czechoslovakia. Her first major encounter with anti-Semitism occurred when the local pastor instructed Emilie that her friendship with Rita Reif, a young Jewess, was not acceptable. Emilie, nevertheless, continued the friendship until 1942 when Rita was murdered by the Nazis in front of her father's store.

Emilie first met Oscar Schindler when he came to her father's farmhouse selling electric motors in 1928. He was tall, handsome, and outgoing and they were married in six weeks. Despite his flaws—overspending, lying, and deceiving his young wife (but then apologizing)—he had a generous heart and she forgave him.

In the 1930s, Oscar joined the Nazi party, seeing opportunities in war. In Kraków, by using bribery and selling black market goods, he gained control of a Jewish-owned enameled-goods factory, Deutsch Emailwaren Fabrik—where he employed mainly Jewish workers, the cheapest labor.

As the brutality of the Nazis accelerated, he began to view Jews also as human beings—mothers, fathers, and children. He used his connections, along with bribery and his wife's help, to risk everything in order to save the 1,300 Schindler Jews from the death camps. Emilie's jewels were sold to buy food, clothes, and medicine. They set up a secret sanatorium in the factory with black-market medical equipment where Emilie looked after the sick. Those who died were given a Jewish burial in a hidden graveyard that was created by the Schindlers.

The factory produced shells for the German Wehrmacht for seven months—not one usable shell was manufactured—but false military travel passes and ration cards were. Toward the end of the war, Emilie alone saved the lives of 250 Jews who were being transported to a death camp by convincing the Gestapo to send these emaciated Jews to the factory camp. Once released to her, Emilie worked to bring them back to life and health.

Oscar encountered a string of business failures after the war. He then fled to Buenos Aires, Argentina, with Emilie, his mistress, and a dozen Schindler Jews. By 1949, they were all farmers and were supported financially by the Jewish organization called Joint and Thankful Jews. However, success eluded Oscar, and in 1957, he went bankrupt and returned to Germany. He remained estranged from his wife for seventeen years before he died in 1974, at the age of sixty-six.

Emilie never saw him again. She remained in Argentina, living on a small pension from Israel and a $650 a month pension from Germany.

In May 1994, Emilie Schindler received the Righteous Among Nations Award, and in 1995, Argentina decorated her with the Order of May, the highest honor given to foreigners who are not heads of state. She returned to Germany and died on October 5, 2001, in a Berlin hospital.

In 1938 the Cohens fled Austria and went to Italy. When the Nazis asked their allies to turn over their refugees in 1941, Mrs. Cohen took her children to Father Anselm, begging him to care for them and send them to Palestine after the war. Instead, the courageous priest hid the family in a car, covering them with a blue church carpet. The priest diverted the sentries at the Swiss border so that the family could escape into Switzerland. Twenty years later, Sarah Cohen, in Haifa, found a similar carpet and she had it embroidered with, "Blessed Be the Righteous Ones" in Latin and Hebrew. She begged officials in charge of the reception to lay out the huge carpet when Pope Paul VI met Israel President Eshkol in 1964. She even arranged for the pope to walk upon it—and sent it to the aged priest's church in Laterina, Italy.

Having a son, I felt, as a German, I should act . . . These were the words of Beate Klarsfeld, who was born in 1939—the daughter of a German soldier and goddaughter of a Nazi official. She became a Nazi hunter after she married a Jew, Serge Klarsfeld, when she was in Paris, when she was twenty-one. When Beate heard about the atrocities committed against Serge's family—and after the 1968 election of a Nazi propagandist as chancellor of Germany—she felt the younger generation of Germans should not tolerate this, and slapped the leader in the face at a rally, thereby marking her as an activist. In 1972, the couple discovered that the notorious Nazi, Klaus Barbie, was hiding in Bolivia and they spent the next eleven years trying to bring him to justice. They finally succeeded in 1983 when he was deported to France, found guilty of crimes against humanity, and sentenced to life in prison. The couple's son, Arno, is an activist and a lawyer.

Nazi-occupied Holland. 1943. Eighteen-year-old Hilde van Straten-Duizer stood facing German soldiers as they hunted for Jews who were hiding at her mother's farm. Hilde and her sister began talking and flirting with the soldiers until they left forgetting about checking the loft where a twenty-two-year-old Jewish friend was hiding in the hay. His parents had already been deported. They were murdered at Auschwitz but he had escaped.

Despite the risk to their own lives, Hilde and her mother Gijsbertje Duizer cared for the young Jewish man, Joop de Van Straten, throughout the war. But more, Hilde fell in love with him, and when Holland was liberated, she converted to Judaism, and they married. In 1951, the couple immigrated to Israel and had four children.

Van-Straten-Duizer and her late mother were recognized on March 31, 2005, by Yad Vashem.

Hungary. March 1944: Maria Olt went to the infirmary to see her Jewish physician, Dr. Kuti Nevo, who was wearing the infamous yellow emblem. The distraught physician told Maria of his concern for his wife Miriam and their newborn child. Miriam Nevo later explained: "Maria . . . had decided to save our baby daughter. She brought the infant to a small village. A few days later she returned . . . and took me to the same village, introducing me as a gypsy who had given birth out of wedlock. . . . She returned once again to the city and brought my husband back with her, hiding him in a small cellar in her father's vineyard. Maria provided us with forged documents, and transferred our daughter to a family . . . in a small village near the Slovakian border, providing her with papers of a Christian child. . . . Maria moved us from place to place. Once

I had reached the point of despair: We saw a convoy of Jews who were being deported to Auschwitz. The train stopped near us. Impulsively, I wanted to join the procession and be rid of my suffering once and for all. Maria prevented me from taking this desperate step. She borrowed money and rented a small apartment in the village for me. After a short time, she brought my husband to the apartment. In another small apartment, near the Gestapo headquarters, Maria hid [and cared for] other Jewish families."

Irene Opdyke was born in 1918, in Poland, to a Catholic family. She was a member of the Polish underground and when she was discovered by Russian soldiers, was beaten and raped and then sent to a hospital. She fled, desperate to locate her family, but was captured by the Germans and placed in a munitions plant, where she collapsed from the heavy labor. She was a pretty Aryan-looking girl and attracted an SS officer, Eduard Rugemer. He arranged for her to have a lighter assignment—in a mess hall. It was here that Irene saw the horrific treatment of the Jews in the ghetto, including a baby flung into the air and shot as though it were hunting game.

She became Rugemer's housekeeper in the Ukraine, which included supervising the workforce, twelve Jews. When she learned of plans to kill them, Irene hid them and cared for them in Rugemer's villa—until he discovered them. She became his mistress—to save their lives, and her own.

Eventually, she married William Opdyke, who was with the United Nations working on behalf of displaced persons from the camps after the war. She came to southern California in 1949.

Though initially silent about her activities, she later started speaking to groups and, in 1999, wrote *Into My Hands*. Irene was recognized by Yad Vashem in 1982.

"I'll remember all my life, the mother that shouted to her child, 'Run, run, run,' and the Swiss customs man shouted, 'Come here, come, come, come to me.' And I didn't even see the horrors they must have then suffered."

The French actress Catherine Samie said these words. At age ten, she helped her mother lead Jews across the mountains into Switzerland to escape occupied France.

Sixty years later, Ms. Samie, a Catholic, performed in the play (2001) and film *The Last Letter* (2003), in which a Jewish woman, awaiting death in the Ukraine, addresses the son she will never see again. As her death looms, she asks him "to be strong and wise," then describes where ditches are being dug, "that's where you'll find the mass grave where your mother is buried." She reassures him her love is "forever . . . indestructible." Ms. Samie has said: "It wasn't acting. It was a testimony."

Ona Simaite was a librarian at Vilnius University. She took advantage of her freedom of movement into the Jewish ghetto— ostensibly to retrieve books loaned to Jews before the war—as a pretext to secure valuable literary works by Jewish authors. She also looked after Jews in hiding outside the ghetto. Ona was arrested during an attempt to smuggle a Jewish girl outside the ghetto and was tortured and sent to a concentration camp. She survived but suffered permanent damage to her health.

Joop Westerweel, a Dutch educator and sworn pacifist, created a clandestine network to help Jewish youth, members of a Zionist pioneering group, avoid detection. He then accompanied them through occupied Belgium and France to the Spanish border. He was eventually apprehended and executed by the Germans.

Dr. Adelaide Hautval was arrested for illegally crossing the demarcation line dividing the two parts of France. While she was in jail awaiting trial, she vociferously protested the inhuman treatment of Jewish prisoners. Censured as a "friend of the Jews," she was sent to Auschwitz, where she refused to join a team of doctors performing pseudo-medical experiments on women. After the war, Hautval testified in the 1964 London trial *Uris vs. Dering*, affirming that it *was* possible to disobey inhuman Nazi orders even in Auschwitz.

Bram Pais, a brilliant physics student, was the last Jew in Holland to receive a PhD before the Nazi ban on higher education for Jews. He and his family were one of the families aided by Tina Strobos, a medical student who lived with her mother and grandmother. These women offered shelter, food, false identification papers, and contact between other Jewish families. Despite the fact that their home was often the target of SS raids, Tina's cool presence of mind convinced them to release captured Jews, thereby saving the lives of numerous Jews in the Nazi-occupied Netherlands.

In 2005, seventy-two-year-old Ruth Gruener, who has two grown sons, finally reunited with the woman who saved her life during the Holocaust—Joanna Zalucka, eighty-one. The tearful reunion occurred sixty years after Joanna hid the then young Jewish girl in her bedroom for eight months and saved her from being murdered by the Nazis in Poland.

Ruth's father put his daughter under his overcoat, and left her with Zalucka's family as he expected to be slaughtered by Ukrainian nationalists.

The child spent her time in a chair, afraid to even look out the window from Joanna's bedroom. Joanna, then eighteen, was in charge of caring for eight-year-old Ruth. The child spent so much time silent and immobilized that she had to relearn how to walk and speak normally.

After the war, Ruth and her family went to Munich, then on to Brooklyn. She eventually married Jack Gruener, another survivor, and started a family.

Had Zalucka been caught, she probably would have faced the death penalty. She was, however, later imprisoned by both the Germans and Soviets as a suspected member of the Polish underground.

Ruth and Joanna, who had been writing to one another, were reunited by the Jewish Foundation for the Righteous. Their meeting was tearful and emotional. "It is just so wonderful that no words can describe how I feel," said Gruener. "It's a miracle," Zalucka added in Polish.

Gruener and her parents, from Lvov, Poland, were the only Jews in their extended family of three hundred who survived the Holocaust.

In 2003, the Karski Foundation in Washington, D.C., announced the 2003 winner of the Jan Karski award of valor and courage. Her name was Irena Sendler.

During the war, Sendler, who worked for the Warsaw health department, was a member of Zegota, the Polish underground. Her code name was "Jolanta."

She rescued 2,500 Jewish children from the Warsaw ghetto at great personal risk by placing them with Christian families. She was also sensitive to the need for these children to eventually reunite with their families, and buried jars containing their real and assumed names in a garden, so that after the war, they could unearth the names of their families.

In 2001, in a small Warsaw apartment, four adoring American students from Uniontown, Kansas, sat with their hero, ninety-one-year-old Irena Sendler, who received a medal from Yad Vashem. When sixteen-year-old Elizabeth Cambers called her a hero, Sendler explained that a hero does extraordinary things. She considered what she did simply a normal thing to do.

The unusual meeting came about when Cambers and her fellow students wrote a play, *The Holocaust and Life in a Jar*, which won a History Day contest. They wrote to Sendler and developed a friendship, and donations financed their trip to Poland.

Capping their trip back into history, the students met a survivor, thanks to Sendler. Elzbieta Ficowska was five months old when a Sendler worker rescued her in July 1942. The rest of her family had died in the ghetto. Had it not been for Irena, she, too, would have perished. Ficowska showed the students a silver spoon that her parents had engraved with her name and date of birth that was carried out with her.

On December 2, 1993, when a brick was thrown through the window of a Jewish home displaying a menorah, the town of Billings, Montana (population 83,000), took action. Another mother, deeply affected by the incident, phoned her pastor and the community immediately rallied together. Menorahs were seen in thousands of Christian, along with Jewish, homes. One store's billboard read: "Not in our town! No hate. No violence. Peace on earth." Eventually the hate crimes died down, but residents continued to support one another. In Billings, when the Jews cry "Never again!"—they're not alone.

BE MAD, MOTHER, BE MAD!
THE HORROR CONTINUES . . .

"The Holocaust reached us here," Faina Saltsman of Brooklyn told the Jewish Telegraph Agency. "My only child was taken from us. We have nothing left of him."

In 1990, years after sixty relatives had been killed in the Holocaust, Saltsman, her husband, Alexander, and son, Arkady, immigrated to the United States from the Soviet Union. Arkady was a premier architect and he was on the 105th floor of the north tower of the World Trade Center on September 11, 2001. After he left a message for his wife, Zhanna, saying he was trapped, she never heard from him again.

On the first Jewish anniversary of her son's death, Faina joined a march through Brighton Beach organized by the Friends of Refugees of Eastern Europe, and helped call out the names of sixteen Russian Jewish victims of September 11.

And she returned from that ceremony "destroyed."

"I am a Jew. My mother is a Jew . . . "

These were reportedly the last words of Daniel Pearl, the thirty-eight-year-old *Wall Street Journal* reporter in Pakistan, before one of his terrorist captors stepped up behind him, slit his throat and then beheaded him on February 2, 2002. Pearl spoke for himself, yet in doing so, spoke for Jews everywhere.

Marine Cpl. Mark Asher Evnin, twenty-one, of South Burlington, Vermont, died in Iraq on April 3, 2003. The former athlete was a scout sniper and the first Jewish serviceman to die in Iraq. On April 15, 2003, the Jewish Telegraph Agency reported that his mother, Mindy, received an emotional outpouring of sympathy from Jews around the world. "I don't know why it is. Maybe it's because the war might help Israel. Maybe because my father was a rabbi. I don't know, but it gives me pleasure." His funeral attracted over 1,000 mourners, including Governor Douglas of Vermont.

Army Spc. Marc S. Seiden, twenty-six, of Brigantine, New Jersey, died in Baghdad, Iraq, on January 3, 2004, when his convoy was ambushed by the enemy who used an improvised explosive device, small arms fire, and a rocket-propelled grenade. His mother Gail told the Fayetteville, North Carolina *Observer* that Seiden was "a daredevil since childhood" and this eventually led him to join the army. "I always had to have twenty-five eyes on him." She added that the terrorist attacks on September 11, 2001, were also part of his reason for enlisting. "He joined because he felt he had a duty. I didn't understand it when he did it. I was angry at him because I knew what could possibly happen. But he felt like he could fight for his country and he wanted to. His unit was scheduled to come back only one month later." Seiden was posthumously awarded a Bronze Star for valor.

Agnes "Aggie" Cohen of Pennsylvania said at the funeral of her son—Michael Ryan Cohen, who was killed in combat on November 22, 2004, near Fallujah in Iraq—that initially she was angry her son was killed. Since that initial reaction, however, she's been trying to understand what her son was fighting for. "Someone has to fight for those who cannot," she said. "Someone has to say, 'Enough. No more.'"

OUR HOMELAND

During the Nazi occupation of Paris an old, well-dressed French Jew entered the offices of a travel company.

"I want to buy a ticket on the next ship out of Cherbourg."

"Certainly, monsieur. Where do you want to go?"

"... May I see that globe?"

"Of course." The clerk placed the globe before the old man, who put on his reading glasses as he slowly turned the globe round and round. After a half hour he removed his glasses and sighed.

"Tell me ... do you have anything else?"

*I*n 1963, my family and I visited Israel. As a child, I recalled my amazement at being in a country where the vast majority of its people were Jewish. After forty years, my grandmother finally saw her family who had survived the war. Her first remark upon seeing them was, "Oy, you changed!"

The country at that time was perhaps the size of Long Island. My cousins Nomi and Moshe took us around. Moshe, with a tattoo on his arm, had survived Auschwitz, then fought for Israeli independence, as did Nomi.

When we went to Jerusalem, a divided city, there were Arab sentries guarding the border, which was maintained by barbed wire.

I was unused to the vagaries of war and life in Israel so I played around, testing the borders with a toe. Moshe pulled me back. "They'll shoot you," he bluntly explained.

It was absolutely remarkable to me what this young country had achieved: On the Israeli side of the border, there was green grass . . . life, and on the other side, there was . . . nothing.

Yet despite all the history, here, I felt safe and accepted, among my own. I knew that whatever happened, we had a homeland that would provide for me, for my children, and theirs, if need be. The Diaspora had ended.

"*I* went to the Wall together with some soldiers . . . only a few hours earlier they had . . . . seen their comrades fall for its sake. Now, standing before the Wall, they wrapped themselves in prayer shawls and wept, and I, too, took a sheet of paper, wrote . . . 'shalom' on it and pushed it into a cranny of the Wall . . . one of the soldiers suddenly . . . laid his head on my shoulder and we cried together. I suppose he needed . . . the comfort of an old woman's warmth."

—Golda Meir, writing of her visit to the Wailing Wall, liberated on the third day of the Six-Day War in 1967

*G*roundbreakers:
"OUR GOLDA"

Golda Meir was the woman who would become the world's third female prime minister (after Sirimavo Bandaranaike of Sri Lanka and Indira Gandhi of India). She was born Goldie Mabovitch in Kiev in 1898, the seventh of eight children born to Bluma and Moshe Mabovitch. Moshe immigrated to Milwaukee three years before his family but didn't prosper. When his wife joined him, Bluma borrowed money and opened a grocery. She wanted Golda to work in the store. Golda, however, wanted to be a teacher and became an activist early. She was haunted by memories of pogroms and was determined to save Jewish children from a similar fate.

During a year in Denver, with an older sister, she discovered Zionism, her life's passion. When she was nineteen she married Morris Myerson and they moved to Palestine in 1921. They had two children, Menachem, a cellist, and Sarah, a kibbutznik, but eventually separated.

In 1940, she was named head of the Histadrut's (the major Jewish labor federation's) political department. When Israel's independence was imminent, as would be a war with the Arab states, Golda was sent to the United States to raise funds for the Jewish armed forces. Meir so convincingly described the urgency of the Jewish cause that she raised $50,000—double the amount requested.

When statehood was declared on May 14, 1948, she was a signer of the Proclamation of Independence. In June 1948, Golda became Israel's ambassador to the USSR, a post she held for seven years. She then served as Israel's foreign minister for ten years and Hebraicized her name from Meyerson to Meir.

When Prime Minister Levi Eshkol died suddenly in early 1969, seventy-one-year-old Meir, although ill with cancer, assumed the post. Her political approach was that of loving grandmother, a straightshooter who won over the world with a simplicity, candor, and warmth that belied her shrewdness and nerves of iron. Even though she and the Labor Party won the elections, she resigned in 1974 in favor of Yitzhak Rabin.

After her death on December 8, 1978, Anwar el-Sádát wrote her children:

"I must record for history that she had been a noble foe during the phase of confrontation between us. . . . I must mention that she had an undeniable role in starting this peace process. . . . She has always proved that she was a political leader of the first category, worthy of occupying her place in your history and worthy of the place she occupied in your leadership."

Golda's quotes:

"Let me tell you something we have against Moses. He took us forty years through the desert in order to bring us to the one spot in the Middle East that has no oil."

"We Jews just refuse to disappear. No matter how strong . . . the forces against us . . . here we are. Millions of bodies broken, buried alive, burned to death, but never has anyone been able to succeed in breaking the spirit of the Jewish people."

And on motherhood: "At work, you think of the children you've left at home. At home, you think of the work you've left unfinished. Such a struggle is unleashed within yourself, your heart is rent."

> "*I* have taught my sons to be good Jews ... to battle for that which is right until the last breath, for man is duty-bound to fight for what he holds dear in life."
>
> —Rivka Gruber

When the Israel-Egypt peace treaty was signed in 1979, Rivka Gruber was among the dignitaries. Rivka, a pioneer settler in what was to become Israel, joined a Jewish Battalion. Her son, Ephraim, joined the Haganah and was killed two months before the establishment of Israel. Her other son, sixteen-year-old Zvi, was killed in battle against the Egyptians three months later.

Rivka went on to teach others in a remote region of Israel, helping to transform the area into a thriving sector.

Chief of neonatology at Assaf Harofeh Hospital in Zerifin, Israel, Dr. Michael Goldberg added another responsibility to his specialty of caring for newborn children. "Every mother who goes home with her baby," said the doctor, "we give her a baby survival kit. This is a plastic tent with long zippers along the side, and its own air pump to filter out noxious agents. What has become normal in Israel is not normal in the rest of the world. This is life for us in Israel."

"Death has cast a shadow over our lives," sighed a weary Nava Barak, wife of Israel's former Prime Minister Ehud Barak. "This has become a country where parents bury their children," reported Tim Boxer. In 2000, Mrs. Barak told media mogul Mort Zuckerman how she tried to console the wife of one of the two soldiers lynched by a mob in Ramallah. "She was married five days before the massacre," Nava said. "She is pregnant. Her child will be born [without a father]. But we will prevail. We have no other land. We are one people with one history and tradition. Now we are one people under attack."

Koby Mandell, thirteen, the oldest son of Sherri and Seth Mandell, and his friend Yosef Ishran, were killed on May 8, 2001. The boys were in a cave in the rocky countryside that surrounds the Mandell home in Tekoa, Israel.

Sherri Mandell has said, "We Jews have never honored cruelty. And we never will. True compassion means tempering kindness with strength. No 'security' fence can stop cruelty. . . . Justice demands that we fight for the lives of our children. We must insist that we are not cruel, even in war."

Sherri Mandell, a director of the Koby Mandell Foundation's Healing Retreat for families struck by terror, is the author of *The Blessing of a Broken Heart*. Although living with horror and grief, she also describes how she managed to return to life and find solace in a personal, spiritual search. Mandell says a part of her died along with her son in the cave that day, however, she decided to not just live with the pain but grow from it.

She refused to give in to anger and hate and become one of the "haters." Revenge, to her, means they have won. And she determined not to let hatred tear her from the world and destroy her.

Mandell and her husband, Seth, a rabbi, have created a foundation in their son's memory that supports, among other things, a free summer camp program for children who have lost parents or siblings. Camp Koby has helped hundreds of youngsters over the years.

In 2002, thirty-six-year-old Jonathan Joseph "J. J." Greenberg, a rising star in Jewish communal service, died in Tel Aviv the night before Yom Kippur. The New Yorker was struck down by a car while riding his bicycle during a visit with his family in Israel. He was the beloved son of Orthodox Feminist leader Blu Greenberg and her husband, Rabbi Irving "Yitz" Greenberg.

He was executive director of the New York-based Jewish Life Network since its inception in 1995 and created such landmark programs as: Birthright Israel, the Makor center on the Upper West Side, the Partnership for Excellence in Jewish Education, Synagogue Transformation and Renewal (STAR), and the Jewish Early Childhood Education Partnership. Jonathan and his father oversaw the national Hillel and the Jewish Heritage Program, as well as many others.

Right before Kol Nidre, visitors to his family home found his parents not just grieving but also comforting others and warmly recalling the impact their son had on so many.

More than any of his other extraordinary accomplishments, Blu Greenberg was perhaps most proud of her son's humanity and love of family—he was an exceptional uncle to his fourteen nephews and nieces, always finding time for each of them.

Rabbi Greenberg, has said that the central principle of Judaism is the triumph of life over death, and that all of the mitzvot are intended to achieve that goal. He therefore made the case for organ donations as "the ultimate mitzvah" in preserving and sustaining life. (Five of J. J. Greenberg's organs were donated for transplants.) This was another way for the grieving parents to deal with their tragedy and heal the world. In keeping with his spirit, Blu Greenberg said her son's liver was donated to an Arab man being treated in an Israeli hospital and that the transplant saved his life. She also spoke of the man's family with affection and said that she envisioned a day when such interactions would be common in both Israel and the occupied territories.

The Web site in tribute of her son is jjgreenberg.org.

Nothing stops the people of Jerusalem from living normal lives, writes Tim Boxer. On a warm June Saturday night, thirty-two relatives and friends gather at Ahavat Hayam, to toast Orit Tsarafi on her thirtieth birthday. They sing, they talk, and they laugh.

But this is Israel and the laughter is leavened with tears.

Orit's husband isn't here. He died in a training accident at an army base, leaving her with an eight-year-old daughter.

Her mother isn't here. She died when a terrorist blew up a bus between Tel Aviv and Jerusalem.

Orit's cousin, Roi, is here. He got a weekend pass.

While partying with his cousins, Roi gets a call from his base that two of his army buddies were just killed in a terrorist ambush. They were both in their early twenties.

This has become a normal way to celebrate a birthday in Israel—with laughter and with tears.

SHALOM

The circle never ends.
No matter what the trials,
The arguments,
The differences between us ...
The bond between mother and
    child
Forms an immutable circle ...

She is the wife ...
She is the mother ...
She is the wellspring, y'know

A wellspring lies deep. ....
Often hidden ... The bounty
    flowing through her ...
to those she loves ...

Often unrecognized ... in the
    expectation of always ...
As a force of nature.
After all, the wellspring is
    forever ...
Forming the eternal core ...

In strife, in struggle, trouble ...
the wellspring is forever ...
And all drink
From her fountain of strength ...

And it's in those times ...
for a brief, shocking instant ...
We see the source.

And wonder how we would
    survive ...
If the wellspring should stop one
    day.
But we know ... it can't. Ever ...
For the core, y'see, flows constant
    ...
Now.
And in the veins of those she
    has nurtured
In the minds of those she has
    taught
In the hearts of those she has
    loved.

For this wife ...
This mother ...
Who has multiplied the
    source ...
And so glorifies the original.
"For you are my child. ..."
And we are all children ...
Wrapped in the circle—
From womb ... into eternity.

—Marnie Winston-Macauley

"My mom was in the hospital dying, when I was eight weeks pregnant," said Mallory Lewis, speaking of her mother Shari Lewis. "After her final surgery and something went wrong, as the doctor came running into the room, she looked at me, and

Mom's last words were, 'I want you to know how happy I am about the baby and how much I love you.'"

> "MOM DIED IN 1998. MY SON WAS BORN IN 1999. WHEN SOMETHING GREAT HAPPENS, I LONG TO TALK TO HER. . . . I'M SHOCKED I DON'T HAVE HER NUMBER."
>
> —Mallory Lewis

There are 1,167 tombstones in the ancient Jewish cemetery of Rhodes. In 1997, when more than two hundred were uncovered during a restoration of the cemetery undertaken by the Jewish community, they found that many dated back to the 1500s and 1600s.

During the 1920s, the Island of Rhodes had an estimated Jewish population of 4,000, mostly of Sephardic origin. The tombstones are chiseled in Hebrew, sometimes utilizing letters of the alphabet for abbreviations such as N.A. ("Nun, Ayin"), which stands for " *Nishmata Eden*" and means "His (Her) Soul in Paradise." These abbreviations are the equivalent to the English usage of "R.I.P." for Rest in Peace.

The poetic passages on the tombstones reflect Ladino, along with lyrics of songs, called "canticas" and "romanzas."

#1847: Blessed be the judge of truth, the sound of crying is heard like a wailing from her husband on the youthful wife. My mouth decorated with silk has drunk a glass of bitterness; she left a son to be suckled; poor bitterness; storm become a pearl; she is the woman, the honorable, the righteous and the pure, Mrs. Miriam, the wife of Shabetai Israel, departed the ninth of the month of Kislev, the year 5607 (1847). May her soul be bound in the bond of life.

#1863: Blessed be the judge of truth. Her husband cries over her that in his smallness he drank the

glass of poison. Cry, crying, night and day, over his
wife, the woman of his youth. Suddenly his house
was ruined prematurely and out of time. Always
remembering the wife of his youth, not to forget.
All of a sudden, in his youth, she went early. She had
hard labor in birth. She is the woman, the strong,
and the humble, Mrs. Caden Linda Tamar, the wife
of Gabriel Pilosof, who died on the second day of
the month of Tamuz, the year 5624 (1863).

Rebekah Gumpert was born in Philadelphia in 1816 to a
Jewish father and Christian mother. She was raised a Jew and
was devout throughout her life. In 1845, she married Benjamin
Hyneman, a jewelry peddler, and officially converted to Judaism.
She was left widowed after five years of marriage. It was thought
that Benjamin may have been robbed and murdered. The young
widow began writing, and became noted for her poetry; many
were Jewish-themed.

Her life was scarred by tragedy. She lost her two sons, Sam,
from a fatal disease, and Elias Leon, a hero, during the Civil War.
Elias had been captured and imprisoned in the dread Andersonville
prison where he died.

Perhaps the most moving sentiments of this Jewish mother
were expressed in her last letter to Elias following the death of
his brother.

Phila'd. June 22/1864
My darling! . . . Oh, my dear one, how can I
write to you feeling so sad and desolate as I do, and
knowing that you are feeling the same. We should
comfort each other, and yet our full hearts will
overflow instead. He died, G-d rest him without a
struggle, without a moan, not a muscle moved, all
was calm as an infant sinking to sleep on its mother's
breast. I could not believe he was going from me, I
willfully shut my eyes to every symptom of it, and
when he calmly told me he was dying and wished

someone to read the prayers for him, I felt as if I could not endure it. . . . He left a kiss for you with his dying lips . . . and loved you to the last. May his pure spirit hover over you, my treasure, and turn aside every weapon that is aimed against you. I do not grieve for him as one without hope, no, thank G-d I am filled with hope, a hope that I may purify myself to meet him and a perfect conviction that he is happy. . . . You say truly you have lost a brother but heaven has gained an angel. . . . The flowers I send were taken from his dear hand just before the coffin was closed, cherish them, and keep them always near your heart, as a last gift from the dead to the living. May G-d forever bless and preserve you my darling. . . . Sorrowing Mother

Elias Hyneman applied for a furlough, but his request was denied. One week after this letter was written, Hyneman's regiment was in a cavalry raid at Reams Station, Virginia (Kautz's Raid). They were surrounded and outnumbered. Hyneman and a compatriot were almost out of the danger zone when the comrade's horse fell, breaking a leg and injuring the rider. Hyneman helped the wounded man onto his own horse, saying he would attempt to escape on foot. Further on, he came upon another wounded comrade, barefoot and bleeding. He gave him his boots. Hyneman was later captured and sent on a transport to the dreaded Andersonville prison where he died of starvation and exposure six months later on January 7, 1865. His family had his remains disinterred and brought home. On April 22, 1866, he was reburied by his brother's side, in Mikveh Israel, the old Jewish cemetery in Philadelphia.

> "[My mother] died two years ago . . . now, there's no one to send articles to."
> —Rabbi Bob Alper

> " Since Mom's death I've gone to cemetery and still have normal conversations with my mother. I report what's going on, with the kids, Larry, Congress . . . she hears. She hears. She drove me crazy my entire life . . . and I will miss her for the rest of my own."
>
> —Congresswoman Shelley Berkley (D-NV) eulogizing her mother, Estelle Auslander, who died July 21, 2002

> "I didn't consider/When I chose your name/ How it would look/On a tombstone."
> —Charlotte Mayerson, "Layout"

Charlotte Mayerson, a writer, poet, and editor, is also a Jewish mother who lost her son, Robert Henry, to AIDS. It was difficult to find comfort, even in religious study. Some solace came from Robert's memory (her own anger and anguish led her to write a collection of poems, *The Death Cycle*), and in recalling the women of the Holocaust. She told the *Jewish News Weekly* of northern California: " . . . as I thought I was going under, I thought of these women. I realized my experience [of not being able to protect my child] wasn't unique. Other women of our tradition have gone through this, too."

A circus act amalgam in a diminutive, square, bustling bundle of energy wrapped up in a "Jewish mother's" body. She had an encyclopedic file of recipes . . . worked fourteen-hour days. . . . There is not a more generous-hearted woman . . . than this woman who came to be my mother when I married her son thirty-three years ago. . . .

Passover came when she stood in her kitchen, . . . staring at the stove, hands lying still and flat on her counter top like dead birds. . . .

. . .

Mama was formally diagnosed . . . with Alzheimer's disease.

Last week, [she] didn't know my name.

. . .

As I visit . . . I focus on the amazing . . . courage with which she has lived [life], the lessons she has taught me about grace, forgiveness, and love. . . . This is where my heart chooses to dwell. . . . It's the whole of it that I will cherish and forever remember.

—Sharon Melnicer, "When the Circus Leaves Town"

"As a parent losing a child you realize that grief leaves you with a permanent hole in your heart. I believe that for me the grieving really began on March 7, 1997, the day my husband, Gary, and I were given the diagnosis of Tay-Sachs," wrote Monica Gettleman in beingjewish.org. "I will never forget the actual pain I felt in my womb when the ophthalmologist told us Brooke had Tay-Sachs.

"In the first few months after Brooke was diagnosed, I would find myself looking at other little girls her age and seeing what they do and longing for what I would never have with my daughter. If I was out, and a mother was close by with her child, I would compulsively ask how old her daughter was. I remember times when I would be in my car and just burst into tears. There was always a feeling that I was being cheated of watching the baby that I carried for nine months grow into a little girl.

"For the next year as I watched Brooke's health deteriorate, I had such an overwhelming feeling of sadness as I saw there was no stopping this disease.

"When Brooke required twenty-four-hour care, Gary and I made the decision to place Brooke in a skilled nursing facility that was thirty minutes from our home. The day after we took her there I literally couldn't move or get out of bed.

"On Friday, December 18, 1998, I had the most amazing visit with Brooke. I took her for a walk and she actually cooed and smiled. After leaving her on that Sunday, we got a call . . . that Brooke was running a fever and didn't look well. We went by ambulance with Brooke to the hospital, where we found out she had a case of pneumonia. Over the next few days, we knew she was dying and it was just a matter of time. What helped me tremendously was holding her in my arms, feeling her heartbeat next to mine, and being able to say goodbye. When we left the hospital on December 23 at 9:00, I knew that was going to be the last time I would see her alive. I woke up in the middle of the night knowing that she was gone; a few minutes later the hospital called, confirming that she passed.

"The biggest adjustment I had was not going to see her every day and holding her. I missed the softness of her skin and the innocence of her being. I knew I had to concentrate on staying healthy for the baby with whom I was four months pregnant. I found myself thinking a lot about what heaven was like and I pictured my daughter there as she physically would look had she not had Tay-Sachs.

"This helped me as I helped our son with his own healing process. I remember one day a few weeks after Brooke had passed I was eating Hershey's kisses with our son Alec, who was six years old. He held up a kiss and said, 'Brooke, this one is for you!'

"As the anniversary of her death approached I found myself reliving the last few days I had with her. I especially think of when I held her in my arms and told her how much I loved her.

"I think of Brooke every day and find peace in knowing that she is no longer suffering. Holidays are still hard but I know they will always come and go. It helps knowing how many lives Brooke touched in her short thirty-four months with us. I know now there was a reason for me being Brooke's mother. Maybe it was to teach me how precious life truly is, or to help others as a mentor with National Tay-Sachs and Allied Diseases. It has certainly made me a much more compassionate and understanding mother to my son and daughter. I always carry with me a tremendous loss for my child, but I know that someday I will be united again with my precious daughter Brooke."

_M_ama, Mama, my regrets for all the pain I caused you crowd in on me in these after-years. Your virtues transcended your faults. Papa knew that and bent his neck to your storms. I had neither his sweet humility nor fortitude.... If only—I could live it over again.

—Fannie Hurst, _Anatomy of Me_, 1958

All I did was grow up . . . not fly away
Where you saw distance, I saw closeness missed.
You felt I soared above you, out of reach
And out of your reach, I felt ungrounded
Because each of us, we're never fully grown
We just complete chapters.
Yet you felt our book had been written.
When I grew up.
But womanhood was just beginning.
Where were you, mom . . .
    when I fell in love again?
    when I was carrying your grandchild?
    when I saw my first gray hair?
Yes, I grew up, but you never believed,
I didn't know how to do any of this—without you.

—Marnie Winston-Macauley, 2006,
for Shirley, my mother (1925–1977)

Epilogue

When Israel's, Rabbi Lau addressed the congregants at one Saturday morning service, he talked of officiating at funerals every week, sometimes going from one to the next.

When he was chief rabbi of Netanya, years ago, he officiated at the wedding of a young girl, Shira. Her family grew.

After the bombing of Sbarro, Shira's sister called him. This time to officiate at the burial of Shira, her husband, and three children.

As he stood silently before the five coffins with tears welling in his eyes, the only words the rabbi could cry out in Hebrew were—"How much longer?"

He went to the hospital to visit the remaining child, now an eight-year-old orphan. Lau looked into her eyes, red with tears, and said, "Miriam, a long time ago there was a little boy, also eight years old, also an orphan. He came here and grew up." He added, "You are looking at him now—a chief rabbi of our nation."

"See what you can become? Be strong. You too can grow up to be a leader of our people."

Throughout the interviews and research for this book, an extraordinary fact emerged.

The Jewish mother is often consumed by the seemingly contradictory values of pessimism in the now . . . yet hope and optimism for the future.

The last question I asked of those I interviewed who were Jewish was, "Will there always be a Jewish mother?" Regardless of any difference of opinion among them, on this singular question, there was absolute agreement.

All wanted to see the Jewish mother remain—always.

"I hope there will always be a Jewish mother," says Blu Greenberg. "It's an honorable title."

"Will the Jewish mother always be there?" says Mallory Lewis. "Yes . . . because God willing . . . there will always be Jews."

"I believe in the continuity of the Jewish existence . . . she will survive," says Theodore Bikel.

"I think the world needs Jewish mothers," says Dr. Eileen Warshaw. "The universality of the Jewish culture affects all cultures, which I believe, is one of the reasons we have survived. There will always be a need to know she's there, providing comfort, safety, caring, and nurturing."

Today, we live in a world of chaos, fear, and disconnection. As neighborhoods have changed and families have scattered, we see "intimacy" by modem—a cold surrogate. In our daily lives, we hear of violence against innocent individuals, made worse, I believe, because our primary supports have fractured. We fear for our homeland and for ourselves.

And we experience a deep-seated, core loneliness, as we leave our roots not only geographically, but spiritually.

My fervent hope is that this book has, in some measure, restored some balance, providing a deeper understanding of the sensibility and range of the Jewish mother against the simplest, often offensive, and ignorant stereotype. And in doing so, we can see the positive values that have permeated our culture, and have given birth to extraordinary children—and ideas. Ideas that have made the world—and our children—more just, more humane, and more civilized. Ideas that took thousands of years to develop. Ideas based on a singular faith that, while at times has been insular, has nevertheless reached out to all as part of our mission to heal the world—not tomorrow or in a next life—but today.

For today, for tomorrow, I, too, pray the Jewish mother will not be lost to us in a faulty haze of misunderstanding and misrepresentation.

I pray the truth of us is acknowledged.

I pray our magnificent ethno-type continues to reconnect us in love and peace.

I pray that we practice, restore, or reclaim our roots, and pass these on to questioning children. Children who will not only understand, but stand by the behavior and beliefs that are the basis of all Jewish thinking.

I pray that now we have struggled, questioned, and come so far in this new world, we are ready and able to return home and embrace all sides of us, so the term "Jewish mother" is once again a source of deep and abiding pride for us all.

And I pray that we thrive as long as humanity occupies this Earth.

WHO MADE YOU?

Seven-year-old Hannah, sitting on her *bubbe*'s lap, was reading Hebrew to the old woman, who was now almost blind from her years in the camps and then the sweatshops.

From time to time, Hannah would take her eyes off the book and take her *bubbe*'s tired hand.

"Did God make you?" she asked.

"Yes, darling," her *bubbe* answered, "God made me a long time ago . . . even before girls could study . . . or lead in the synagogue."

"Really, *bubbe*?" asked Hannah, pondering. "I want to be a doctor . . . or an astronaut . . . or a rabbi—and a mommy."

"That, my *kinder*, you can now do."

She kissed *bubbe*'s wrinkled cheek. "*Bubbe*, did God make me too?"

"Yes, indeed, sweetheart," she said, "God made you just a little while ago."

After thinking this over, Hannah observed, "God is getting better at it."

The Aleph-baiz of Jewish Mother Humor

A: ASSISTANCE

Rachel, Sheva, and Rosalie, visited Gittel, mother of four, who was laid up with a bad back.

"Oy . . . such a shame," exclaimed Rachel, sipping her tea.

"I know," agreed Sheva. "The pain, and now the operation . . . such *tsouris* you have."

"Well, let me tell you, darling," said Rosalie. "We'll pray for you every night!" as the other women nodded vehemently.

"Every night, instead," said Gittel, "wash my dishes. Praying I can do myself."

B: BUSINESS

Selma, Abie, and their four children ran a dry goods store on the Lower East Side. Over forty years, they expanded and made a fortune so they decided to go big time and buy a department store—Macy's. They toured the huge store with Mr. Macy himself. Afterward, Abie wrote a check for the $10 million down payment, when Selma tugged at his sleeve.

"Abie, don't buy!" she whispered adamantly.

"Why not?"

"You didn't notice? There's no apartment in the back!"

C: CEZANNE

Jake was very wealthy. For his mother's birthday he went to a Sotheby's auction, bought her a painting, and couldn't wait to call her.

"Mama!" he said, "for your birthday, I bought you a Cezanne."

"Wha . . . ? You mean that nice girl in the deli?"

"No, Mama. That's *Suzanne*. Paul Cezanne is a great painter!"

"Who knew?" she said. "*Bubbeleh*, ask him how much he'll charge to paint mine ceiling."

ⅅ: DON'T ASK

Frieda and Shana, old friends, ran into each other in the deli.

"So how's your Morty?" asked Frieda.

"Oy . . . a bad cold."

"And your children?"

"They, thank God, perfect."

"And the business?"

"Never better. Listen, I'm in a hurry so—"

"Wait a minute," said Frieda. "How come you never ask about me and mine?"

"You're right. OK, darling, how's by you?"

"Don't ask."

ℰ: ENOUGH

Jewish mama, Rivka, tottered into a lawyer's office and told him she wanted a divorce.

"A divorce?" asked the shocked lawyer. "Tell me, how old are you?"

"Ninety—this July," answered Rivka.

"And how old is your husband?"

"He's ninety-two."

"And how long have you been married?" he asked in disbelief.

"September will be seventy years."

"And children?"

"Four. Gorgeous."

"Why would you want a divorce now?"

"Because," said Rivka . . . "*enough is enough*."

ℱ: THE FLASHER

A Yiddishe mama is walking in the park at dusk. All of a sudden a strange man, who was walking in front of her, blocks her path, opens his raincoat, and flashes her.

Unruffled, she takes a look, shakes her head, and remarks, "This you call a lining?"

𝒢: THE GIFT

Sidney Cohen couldn't believe God sent him Esther, such a perfect wife and mother.

"God," he asked, "why did you make Esther so kind-hearted?"

God said, "so you could love her, my son."

"And why so good-looking?"

"So you could love her, my son."

"And such a cook?"

"So you could love her, my son."

"And such a mother!"

"The only thing, God," he said, "why with those gifts did you make her so stupid?"

"Oy . . . so, she could love *you*, my son."

𝓗: HINT

Myrna and David dated all through college, yet not once did David bring up the subject of marriage. Finally, Myrna's mother sat her down.

"Darling, although David's a doll, I think you've waited long enough. The very next time you're out, try giving him a little hint, OK, *Mamala*?"

The following Sunday night, David took Myrna to their favorite kosher Chinese restaurant. As he read the menu, he casually asked her, "Myrna, darling, how do you want your rice? Boiled? Or fried?"

Without hesitating, Myrna looked up at him, and replied, "Thrown."

𝒥: INSOMNIA

Dr. Friedman had been caring for an elderly *bubbe*, Mrs. Kantor, for over thirty years.

When he retired, he turned over his patients to young doctor Siegal, who asked Mrs. Kantor to bring her list of medications. Shocked, he saw the seventy-five-year-old had a prescription for birth control pills.

"Mrs. Kantor," he said, "do you know that these are birth control pills?"

"Of course, doctor," she replied. "They help me sleep at night."

"Look, there is absolutely nothing in birth control pills that could help you sleep better."

Hearing this, Mrs. Kantor patted the young doctor on his knee. "I know this," she said, "but every morning I get up at six, grind up one of the pills, and mix it in the cereal for my sixteen-year-old granddaughter. After she's has breakfast, oy, do I sleep better!"

$\mathcal{F}$: JEWISH SURVIVAL

A new flood was predicted and nothing could prevent it. In three days, the waters would wipe out the world.

The Dalai Lama appeared on worldwide media and pleaded with humanity to follow Buddhist teachings to find nirvana in the wake of the disaster.

The pope issued a similar message, saying, "It is still not too late to accept Jesus as your Savior."

The chief rabbi of Jerusalem took a slightly different approach: "My people," he said, "we have three days to learn how to live under water."

$\mathcal{K}$: KREPLACHAPHOBIA

Fanny's ten-year–old son, Marvin, went into a panic whenever she served kreplach. So she took him to a psychiatrist, who suggested the boy watch her prepare the dish, and once he saw the ingredients, the problem would be solved. That night, Fanny let Marvin watch her. She showed him the mound of dough and chopped meat.

"See, darling? Is there anything to worry about?"

"No, Ma," said Marvin.

"Now I'm putting meat in the center of the dough and folding one corner." Marvin was smiling. She folded a second and third corner. All was going terrifically.

Finally, she folded the final corner. Suddenly Marvin shouted: "Oy vey, kreplach!!"

𝓛: LITTLE LOST BOY

A Jewish mother took her son shopping. The mall was a madhouse and the two were separated. The four year old started to wail until security came.

"Why are you crying, little boy?" asked the guard.

"I lost my mommy," he said.

The guard brought him to the security desk. "What's your name, little boy?" they asked.

"Shayna punum."

𝓜: THE MIGRAINE

Thelma went to see her rabbi about her migraines.

"Rabbi, my head's thumping like a giant hammer."

"What's wrong?" asked the rabbi.

"I haven't told a soul, but my son dropped out of dental school to become a clown. My daughter finally has a 'significant other'—who's married. My other daughter got her nose pierced. And worse, my younger son joined Jews for Jihad!"

"Oy-oy-oy," said the rabbi, who commiserated.

"You know, rabbi," said Thelma, "talking to such a learned man has cured me! My migraine's gone!"

To which the rabbi replied, "No, it's not. *I* have it now."

𝓝: NEVER MIND

Rosie's husband Max didn't come home from work one day, so her daughter suggested she call the police.

When the officer arrived, she said, "I can't live without him. Please help me."

"Calm down, madam," he replied, "I need you to answer some questions."

"Of course."

"Can you describe him?"

"Well, officer, he's fifty-two with gray hair—what's left of it. He's seventy pounds overweight. And he sweats from every-where. He also screams a lot. He was wearing a brown suit, ten years old, with a stained white shirt . . . He fools with women

. . . and . . . he smells of herring. And . . . wait a minute, officer, on second thought . . . *never mind.*"

☉: ONLY ONE THING

A widowed mama was talking about her recent breakup with the businessman she was seeing, telling all to her married daughter.

"So, Mama, why did you stop seeing that nice senior businessman? You told me how much alike you are. You both love art and hate opera; you both love cats and hate dogs; you both love tea and hate coffee—"

"And," added Mama, "we both love our Social Security checks and hate each other."

𝒫: THE PRAYER

A rabbi was talking to precocious six-year-old Mendel.

"So, you tell me that your mother says your prayers for you each night. That's very commendable. What does she actually say?"

Little Mendel replied, "Thank God he's in bed!"

𝒬: THE QUESTION

Maya went into labor for thirty-six hours. Finally Dr. Shlockman comes in.

"Oy-oy-oy!" yelled Maya, "I'm suffering terrible pains!! Please. Advice!!"

Dr. Shlockman replied, "*Nu*, so what did you think? You were going to *enjoy* them?"

𝓡: THE RULES

Mrs. Bronstein greeted the newest member of the canasta club to the tables.

"So, welcome to our group. As president, it's incumbent upon me to welcome you to the group, and tell you our rules. We never tell a lady how she should have played a hand. We don't discuss our husbands. We don't boast about our grandchildren. Finally, we never discuss S-E-X. The way we all feel is: What was, was!"

$\mathcal{S}$: SPIN

Two vacationers, Mrs. Shulman and Mrs. Feinberg, were rocking on the porch of a resort when a young man approached.

"*Gottenyu*!" exclaimed Mrs. Feinberg in a loud whisper. "Look at that boy! Did you ever see such a nose? And those crossed eyes? A mouth, oy, the size of a latke."

Mrs. Shulman icily replied, "It so happens, you're talking about my grandson!"

"Lis-ten," said Mrs. Feinberg quickly, "on *him*, it's becoming!"

$\mathcal{T}$: TWO JEWS THREE OPINIONS

After forty years together and five children, Isaac and Sylvia were not doing too well in the marriage department. After consulting the rabbi, they reconciled, but it was a no go, and they wound up in divorce court. The judge turned to Isaac.

"What terrible thing has brought you to this point that you can't keep your forty-year marriage together?"

Isaac answered, "Your honor, not one thing could Sylvia and I agree on in the three weeks we were back together—"

"Excuse me, Your Honor," interjected Sylvia, "Make that two weeks!"

$\mathcal{U}$: THE UNIVERSE

Melvin was reading the paper when he noticed an interesting item.

"Mama," he said. "It says in the paper that the world is getting smaller."

"This, I don't believe," answered mama, adamantly.

"It's here—in black and white."

"OK, OK," said she. "But if the universe is getting smaller, so why is it taking your father longer to get home each night?"

$\mathcal{V}$: "VELL . . . ?!"

The following is a true story. When I was in my twenties, I developed a blood clot and was hospitalized. My grandmother called me—not to find out how I was. She had a more important agenda:

"Darling, so you've been laying there ten days. *Vell?* Did you meet a doctor yet?"

"Well . . . actually, I did meet an opthomologist . . . "

"Eyes!" she cried. "Vat kind of doctor's that! From hearts, from brains—now *dat's* a doctor. *Vell . . . ?!*"

𝒲: WHERE'S THERE'S A WILL THERE'S A WIFE

Seymour worked hard and became wealthy. As he lie dying, he talked to his wife.

"Minnie . . . here are my last wishes."

"Whatever you want, I'll do."

"First, the business I leave to Morty, our eldest."

"Morty!" Minnie protested. "Morty's always with the girls. Better to leave it to Jeffrey."

"OK, Jeffrey," he sighed. "Now, the bonds I leave to Thelma."

"Better me," argued Minnie. "In two days, she'll spend at Bloomingdale's."

"Alright. The summer house I leave to our Adah."

"She's not spoiled enough? Leave it to Morty."

Finally, summoning his last ounce of strength, Seymour lifted himself up and said, "Minnie . . . who's dying here—me or you?"

𝒳: X-AXIS

Little Irving sat down with his mama, as always, to do his homework.

"Mama . . . what's an x-axis?"

"Darling, what do I know from x's? But it's a good question."

"Well, what about stem cell research?"

"The only stems I know are on fruit," she answered.

"Well, why does lightning come before thunder?"

"I forgot, but I'll look it up later."

Then little Irving asked, "Do you mind me asking you all these questions?"

"*Mamala!* If you don't ask, how can you learn!"

ℐ: THE YACHT

Morty made a killing in the stock market, so he bought a yacht and all the fittings—a fancy "captain's" uniform with white jacket, hat, and epaulettes. One Sunday, he invited his mama from the Bronx to take a look.

"Some yacht, huh, Mama? So, what do you think of your boychick now?"

"Very nice," she murmured.

"See?" Morty said, pointing to his epaulettes. "I'm a regular captain now!"

Mama rolled her eyes.

"Well," said Morty, indignant. "You don't seem very impressed."

"Morty darling," his mother said. "By the world you're a captain, by me you're a captain—but believe me sonny, by a *captain*, you're no captain!"

ℨ: THE ZIONIST BIG SHOT

At a banquet for a rich Zionist, forty people, including the mayor, celebrities, and other *machers* (big shots) gave huge testimonials about the guest of honor. They all gushed over his generosity, his humanity, and his contributions to Israel. Mama Greenbaum's son, Morris, a kidney specialist, brought her along. After the thirtieth speech extolling the man's greatness, she turned to her son.

"Morris," she whispered. "Why does such a big shot need so many character witnesses?"

APPENDIX 2

From These Roots:
JEWISH MOTHERS TO US ALL

All the women included are mothers, or contributed mightily to motherhood. The list could go on and on and is by no means exhaustive.

Bella Abzug, Paula Ackerman, Sara Adler, Stella Adler, Mary Antin, Joyce Antler, Ruhama Avraham, Diane Arbus, Rose Arensberg, Beatrice Fox Auerbach, Lauren Bacall, Jennie Loitman Barron, Charlotte Baum, Matilda Blaustine, Beatrice Alexander Behrman, Gertrude Berg, Shelley Berkley, Helen Beverley, Stella Blits-Agsteribbe, Judy Blume, Naomi Blumenthal, Barbara Boxer, Fanny Brice, Fanny Brin, E. M. Broner, Joyce Brothers, Hortense Calisher, Rachel Calof, Aviva Cantor, Shoshana Cardin, Peggy Charren, Betty Comden, Elizabeth Levy Cooper, Dr. Gerty Theresa Radnitz Cori, Carolyn Blumenthal Danz, Helene Deutsch, Bettina Donau, Jennie Migel-Drachman, Rosa Katzenstein-Drachman, Anna Dresden-Polak, Celia Dropkin, Amy Eilberg, Judith Kaplan Eisenstein, Hannah Bachman Einstein, Nora Ephron, Judith G. Epstein, Dianne Feinstein, Merle Feld, Tovah Feldshuh, Clara Ferrin-Bloom, Terese Marx Ferrin, Dorothy Fields, Marilyn Fierro, Julia Frank, Bilhah Abigaill Levy Franks, Betty Friedan, Ruth Cohen Frisch, Ruth Bader Ginsburg, Judy Gold, Francine Goldberg, Caroline Goodman, Lee Grant, Rebecca Gratz, Blu Greenberg, Bernice Degginer Greengard, Jennie Grossinger, Ruth Gruber, Minnie Guggenheimer, Ruth Handler, Ida Handwerker, Myrna Hant, Goldie Hawn, Esther Hays, Carolyn Heilbrun, Gladys Heldman, Lee M. Hendler, Fannie Hurst, Paula Hyman, Rebekah Hyneman, Fannie

Jaffe, Janet Rosenberg Jagan, Ruth Prawer Jhabvala, Regina
Jones, Pauline Kael, Florence Prag Kahn, Andrea Kalinowski,
Ida Kaminska, Deborah Kaplan, Bel Kaufman, Lainie Kazan,
Judith Kaye, Agnes Keleti, Faye Kellerman, Carole King, Irena
Kirszenstein-Szewinska, Minna Kleeberg, Melanie Klein, Lea
Kloot-Nordheim, Blanche Wolf Knopf, Syd Koff, Rebekah
Kohut, Annie Cohen Kopchovsky, Bonnie Koppell, Lilli Cohen
Kretzmer, Mathilde Krim, Madeleine Kunin, Hedy Lamarr,
Estée Lauder, Esther Lederer, Francis Lehman Loeb, Anne
Lapidus Lerner, Gerda Lerner, Lena Levine, Flora Lewis,
Mallory Lewis, Shari Lewis, Hadassah Lieberman, Irma
Levy Lindheim, Helen Levinthal Lyons, Regina Margareten,
Lane Bryant Malsin, Elaine May, Charlotte Mayerson, Golda
Meir, Adah Isaacs Menken, Annie Nathan Meyer, Lenore
P. Meyerhoff, Marilyn Michaels, Sonya Michel, Gertrude
Michelson, Bette Midler, Abigail Minis, Ida Mintz, Yocheved
Mintz, Penina Moise, Kadia Molodowksy, Belle Moskowitz,
Rahel Musleah, Barbara Myerhoff, Bess Myerson, Dona Gracia
Nasi, Joan Nathan, Maud Nathan, Joan Nathanson, Louise
Nevelson, Tillie Lerner Olsen, Fredele Oysher, Cynthia Ozick,
Grace Paley, Gail Parent, Mollie Parnis, Dalia Rabin Pelossof,
Roberta Peters, Irna Phillips, Eugenia Levy Phillips, Rebecca
Machado Phillips, Molly Picon, Letty Cottin Pogrebin, Susan
Polgar, Eve Pollard, Sally Priesand, Judith Raskin, Fanny
Reading, Freda Resnikoff, Adrienne Rich, Joan Rivers, Nacha
Rivkin, Annie Rochlin, Roseanne Ida Rosenthal, Esther
Roth, Helena Rubinstein, Muriel Rukeyser, Esther Ruskay,
Aline Bernstein Saarinen, Summer Sanders, Sandy Eisenberg,
Sasso Mathilde Schechter, Susan Weidman Schneider, Allyson
Schwartz, Barbara Seaman, Frances "Fannie" Sheftall, Naomi
Shemer, Dinah Shore, Sylvia Sidney, Beverly Sills, Joan Micklin
Silver, Anna Sokolow, Anna Freudenthal-Solomon, Hannah
Greenebaum Solomon, Rosa Sonnenschein, Susan Sontag, Flora
Spiegelberg, Fanny Goldberg Stahl, Dawn Steel, Bettina Donau
Steinfeld, Julia Kaufman Strauss, Barbra Streisand, Eva Szekely,
Linda Kaplan Thaler, Chana Timoner, Dara Torres, Barbara
Tuchman, Sophie Tucker, Lillian Vernon, Barbara Walters,

Eileen Warshaw, Wendy Wasserstein, Lotus Weinstock, Margaret Whitman, Shelley Winters, Rosalyn Sussman Yalow, Julia Frank Zeckendorf, Lydia Hatoel-Zuckerman.

Selected Biographies

MARTY ALLEN: The "Hello, Dere!" man with the Don King locks and ping-pong ball eyes is still making crowds howl. He performs with his wife, the super singer and straight lady Karon Kate Blackwell, in Las Vegas venues, clubs around the world, and on cruise ships. When Nat King Cole put the comic legend together with Steve Rossi, they became the biggest duo since Martin and Lewis. Mr. Allen, a soldier's medal recipient, is a tireless charity performer (particularly Holocaust-related), actor, and an art and book expert.

RABBI BOB ALPER: Rabbi Alper is a stand-up comic with a fresh, "unorthodox" style that delights audiences of all backgrounds from Hollywood's IMPROV to the Montreal Comedy Festival. He is the first Jewish person to ever earn a doctorate from the Princeton Theological Seminary and still conducts High Holiday services in congregations both in Buffalo and Philadelphia. He's been seen on *Good Morning America*, Showtime, the BBC, CNN, and *Extra*. Rabbi Alper performs nearly one hundred shows per year, often with Muslim/Arab comedian Ahmed Ahmed. He is the author of *Life Doesn't Get Any Better Than This*, and *A Rabbi Confesses*, an award-winning cartoon book. He has also created two best-selling comedy CDs. (BobAlper.com)

KAYE BALLARD: Ms. Ballard was fifteen when she made her debut in a USO show in her hometown of Cleveland. Two years later, she was a solo performer on the RKO vaudeville circuit. She's distinguished herself in film but is known primarily for her work in cabaret, theater, and televison. She starred in the sitcom, *The Mothers-in-Law*, and was later seen on *The Doris Day Show* and *The Steve Allen Comedy Hour*, among others. She received the Hal Erickson, All Movie Guide Award and was nominated for a Drama Desk Award. A powerhouse since 1950, she remains a much-in-demand cabaret and stage performer. Ms. Ballard has appeared in *Quartet* with Simon Jones, but claims her best role was Mama, in *Gypsy*.

CONGRESSWOMAN SHELLEY BERKLEY: She began serving in the U.S. House of Representatives in January 1999, representing constituents living in the First Congressional District of Nevada. She is the mother of two sons: Sam, a student who recently returned from studying in Israel, and Max, a graduate of the University of Arizona. In March of 1999, she married Dr. Lawrence Lehrner, a nephrologist, who has two children of his own: David, putting his graduate degree from Indiana University to use at MGM Mirage, and Stephanie, a family practice physician. Congresswoman Berkley enjoys historical fiction and entertaining guests with her gourmet cooking.

THEODORE BIKEL: The Viennese-born Emmy-winning actor, singer, author, linguist, and activist is a true Renaissance man. He created the role of Baron von Trapp in *The Sound Of Music* on Broadway, and has played Tevye in *Fiddler on the Roof*, over 2,000 times. His films include *The Defiant Ones*, *The African Queen*, *My Fair Lady*, *The Russians Are Coming, The Russians Are Coming*, and *Shadow Conspiracy*. Mr. Bikel is politically active and was elected as a delegate to the 1968 Democratic Convention. Among many appointments, he was also senior vice president of the American Jewish Congress, president of the Actors' Equity Association, and, by presidential appointment, a member of the National Council on the Arts. He is currently president of the Associated Actors and Artists of America. Mr. Bikel has two sons.

NATE BLOOM: Mr. Bloom regularly publishes uplifting and inspirational stories for *JWR*. He writes on popular culture and celebrity Jews for the *Detroit Jewish News*, *Baltimore Jewish Times*, *Cincinnati American Israelite*, *New Jersey Jewish Standard*, and *JWeekly* (San Francisco).

Mr. Bloom is the editor of Jewhoo.com, which is a smorgasbord of information on Jewish cultural figures, including Jewish actors, actresses, comedians, musicians, scientists, and others.

AMY BORKOWSKY: She is a successful comedian and author, and has published *Amy's Answering Machine/Volume One: Messages from Mom* and *Volume Two: More Messages from Mom* books and CDs. Ms. Borkowsky has appeared on the *Today* show, and has been featured in *People, Life, Mademoiselle, Jane*, as well as the *New York Times, L.A. Times*, and *Chicago Tribune*. Her latest book is *Statements: True Tales of Life, Love, and Credit Card Bills*. Prior to comedy, she was executive vice president and creative group head at a major Manhattan ad agency where she won five Clios, three Cannes Festival Lions, and an Emmy. (SendAmy.com.)

TIM BOXER: Is there someone he doesn't know? I doubt it. For years, Mr. Boxer was the guiding force behind Minyan of the Stars, a group of Jewish celebrities shmoozing and celebrating their heritage. I was fortunate to be a member and had some memorable nights, thanks to his remarkable get-togethers. Mr. Boxer has been writing a celebrity column for three decades for the *New York Jewish Week*. He is also editor and publisher of 15MinutesMagazine.com, and author of two books, *Jewish Celebrity Hall of Fame* and *Jewish Celebrity Anecdotes*. He was formerly an assistant to the legendary Broadway columnist Earl Wilson of the *New York Post*.

SEYMOUR "SY" BRODY: He is the author of *Jewish Heroes and Heroines of America: 150 True Stories of American Jewish Heroism*, and may have written more biographies of famous Jews than any other single individual. Mr. Brody is a former editor of *The Jewish Veteran*. He has also created six exhibits of Jews in America for the Web site of the Molly Freiberg Judaica Collections of Florida Atlantic University. He is president of the Jewish Heroes and Heroines of America Foundation.

JULIE COBB: Ms. Cobb was born into a theatrical family. Her mother was Yiddish stage and film actress Helen Beverley, and her father was the Tony Award–winning actor Lee J. Cobb. Ms. Cobb has appeared in over seventy TV programs, including *Charles in Charge, Knot's Landing, Family Ties, Magnum P.I., Hearts Afire*, and *Judging Amy*, among others. She won the Los Angeles Drama Critics Circle Award for her performance in *After the Fall* and the Dramalogue Award for her direction of *Twelve Angry Men*. Her daughter, Rosemary Morgan, is also an actor and continues the family tradition. Ms. Cobb is a licensed coactive life coach. She says her dog Seamus reflects her values—unconditional love, acceptance, and the ability to find fun in challenging times.

LORRIE COHEN: This Canadian-born journalist, comic, and mother of three is currently the assistant news editor at the *Tucson Citizen*. In addition to editing, Ms. Cohen has written numerous news stories, and has a strong background in celebrity interviews. When she's not writing and editing, she can be found doing her own material at comedy clubs in Tucson and all over the country. Her family sometimes provides her comic fodder—as does her lifelong struggle with weight. She swears her model-slim mother had a one-nighter with Danny DeVito.

BILL DANA: "My name: José Jiménez," soared the comedian, writer, and producer to fame. He was a head writer for *The Steve Allen Show*, and wrote the classic *All in the Family* episode, "Sammy Davis Visits Archie Bunker," and *The Laughter Prescription* with Dr. Laurence Peter. He starred in *The Bill Dana Show*, and has headlined in clubs across America. The National Hispanic Media Coalition awarded him their first Impact Award and he serves on their advisory board. When "José Jiménez" acted the reluctant astronaut, he became a part of that "family." He's on the advisory board of the Astronaut Scholarship Foundation and the nominations committee of the National Aviation Hall of Fame. He received a lifetime achievement award from the Pacific Broadcast Pioneers and is currently developing the American Comedy Archives with his alma mater, Emerson.

ZORA ESSMAN: She is the mother of comic Susie Essman, who costars on *Curb Your Enthusiasm*, and is a widowed mother of four. Her husband Leonard was a physician who died in 2001. Susie is her third child. All the Essman children are highly creative individuals: composers, pianists, and producers. Mrs. Essman was born in New York City, educated at Brooklyn College, and holds a master's degree from Middlebury College. She's also a multilingual scholar, has taught Slavic languages at NYU and Sarah Lawrence, and has translated books, plays, and poetry.

TOVAH FELDSHUH: Ms. Feldshuh is the quintessential performer—in theater, film, TV, and cabaret. She has earned Tony nominations, and won Drama Desk Awards, Outer Critics Circle Awards, an Obie, and Theatre World Awards. In October 2003, *Golda's Balcony* opened on Broadway, which earned her a Drama Desk Award. Her TV appearances have included her portrayal of a Czech freedom fighter in *Holocaust*. In film, she appeared in *Kissing Jessica Stein* and *A Walk on the Moon*, among others. Ms. Feldshuh is a supporter of Seeds of Peace, which helps teenagers from regions of conflict. She is a recipient of the Eleanor Roosevelt Humanitas Award, the Israel Peace Medal, and the National Foundation for Jewish Culture's Jewish Image Award. She is married and has two children.

EILEEN FULTON: She was the first "Bad Girl" on TV, in 1960, when she played Lisa Miller on *As The World Turns*. Her many honors include the Lifetime Achievement Emmy in 2003, and Ms. Fulton has coauthored autobiographies, *How My World Turns* and *As My World Still Turns, Soap Opera*, and six murder mysteries. Ms. Fulton is an acclaimed cabaret star who performs in top venues. Ms. Fulton has appeared in independent films including *Signs of the Cross*, receiving the Achievement in Television and Film Award from the Independent Filmmakers. She actively supports UNICEF, the March of Dimes, Cerebral Palsy, the Lupus Foundation, Martha's Table, and has established creative scholarships in her family's name at Brevard College and at her alma mater, Greensboro College, where she was awarded an honorary doctorate in 2005.

RONA GINOTT: She is CEO of Rayburn Musical Instruments Company, Inc. in Boston, and she is also passionately involved in Democratic politics, as Connecticut state chair of the Women's Leadership Forum of the DNC. Ms. Ginott is a former teacher and educational consultant. Her husband, David Ginott, died in 2003 leaving her a mother with two daughters. Her oldest is a Harvard graduate who is currently attending Yale Law School. Her younger daughter is finishing high school. Ms. Ginott is also a niece by marriage to the famed child psychologist, Haim Ginott.

JOANNA GLEASON: Ms. Gleason, the daughter of Monty Hall, is a distinguished theater actor. She won the Tony, Drama Desk, and Outer Critics Circle Awards for performances in *Dirty Rotten Scoundrels. I Love My Wife, Into the Woods, Joe Egg*, *Social Security*, and *Nick and Nora*. She has appeared in many films, including *Hannah and Her Sisters, Crimes and Misdemeanors, Heartburn, FX2, Boogie Nights, Fathers and Sons, Mr. Holland's Opus, The Wedding Planner*, and *The Pleasure of Your Company*. On TV she has been featured in *Love and War, The West Wing, ER, The Practice, Tracey Ullman*, and *Bette*. Ms. Gleason has directed *Love and War, Louie, Oh, Baby*, and many theater productions. She and her actor husband, Chris Sarandon, have four children between them.

JUDY GOLD: This former gangly "band nerd" has turned into one of America's leading cutting-edge comics, actors, and writers (winning two Emmys for the *Rosie O'Donnell Show*). The lesbian mother of two was in the sitcom, *Living in LA*, which was followed by an HBO special (and a Cable Ace Award). She is the host of HBO's *At the Multiplex with Judy Gold*. She has also hosted Comedy Central's *100 Greatest Stand-Ups of All Time*, and the GLAAD Media Awards. Her specials include *Judy Gold, Comedy Central's Tough Crowd Stands Up*, and she has been seen in *The Aristocrats*, and TV's *Law and Order*. She's also guested on *The Tonight Show with Jay Leno*, and *Late Night with Conan O'Brien*. Her most recent hit is her critically acclaimed show *25 Questions for a Jewish Mother*.

MAYOR OSCAR GOODMAN: The nineteenth mayor of the city of Las Vegas, Oscar B. Goodman calls himself "the happiest mayor in the world." He was born in Philadelphia and received his law degree from the University of Pennsylvania Law School. As a criminal defense attorney, he was named one of the Fifteen Best Trial Lawyers in America by the *National Law Journal*. Mayor Goodman also serves on the advisory board of the U.S. Conference of Mayors. The colorful mayor (who was featured in *Of Rats and Men*, and portrayed himself in the movie *Casino*) and his wife, Carolyn, have four children. "When Carolyn and I came here, Las Vegas was truly a land of opportunity," the mayor says. "You could establish a career, make something for yourself, and enjoy a great quality of life. I want to make sure that never changes."

BLU GREENBERG: Since 1973, Ms. Greenberg has been a leading voice in bridging feminism and Orthodox Judaism. Her books include *On Women and Judaism: A View from Tradition*, *How to Run a Traditional Jewish Household*, and *Black Bread, Poems After the Holocaust*, among others. She is the founding president of the Jewish Orthodox Feminist Alliance, and in 1997 and 1998, she chaired the International Conference(s) on Feminism and Orthodoxy. She has served on numerous boards, including Covenant Foundation, Project Kesher, and U.S. Israel Women to Women. She was first chair of the Federation Task Force on Jewish women and serves on the editorial board of *Hadassah* magazine and the advisory board of *Lilith* magazine. In 2000, she founded One Voice: Jewish Women for Israel. Ms. Greenberg was cofounder of Women of Faith and has been active in the Dialogue Project, which includes Jewish and Palestinian women. In 1990 she participated in the Jewish Tibetan encounter in Dharmasala, and in 2002, the World Conference of Religious Leaders in Bangkok. Ms. Greenberg is listed in *Who's Who in America* and *Who's Who in World Jewry*. She is married to Rabbi Irving (Yitz) Greenberg. They are the parents of five children and nineteen grandchildren.

DR. HOWARD M. HALPERN: Dr. Halpern, a psychotherapist and noted author, wrote *How to Break Your Addiction to a Person*, *Cutting Loose: An Adult Guide to Coming to Terms with Your Parents*, and *Finally Getting It Right*. He also wrote the syndicated newspaper column called "On Your Own," and has appeared on *Donahue*, the *Today* show, *20/20*, and CNN. He received his PhD in clinical psychology from Columbia University in 1954 and has taught, practiced, and consulted at several New York colleges and clinics. He is past president of the American Academy of Psychotherapists.

DR. MYRNA A. HANT: Dr. Hant is a visiting scholar at the Center for the Study of Women at UCLA and an instructor in gender studies at UCLA Extension and Chapman University.

Her research focus is popular culture/television with an emphasis on portrayals of mature women in the media. She is the author of a number of articles and papers on Jewish mothers and the media. She is also chair of the board of P.A.T.H. (People Assisting the Homeless), a nationally acclaimed nonprofit organization that reduces the homeless population by teaching job skills and by providing affordable housing. Previously, she was a college administrator at Chapman University. She holds a master's in English (Cal State Northridge), an MBA (Loyola Marymount University), and a PhD from UCLA.

LEE M. HENDLER: Lee Hendler, daughter of Lenore (Lyn) Pancoe Meyerhoff, is past president of Chizuk Amuno congregation in Baltimore, and the author of *The Year Mom Got Religion*, an autobiographical memoir of midlife learning and transformation. She is the mother of four children, and a well-known speaker on inter-generational philanthropy and issues of Jewish identity. Ms. Hendler and her family, the Meyerhoffs, are well-known philanthropists. She has two sons, two daughters, and two daughters-in-law.

BINYAMIN JOLKOVSKY: Mr. Jolkovsky is the publisher of *JWR*, the *Jewish World Review* (jewishworldreview.com, and PoliticalMavens.com). He is an Orthodox Jewish newspaperman from the Flatbush section of Brooklyn. His newspaper communicates traditional Jewish values to counter the growing indifference among young Jews to their religious heritage. PoliticalMavens.com stimulates dialogue from scholars and cultural leaders. Jewish contributors include terrorism scholar Daniel Pipes, *Jerusalem Post* columnist Jonathan Rosenblum, Nat Hentoff, (and yours truly), along with over two hundred columnists of all backgrounds (including Tony Snow, Thomas Sowell, and Walter Williams). Mr. Jolkovsky and his Web sites are regularly cited by national and international media.

LAINIE KAZAN: The multitalented Ms. Kazan is known for her electric voice and superb acting skill. She hosted her own special for NBC, and opened her own rooms at the Los Angeles and New York Playboy Clubs. She has received a Golden Globe nomination for *My Favorite Year* (which she reprised on Broadway as a musical), and her films include *Delta Force*, *Beaches*, *Harry and the Hendersons*, *The Associate*, and the blockbuster *My Big Fat Greek Wedding*. Kazan has also received award nominations for *St. Elsewhere* and *The Paper Chase*. Her TV work includes recurring roles on *The Nanny*, and on *Veronica's Closet*. She appears in top nightclub venues worldwide and in 1990, she received the Israeli Peace Award. On her CD, *Lainie Kazan—In the Groove*, she sings with her daughter, Jennifer Bena.

MARY KEATING: Ms. Keating is an actress, singer, and composer. She is married to actor Charles Keating and has created a CD called *Song Stories for Children* that was inspired by her relationship with her grandchildren. The compositions on the CD were designed to encourage creativity and develop imagination, using the animal kingdom. Ms. Keating began her acting career at the Cleveland Play House, where she met her future husband. The couple has two sons and six grandchildren. Although Ms. Keating wrote and sang the songs, she credits her son James for arranging, performing, and producing the CD.

RABBI BONNIE KOPPELL: Rabbi Koppell was one of the first women to be ordained as a rabbi in the United States, and the first female Jewish chaplain in the U.S. military. She is assigned to the Fifth U.S. Army and is currently the guest rabbi at Beth Hagivoth and Havurat Emet, interim associate rabbi of Temple Chai, and chaplain for the center for life enrichment of the Jewish family and children's service. She's a full colonel in the army reserve and has received many awards, including the Global War on Terrorism medal for her service in Iraq in 2005. In 2006, she visited with the Jewish military in Kuwait and Afghanistan and spent Passover in Iraq. She is listed in *Who's Who in Religion* and received the Celebration of Success award from Impact for Enterprising Women. Rabbi Koppell's writings can be found in numerous publications. She is married to David Rubenstein, an internationally known astrologer, and they have two children.

HARRY LEICHTER: Mr. Leichter considers himself an "open source researcher" who, since 1990, has created over 5,500

Jewish Webpages (mostly under www.Haruth.com), to educate people worldwide. To help promote his "kosher project" (to convince local store managers to carry more kosher foods), he created what is now called the *Schmooze News* (www.schmooze news.com), which includes a hundred stories of Jewish interest from international news and kosher recipes, to a classified section and calendar of events for the Jewish community. The news goes out to 2,000 worldwide subscribers and gets a million and a half "hits" per month. His information is often cited by universities as part of their curriculum. Mr. Leichter and his wife have one son.

MALLORY LEWIS: Mallory Lewis is the daughter of TV pioneer, Shari Lewis, and is an entertainer, producer, and Emmy award–winning writer. After writing and producing *Lamb Chop's Play-Along*, Lewis assumed the responsibilities of her mother's prime-time variety specials, and was executive story editor and producer of *The Charlie Horse Music Pizza*. Today, she appears with Lamb Chop at live and televised events, performing in more than two hundred shows in such venues as the Magic Castle and aboard the *Queen Elizabeth 2*. Mallory has also toured with the USO. She's the author of twenty children's novels, and her favorite reader is her son Jamie, who not only enjoys his mother's work, but also tells "his secrets" to Lamb Chop!

JODY LOPATIN: Ms. Lopatin, the former head mistress of an Orthodox Danish preschool, was the first Jewish president of the American Womens' Club in Denmark and served on the board of the International American Women's Foundation. She left Denmark as a result of growing anti-Semitism, but her husband stayed behind. She is divorced, and has four grown sons.

GIL MANN: Mr. Mann is a journalist and self-made entrepreneur. He adeptly uses both of those careers to help others understand their Judaism. His book, *How to Get More Out of Being Jewish Even If: A. You Are Not Sure You Believe in God, B. You Think Going to Synagogue Is a Waste of Time, C. You Think Keeping Kosher Is Stupid, D. You Hated Hebrew*, has been critically acclaimed. He lectures and conducts an online bulletin board called "Why Be Jewish Anyway?" After three years as a fellow of the Wexner Heritage Foundation, Mr. Mann decided to learn more about unaffiliated Jews. He saw that "the product is excellent but sales haven't been so hot." He also wanted to know what other Jews think of Judaism. So he asked and continues to ask. Mr. Mann publishes the *Being Jewish* magazine that goes to about 100,000 homes. (BeingJewish.org)

STACEY MARCUS: Stacey Marcus is a senior contributing editor at *New England Bride* and *New England Corporate Events*, and has been a popular columnist for the *Jewish Journal of the North Shore*. She is also a freelance contributor to many area publications in the Boston area. Ms. Marcus owns and operates Grapevine Communications, which provides public relations and marketing counsel for nonprofit organizations and small businesses. She and her husband, Mitchell, reside in Marblehead, Massachusetts, with their two daughters, Rachel and Emily.

MICHAEL MEDVED: Mr. Medved, an Orthodox (or "Observant") Jew, is a nationally syndicated conservative radio talk-show host, film critic, and author. He left Yale Law School, to serve as a Democratic campaign consultant and worked for Robert Kennedy's election. After that he had a brief stint for Congressman Ron Dellums of California, which pushed him away from the "left." Mr. Medved then worked for the election of Ronald Reagan and became a vocal supporter for conservatism and the Republican Party. Medved has reviewed movies for CNN and the *New York Post* and was also cohost of *Sneak Previews*, on PBS. He is on the board of contributors to *USA Today* and does op-ed pieces for the *Wall Street Journal*. His daily three-hour talk radio program reaches 140 markets. In 2005, he published his autobiography, *Right Turns: Unconventional Lessons from a Controversial Life*. He's also written the bestseller *What Really Happened to the Class of '65*, as well as *The Shadow Presidents* and *Hollywood vs. America,* among others. He collaborated with wife, Dr. Diane Medved, a clinical psychologist, on *Saving Childhood: Protecting Our Children from the National Assault on Innocence.*

SHARON MELNICER: Ms. Melnicer is a freelance writer, visual artist, and teacher living in Winnipeg. She is also a regular contributor to the *Jewish Post and News*, the *Winnipeg Free Press*, and other publications.

MARILYN MICHAELS: Ms. Michaels is the winner of an Outer Critic Circle Award and a Drama League Award for her work in *Catskills On Broadway*. The woman "of a thousand faces and voices," she was a star of the Emmy-winning series *The Kopykats*. Today she performs in clubs from New York to Las Vegas. But then what would you expect from a child of the theater, whose mother was the famed female cantoress, Fraydele Oysher, and her uncle, the legendary Moishe Oysher? Ms. Michaels is also an accomplished artist whose paintings and celebrity artworks have appeared in fine galleries. Her new art poster, the Fabulous Blondes, depicts filmdom's movie goddesses. Her son, Mark, who is also in "the family business," can be heard on her CD, *A Mother's Voice*.

RABBI YOCHEVED MINTZ: Rabbi Mintz has been involved in Jewish education as teacher and principal for over forty-five years. She was ordained in 2004 and is the spiritual leader of the Valley Outreach Synagogue of Las Vegas, Nevada's only Reconstructionist congregation. She is a member of the board of rabbis of southern Nevada, the Clark County Ministerial Association, and the Interfaith Council of southern Nevada. Rabbi Mintz is also managing director of the Las Vegas Jewish Center for Education, Media, and the Arts. Her other memberships include: the Chevra Kaddisha, president of the Academy for Jewish Religion/CA Alumni Association, and associate member of the Reconstructionist Rabbinical Association. She is also on the board of OHALAH, the Rabbinical Association of the Renewal Movement. Rabbi Mintz is the eighteenth generation of rabbis on her paternal (Porath) side. She is married to physician and entrepreneur Dr. Alan Mintz. They have four sons and thirteen grandchildren.

RAHEL MUSLEAH: Ms. Musleah is an award-winning journalist, author, singer, storyteller, and educator. Her articles have appeared in numerous publications including: the *New York Times*, *Family Circle*, *Publishers Weekly*, *Hadassah* magazine, *Reform Judaism*, and *Jewish Woman*. Her books include:

Apples and Pomegranates: A Family Seder for Rosh Hashanah, Why on This Night? A Passover Haggadah for Family Celebration, Sharing Blessings: Children's Stories for Exploring the Spirit of the Jewish Holidays, B'Kol Arev: Songs of the Jews of Calcutta, and *Journey of a Lifetime: The Jewish Life Cycle Book.* She has also created the CD *Hodu: Jewish Rhythms from Baghdad to India.* She was born in India, and is the seventh generation of a Calcutta Jewish family. Ms. Musleah also presents programs on the Jewish communities of India. www.rahelsjewishindia.com.

DR. RENA NORA: Dr. Nora is a preeminent expert in gambling problems. She is clinical professor of psychiatry at the University of Nevada School of Medicine, former chief of psychiatry at the VA Southern Nevada Health Care System and the Mike O'Callaghan Federal Hospital, and commissioner on the Nevada's governor's Commission on Mental Health and Developmental Services. She serves on the Nevada Board of Examiners for Drug, Alcohol, and Gambling Counselors, and is medical advisor for the American Foundation for Suicide Prevention (Nevada) and the Nevada Council on Problem Gambling. She has published numerous articles on suicide, problem gambling, and mental health issues, Dr. Nora, a retired Lt. Col. U.S. Army Reserve, is known for her impressive ability to manage the roles of mother, physician, teacher, administrator, writer, researcher, and community leader.

ALLYSON RICE: Ms. Rice is co-owner and director of Earth-Heart. She is a gifted, intuitive individual who works with others using the body as an energetic map of life experiences and as a vehicle for healing. She facilitates workshops, quests, healing retreats, and women's retreats around the country. Ms. Rice is a former actress, who was a star of *As the World Turns,* and has since had extensive training in advanced energy healing based in ancient Native American and Tibetan healing arts. She is an internationally certified kundalini yoga instructor through the Kundalini Research Institute. She has a private energy healing practice in the Los Angeles area and is a powerful and compassionate teacher, dedicated to unleashing the awareness and creative potential of her clients.

MARTA SANDERS: Ms. Sanders is the recipient of the Outstanding Female Vocalist award from the Manhattan Association Cabarets. She comes a family that loved to perform. Her mother and two aunts were regulars on *Major Boles* and two of her siblings (Jay O. Sanders and Fred Sanders) are successful actors. Her father's career in education and social service brought the family to Bogotá, Colombia, where Marta took voice lessons in classical music. At nineteen, she moved to New York and attended the American Music and Dramatic Academy. She appeared in *The Best Little Whorehouse in Texas* and today, she is a world-renowned cabaret artist. Her current performances include her one-woman show *It's a Mother*, which incorporates songs of the great mamas of Broadway. Ms. Sanders is also producing a Spanish CD of Latin ballads. She and her husband have two daughters.

DR. ELIEZER SEGAL: Dr. Segal, originally from Montreal, is a professor of religious studies at the University of Calgary and specializes in Judaism. He also holds a PhD in Talmud from the Hebrew University of Jerusalem. His primary areas of research include rabbinic literature, Jewish law and homiletics, and comparative biblical interpretation. His publications include scholarly monographs, popular scholarship, a children's book, and many articles and book chapters. He also maintains an extensive Web site, ucalgary.ca/~elsegal. He is married to Agnes Romer Segal, and has three sons and two "extraordinary" grandsons.

KAREN L. SMITH: Ms. Smith, MSS, LSW, is a clinical social worker and director/founder of Full Living: Resources for Celebrating Body/Self, which offers national consulting services to organizations, schools, and clinics. She speaks nationally on the topics of eating disorders, body image, sexuality, sexual orientation and gender, and maintains a private outpatient practice in Philadelphia.

RABBI SHIRA STERN: Rabbi Shira Stern, BCC, is the daughter of famed violinist, Isaac Stern, and is a member of the advisory board of PlainViews, and director of the Jewish Institute for Pastoral Care of the HealthCare Chaplaincy in New York City. She serves on the National Association for Jewish Chaplains' board of directors and is a member of its executive committee.

In 1983, Rabbi Stern was among the early group of women ordained by the Hebrew Union College-Jewish Institute of Religion. She was pulpit rabbi of the Monroe Township Jewish Center in New Jersey for thirteen years, East Coast director of MAZON: A Jewish Response to Hunger, and Middlesex County's director of Jewish chaplaincy. She has been an acute-care hospital chaplain and has a private pastoral counseling practice in Marlboro, New Jersey. She lectures and teaches in synagogues, JCCs, and Healing Centers, and leads services at two area independent and assisted living facilities.

JOHN STOSSEL: Mr. Stossel is an award-winning news correspondent, anchor of *20/20* and the *John Stossel Specials*, and the *New York Times* best-selling author of *Myths, Lies and Downright Stupidity: Get Out the Shovel— Why Everything You Know Is Wrong*. Mr. Stossel is also known for his "Give Me a Break" features that take a skeptical look at a wide array of issues—from pop culture controversies to government regulations. His specials tackle topics with purpose: to expose frauds, myths, and nonsense and convey the truth—from hard news to human nature to science (or junk science). He has received nineteen Emmys, been honored five times for excellence in consumer reporting by the National Press Club, and, among other honors, received the George Foster Peabody Award. Mr. Stossel is a graduate of Princeton University, with a BA in psychology. He is married and has children.

RABBI JOSEPH TELUSHKIN: Rabbi Telushkin is a preeminent scholar and best-selling author. He has written *The Book of Jewish Values and Words that Hurt, Words that Heal,* and *Jewish Humor: What the Best Jewish Jokes Say About the Jews* along with a myriad of other widely read books on Judaism. He is also the author of the *Rabbi Daniel Winter* murder mysteries. He lives in New York City and lectures widely throughout North America.

ROBIN TYLER: Robin Tyler is the executive director of the Equality Campaign. She is a leading activist, as well as a special event producer for the lesbian/gay, AIDS, women's, and anti-war movement. She has distinguished herself as the main stage producer of the 1979, 1987, and 1993 marches on Washington for lesbian and gay rights, the producer of the Women's Philharmonic at the Kennedy Center, and producer/executive director of the first International Gay Comedy Festival in Sydney, Australia. She also produced the Stonewall Democratic Federation Convention in Palm Springs, in addition to twenty-five major outdoor women's music and comedy festivals. Robin was also one of the first "out" gay or lesbian comics in the 1970s. Her first comedy album was called *Always a Bridesmaid, Never a Groom*.

DR. EILEEN WARSHAW: Dr. Warshaw is the executive director of the restored Jewish Heritage Center in Tucson, Arizona, which was the first Jewish House of Worship (1910) in the territory. The center houses collections and a research library. Dr. Warshaw has also helped restore four other synagogues, including the original synagogue in Dublin, Ireland. A historic preservationist, Dr. Warshaw received her PhD from Trinity College, Dublin. She has served on the board of advisors for the National Trust for Historic Preservation, and a number of preservation societies and heritage boards. She has published articles on preservation and written a book on Irish genealogy. Dr. Warshaw and her husband Alan have four daughters and seven grandchildren. She is the second-oldest girl of a traditional Roman Catholic family of seventeen children. She chose Judaism twenty-five years ago and never knew how Jewish her *mother* was until she became one!

MARJORIE GOTTLIEB WOLFE: Ms. Wolfe, author of *Are Yentas, Kibitzers, and Tummlers Weapons of Mass Instruction? Yiddish Trivia*, is a retired business educator and freelance writer. Her articles have appeared in the *New York Times*, *Smart Money* magazine, *Playbill* magazine, *Reunions* magazine, the *National Business Employment Weekly*, the *Jewish Press*, *Long Island Jewish World*, GantsehMegillah.com, and many other publications. She "learned" Yiddish from Leo Rosten, Uriel Weinreich, Fred Kogos, Rabbi Benjamin Blech, Arnold Fine, Jackie Mason, Jerry Stiller, Pakn Treger, the magazine of the National Yiddish Book Center, and her mother, Jeanette Gottlieb.

Selected Bibliographies

T housands of sources were used and all were highly valuable. Many sources have already been cited within the book. Those below were major sources.

BOOKS

All in a Lifetime: An Autobiography, Ruth Westheimer, Ben Yagoda. Warner Books, 1987.

All My Best Friends, George Burns, David Fisher. Perigee, 1990.

Amy's Answering Machine, Amy Borkowsky. Pocket Books, 2001.

An Empire of Their Own: How the Jews Invented Hollywood, Neal Gabler. Crown, 1988.

The Art of Jewish Cooking, Jennie Grosssinger. Bantam, 1965.

Asimov Laughs Again, Isaac Asimov. HarperPerennial, 1992.

Bachelor Girls, Wendy Wasserstein. Vintage, 1991.

The Big Book of Jewish Humor, William Novak and Moshe Waldoks. HarperPerennial, 1981.

The Book of Lists 90s Edition, David Wallechinsky and Irving Wallace. Little, Brown, 1993.

The Book of Lists 2, Irving Wallace. Bantam Books, 1980.

Book of Jewish Values, Rabbi Joseph Telushkin. Crown, 2000.

Born This Day, Ed Morrow. Carol Publishing, 1995.

Born to Kvetch, Michael Wex. St. Martin's, 2005.

Bread and Rice, Doris Macauley. Lyons Press, 2004 (orig. Macauley Publishing, 1948).

Children of the Holocaust, H. Epstein. Penguin, 1979.

Children of Loneliness, Anzia Yezierska. Funk and Wagnalls, 1923.

Deborah, Golda, and Me: Being Female and Jewish in America, Letty Cottin Pogrebin. Anchor Books, 1991.

A Dictionary of Yiddish Slang and Idioms, Fred Kogos. Citadel, 1998.

Dr. Burns' Prescription for Happiness, George Burns. Putnam, 1984.

Encyclopedia of Jewish Humor, Henry D. Spalding. Jonathan David, 2001.

Encyclopedia of Jews in Sports, Bernard Postal, Jesse Silver, and Roy Silver. Bloch Publishing, 1965.

Enter Whining, Fran Drescher. ReganBooks, 1996.

Every Mother is a Daughter, Perri Klass and Sheila Solomon Klass. Ballantine, 2006.

The Feminine Mystique, Betty Friedan. W. W. Norton and Company, 2001.

Fifty Jewish Women Who Changed the World, Deborah G. Felder and Diana Rosen. Citadel, 2003.

Fighting to Become Americans: Assimilation and the Trouble between Jewish Women and Jewish Men, R. E. Prell. Beacon, 1999.

First Facts in American Jewish History, Tina Levitan. Jason Aronson, 1996.

From Lokshen to Lo Mein: The Jewish Love Affair with Chinese Food, Donald Siegel. Gefen, 2005.

Funny People, Steve Allen. Stein and Day, 1981.

Funny Women: American Comediennes, 1960, 1985, Mary Unterbrink Mcfarland and 1987.

The Genius of the Jewish Joke, Arthur Asa Berger. Transaction, 2006.

Goddesses in Every Woman: A New Psychology of Women, Jean Shanoda Bolen. HarperPerennial, 1985.

Great Jewish Quotations, Alfred J. Kolatch. Jonathan David, 1996.

Great Jewish Quotes, Noah benShea. Ballantine, 1993.

Great Jewish Women, Elinor Slater and Robert Slater. Jonathan David, 1998.

Great Jews in Sports, Robert Slater. Jonathan David, 2000.

Great Jews on Stage and Screen, Darryl Lyman. Jonathan David, 1987.

Groucho: The Life and Times of Julius Henry Marx, Stefan Kanfer. Vintage, 2001.

Her Face in the Mirror, Faye Moskowitz. Beacon, 1994.

A History of the Jews in America, Howard M. Sachar. Knopf, 1992.

Hooray for Yiddish, Leo Rosten. Simon and Schuster, 1982.

How to Be a Jewish Mother, Dan Greenburg. Price Stern Sloan, 1979.

How to Get More Out of Being Jewish Even If: A. You Are Not Sure You Believe in God, B. You Think Going to Synagogue Is a Waste of Time, C. You Think Keeping Kosher Is Stupid, D. You Hated Hebrew, Gil Mann. Leo and Sons Pub; 2nd edition, 1996.

How to Curse in Yiddish, Joe Singer. Ballantine, 1977.

How to Survive a Jewish Mother, R. Steven Arnold. CCC Publications, 1996.

I Am My Mother's Daughter: Making Peace with Mom Before It's Too Late, Iris Krasnow. Perseus, 2006.

Isaac Asimov's Book of Facts, Hastings House, 1992.

Jackie Mason's "The World According to Me!" Simon and Schuster, 1987.

Jackie Mason and Raoul Felder's Guide to New York City. Avon, 1997.

The Jazz Singer, Robert L. Carringer, ed. University of Wisconsin Press, 1979.

Jewish American Literature: A Norton Anthology. Jules Chametzky, John Felstiner, Hilene Flanzbaum, Kathryn Hellerstein, eds. W. W. Norton and Company, 2000.

Jewish and Female: Choices and Changes in Our Lives Today, Susan Weidman Schneider. Simon and Schuster, 1984.

The Jewish Book of Lists, Joel Samberg. Citadel, 1999.

The Jewish Book of Why, Alfred J. Kolatch. Jonathan David, 1981.

Jewish Celebrity Anecdotes, Tim Boxer. Jonathan David, 1996.

The Jewish Comedy Catalog, Darryl Lyman. Jonathan David, 1989.

The Jewish Connection, M. Hirsh Goldberg. Bantam, 1979.

Jewish Cooking in America, Joan Nathan. Knopf, 1998.

The Jewish Dietary Laws, Samuel Dresner, Seymour Siegel. United Synogogue Book Service, revised 1980.

The Jewish Festival Cook Book, Fannie Engle and Gertrude Blair. Warner, 1966.

Jewish Heroes and Heroines of America, Seymour "Sy" Brody. Lifetime Books, 1996.

Jewish Humor: What the Best Jewish Jokes Say About the Jews, Rabbi Joseph Telushkin. Morrow, 1998.

Jewish Literacy, Rabbi Joseph Telushkin. William Morrow, 1991.

Jewish Mothers, Paula Ethel Wolfson and Paul Wolf. Chronicle, 2000.

Jewish Mothers' Hall of Fame, Fred A. Bernstein. Doubleday, 1986.

The Jewish People's Almanac, David C. Gross. Hippocrene, 1994 (revised).

Jewish Pioneer Women, Andrea Kalinowsky (art). Museum of New Mexico, 2002.

Jewish Pioneers in America, Anita Libman Lebeson. Behrman's Jewish Book House, 1938.

The JPS Guide to Jewish Women, 600 B.C.–1900 C.E. Emily Taitz, Sondra Henry, Cheryl Tallan. Jewish Publication Society of America, 2003.

Jewish Responses to Nazi Persecution, Isiah Trunk. Stein and Day, 1979.

Jewish Sports Legends, Joseph Siegman. Brassey's, 2000.

Jewish Stars in Texas, Ava Weiner Hollace. Texas A&M University Press, 1999.

Jewish Women in America, Paula E. Hyman. Routledge, 1997.

The Jewish You Wouldn't Believe It Book, M. Hirsch Goldberg. Shapolsky Publishers, 1988.

Jews on the Frontier, Harold I. Sharfman. Henry Regnery, 1977.

The Joys of Yiddish, Leo Rosten. Pocket Books, 1970.

The Joys of Yinglish, Leo Rosten. McGraw-Hill, 1989.

Keeping Passover, Ira Steingroot. HarperCollins, 1995.

Leo Rosten's Giant Book of Laughter, Leo Rosten. Random House, 1985.

Life Is with People: The Culture of the Shtetl, Mark Zborowski, E. Herzog. Schocken Books, 1962.

A Little Joy, A Little Oy, Marnie Winston-Macauley. Andrews McMeel, 2001.

Meet the Folks, Sammy Levenson. Citadel, 1949.

Memoirs of American Jews, 1776–1865, Jacob Rader Marcus, ed. KTAV Publishing, 1974.

Molly!, Molly Picon. Simon and Schuster, 1980.

Molly Goldberg Jewish Cook Book, Gertrude Berg and Myra Waldo. Pyramid, 1976.

More Funny People, Steve Allen. Stein and Day, 1982.

Motherless Daughters: The Legacy of Loss, Hope Edelman. Dell, 1994.

My Life, Golda Meir. Dell (reissue), 1976.

The Official Jewish Mothers' Hall of Fame, Fred A. Bernstein. Doubleday, 1986.

The New Joys of Yiddish, Leo Rosten (revised by Lawrence Bush). Three Rivers, 2001.

One Foot in America, Yuru Suhl. Paperback Library, 1968.

Our Crowd: The Great Jewish Families of the New York, Stephen Birmingham. Harper and Row, 1967.

Pictorial History of the Jewish People, Nathan Ausubel. Crown, 1966.

People's Almanac 2, David Wallechinsky and Irving Wallace. Morrow, 1978.

The Portable Curmudgeon, Jon Winokur. New American Library, 1987.

Portnoy's Complaint, Philip Roth. Bantam, 1970.

Prairie Dogs Weren't Kosher, Linda Mack Seldoff. Minnesota Historical Society Press, 1977.

The Quotable Einstein, Alice Calaprice. Princeton, 1997.

The Quotable Jewish Woman, Elaine Bernstein Partnow, ed. Jewish Lights, 2004.

Rachel Calof's Story: Jewish Homesteader on the Northern Plains, Rachel Calof. Indiana Univerity Press, 1995.

The Red Tent, Anita Diamant. Picador USA, 1998.

Roseanne, My Life as a Woman, Roseanne Barr. Harper&Row, 1989.

The Second Jewish Book of Why, Alfred J. Kolatch. Jonathan David, 1995.

The Seinfeld Scripts, Jerry Seinfeld and Larry David/Castle Rock Entertainment. HarperPerennial, 1998.

Sheila Levine Is Dead and Living in New York, Gail Parent. Bantam, 1973.

Schindler's List, Thomas Keneally. Touchstone, 1982.

Shabbat Shalom, Susan R. Friedland. Little, Brown and Company, 1999.

The Spirit of the Ghetto, Hutchins Hapgood. Funk and Wagnalls, 1965.

Stars of David, Abigail Pogrebin. Broadway Books, 2005.

The Story of Yiddish in America, Sol Steinmetz. University Alabama Press; 2nd edition, 2001.

Talking Back: Images of Jewish Women in American Popular Culture,
  Joyce Antler, ed. Hanover and London: Brandeis University Press.

*The Tapestry of Jewish Time: A Spiritual Guide to Holidays and Life-
  Cycle Events,* Nina Beth Cardin, Ilene Winn-Lederer (Illustrator).
  Behrman House, 2000.

A Treasury of Jewish Folklore, Nathan Ausubel. Crown, 1975.

A Treasury of Jewish Humor, Nathan Ausubel, ed. Galahad, 1993.

Treasury of Jewish Quotations, Leo Rosten. Bantam, 1978.

Treblinka, Jean-Francois Steiner. Simon and Schuster, 1967.

The 2,000 Year Old Man in the Year 2,000, Mel Brooks and Carl
  Reiner. Cliff Street, 1997.

Vagabond Stars, Nahma Sandrow. Seth Press, 1986.

Véra: Mrs. Vladimir Nabokov, Stacy Schiff. Modern Library, 2000.

We'll Always Have Paris, Robert A. Nowland and Gwendolyn W.
  Nolan. HarperCollins, 1995.

Without Feathers, Woody Allen. Random House, 1975.

What Jews Say About God, Alfred J. Kolatch, ed. Jonathan David,
  1999.

Why Didn't I Learn That in Hebrew School, Eliezar Segal. Rowen and
  Littlefield, 1999.

*Women Who Would Be Rabbis: A History of Women's Ordination
  1889–1985,* Pamela Nadell. Beacon, 1998.

Woody Allen: A Biography, John Baxter. Carroll and Graf Publishers,
  1999.

Woody Allen: A Biography (2nd edition, revised), Eric Lax. Da Capo
  Press, 2000.

Words that Hurt, Words that Heal, Rabbi Joseph Telushkin. William
  Morrow, 1996.

World of Our Fathers, Irving Howe. Harcourt Brace Jovanovich,
  1976.

Yentl the Yeshiva Boy, Isaac Bashevis Singer. Farrar, Straus and
  Giroux, 1983.

Yiddish, A Nation of Words, Miriam Weinstein. Steerforth, 2001.

Yiddish Slang and Idioms, Fred Kogos. Citadel, 1998.

PAPERS/ARTICLES/SERMONS/POEMS

Leo M. Abrami: "Laughing Through the Tears Jewish"

Joyce Antler: "The Gift of Jewish Women's Comedy"

Isaac Asimov related this story about his Jewish mother in "It's Been a Good Life."

Marianna Belenkaya: "Russia's Jewish Warriors"

Rabbi Barry H. Block: "Whose Body Is It Anyway?"

Bruce Bower: "Trauma syndrome transverses generations"

Tim Boxer: "Life in Jerusalem Normal: Joy Mingled with Tears"

Gabriella Burman: "Savoring Yiddish"

Jules Chametzky: "Jewish Humor"

Rodger Kamenetz: "A Buccaneer's Secret"

Susan J. Landau-Chark: "Whither the Rebbetzin in the Twenty-first Century?"

Judy Cohen: "Lessons Learned from Gentle Heroism: Women's Holocaust Narratives"

Rabbi Dovid Dubov: "What Is the Role of the Woman in Judaism?"

L. Ehrlich, S. Bolozky, R. Rothstein, M. Schwartz, J. Berkowitz, and J. Young: "Textures and Meaning: Thirty Years of Judaic Studies at the University of Massachusetts Amherst"

Michael Feldberg: "Mordecai Sheftall and the Wages of War"

Joan Fisher: "Resistance and Triumph: an Interview with Gerda Lerner," *Wisconsin Academy Review*

Garance Franke-Ruta: "Liebermama"

Monica Gettleman: "A Mother Shares Her Grief"

D. Giacomo and M. Weissmark: "Toward a Generative Theory of the Therapeutic Field" Family Process

Avivi Gidi, Ben-Nun, Sagui. "Naomi Shemer: First Lady of Israeli Song," Haaretz (June 27, 2004)

Sheri Goldstein Gleicher: "Flora Spiegelberg: Grand Lady of the Southwest Frontier"

Rabbi Joshua J. Hammerman: "Kosher Today"

Myrna Hant: "TV Jewish Mothers: The Creation of a Multiethnic Antiheroine" and "Creation of the Yiddishe Mammeh Stereotype"

Lee M. Hendler: "Recollections of Lenore Pancoe Meyerhoff"

Steve Hochman: "Who knew Woody Guthrie wrote a trove of Jewish-themed songs? His son Arlo, for one"

Rav B. Horovitz: "A Diet for the Soul?"

Carol K. Howell: "Portraits of Grief: Focus on Survivors"

Ellen Jaffe-Gill: "Bias Hits Rabbis on Mommy Track"

Adam Katz-Stone: "Philanthropists offer tips on teaching tzedakah to kids"

Janet Liebman Jacobs: "Women, ritual, and secrecy: the creation of crypto-Jewish culture"

Journal of Mrs. Eugenia Levy Phillips, 1861–1862

Fara Kaplan: "Holocaust Survivors and Their Children: A Search for Positive Effects"

Alexander Kimel: Holocaust stories

B. H. Levy and Rabbi Arnold Mark Belzer: "Jews of Savannah"

Charlotte Mayerson: "Layout"

Joan Nathan: "Family Treasures Hold Kosher America's Roots"

New England Literacy Resource Center: "Light in Montana: How One Town Said No to Hate"

Chaya Ostrower: Doctoral dissertation, "Holocaust Thesis." Tel-Aviv University

Cynthia Ozick: "The Meaning of Life"

Naomi Pfefferman: "Lainie Kazan"

Dr. Steven Carr Reuben: "Jews, Food, and Holiness"

Alan Riding: "A Mother's Last Words, an Actress's Memories"

Michael Rogin: "Blackface, White Noise: The Jewish Jazz Singer Finds His Voice"

Nola Ross: "Jean Lafitte: Louisiana Buccaneer"

Jackie Ruben: "In My Grandmother's Kitchen"

Vickie R. Rumble: "Notable Women in Alabama History"

Irv Saposnik: "Jolson, the Jazz Singer and the Jewish mother: or how my Yiddishe momme became my mammy"

Monika Scislowska: "Kansas Students Meet Holocaust Hero"

Louise Scodie: "A Forgotten Pioneer of Faith"

Eliezer Segal: "Why Didn't I Learn This in Hebrew School"

Nicholas Simon: Dr. Bruno Halioua, author of "*Meres Juives des Hommes Celebres*" ("Jewish Mothers of Famous Men")

Eleanor Cohen Seixas: "Southern Patriot: Diary, February 28, 1865–September 10, 1865"

Jonathan Singer: "Cultural Differences Among Elderly Women in Coping With the Death of an Adult Child"
Karen L. Smith: "Jewish Women and Eating Disorders"
Allison J. Waldman: "Barbra Streisand Scrapbook"
Benjamin Wallace-Wells: "Private Jihad: How Rita Katz got into the Spying Business"
Jack Wertheimer: "The Politics of Women's Ordination: Jewish Law, Institutional Power and the Debate over Women in the Rabbinate"
Alex Witchel: "Eating Hollywood Style, With Thin Air on the Side"
Philip Whitten: SwimmingWorldMagazine.com
Jill Gold Wright: "How Deep Is the Ocean? How High Is the Sky?"
Peter Zheutlin: "Chasing Annie"

PLAYS, FILMS, AND TELEVISION
Biloxi Blues, Neil Simon. Random House, 1986
Brighton Beach Memoirs, Neil Simon. Random House, 1984
Broadway Bound, Neil Simon. Random House, 1987
Enter Laughing, Joseph Stein, adapted from novel by Carl Reiner. Samuel French, 1964
Fiddler on the Roof, Joseph Stein. Pocket Books, 1971
Lost in Yonkers, Neil Simon. Random House, 1991
Annie Hall, 1977
Sunshine, 1999
A Laugh, A Tear, A Mitzvah, Roy Hammond, executive producer; Roman Brygider, producer/director; Ron Rudaitis, producer; Sam Toperoff, writer. Produced by WLIW21 Productions, Long Island, NY, 1996 Heritage

INTERNET
aaets.org; aafla.org; abcnews.go.com; adherents.com; aegis.com; Ahavat-Israel.com; aip.org; aish.com; ajcongress.org; ajhs.org; alanabel.com; americanrevolution.org; amfar.org; amres.com; anecdotage.com; acs.ucalgary.ca/~elsegal; askarabbi.com; askmoses.com/article.html; asknoah.org; ats.org/news; auschwitz.dk; autry-museum.org; awordinyoureye.com; bbc.co.uk; beatl.barnard.columbia.edu; BeingJewish.org;

berdichev.org/the_last_letter.htm; Bloom Southwest Jewish
   Archives; bnaibrith.org; boston.com; brainyquote.com;
   brandeis.edu; Brittanica.com; brown.edu;
   Ken Brown brownk@ucalgary.ca; burlingtonfreepress.com;
   ceemast.csupomona.edu; chabad.org; charlottemayerson.com;
   cinema.com; cjh.org; columbia.edu; cornellsun.com;
   csupomona.edu;
dartmouth.edu; dawnschuman.org;
   diduknow/jrpguide; digital.net/~klane; discovery.org; dvar.org.il;
   eddiecantor.com; education-world.com;
fau.edu; 15minutesmagazine.com; filmforum.org; filmsite.org;
   fortune.com; forward.com; fullliving.com;
geocities.com; goldamagazine.com; goldasbalcony.com;
   guyanafilm.org;
havelshouseofhistory.com; henkbrouwer.tripod.com;
   herstoryfreehomepage.com; historycooperative.org; home.flash.net;
   hospitalityguild.com; humboldt.edu;
ic.arizona.edu; ideafinder.com; imdb.com; iml.jou.ufl.edu;
   innernet.org.il. iparenting.com;
Jewhoo.com; jewish.com; Jewish-American Hall of Fame
   (Jewish Museum in Cyberspace); Jewish-American History
   Documentation Foundation, Inc.; jewishaz.com; jewishbulletin.ca;
   jewishencyclopedia.com; JewishGates.org; jewish-history.com;
   jewishjournal.com; jewishpress.com; Jewishsf.com;
   The Jewish Student Online Research Center (JSOURCE);
   jewishstarsintexas.com; jewish-theatre.com; jewishvirtuallibrary.org;
   thejewishweek.com; jewishworldreview.com; jewmag.org;
   jewsinsports.org; jpost.com; jta.org; jtsa.edu; jwa.org; jwv.org;
kansascity.com; kimel.net; kobymandell.org;
latimes.com; libraries.psu.edu; library.arizona.edu; library.csi.cuny.edu;
   lilithmag.com; lilith.org; lillianvernon.com; likud.nl/ref27.html;
   learn.jtsa.edu;
Magazine Americana: The American Popular Culture Online Magazine;
   mendelmeyers.com; militarycity.com; mindfully.org; miriamscup.com;
   mit.edu; mljewish.org; momentmag.com; monmouth.com;
   MSNBC.com; museum.tv/archives/etv/G/htmlG/goldbergsth/
   goldbergsth.htm; myjewishlearning.com;

ncof.com; New Jersey Jewish News; newyorker.com; Nizor.org;
   Noetic Sciences Review # 39; noticiasaliadas.org; now.org; nps.gov;
   nwhp.org; nytimes.com;
oswego.edu; Oyvey.co.il;
parentseyes.arizona.edu; pbs.org; pbs.org/wnet; portalwisconsin.org;
   prospect.org;
rabbibjk@cox.net; radio-electronics.com; radiohof.org; remember.org;
   rhodesjewishmuseum.org; row2k.com; ruedefrance.com;
s2k.org; schmoozenews.com; science.nasa.gov; scottsdalepublicart.org;
   sendamy.com; sfgate.com; sfmuseum.org; shop.nathansfamous.com;
   signonsandiego.com; sil.si.edu; sip.armstrong.edu; soapboxinc.com;
   sympatico.ca/mighty1/essays/lessons1.htm;
templeganelohim.org; tennisfame.org; thenation.com;
   The Rabbi's Study: TheRabbisStudy@groups.msn.com;
   theroyalforums.com;
u.arizona.edu; ucalgary.ca/~elsegal; ukonline.co.uk/m.gratton;
   umass.edu; usadojo.com; uscj.org; usfca.edu; ushistory.org;
   usoc.org; usps.gov;
vcn.bc.ca/doxa/2005press/Abelraisescain_epk.pdf; vitebsk.by/eng/
   vitebsk/chagall/house/lavka.html;
washingtontimes.com; wedding.ziemkowski.com; weeklywire.com;
   wgbh.org; wic.org; wlcj.org; wm.edu; womenshistory.about.com;
   womensenews.org; online.wsj.com;
yadvashem.org

Marnie Winston-Macauley

"**M**y mother kept telling me my teachers told her I was terrific . . . only not in their subjects," says Ms. Winston-Macauley. Quirky, no-nonsense, funny, she is a straight shooter, who has a unique voice and takes on the world in her books and advice column, "Ask Sadie." Her hallmark statement? "People aren't pantyhose. We're each a custom job." She loathes pretension and can nail it from a well-honed distance. Ms. Winston-Macauley holds a BA in psychology, and an MS degree from the Columbia University School of Social Work, where she won the first Judith L. Ginsberg Memorial Scholarship. She is the author of the advice column, "Ask Sadie" (which was syndicated through Tribune Media Services), writes an advice and parenting column for the *Tucson Citizen,* is a columnist for *Jewish Life and Style,* and a contributing columnist for JWR. She has written over twenty books/calendars, including the series, *A Little Joy, A Little Oy,* was a writer for the daytime drama, *As the World Turns,* which garnered her both Emmy and Writers Guild award nominations, has written two science fiction novelettes for the *Magazine of Fantasy and Science Fiction, Realms of Fantasy,* and *Fantom* (Russian). She has written hundreds of relationship articles for women's magazines and newspapers, including *Woman, First, Women's World, Theater Week,* the *Star,* the *New York Times,* and the *Rocky Mountain News Co.,* among others. A popular media presence, in addition to hosting her advice radio show, *Ask Sadie Live!,* she was a regular advice maven on *The Karen Grant Show,* in Monterey, California, and has appeared on hundreds of other radio and television shows, including *Lifetime for Women, Mike and Maty, The Mark Wahlberg Show, The Pat Bullard Show,*

USA Live, Charles Perez, and *Bill O'Reilly* (Fox). In 2003, she starred in a relationship-advice pilot for the Discovery Networks. Ms. Winston-Macauley was a graduate-level supervisor and has clinically supervised for both Columbia University and the Adelphi School of Social Work. She also taught at the New York City Correctional Academy. Ms. Winston-Macauley has smashed the glass ceiling more than once. Before turning to writing, she was a senior administrator, as well as clinician for the New York City Department of Correction. She was appointed director of Pre-Trial Services in Westchester County, New York, the first women to hold a directorship in criminal justice in that county. Her agency received an Exemplary Project Award from the federal government. Ms. Winston-Macauley was a member of the Curriculum committee, at Columbia University; served on the Criminal Justice Committee to the Advisory Council, New York State Senate; was vice president of the State Association of Pre-Trial Service Agencies, and on the board of the National Association. She also served on the board of Headstart (Rockland County, New York) and on the Rockland Psychiatric Center Advisory Committee. She is currently associated with the Las Vegas Jewish Center for Education, Media, and the Arts. She is married to a former *New York Times* senior editor. The couple has one son, and she has five stepchildren. Ms. Winston-Macauley is in *Who's Who in America,* 2007.

Interviews

Liz Abzug, Marty Allen, Rabbi Bob Alper, Rabbi Bruce Adler, Kaye Ballard, Jeanne Bavaro, Congresswoman Shelley Berkley, Theodore Bikel, Robert Kim Bingham, Janel Bladow, Amy Borkowsky, Tim Boxer, Nancy Byrne, Frances Coyle Brennan and Thomas Brennan, Pat Caso, Julie Cobb, Lorrie Cohen, Jennifer Collet, Bill Dana, Zora Essman, Tovah Feldshuh, Mary Fischer, Eileen Fulton, Julie Gans, Monica Gettleman, Joanna Gleason, Judy Gold, Dr. Carolyn Goodman, Rabbi Felipe Goodman, Mayor Oscar Goodman, Rona Ginott, Blu Greenberg, Dr. Ruth Gruber, Dr. Bruno Halioua, Dr. Howard Halpern, Dr. Myrna Hant, Lee M. Hendler, Binyamin Jolkovsky, Lainie Kazan, Mary Keating, Rabbi Bonnie Koppel, Irwin Keller, Murray and Edith Klein, Harry Leichter, Mallory Lewis, Sig and Rose Lee Liberman, Jody Lopatin, Jackie Mason, Charlotte Mayerson, Michael Medved, Marilyn Michaels, Rabbi Yocheved Mintz, Dr. Rena Nora, Michelle Patrick, Rabbi Sally Priesand, Allyson Rice, Shari Ritter, Marta Sanders, Ben Schatz, Rabbi Shira Stern, John Stossel, Melanie Strug, Ginger Tafoya, Robin Tyler, Dr. Eileen Warshaw, Siofra Willer, Marjorie Gottlieb Wolfe